THE
BACKWARD
ART OF
SPENDING
MONEY

Wesley Clair Mitchell

THE BACKWARD ART OF SPENDING MONEY

with a new preface,
introduction, and afterword by
Eli Ginzberg

Routledge
Taylor & Francis Group

LONDON AND NEW YORK

Originally published in 1937 by McGraw-Hill Book Company, Inc.

Published 1999 by Transaction Publishers

Published 2017 by Routledge
2 Park Square, Milton Park, Abingdon, Oxon OX14 4RN
711 Third Avenue, New York, NY 10017, USA

Routledge is an imprint of the Taylor & Francis Group, an informa business

New material this edition copyright © 1999 by Taylor & Francis

Library of Congress Catalog Number: 99-24855

Library of Congress Cataloging-in-Publication Data

Mitchell, Wesley Clair, 1874–1948.
    The backward art of spending money / Wesley Clair Mitchell ; with a new preface, introduction, and afterword by Eli Ginzberg.
        p. cm.
    Originally published: The backward art of spending money, and other essays. New York ; London : McGraw-Hill Book Co., 1937.
    Includes bibliographical references and index.
    ISBN 0-7658-0611-8 (paper : alk. paper)
    1. Money. 2. Business cycles. 3. Economics. I. Title.
HG221.M6757   1999
332.4—dc21   99-24855
                                                                              CIP

ISBN 13: 978-0-7658-0611-6 (pbk)

Contents

Preface to the Transaction Edition   vii
  Eli Ginzberg

Introduction, "Wesley Clair Mitchell"   ix
  Eli Ginzberg

Prefatory Note   xxxvii

1. The Backward Art of Spending Money   3

2. Quantitative Analysis in Economic Theory   20

   Appendix: The Present Status and Future
   Prospects of Quantitative Economics   37

3. Statistics and Government   42

4. Institutes for Research in the Social Sciences   58

5. Research in the Social Sciences   72

6. Social Science and National Planning   83

7. Intelligence and the Guidance of Economic Evolution   103

8. Making Goods and Making Money   137

9. The Role of Money in Economic Theory   149

10. Bentham's Felicific Calculus   177

11. Postulates and Preconceptions of Ricardian Economics   203

12. Wieser's Theory of Social Economics   225

13. Sombart's Hochkapitalismus   258

14. Thorstein Veblen   279

15. Commons on Institutional Economics   313

16. The Prospects of Economics   342

17. Economics, 1904–1929   386

18. Business Cycles   416

Afterword, "The Optimistic American Empiricist"   454
  Eli Ginzberg

Index   459

Preface to the Transaction Edition

M Y FRIEND, Irving Louis Horowitz, the long-time head of Transaction Publishers, who has done so much to print and reprint the work of leading American social scientists for the benefit of researchers, students, and the reading public, has another credit to his account. It was his idea to republish a collection of essays by Wesley Clair Mitchell, the acknowledged leader of American economists during the first half of this century.

Regrettably, the passage of time can blur and even obliterate the reputation and achievements of yesterday's leaders of ideas and actions. Although the National Bureau of Economic Research which Wesley Mitchell helped to found and which he led in the 1920s and 1930s remains an important research institution as this century draws to a close, I surmise that relatively few of its research associates who represent the elite among U.S. academic economists have any first-hand acquaintance with Mitchell's work. I therefore responded enthusiastically to Horowitz's suggestion that I cooperate with him in preparing a volume of Mitchell's essays that would make it easier for today's and tomorrow's economists and social scientists to become acquainted with Mitchell's many scholarly contributions.

I found among my own books a volume of Mitchell's essays entitled The Backward Art of Spending Money that McGraw-Hill had published in 1937, which if reprinted would go a long way, but not all of the way, to filling the lacuna. The earlier publication did not include any of Mitchell's contributions to the analysis of business cycles, the area that commanded most of his scholarly efforts. Fortunately, the omission was easily remedied. Mitchell had contributed a multi-page article on "Business Cycles" to the Encyclopedia of Social Sciences, published by Macmillan in 1929 which is reprinted in the current volume.

It was Horowitz's judgment that my long delayed essay on "Wesley Clair Mitchell," written in 1931 and published for the first time in 1997, would be an appropriate introduction to this new volume of Mitchell's essays. We agreed that the Afterword would contain the core of my remarks delivered at the fiftieth anniversary of Mitchell's death at the meeting of the Allied Social Sciences Association held in Chicago early in 1998.

Eli Ginzberg

Wesley Clair Mitchell

I WROTE "Wesley Clair Mitchell"—which follows this brief introductory statement—during the summer of 1931 after having been enrolled as a college senior in Wesley Mitchell's graduate class on "Current Types of Economic Theory" during the preceding two semesters. On several occasions during the two semesters, I talked after class with Mitchell about his views as to when the worsening depression was likely to end and the public policy interventions that might contribute to turning the economy around, only to be amazed and disappointed to have him reply that he had not yet done sufficient research to know the answers.

I had begun to read systematically through Mitchell's bibliography, and at the end of the course I told him that I planned to undertake a "psychoanalytic" assessment of his work. He responded that he would be more interested in the outcome than anybody else and that he looked forward to reading it once it was completed.

Mitchell spent the academic year 1931–32 as the second visiting Eastman Professor at Oxford University and returned in mid-1932 to his summer home at Huckleberry Rocks in Greensboro, Vermont. I forwarded my draft essay to him there and asked whether I could stop by on my forthcoming visit to the Adirondacks to review the paper with him. I received a warm note in reply to send the paper along and to let him know when I would be coming by to discuss it. When I

Originally published in the *History of Political Economy* 29:3 by Duke University Press (1997).

arrived a fortnight or so later and asked a lady working on a barn at the entrance to the property where I might find Mitchell, she asked, "Who are you?" When I told Mrs. Mitchell my name, she said, "Oh, you are the young man who has upset Wesley. He's out playing golf, but you can go down the hill to the house and wait for him." Some twenty minutes later Mitchell arrived and welcomed me warmly. However, I was shocked to find that his hair had turned completely gray during his year abroad. Without further ado, he found his copy of my paper, and starting on page 1 and continuing to the end he challenged me on a great many points where he disagreed with my assessment or sought clarification. The session lasted about three hours and was interrupted only briefly when Mrs. Mitchell joined us to serve tea. At the end of the session, Mitchell asked me what I planned to do with the paper, and when I indicated that I would like to revise and then publish it, he said that he would be pleased to have it published.

That night I stopped at the nearby home of Frederick C. Mills, another of my teachers and a longtime colleague of Mitchell's both at Columbia and at the National Bureau of Economic Research (NBER), who asked for details of my visit to Mitchell, since he had not caught up with him since his return from England. After I filled him in, he indicated that I should do nothing about publishing the paper until we met again when classes resumed. He alerted me that he had heard that Mitchell had had a disturbing and disappointing year at Oxford, and he was sure that I would not want to do anything to upset him further. When we next talked at Columbia in the early fall, we were in full agreement that it was best not to publish the paper.

I recently found a copy of the paper and asked my good friend Moses Abramovitz of Stanford University—a student of Mitchell's and his long-term associate at the NBER—whether

INTRODUCTION

he thought I should publish it at this late date. He encouraged me to do so but to add a few introductory statements about the place of Wesley Mitchell in American economics at the time when this brash Columbia College senior first encountered him.

Wesley Clair Mitchell in 1931 was recognized as the country's outstanding empirical economist, the father of business cycles research, the cofounder and director of the National Bureau of Economic Research, whose own research and the research of his collaborators at the NBER turned economics from a system of theoretical speculations about how markets operated into the quantitative analysis of economic developments in which the analysis of statistical data provided the foundation for the assessment of economic changes in the real world. It was my appreciation of Mitchell's unique position as the principal architect of quantitative economics that led me to explore how it happened that he stayed on the sidelines, refusing to assess what turned into the most severe depression in the nation's history and unwilling to formulate any recommendations that might help to reverse the ever worsening downward spiral. I looked for the key to this dilemma in Mitchell's personality and in his value system. My willingness to publish this essay after such a long interval rests on two convictions. First, present and future generations of American economists need to know more about Mitchell's life and work. And I believe that my brash insights provide an important clue to the understanding of the work and life of one of America's most gifted economists.

Wesley Clair Mitchell

Scientific criticism has concerned itself to an ever-decreasing degree with personalities. The investigations have dwarfed the investigators—witness Einstein's violin shrinking into oblivion beside the awe-inspiring system of relativity. The work of Freud and his school has illustrated the usefulness of analyzing the creator as well as the creation of scientific disciplines.

Most critics would ascribe a place of priority to the institutional-descriptive-quantitative tendencies among American economists in the complex of current thinking. And Mitchell would doubtless be recognized as the leader of this school (Seligman 1925, 155; Homan 1928, 337).[1] A study of Mitchell's preconceptions and emotional characteristics as reflected in his writings will perhaps prove enlightening in an appraisal of the statistical approach to economics. Psychoanalysis without the patient is dangerous, if not impossible. But acknowledging the limitations, the scrutiny of written materials might offer a substitute for the analysis of personal recitals. We are exceedingly fortunate to possess a long letter in which Mitchell, responding to a pressing request, ventured an attempt at self-analysis (Clark 1931, 662). This illuminating and elegant memorandum—an excellent example of Mitchell's stylistic abilities—might well serve as a point of departure for the present interpretation.

The hereditary and early environmental forces that helped to mold Mitchell are unknown to us. Mitchell, however, has summarized some childhood theological discussions with his grandaunt. This account is a rather succinct commentary on the intellectual and emotional predilections of the midwestern youngster prior to his college days. He looked askance at speculation, and continuously attempted to supplant the metaphysical with the empirical. The pragmatism of his later life is therefore not solely the product of his university schooling. Veblen, and to a much greater degree Dewey, only rein-

[1] Seligman describes Mitchell as the ablest of the slightly younger school of economists (1925).

forced the skepticism of the Illinois lad toward things he could not see or handle.

His Chicago apprenticeship explains much of his later work. By and large, he deviated only slightly from the path on which he started in his undergraduate days. He studied philosophy and economics and soon came to the conclusion that the two disciplines were distinctly similar. He "could spin speculations by the yard," but considered his "deductions" futile (Clark 1931, 676). He was acutely conscious of this ability. His facility in mastering the method led him to doubt the utility of the approach. The earlier economists had undervalued observation; Mitchell considered facts much more important than theories built up in a large degree without any intimate knowledge of the facts. Dewey had made him suspicious of logic. "My grandaunt's theology; Plato and Quesnay; Kant, Ricardo, and Karl Marx; Cairnes and Jevons, even Marshall were much of a piece. Each system was tolerably self-consistent—as if that were a test of truth!" This disdain of the pillars of learning was not unique among American college youth. Although Mitchell's reaction to the learned and revered idols of civilization might have been typical of most of his contemporaries, it was predicated on more than a general wariness of philosophical systems. After reading the prophets' prolegomena to salvation, he concluded that they had not only failed to save the masses, but were unable to rescue themselves. Their works were not tests of the truth. Mitchell was unable to react sympathetically to these artistic creations. He thought, rather, that they had been put to trial and found wanting. Mitchell ceased worshipping philosophy—the idol of old—and set out in search of the true god, science.

"There seemed to be one way of making real progress, slow, very slow, but tolerably sure. That was the way of natural science."[2] Veblen thought that economics had much to learn from biology, but Mitchell desired to emulate physics and chemistry. These sciences depended largely on observation and experimentation. "They had been built up not in grand systems like soap bubbles." His was a continuous predilection for the concrete, for problems that he could treat with some approach to scientific methods. One can search in vain for epistemological formulations in Mitchell. Test tubes, scales, and rulers had been instrumental in furthering progress in the physical sciences. Mitchell was fascinated by both the techniques and the results. He hastened to experiment with these same tools. He did not inquire whether the phenomena of the social sciences could be isolated, weighed, and measured. There was no a priori solution possible. For forty long years he has sought the answer. His energies have been entirely absorbed by his original experiment—to establish in economics a method similar to those of physics and chemistry. He has restrained himself in his desire to achieve speedy results, and devoted little time to elaborating a systematic approach. In answer to J. M. Clark's query concerning the relation of his analytic description to causal theory, Mitchell stated that he had "no clear ideas—though I might develop some at need."

What led Mitchell to adopt statistics as the staff that was to support him through the deep, unexplored morasses of economic phenomena? We have already referred to his skepticism of speculation. The work of the leading neoclassical economists in America he judged to be utopian. He had run the gamut from Quesnay to Marshall and considered the output

[2] With characteristic modesty Mitchell continues: "I really knew nothing of science and had enormous respect for its achievements." Mitchell has stated on several occasions that he is not completely at home in the realms of advanced mathematics and statistics. Did he accept this new technique somewhat uncritically?

INTRODUCTION

insignificant: "It seemed to me that the people who took seriously the sort of articles which were then appearing in the Q.J.E. might have a better time if they went in for metaphysics proper." Mitchell's evaluation of 'the then dominant trend in economics was hardly flattering to the authorities of the day. His studies with Veblen probably did little to revise his estimate of orthodox economic writings. The agnostic student was reinforced in his criticism of economists by his skeptical teacher. The latter couldn't, however, be certain that this young disbeliever would later not turn his incredulity against his teacher. In fact, Mitchell became highly dubious of the results that Veblen was able to achieve despite his superior intellect and keener insights (Clark 1931, 677).[3]

The iconoclastic youngster made rapid progress during his period of maturation. Before leaving Chicago, he had definitely broken with the main tradition in economics. It was not his intention to do what classical economists had done— "to think out a deductive scheme and then talk of verifying that." This determination to break with the old closed for him the customary channels of economic research. But the dissenters were not ideal foster parents. Veblen appealed to him because of his "artistic side. " He grouped the outstanding critic of classical economics, Karl Marx, with Kant and Ricardo as an architect who had deluded himself into constructing a strictly logical account of the world and man's origin. The conservatives as well as the radicals had manufactured "theories for their spiritual comfort and practical guidance which ran far beyond the realm of fact without straining their powers of belief." Mitchell was as ill at ease with the censors as he had been with the censored. The subtleties and sardonic humor of Veblen might have attracted

---

[3] "Veblen got nothing more certain by his dazzling performances with another set of premises."

[xv]

him aesthetically, but intellectually and emotionally they proved unsatisfying. The zest to work, to work constructively, predominated. The instinct of workmanship was supreme. He was doubtful whether the inherent potentialities of Veblen's approach could satisfy his propensity for solid outputs.

Mitchell's ancestors had transformed a virgin forest into a world empire. His early life, his intimacy with the land, had engendered in him a deep respect for hard work. A house could be erected only after the tree had been felled, the wood cut and planed, the boards grooved and nailed. Achievement depended on the successful performance of a series of consecutive steps.

The natural sciences, especially chemistry and physics, conformed most closely to this unconscious pattern that had ruled Mitchell since childhood. The magnificent achievements of the white-robed investigators in the laboratories of Germany, England, and the United States were the source of his conscious admiration. Both woodsman and scientist obtained results by making progress step by step. He inclined, however, to the social sciences. Mathematics was the indispensable tool in physical research. In economics, "there was plenty of need for rigorous thinking—but it was inside the investigation," and Mitchell discovered the counterpart to mathematics, the instrument that would contribute to precise thinking in the social sciences—statistics. Was this choice predictable in terms of the situation? Mitchell himself quoted the statement of Schumpeter that American institutionalism bears a close resemblance to the Historical School of Schmoller's day. The difference is slight; statistical series supplanted the historical monographs (Mitchell 1928, 40).

It will be remembered that Schmoller and his predecessors were concerned with superseding the technique of the classical school. At the same time they desired to avoid the involved polemics of the Marxian socialists. Admitting the validity of Schumpeter's analogy, Mitchell's solution was less naive. He did not believe that statistics of monthly deposits of the London goldsmiths would shed material light on the idiosyncracies of our modem banking system.

Did statistics appeal to Wesley C. Mitchell for any other reasons? I am forced to conjecture, and am probably unwarranted in my interpretation. But I shall place the blame on his unconscious—and proceed. It has already been emphasized that Mitchell was a dissenter without being a radical. My later analysis will indicate that there has existed in Mitchell a deep resistance to establishing clearly his position on issues of practical or theoretical significance. One may well inquire therefore whether—on the assumption that this trait has been present since childhood—statistical investigations did not afford him an excellent opportunity to tolerate this inhibition without compromising his ability to work or restricting his influence. This hypothesis need not be affirmed or denied at present, but it may well serve as a point of departure for a detailed analysis of the underlying attitudes, conscious and unconscious, in Mitchell's writings.[4]

The key to an understanding of Mitchell's approach to economics is his assessment of the methods employed in the physical sciences at the beginning of the present century.[5] It was the technique of the physicist and chemist that he hoped to replicate. Mitchell has written of himself that his was not so much a "predilection for the concrete" as it was a "predi-

---

[4] For the purposes of the following analysis I shall deal with most of Mitchell's writings except for his volumes on business cycles. Only occasional reference will be made to the latter. A discussion of this material would only be confusing. Furthermore, he hopes to publish in the near future the second volume of his revised treatise. Accordingly, it was thought best to defer until such time a critical appraisal of this phase of his work. See *A Bibliography* 1931, 201, for a comprehensive list of Mitchell's publications.

lection for problems one can treat with some approach to scientific method" (Clark 1931, 678). His concern with method transcended his interest in problems. The former became the determining force in his scholarly work. What little we know about scientific method would lead us to believe that we are confronted with an anomalous situation. Instead of the problem dictating the tools to be employed, the tools go in search of the problem.

Economics in Mitchell's opinion had been more art than science. And he "was a workman who wanted to become a scientific worker-who trusted only what we see in the light of the common day" (Clark 193 1, 678). He never deliberated on justifying the introduction of *scientific methods* into economics. His faith in the efficacy of the medium sustained him. He felt assured that he would not run into a cul de sac. He has declared his belief in the futility of the old, *artistic* economics on frequent occasions and in no uncertain terms. He has reacted with especial intensity against the subjective and speculative approaches of all of his predecessors and most of his colleagues. In order to establish an objective science of economics based to the greatest degree on statistical investigations, it was essential for Mitchell to take up the cudgels against the older, evaluative approach.

The investigator in the social sciences dares not inject his scale of values into his research. "The socio-ethical element in the work of many German economists—does not seem to me to be economic theory, or to have a scientific character" (Mitchell 1916, 159). Any attempt of writers to inculcate their ideals of social welfare necessitates, in Mitchell's opinion, their withdrawal from the ranks of economists. "They exercise the functions of preachers and statesmen rather than the

[5] See note 2.

functions of investigators" (Mitchell 1916, 159). Objective economics must be *wertfrei*.

In a formal confession of faith (Mitchell 1925, 4), Mitchell maintained that economists following qualitative methods undertook excursions into the subjective. In his opinion, these excursions were unnecessary. In an earlier and equally carefully prepared address (Mitchell 1919), he leveled strong invectives against the naive, subjective investigators. "In part the Social Sciences represent not what is, so much as what their writers think ought to be. In short, the Social Sciences are still childish" (Mitchell 1919, 230). Plato in *The Republic* and Marx in *Das Kapital* did not distinguish between their objective analyses and subjective aspirations. Would it be justifiable to brand their work *childish?*

Mitchell would be the last to deny that the choice of method in scientific research is determined by the predilections of the investigator. He stated that his own inclinations prompted him to employ *scientific methods* in economics. However, the personal commitments of the investigator will largely determine how he applies his techniques. The labor theory of value, applied to identical phenomena, yielded entirely different results at the hands of David Ricardo and Karl Marx. The problem of evaluation is the problem of science! And all values are subjective. Mitchell's own work in the field of index numbers is a telling challenge to his own philosophy (Mitchell 1921). He considered the rationalization of weighting to be the crucial problem of index numbers. And different individuals, with different values, will pursue different weighting schemes.

Mitchell's shyness of the subjective is matched by his fear of the speculative. He frequently has contrasted the scientific with the metaphysical (Mitchell 1928, 4). The older economists were speculative, though Mitchell would not deny that they achieved "real wonders" despite this handicap. But Ricardo, Jevons, and Marshall "got good results only with the simplest of problems" (Clark 1931, 678). He remarked of himself that he "could spin speculations by the yard" (Clark 1931, 676). But he felt instinctively that these deductions were futile. Unfortunately many terms remain undefined in Mitchell, and one is forced to infer the implications of contrasting the scientific and the metaphysical. Sodium and chloride combine. A consistent, replicable explanation of this phenomenon is scientific. Continuous experimentation is able to establish the validity of the theory. Marx's laws of capitalistic development would be considered metaphysical. A confirmation of his hypotheses is not feasible.

The mechanistic philosophy reigned supreme in the sciences to which Mitchell looked for guidance during his college studies. He became thoroughly imbued with this *Weltanschaungslehre*. Since then, a quarter of a century has passed. The work of Einstein alone should have raised some doubts in Mitchell's mind concerning the position of speculative thought in science, even in the physical sciences. Surely, the followers of the discoverer of relativity did not trust "only what we see in the light of the common day" (Clark 1931, 678). But Mitchell remained a nineteenth-century mechanist. He conceived of an antithesis between science and metaphysics, interpreting science to be a discipline concerned with facts. His ideal was to make economics an objective science. The key to his concept of objectivity was the role of facts in the scheme of things (Clark 1931,678).[6]

In one of his early articles, essentially a review of McDougall's book, *Social Psychology,* Mitchell states that he is glad to learn that psychology is becoming increasingly dependent on *objective observation* (Mitchell 1910, 100). And this science is important in Mitchell's estimation. "It is because they are developing a sounder type of functional psychology that we may hope both to profit and to share in the work of the contemporary psychologists" (Mitchell 1914, 47).

Mitchell disliked the subjective approach because the investigator introduced value judgments into his analyses. He prized the objective attitude highly because it alone insured the absence of an evaluative process. He constantly equated quantitative with objective data. Facts are objective; economics should be factual, for only then will it be objective.

The religion of *facts* was first preached as gospel truth, and only after a period of time was it institutionalized. The central dogma was loudly proclaimed at the dedication of the new church (Mitchell 1922a). "Its effort is to reduce economic and industrial problems to definite facts and authoritative figures" (Mitchell 1922a, foreword). Through what process can problems ever be turned into facts? Mitchell had become a metaphysician. The size of the national income is a factual question. But the *problem* of its distribution is clearly not factual. Mitchell desires "that social problems of whatever sort should rest whenever possible on objective knowledge of fact and not on subjective impressions" (Mitchell 1922a, 6). Two distinct issues are being confused. Every research worker would benefit if his data were more critically tested. It is certainly helpful to the taxation expert to know what proportion of the total income is earned by laborers, what percentage is distributed in the form of dividends, and so forth. But Andrew Mellon and Senator Norris would continue to disagree as to the most efficacious system of taxation despite their acceptance of the revenue estimates.

Mitchell once distinguished statesmen from economists. It

[6] It is hoped that the author's statements with reference to the problems discussed here have not been seriously distorted.

is not clear from the scattered references whether he would consider the construction of a taxation program the work of the statesman or the economist (Mitchell 1923a).[7] In a review of Von Wieser's "Social Economics" (Mitchell 1917, 115) he injects an obiter dictum on the duties of the economist who, he says, "should observe and record what men do in business, as the meteorologist observes and records the weather." This statement would lead one to believe that Mitchell desires to circumscribe radically the scope for economic investigation.[8] It is, however, debatable that observation and tabulation are ipso facto *objective* undertakings. A knowledge of the national income would be a great boon to many investigators.[9] It has been possible for two experts to estimate the same figures and discover, despite the employment of different methods, a marked similarity in their results (NBER 1921, 10–11). A decade after the original investigation, another student reworked the materials and admitted that certain of his estimates might contain a 30 to 40 percent margin of error (King 1930, 34). And this through no fault of his own: the materials at his disposal were woefully inadequate. Mitchell has been concerned with filling these appalling gaps in our knowledge of the facts. The justification for this task is evident. But these essays are spade work. Only the topsoil has been prepared for ploughing. Perfect arrays of facts and figures would still remain so much refuse unless selected, sorted, and interpreted.[10]

[7] He expresses the hope that accountants will soon usurp important advisory functions in the determination of business policies.

[8] See note 7. This address was delivered about six years after the review was written. It is doubtful whether Mitchell changed his viewpoint during this period. The seeming contradiction can perhaps be accounted for by the cursory attention that he has paid to these problems.

[9] Mitchell and several research associates at the National Bureau of Economic Research have been grappling with this problem for more than a decade, but as yet have evidenced no great satisfaction with their results.

INTRODUCTION

Science is systematized knowledge. Knowledge without insight is worthless. Mitchell's statement that "the fact that we can all agree in finding the facts concerning social issues is the best practical demonstration that any group of men has given that scientific method can be applied to the treatment of social problems" (1922a, 14) is far from self-evident. Mitchell has been ardent in his advocacy of *scientific methods* in economics. Such an approach can inhibit the expression of opinion on the part of the investigators. To talk of facts as being objective is specious. The student alone gives meaning to the facts. The preconceptions, the conscious and unconscious attitudes, the approach of the individual investigator will determine beyond a measure of doubt his solution. Neither the test tube nor the adding machine has ever answered a single query of man.

Mitchell's devotion to the facts derived from his youthful admiration for the natural sciences. He aspired to transmit the methods of the physical sciences to economics. Arguing by analogy, he contended that the social sciences should initiate and play a role in progress not dissimilar to that of physical science (Mitchell 1926, 84). "They have not won such confidence because they do not merit it. They do not merit it because they are less exact and less certain in their conclusions" (Mitchell 1926, 84). Is the difference one of exactness and certainty? Perhaps the essential dissimilarity is one of quality not quantity. The chemist has no predilection to discover that A and not B is the potent agent in a reaction. His disinterestedness can reach a very high order. His training and general preconceptions might impede him in his research, though his likes and dislikes are apt to be without the

---

[10] The voluminous collections of statistical data in the census monographs are some indication of the worthlessness of undigested statistics (facts).

slightest influence."[11] Unfortunately, the social scientist is in no such happy situation. It always has been, and probably always will be impossible for men to live without a scale of preferences. Neutrality on social issues is impossible. The economist who deals with contemporary materials should realize that his interpretations will help support or undermine existing social institutions.[12] To throttle his emotional interests would alone insure objectivity to his scientific work. And this would be the death of science!

The experimental method was in no small measure responsible for the rapid progress of the physical sciences. Mitchell, ever anxious to model the social sciences in the light of his ideal, endeavored to introduce the laboratory into economics. He hoped that the problems with which Ricardo and Marshall grappled would "cease to be a system of pecuniary logic, a mechanical study of static equilibria under non-existent conditions and become a science of human behavior" (Mitchell 1914, 47). Experiments in human behavior would increase knowledge and quicken progress. Mitchell foresaw the specific difficulties of experimenting in the social sciences. But his fundamental optimism permitted him to minimize the obstacles. "Social experimentation, based on clearly thought out hypotheses and accompanied by careful recordkeeping is one of the essential processes in increasing social knowledge and gaining social control" (Mitchell 1923c, 18). The most significant social experiment of modern times

[11] Revolutionary concepts have not always met with favorable receptions in the physical sciences, especially when general social or religious doctrines were implicitly attacked by the newer approach. (Consider Copernicus, Darwin, and Freud.) However, it is comparatively simple for the scientist to lead a Jekyll and Hyde existence, as with the religiosity of Newton and his mechanistic philosophy.

[12] This interpretation is not completely alien to Mitchell. "For the results of the most careful measurements may be interpreted in diverse ways" (Mitchell 1920b, 130).

was engendered by a group of intellectual agitators working with word, pen, and sword. The Russian Communists had a vehement hatred of the old regime. With opportunity in the offing, they used every means fair and foul to achieve their ends. Would Mitchell view with favor this experiment in social adaptation? No—for he holds "no brief for experiments which are based mostly upon emotional reaction to social ills" (Mitchell 1923c, 18).

Mitchell's disavowal of social movements that derive their principal strength from the emotional involvement of the participating members is significant in evaluating his approach to economics. Where is one to look for the dynamics of change if rejection of authority is banned? The courtiers of Louis XVI did not spend their free hours engineering the Revolution. The English Parliament, composed mostly of wealthy landowners and bourgeois merchants, would never have passed the social legislation of the 1850s had it not been frightened into action by the Chartists. And the latter were assuredly not motivated by abstract scientific theories. But Mitchell believed that "reform by agitation or class struggle is a jerky way of moving forward" (Mitchell 1919, 229). Admitting the validity of this contention, what are we offered as an alternative? Mitchell believed that we can make our peace with the world "through intelligent experimenting and detailed planning rather than agitation or class struggle" (Mitchell 1919, 230). Mitchell did not agree with Marx's analysis that "the history of the world has been the history of class struggles"; or perhaps he did not sympathize with the concluding appeal of the Communist manifesto. Both positions are entirely tenable. Who will be interested in "intelligent experimenting"? If the jerky process of agitation is shunned, one must look elsewhere for the launchers of experiments. Those groups that stand to gain by the retention of the status quo will not support or applaud innovations in the social structure.

Mitchell has looked askance at the methods of achieving progress in the past. They have been *unscientific*. His failure to offer any constructive suggestions—except to enunciate a sublime optimism in the world of the future—weakens one's faith in the potentialities of the scientific approach to economics.

Experiments should be undertaken only after we are in command of the facts. The National Bureau of Economic Research is "Prevented from making positive recommendations on any question of social policy except the policy of basing action on ascertained facts" (Mitchell 1923c, 15). It is implicitly assumed that experiments based on the facts will be scientific. During the last ten years, the NBER has published important factual materials dealing with our economic society. The data suggested the advisability of undertaking reforms; but Mitchell failed to act. He complained at one time of the "under-developed public appreciation of the social importance of careful study as the basis for social action" (Mitchell 1923c, 16). It is doubtful that the country was unappreciative of the scientific labor expended in the accumulation of facts and figures. Professorial treatises analyzed the dangers of the present distribution of income. But the American public smiled cynically as it watched Congress lower inheritance taxes. Social action, despite Mitchell's fervent wish, will never be determined by a knowledge of the facts in an institutional setting like modem capitalism. An individualistic system cannot achieve social ends through a rational process.

The religion of facts has given an optimistic hue to Mitchell's approach. Innate human abilities need not improve. Progress will be hastened through pyramiding our factual knowledge. There is a strong, submerged belief in the ameliorative trend of events. Much of Mitchell's statistical technique can be appreciated only in terms of these preconceptions. His methodology was patterned after chemistry and physics, but his philosophy and general outlook were largely conditioned by Darwinian biology. "Most important of all, the influence of nurture may be cumulative. Every increase in social wisdom may be applied in bettering the nurture given to the generation that follows, so that this generation in turn may give its successor training better than it received" (Mitchell 1914,7). Mitchell was following Lamarck more closely than Darwin. He believed that it would be feasible to transmit the scientific discoveries of one generation to the next. Knowledge would grow by accretion. Hence the development of social sciences would more closely approximate that of the natural sciences. They would break with their past, for they would no longer depend on the manipulation of concepts (Mitchell 1928, 7).

Mitchell appealed to history through the medium of statistics. Wisdom as well as knowledge would accumulate through the ages. Postulating a pliability in human nature, his philosophy is optimistic. "Every one who does not emphasize the fact that human nature of each generation of men is determined chiefly by its nurture at the hands of the preceding generation misses the most potent single factor in social psychology" (Mitchell 1914, 15). Has man been able to profit from the experiences of his forefathers? To appeal to history is a paradox. Our chronicles testify to the recurring fratricidal massacres in which the descendants of Adam engage. True, they might learn much from the past about the techniques of existing, but the way of life they are forced to discover for themselves.

Mitchell's is a rational approach to economics. "In singling out institutional factors as the basis of rationality, current economics is also in line with current psychology" (Mitchell 1916, 155).[13] His technique has forced him to disregard the nonrationalistic elements. He is the supreme intellectualist. Collect data, derive trend lines, determine deviations—this is Mitchell's attack on business cycles!

THE BACKWARD ART OF SPENDING MONEY

His reflections on the crisis of 1920 illustrate his overwhelming faith in *science*. "We are justified in hoping that in the future such exigencies will seldom arise to prevent the Federal Reserve Board from adopting the policy which seems wise in the economic interest of the public" (Mitchell 1922b, 23). What reason has one to anticipate a phenomenal increase in either the ability or integrity of American banking interests? The Board erred once and it will probably err again. But Mitchell thought otherwise; he hoped that the mistakes of the past would not be repeated. The commission of errors at one period holds a promise if not a guarantee that they will not be repeated. Life becomes a mathematical problem for Mitchell. Having failed to obtain the correct answer by addition, one tries subtraction, forgetting that addition might be a faulty technique at one time, and subtraction equally ill-suited at another. Economic problems are never mechanical; their solution always involves judgment. The phrase *economic interest of the public* should have warned Mitchell that he was not confronted with a single problem. To experiment with sulphur and hydrochloric acid is one thing; to treat with the "public interest" is another. England desired to stabilize the pound in 1925. The Federal Reserve Board was asked to cooperate. Perfect statistical series covering discount rates in both markets would not have facilitated the Board's decision. These men were confronted with a unique situation. History inevitably failed them in their hour of need.

Mitchell was antagonistic to the "mechanics of utility" approach, and desired to mold economic theory along evolutionary lines (Mitchell 1924). His was a faith in a more scientific

---

[13] Mitchell wrote this essay in 1916. It is doubtful that the Freudian school was not already sufficiently prominent to cast suspicion on his assertion that modem psychology was concerned primarily with the rational.

type of economic theory—a type which looks at the material from the evolutionary point of view (Mitchell 1910, 110).

For the elements and compounds of the chemist, Mitchell substituted in his laboratory the literary and statistical records of the past. His method and objective were intimately related. He was confident that we can face the future unafraid, for our knowledge slowly accumulated in the past will serve as our guide. But one may well inquire whether history is anything more than "the story of how people have taken things into their own hands, and got themselves or others into and out of trouble over it" (Galsworthy 1931, 329).

Mitchell has had occasional misgivings concerning his technique. Life never repeats itself, and when analogies with the past are tenuous his difficulties mount. Business conditions in 1920 presented an enigma to both the economic historian and the men of affairs. Only a prophet would have ventured to forecast. Mitchell acknowledged the serious limitations of his method. "We therefore stand a better chance of forming correct anticipations of what will happen to prices and business in the early nineteen twenties by analyzing the present situation than by studying earlier economic history."[14] Business conditions corrected themselves rapidly after the crisis of 1920–21. The next eight years did not give Mitchell further cause to question his method of approach. The period was especially conducive to the development of an optimistic economics.

Socioeconomic adjustments are viewed by Mitchell in the light of technical difficulties. In discussing the control of the business cycle, he remarked that "one has slender confidence in the vitality of the race and in the power of the scientific method if he thinks a task of this technical sort is beyond man's power" (Mitchell 1923b, 53). Mitchell approached the problems of modem civilization in much the same way that a mechanic grapples with repairs. He believed that most defects could be eradicated by technical improvements. Social institutions are to undergo a steady process of reform. His concern with details did not permit him to consider scrapping the entire machine. His admiration for modern civilization always exceeded his criticism of specific aspects.

"Many businessmen regard themselves primarily as servants of the common welfare and do the very best they can to supply the community with wholesome products at reasonable prices" (Mitchell 1923a, 163). This is Mitchell in a wishful but not an analytic state. He considered capitalism to be "the best system of economic organization which the wit of man has so far devised" (Mitchell 1923a, 163). Not that he denied the existence of serious shortcomings, but he believed them to be remediable. His suggestions were assuredly not radical. Accountants were to assume more prominent positions as economic advisors because "every business concern which does manage to forecast the course of events which affects its operations-benefits the general public" (Mitchell 1923a, 170). Mitchell has studied business cycles thoroughly in their institutional setting of modern capitalism.[15] Yet he believed that the individual concern can affect materially the course of business fluctuations. The acuity of his analysis is matched by the weakness of his nostrums. He has never lost faith in the potentialities of his method. His reluctance to contemplate radical alterations in the status quo can be ascribed in part to this never failing trust. Not by faith but by knowledge will humankind be saved. "The more all of us try to achieve the scientific method-die more likely are we to make the world better (Mitchell 1926, 85). It constantly has

---

[14] Mitchell 1920a. Mitchell enunciated the same thesis in December 1919 at the annual meeting of the American Economic Association (Mitchell 1920b, 129).

been Mitchell's contention that ignorance of fundamental facts has been a much more serious impediment in the path of social progress than bad reasoning or bad motives and bad actions (Mitchell 1922a, 14). Did the Romans not foresee what their policy of ruthless exploitation would portend? Were the military leaders of France ignorant of the consequences that would follow the adoption of their policy to strip the Ruhr? By no means. In both cases the eagerness for immediate gains outweighed the fear of future reverses. Mitchell's (1919, 230) optimistic conviction that "not good will but knowledge is lacking" demands revision in light of these examples. The relation of Mitchell's method to his objective is best illustrated by a quotation from his writings, in which he encourages "cultivating an experimental habit of mind and endeavoring to add. our mites to the knowledge that may some day give mankind control over their own behavior" (Mitchell 1922b, 32).

Along what lines does Mitchell anticipate an advance in economics? In his presidential address to the American Economic Association he offered a fourfold program: (1) the compilation of new statistics, (2) the invention of new technical methods, (3) the refinement of the older methods, and (4) the design of experiments in behavior (Mitchell 1928, 7).

Some years earlier, shortly after the depression of 1920, Mitchell had drawn up a set of objectives for economic science, in which three things must be accomplished: (1) a more thorough use of quantitative analysis must be undertaken; (2) a better understanding of the role of institutions must be attained; and (3) a courageously constructive attitude must be adopted. What underlay the choice of these objectives?

---

[15] See Mitchell 1930, in which he discusses with consummate acuity business fluctuations in modern capitalism.

THE BACKWARD ART OF SPENDING MONEY

The concluding section of this essay will attempt to illustrate the existence of a basic congeniality between the scientific methodology and the social aspirations of Wesley Clair Mitchell. The riddle of the universe can be solved, if at all, by a study of men.

The Illinois youngster who came to Chicago in 1892 was gifted and ambitious. He chose the social sciences as his field of study. He reacted adversely to European idealism and realism. He was an American empiricist. The revolutionary doctrines of Continental agitators fell on deaf ears.[16] Nothing in the American scene suggested the need for destruction. Rather the reverse was true; the country was still in its period of adolescence, in need of all of its strength.

We have seen how the bright youth soon became dissatisfied with, one might almost say disdainful of, the idols of his intellectual community. He discovered that they had eyes that could not see, and ears that could not hear. His was a desire to breathe the breath of life into these wooden images. Unlike Marx, he did not desire to demolish the false gods by sword and fire. He would teach the heathens to forgo their idol worship.

Statistics offered Mitchell a means of escape from reality— for he was a realist who feared reality. Statistical laboratories became his haven of refuge. There he found asylum while he searched for the magic formula that would cure the stricken world of its many maladies. Disease became more rampant, but still the investigator sought his opiate. Suddenly, it became clear that if the search were much prolonged, the world would succumb while the scientist searched.

Mitchell pursued quantitative analysis in economics for more than thirty years. He perfected a most powerful technique.

[16] The dislike of social reformers has remained with him throughout his life (Mitchell 1919, 229).

INTRODUCTION

But the creator fell in love with his own creation. One is reminded of the legend of Narcissus. Grandiosity, according to the Freudians, is frequently associated with profound feelings of inferiority. Mitchell devised a beautiful rifle, but his fear of blood stayed him from shooting.[17] To compensate for this inherent deficiency, he continued to devise ever more elaborate weapons. Like the pacifist who placed national security first, this economist strived more for knowledge than reform. But peace does not thrive on armaments, nor life on statistical series. A police force is necessary to insure the tranquility of a society, just as knowledge is essential for progress. One of the wisest men of the Occident realized the tragedy of the paradox:

> How hard it is to master ways and means
> By which a man may reach the fountain-head!
> And, ere he's half-way there, fate intervenes:
> Before he knows it, the poor devil's dead.
> (Goethe 1949)

ELI GINZBERG

References

A Bibliography of the Faculty of Political Science, Columbia University, 1880–1930. 1931. New York: Columbia University Press.

Clark, John Maurice. 1931. Wesley C. Mitchell's Contribution to the Theory of Business Cycles. In *Methods in Social Science, A Case Book*, edited by Stuart A. Rice. Chicago: University of Chicago Press.

---

[17] The "fear complex" in Mitchell can best be demonstrated by the following examples. He frequently recognizes and emphasizes highly significant issues, only to shy clear of them at the crucial point when he is forced to commit himself specifically, not generally: (1) See his allusion to the problem of stabilization in 1920 and his failure to establish his position clearly, in Mitchell 1920a, 6; (2) see his reference to the need for a "courageously constructive attitude" and his failure to amplify this remark in Mitchell 1922b, 32; and (3)

Galsworthy, John. 1931. *Maid in Waiting*. New York: Charles Scribner's Sons.

Goethe, Johann Wolfgang von. 1949. *Faust: Part 1*. Translated from the German by Philip Wayne. New York: Penguin.

Homan, Paul T. 1928. *Contemporary Economic Thought*. Freeport, N.Y.: Books for Libraries Press.

King, Willford Isbell. 1930. *The National Income and Its Purchasing Power*. New York: National Bureau of Economic Research.

Mitchell, Wesley C. 1910. The Rationality of Economic Activity (part 1). *Journal of Political Economy* 18.2 (February): 97–113.

———. 1914. Human Behavior and Economics: A Survey of Recent Literature. *Quarterly Journal of Economics* 29.1 (November): 1–47.

———. 1916. The Role of Money in Economic Theory. *Supplement of the American Economic Review* 6.1 (March): 140–6 1.

———. 1917. Wieser's Theory of Social Economics. *Political Science Quarterly* 32 (March): 95–118.

———. 1919. Statistics and Government. Presidential address at the Eightieth Annual Meeting of the American Statistical Association, Richmond, Virginia, December 1918. *Publications of the American Statistical Association*, n.s., 125 (March): 223–35.

———. 1920a. Prices and Business in the Near Future. *Bankers Statistics Corporation* (N.Y. weekly) 1.17 (10 February): sec. 2.

———. 1920b. Prices and Reconstruction. *Supplement of the American Economic Review* 10.1 (March): 129–55.

———. 1921. The Making and Using of Index Numbers. *Bulletin of the United States Bureau of Labor Statistics*, rev. ed., 284 (October): 7–114.

———. 1922a. *A Bold Experiment: The Story of the National Bureau of Economic Research*. New York: National Bureau of Economic Research.

———. 1922b. The Crisis of 1920 and the Problem of Controlling

see his allusion to "social experimentation" which likewise remained undefined in Mitchell 1923c, 18. These examples could be multiplied many times over. Mitchell's desire to avoid controversy ("I look forward to the day when a round table such as we are now holding will be an anachronism" [Mitchell 1928]) and his attempt to rid economics of its "socio-ethical" elements are objective manifestations of his unconscious reactions. A study of the emotions is key to an understanding of man and his work.

INTRODUCTION

Business Cycles. *Supplement of the American Economic Review* 12.1 (March): 20–32.

———. 1923a. Accountants and Economics with Reference to the Business Cycle. *Journal of Accountancy* 35.3 (March): 161–7 1.

———. 1923b. The Problem of Controlling Business Cycles. In *Stabilization of Business,* edited by Lionel D. Edie. New York: Macmillan.

———. 1923c. Unemployment and Business Fluctuations. *American Labor Legislation Review* 13 (March): 15–22.

———. 1924. The Prospects of Economics. In *The Trend of Economics,* edited by Rexford G. Tugwell. New York: Knopf.

———. 1925. Quantitative Analysis in Economic Theory. (Presidential address before the American Economic Association.) *American Economic Review* 15.1 (March): 4–12.

———. 1926. The Contribution of the Social Sciences in Solving Social Problems. *American Labor Legislation Review* 16 (March): 84–85.

———. 1928. Round Table Discussion. *Supplement of the American Economic Review* 18.1 (March): 39.

———. 1930. Business Cycles. In *Encyclopedia of the Social Sciences,* edited by Edwin R. A. Seligman. Vol. 3. New York: Macmillan.

National Bureau of Economic Research (NBER). 192 1. *Income in the United States, Its Amount and Distribution, 1909–1919- 1.* New York: Harcourt, Brace.

Seligman, Edwin R. A. 1925. *Essays in Economics.* New York: Macmillan.

Prefatory Note

THIS collection of essays was made by my friend Joseph Dorfman. The plan was his, the selections are his, the execution is his, and to him I render thanks. But I must confess to being an accessary before the fact. At Dr. Dorfman's request, I have reread the papers he has chosen, some of which had grown vague in my memory. As I read, the editorial passion gripped me. I could not suppress impulses to mend awkward expressions, though I tried not to go beyond making the original meaning clearer. That I would not now write certain passages as they are here republished means, I like to believe, that I have learned something as the years have passed.

Since the essays were prepared for different occasions at intervals irregularly distributed over a quarter century, the book contains several repetitions, of which the most conspicuous are pointed out in footnotes. There are presented numerous diagnoses of the ills from which economics suffers, as well as prescriptions for alleviating some among them; but my experiments as a practicing economist in taking my own medicine are either too technical or too elaborate for a book of essays, and Dr. Dorfman did well to omit them. Without submitting the evidence here, I venture to claim on the basis of personal experience that, when taken in the proper way, the medicine often has beneficial effects.

WESLEY C. MITCHELL.

NEW YORK, N. Y.,
March, 1937.

[xxxvii]

THE BACKWARD ART OF SPENDING
MONEY AND OTHER ESSAYS

THE BACKWARD ART OF SPENDING MONEY[1]

IN THE scheme of modern life, making money and spending money are strictly correlative arts. Of the two, spending is rated as both pleasanter and easier to practice. Certainly for most of us it is not less important. A few, indeed, make so much money that they can slight the art of spending without suffering discomfort, but the vast majority would gain as much from wiser spending as from increased earning.

Important as the art of spending is, we have developed less skill in its practice than in the practice of making money. Common sense forbids our wasting dollars earned by irksome efforts; and yet we are notoriously extravagant. Ignorance of qualities, uncertainty of taste, lack of accounting, carelessness about prices—faults that would ruin a merchant—prevail in our housekeeping. Many of us scarcely know what becomes of our money; though well-schooled citizens of a money economy ought to plan for their outgoes no less carefully than for their incomes.

For this defect in our way of living we are often taken to task, not only by thrifty souls who feel that waste is sin, but also by men of large affairs who wish that we might ask less insistently for higher wages and save more money to invest in their securities. No doubt there is sufficient reason for faultfinding, and no doubt much of the free advice given

[1] Reprinted by permission from *American Economic Review*, vol. II, pp. 269–281, June, 1912.

on mending our ways is sound. Conscience admits the first, common sense the second. But in our haste to plead guilty we forget certain mitigating circumstances which might go far toward recommending us to the mercy of an impartial court. To spend money is easy, to spend it well is hard. Our faults as spenders are not wholly due to wantonness, but largely to broad conditions over which as individuals we have slight control.

Under the less complicated economic organization of barter and the nascent use of money, the family was the unit in large measure for purposes both of producing and of consuming goods. By the time of American colonization, English society had grown out of such simple conditions. But the earlier colonists were forced by their isolation to revert to practices that the mother country had long since abandoned. The family became again a unit of producers, caring for one another's wants. Foodstuffs and other raw materials were produced by the men, assisted by the women and children; these materials were prepared for family use by the women, assisted by the children and men. While this form of organization was transient in any one district, it kept reappearing on the frontier, so that for generations production was based in part upon the family as a unit.

Denser settlement would have sufficed by itself to enable Americans to develop division of labor and regular markets corresponding to those of seventeenth- and eighteenth-century England. But in addition there came the industrial revolution and the railway. These factors in combination gradually deprived the family of its old importance as a unit for producing goods. For the factory made, the railway brought, the shop kept a great variety of articles that the family once provided for itself. Production was reorganized on the basis of a new unit—the business enterprise —in which the members of many families were employed. And the new unit proved vastly more efficient than the old. It made possible more elaborate specialization of labor and machinery, more perfect coordination of effort and greater reduction of waste than could be attained by the family. There resulted a gigantic increase in the volume of goods produced and in the aggregate incomes earned.

Meanwhile as a unit for consuming goods, for spending money, the family has remained substantially where it was in colonial days. Division of labor in spending has not progressed beyond a rudimentary division between the adult men and women of the family—the women bearing the heavier burden of responsibility. Housework has been lightened by the growth of industry; but housewives still face essentially the same problems of ways and means as did their colonial grandmothers. No trade has made less progress than this, the most important of all trades.

It is because we have not wanted to that we have not developed a larger and more efficient unit for spending money than the family. Our race-old instincts of love between the sexes and parental affection, long since standardized in the institution of monogamy, are a part of experience at once so precious and so respectable that we have looked askance at every relaxation of the family bond, whatever material advantages it has promised. While we have become increasingly dependent upon other men for the goods we buy and for the sale of our services, we have jealously insisted upon maintaining the privacy of family life, its freedom from outside control, so far as our circumstances have permitted. Reluctantly we have let the factory whistle, the timetable, the office hours impose their rigid routine upon our money-making days; but our homes we have tried to guard from intrusion by the world of machinery and business. There are strains in our stock, to be sure, that can adapt themselves more readily to the lock step of life organized by others; such people fill our family hotels. But most of us still prefer a large measure of privacy, even though we pay in poor cooking. So long as we cling fondly to home life, so long will the family remain the most important unit for spending money. And so long as the family remains the most important unit for spending money, so long will the art of spending lag behind the art of making money.

The dominance of women in spending, which the family form of organization establishes, may explain in some measure the backwardness of the art. An effective contrast might be drawn between the slipshod shopping of many housewives and the skillful, systematic buying done for business enterprises by men. But the fair comparison is between the housewife's shopping for the family, and her husband's shopping for strictly personal wants. Current opinion certainly represents women as more painstaking than men in making selections, and more zealous in hunting for bargains. Doubtless if men had to do the work they would do it otherwise in some ways, and doubtless they would think their ways better. But if men had to spend money under the limitations now imposed upon women by family life, they would certainly find the task exceedingly difficult. It is the character of the work more than the character of the women that is responsible for poor results. Indeed, the defects of the workers are partly effects of the work. The lack of system, which reduces the efficiency of so many housewives, comes in a measure from the character of their daily tasks, like the pedantry that makes so many teachers uninspiring.

The housewife's tasks are much more varied than the tasks that business organization assigns to most men. She must buy

[6]

milk and shoes, furniture and meat, magazines and fuel, hats and underwear, bedding and disinfectants, medical services and toys, rugs and candy. Surely no one can be expected to possess expert knowledge of the qualities and prices of such varied wares. The ease with which defects of materials or workmanship can be concealed in finishing many of these articles forces the purchaser often to judge quality by price, or to depend upon the interested assurances of advertisers and shopkeepers. The small scale on which many purchases are made precludes the opportunity of testing before buying, and many articles must be bought hurriedly wherever they are found at whatever price is asked. If this work could be taken over for many families and conducted by a business enterprise it would be sub-divided into several departments, and each department would have its own minute division of labor. There would be the commissariat with its trained corps of purchasing agents and chemists, each giving his whole working day to the buying or testing of meats, or vegetables, or groceries. There would be departments of building and grounds, of furnishing, of fuel and lighting, of the laundry, of clothing, of the nursery, and the like—all bringing specialized knowl-edge to the solution of their problems, all having time and opportunity to test qualities and find the lowest prices. The single family can no more secure the advantage of such division of labor in caring for its wants as consumers than the frontier family could develop division of labor in production.

Nor can the family utilize labor-saving machinery to reduce the cost of living more effectively than can the very small shop utilize it to reduce the cost of production. The economical use of machinery requires that the work to be done be minutely subdivided and that each successive operation be standardized. The family unit is so small, the tasks are so various, and the housework is so scattered from cellar to attic as to make machinery more troublesome than useful. Even if a housewife were supplied with an elaborate mechanical equipment, and if she knew how to operate each machine and keep it in order, she could make but brief use of each device as she turned from one of her endless tasks to the next. A machine that is to stand idle ninety-nine hours in a hundred must possess extraordinary advantages, or cost but a trifle, to warrant its being installed even in a factory. Hence, the equipment that can be employed economically in the household falls into the class of inexpensive utensils and hand tools; even in this age of steam and electricity, a family must be cared for by hand.

Again, the general managers of households, unlike the general managers of business enterprises, are seldom selected upon the basis of efficiency. Indeed, there are grounds for believing that in this country less attention is paid than formerly to housewifely capacity in choosing wives. The young farmer going west to take up land knew that his success would depend largely upon the efficiency of his helpmate. Perhaps his grandson exercises as much worldly wisdom in choosing a wife, but he thinks more of how much an available *parti* can add to his income than of the skill with which she can manage what he earns.

However chosen, the young wife seldom approaches her housework in a professional spirit. She holds her highest duty that of being a good wife and a good mother. Doubtless to be a good manager is part of this duty; but the human part of her relationship to husband and children ranks higher than the business part. In a sense the like holds true for the man; but in his case the role of husband and father is separated more sharply from the role of money-maker.

[8]

The one role is played at home, the other role in the fields, the shop, or the office. This separation helps the man to practice in his own activities a certain division of labor conducive to efficiency in money-making. He can give undivided attention during his working hours to his work. But the woman must do most of her work at home, amidst the countless interruptions of the household, with its endless calls from children and friends. She cannot divide her duties as a human being so sharply from her duties as a worker. Consequently, her housekeeping does not assume objective independence in her thinking, as an occupation in which she must become proficient. Household management, under the conditions of family life, is not sufficiently differentiated from other parts of the housewife's life to be prosecuted with the keen technical interest which men develop in their trades.

Upon the household manager, capable or not as she may be, family life commonly throws an exhausting routine of manual labor. In large business enterprises matters are managed better. The man who makes decisions, who initiates policies, who must exercise sound judgment, does no work with his hands beyond signing his name. He is relieved of all trivial duties, protected from all unnecessary intrusions. One of the handicaps of the small enterprise is that its manager must also keep the books, write the letters, or work in the shop—must disperse his energy over many tasks. In the great majority of homes the housewife labors under a like handicap. If she has no servant, then cooking and sweeping, mending and shopping, tending the children and amusing her husband leave her little leisure and less energy for the work of management proper. Tired people stick in ruts. A household drudge can hardly be a good household manager. Even with one or two servants to assist them, many

[9]

wives work longer hours than their husbands, and work under conditions that are more nervously exhausting. The number of housewives who have leisure to develop the art of spending money wisely must be a very small percentage.

Though so many conditions of family life conspire to make hard the housewife's task, a surprising number of women achieve individual successes. If housekeeping were organized like business, these efficient managers would rapidly extend the scope of their authority, and presently be directing the work of many others. Then the less capable housewives, like the mass of their husbands, would be employed by these organizing geniuses at tasks that they could perform with credit to themselves and profit to the community. By this system we get the full use of our best brains in making money. But the limitations of family life effectually debar us from making full use of our best domestic brains. The trained intelligence and the conquering capacity of the highly efficient housewife cannot be applied to the congenial task of setting to rights the disordered households of her inefficient neighbors. These neighbors, and even the husbands of these neighbors, are prone to regard critical commentaries upon their slack methods, however pertinent and constructive in character, as meddlesome interferences. And the woman with a consuming passion for good management cannot compel her less progressive sisters to adopt her system against their wills, as an enterprising advertiser may whip his reluctant rivals into line. For the masterful housewife cannot win away the husbands of slack managers as the masterful merchant can win away the customers of the less able. What ability in spending money is developed among scattered individuals, we dam up within the walls of the single household.

There are, however, reasons for the backwardness of the art of spending money other than the organization of expenditure on the basis of the family. Grave technical difficulties inhere in the work itself, difficulties not to be wholly removed by any change of organization.

The rapid progress made and making in the arts of production rests upon progress in scientific knowledge. All the many branches of mechanics and engineering are branches of the tree of knowledge, nourished by the roots of research. Among the various sciences the most important for industry are physics and chemistry. It is by applying in practice the physical and chemical laws learned in the laboratory that recent generations have been able to develop not only their complicated machinery, but also their effective processes of modifying materials. Now physics and chemistry happen to be the sciences that deal with the subject matter that is simplest, most uniform, and most amenable to experimental control. They are therefore the sciences of which our knowledge is most full, most precise, and most reliable.

In similar fashion, progress in the arts of consumption rests upon progress in science—or rather waits upon progress in science. To secure the better development of our children's bodies we need a better knowledge of food values and digestive processes, just as we need better knowledge of electricity to reduce the waste of energy on long transmission lines. To secure the better development of children's minds we need better knowledge of the order in which their various interests waken, just as we need better knowledge of physical chemistry to control the noxious fumes of smelting plants.

But, unfortunately for the art of spending money, the sciences of fundamental importance are not physics and chemistry, but physiology and functional psychology. While the latter may be ultimately capable of reduction to a

[11]

physicochemical basis, they certainly deal with subject matters far less simple, less uniform, and less amenable to experimental control than does physics or chemistry proper. Hence, they are in a relatively rudimentary condition. As now written they are easier for the layman to read, they present fewer superficial difficulties; but that is precisely because their real difficulties have not been mastered and elucidated.

Accordingly, even the housewife who is abreast of her time labors under a serious disadvantage in comparison with the manufacturer. The latter can learn from an industrial chemist and a mechanical engineer far more about the materials he uses, the processes at his disposal, the machinery best adapted to his purpose, than the housewife could learn from all the living physiologists and psychologists about the scientific laws of bodily and mental development. No doubt the sciences that will one day afford a secure basis of knowledge for bringing up a family are progressing; but it seems probable that they will long lag behind the sciences that serve industry. Hence, the housewife's work presents more unsolved problems, is more a matter of guesswork, and cannot in the nature of things be done as well as the work of making and carrying goods. Until such time as science shall illuminate the housewife's path, she must walk in the twilight of traditional opinion.

If the art of making money has advantages over the art of spending on the side of scientific technique, it has equal advantages on the side of business method. Money-making is systematized by accounting in which all the diverse elements in a complicated series of bargains are adequately expressed in terms of one common denominator—the dollar. Thus a businessman is enabled to compare the advantage of granting long credits with the advantage of selling on closer margins for cash; he can estimate whether it would be cheaper to buy a higher grade of coal or to let his fireboxes burn out rapidly; he can set off the cost of additional advertising against the cost of more traveling salesmen. And since profits are also expressed in dollars, the businessman can control all items of expense on the basis of their estimated contributions toward his gains. In making money, nothing but the pecuniary values of things however dissimilar need be considered, and pecuniary values can always be balanced, compared, and adjusted in an orderly and systematic fashion.

Not so with the housewife's values. A woman can indeed compare costs as long as they consist solely in the money prices she is charged for goods. But she cannot make a precise comparison between the price of a ready-to-wear frock and the price of the materials plus her own work in making. Still less can she compare costs and gains. For her gains are not reducible to dollars, as are the profits of a business enterprise, but consist in the bodily and mental well-being of her family. For lack of a satisfactory common denominator, she cannot even make objectively valid comparisons between the various gratifications which she may secure for ten dollars—attention to a child's teeth, a birthday present for her husband, two days at a sanatorium for herself. Only in the crudest way can subjective experiences of different orders occurring to different individuals be set against one another. Opinions regarding their relative importance change with the mood and flicker with the focus of attention. Decisions made one hour are often cause of regret the next. In fine, spending money cannot conceivably be reduced to such a system as making money until someone invents a common denominator for money costs, and for all the different kinds and degrees of subjective gratifications that money can procure for people of unlike temperaments. Such household accounts as are kept doubtless have their value; but the most painstaking efforts to show the disposition of every cent spent still leave unanswered the vital question of what has been gained.

And what does the housewife seek to gain? The businessman in quest of profits can answer such a question for himself in terms distinctly definite. To make money becomes an end in itself; to spend money involves some end beyond the spending. When the housewife pursues her problem to this final query she comes upon the most baffling of her difficulties. Doubtless she can tell herself that she seeks the happiness of her husband and herself, the fair development of their children. But before these vague statements can serve as guides in the intensely practical problem of spending money, she must decide what happiness and development mean in concrete terms for her particular husband and children. Of course, our housewives are seldom philosophers, and if they were they could not let the dishes go unwashed while they wrestled with the question of what is best worth while in life. Most women, indeed, do their work in an empirical spirit, so busied with obvious difficulties of detail that they are saved from seeing the deepest perplexities of their position. It is commonly the very young wife whose conscience is worried about the ultimate aims of her spending; and she is more likely as the years go by to stop thinking about this problem than to think it out.

In accounting for the defects of the art of spending, as that art is currently practiced, there is little need to lay stress upon difficulties that are neglected by the great mass of practitioners. But there is one end which women assuredly do seek in spending, albeit unconsciously for the most part, which deserves attention because it is subversive of economical management.

Nassau Senior long ago pointed out the important role played by the desire for distinction in guiding conduct; and more recently Thorstein Veblen has developed the theme with much subtlety in his satirical *Theory of the Leisure Class*. We are all prone to draw invidious comparisons between ourselves and our neighbors. Such comparisons give us much edifying satisfaction when they can be twisted to our advantage, and produce a corresponding sense of discomfort when we cannot disguise our own inferiority. The subject matter of these invidious comparisons is drawn from the whole range of our experience, from appreciating Browning to catching trout, from observing the Sabbath to the weight of our babies. In the money economy of today, where so much of our attention is devoted to business, these comparisons turn with corresponding frequency upon our pecuniary standing. Money income is a crude, tangible criterion of worth that all of us can understand and apply. It needs a certain originality of character or a certain degree of culture to free us even in a measure from the prevailing concern with commercial standards. Most of us who are rich like to feel that the fact is known to all men; most of us who are poor strive to conceal the petty economies we are compelled to practice. Of course, we see this unamiable trait of human nature more clearly in others than in ourselves; but in most of us that is but a subtle exercise of our inveterate habit of drawing biased comparisons between ourselves and others.

Now, the simplest and most effective way of providing material for a soul-satisfying comparison with others on the basis of pecuniary competence is to show that we are

[15]

better off by living in larger houses, wearing more stylish clothing, taking more leisure, and the like. Thus the money economy forms in us the habit of extravagant expenditure for the unacknowledged purpose of impressing both ourselves and our neighbors with an adequate sense of our standing. Of course, indiscriminate vulgarity in wasting money offends our taste. The ideal toward which we learn to strive is an ideal of refined elegance, such as is reputed to be the legitimate offspring of generations of wealth and leisure. But for working purposes, all classes of society exhibit the same species of impulse in a vast number of variants. The gaudy ribbons of the shopgirl are close kin to the paste jewels worn by the heiress to show that she keeps genuine jewels locked up in her safe-deposit box.

In their task of spending money the mass of housewives come under the sway of this paradoxical impulse. Not for themselves alone, but also for the sake of their husbands and their children, must they make it appear that the family stands well in a world where worth is commonly interpreted as dollars' worth. An appearance of poverty in comparison with their associates may disturb the husband's complacency and may handicap the children's chances of forming pleasant and profitable associations. Worldly wisdom, therefore, counsels the housewife to make as brave a show as may be with the income at her disposal. She must buy not only gratifications for the appetites and the aesthetic senses, but also social consideration and the pleasant consciousness of possessing it. The cost of the latter is an air of disregarding cost.

If this analysis of the reasons why the art of spending money is in so backward a state be sound, it follows that homilies upon the ignorance, foolish extravagance, and lack of system among our housewives are a vain exercise, productive of slight effect beyond the temporary indignation they arouse. However edifying such preachments may be made, they cannot remove the limits set by family life to a more effective organization of expenditure, they cannot increase our knowledge of physiology and psychology, they cannot give us a common denominator for costs and gains in living, they cannot define our aims with definiteness, and they cannot cure us of seeking social consideration by living beyond our means.

What prospect of improvement can be seen lies in the slow modification of the broad social conditions that make woman's work so difficult at present. Despite certain relaxations of the family bond, we are seemingly inclined to maintain the essential features of the family group, with its large measure of privacy. Nevertheless, we are reorganizing certain forms of family expenditure on the basis of larger groups. Some among these tentative efforts may survive initial blunders and increase mightily in the years to come. The apartment building with its steam heat, janitor service, and common washtubs seems likely to increase in favor and perhaps will increase in the facilities it offers. The family hotel, which still seems to many of us the worst place for a family, may please a larger number of our children. Cooperative kitchens look promising on paper and may prove endurable in practice—particularly if wages of competent cooks continue to rise. Pure food laws, municipal certification of milk, and the like render easier the task of the housewife who is intelligent, though they doubtless disquiet her easygoing sisters by emphasizing dangers of which they had been but dimly conscious. Finally, our cities are providing with a larger liberality playgrounds, parks, library stations, day nurseries—a socialized spending of money with a neighborhood instead of a family as the unit. In spite of the fact that all these forms of arranging expenditure for larger groups may be so managed as to increase the cost and diminish the benefit, they at least represent promising experiments that may result in solid gains. For one thing they give men a larger share in organizing expenditures, and men bring to the task a trained capacity for cooperation and the development of system—qualities to which the greater size of the unit allows free scope.

With greater confidence we may rely upon progress in physiology and psychology to make wider and more secure the scientific foundations of housekeeping. But such progress will have little practical effect unless the results of research are made available to far larger circles. This work of popularizing scientific knowledge, however, promises to become increasingly effective. Most of the magazines for women have departments devoted to matters of technical interest to housewives—channels through which trebly diluted applications of science may trickle to thousands of untrained readers. The ever-increasing number of women's clubs, with their ever-increasing membership, are other promising centers for the dissemination of knowledge concerning scientific cooking, domestic hygiene, sanitation, and the like. Probably of more importance will be the growing attention to "domestic science" in the schools, and the efforts of colleges and universities to meet the popular demand for adequate instruction in the matters of gravest import to future wives and mothers. At best, however, a small percentage of women can secure this more elaborate training. And the more we learn about the sciences involved, the more prolonged, more difficult, and more expensive will such training become. Perhaps we may solve the problem by developing a professional class of Doctors of Domestic

Science, who will be employed in organizing households, giving expert counsel to the newlywed, holding free dispensaries of advice for the indigent, assisting in diverse municipal ventures in welfare work, and the like. Then the training of the mass of women may be confined to such an exhibit of the complexities and responsibilities of their work as will induce them to employ these elect as freely as they now employ physicians.

But even after many of the housewife's present cares have been reduced by the extension of business enterprise and municipal housekeeping, and after the housewife has received better training herself and can command the expert advice of a professional class, her task in spending money will still remain perplexing to one who takes it seriously. For the ultimate problem of what is worth while to strive for is not to be solved by sounder organization, by better training, or by the advance of science. Doubtless most women, like most men, will ever continue to accept uncritically the scale of conventional values which their day and generation provides ready-made. To such souls the only nontechnical problems will be problems of reconciling minor inconsistencies, or striving to attain the more decorous standards of a higher social class. But to women of conscience and insight the ends of living will always be a part of the problem of spending money—the part that is most inspiring and most baffling. In this aspect the art of spending money differs from the technical pursuits of business and science, and is allied to philosophy and ethics. There is a scheme of values embodied in every housewife's work, whether she knows it or not, and this scheme affects for good or ill the health, the tastes, the character of those for whom she cares and those with whom she associates.

2

QUANTITATIVE ANALYSIS IN ECONOMIC THEORY[1]

EIGHTEEN years have passed since Dr. Alfred Marshall, addressing the Royal Economic Society, said that "qualitative analysis has done the greater part of its work" in economic science, and that the "higher and more difficult task" of quantitative analysis "must wait upon the slow growth of thorough realistic statistics."[2]

These dicta of the great teacher, to whom we owe so much, have an almost provocative ring. Were we like-minded with our predecessors of the eighties, we might find the makings of a new *Methodenstreit* in the saying that "qualitative analysis has done the greater part of its work." It is a cheering evidence of progress that no such futile disputation seems to be in process or in prospect. We do not speak of qualitative *versus* quantitative analysis. We do not seek to prove even that one type should predominate over the other. Instead of dogmatizing about method at large, we are experimenting with methods in detail. In the measure of our proficiencies, we all practice both qualitative and quantitative analysis, shifting our emphasis according to the tasks we have in hand. And we are all eager to see our colleagues develop both types of analysis to the limits of efficiency in whatever tasks they essay. Such differences of opinion as flourish among us

---

[1] Presidential address delivered at the Thirty-seventh Annual Meeting of the American Economic Association, held in Chicago, Dec. 29, 1924. Reprinted by permission from *American Economic Review*, vol. XV, pp. 1–12, March, 1925.

[2] "The Social Possibilities of Economic Chivalry," *The Economic Journal*, vol. XVII, pp. 7, 8, March, 1907.

turn chiefly on our expectations concerning the relative fruitfulness of qualitative and quantitative work in the near future—the future within which we and our associates can hope to be counted among the workers.

In discussing these expectations, I shall say little of qualitative analysis beyond making the obvious remark that it cannot be dispensed with, if for no other reason, because quantitative work itself involves distinctions of kind, and distinctions of kind start with distinctions of quality. The problematical and therefore interesting point is: What can we hope from quantitative, the less thoroughly proven type of analysis?

I

Since Dr. Marshall said that quantitative analysis "must wait upon the slow growth of thorough realistic statistics," the situation and outlook have changed in vital particulars.

In the United States, Canada, and somewhat less decisively in other countries, the "growth of thorough realistic statistics" has been accelerated. We may still fume about this growth as slow—it is slow in comparison with the demands of economic statisticians—but it is not so slow as it was before 1907. Quantitative analysis still waits upon the gathering of data in numerous fields; but in other fields the lack is of analysts—analysts with the imagination, technique, and resources required to wring fresh knowledge from the accumulating masses of data. And the prospects seem bright that the recent rate of growth will be maintained. For the increasing complexity of economic organization makes more pressing our need of definite knowledge of our requirements and the resources for meeting them.

Nor is it merely in the range and quality of the "realistic statistics" at their disposal that the prospects of the quantitative workers have grown brighter. A second gain is the steady improvement in the technical methods of statistical analysis. On this side, progress is not less rapid in other countries than in the United States.

In still a third respect prospects are improving. One of the chief obstacles in the way of quantitative analysis in economics has been the heavy burden of routine labor involved. A qualitative worker requires hardly any equipment beyond a few books and hardly any helper except a typist. A quantitative worker needs often a statistical laboratory, a corps of computers, and sometimes a staff of fieldworkers. Few economists command such resources. But of late the endowment of economic research has begun on a scale that reduces this handicap upon quantitative research and promises to reduce it further in the near future. Numerous government agencies and large business enterprises have created research staffs that have considerable latitude in the choice of their problems, and so find opportunity to do work of scientific significance. Still freer to choose their own problems are the organizations created specifically to do research work, such as the Harvard Committee of Economic Research, the Pollak Foundation, the Institute of Economics, the National Bureau of Economic Research, the Food Research Institute, and the university bureaus of business or industrial research. The Social Science Research Council promises to become an agency through which important projects can obtain support. And there are signs that some of our universities presently will provide funds for aiding the researches of their faculties of social science.

II

Thus the economist of today has at his disposal a wider array of "thorough realistic statistics" than had the economist of yesterday, a more powerful technique, and more opportunities to get assistance. All this is recognized by everyone. But the crucial question remains: What use can we make of these data, this refined technique, and these research assistants in solving the fundamental problems of economic science? Are not these the problems qualitative analysis has posed? When a theorist puts any one of his problems to a statistician, does the answer he gets ever quite meet his questions? And when a statistician attempts to test an economic theory, is his test ever conclusive? In fine, what evidence have we that quantitative analysis is taking over the task upon which qualitative analysis, with all its shortcomings, does make headway?

One view is that, despite all the gains it has made, quantitative analysis shows no more promise of providing a statistical complement of pure theory than it showed when Dr. Marshall pronounced his dicta. I think this view is correct, if the pure theory we have in mind is theory of the type cultivated by Jevons, or by Dr. Marshall himself. Indeed, I incline to go further and say that there is slight prospect that quantitative analysis will ever be able to solve the problems that qualitative analysis has framed, in their present form. What we must expect is a recasting of the old problems into new forms amenable to statistical attack. In the course of this reformulation of its problems, economic theory will change not merely its complexion but also its content.

Let me illustrate the reaction of methods upon problems by citing an example. In the course of his investigations into economic cycles, Professor Henry L. Moore needed to formulate "the concrete laws of demand for the representative crops." He approached this task by quoting Dr. Marshall's qualitative analysis of demand. But with Marshall's formulation of the problem it was impossible to get quantitative results. For Marshall treated the relation between demand

and price on the assumptions (1) that the changes in the two variables are infinitesimal, (2) that the conditions remain constant, and (3) that the shape of the demand curve is known. Professor Moore, on the contrary, had to derive his curves of demand, and to deal with the real world where no factor is known to remain constant and where changes in demand and price are finite. Attacking his problem by mathematical statistics, Moore obtained equations expressing the relations between the demands for and the prices of corn, hay, oats, and potatoes; he determined the precision of these equations as formulas for predicting prices, and he measured the elasticity of demand for each crop. As he pointed out in concluding the discussion, his results do not solve Marshall's problem. But is not Moore's problem more significant theoretically, as well as more relevant to economic practice? If quantitative analysis can give us empirically valid demand curves and coefficients of elasticity for numerous commodities, shall we not have a better theory of demand than qualitative analysis can supply?[3]

From this concrete illustration of the reaction of quantitative method upon economic theory, we may pass to a broader range of considerations. Jevons preached that "The deductive science of Economics must be verified and rendered useful by the purely empirical science of Statistics." But the deductive theory for which Jevons wished a statistical complement was "based on a calculus of pleasure and pain."[4] Today there seems little likelihood that we shall have a quantitative proof—or disproof—of the calculus of pleasure and pain. That problem is passing off the stage.

[3] Henry Ludwell Moore, *Economic Cycles: Their Law and Cause*, Chap. IV, "The Law of Demand," New York, 1914.

[4] W. Stanley Jevons, *The Theory of Political Economy*, pp. 22, 23, 4th ed., London, 1911.

QUANTITATIVE ANALYSIS IN ECONOMIC THEORY

Belonging to a younger generation than Jevons, Dr. Marshall formally repudiated hedonism; but he conceived of economic behavior as controlled by two opposing sets of motives, the motives that impel us toward consumption and the motives that repel us from labor and waiting. Money was to him "the center around which economic science clusters" because it is the economist's instrument for measuring the force of these motives.[5] One task that he hoped quantitative method would perform was that of rendering these measures more precise. Is there a better chance that we shall attain a statistical measurement of the force of motives than that we shall measure pleasures and pains?

I doubt it. For the quantitative data of the economist are limited to objective phenomena. Of course, the theorist who so wishes may interpret these data in subjective terms, such as pleasure or the strength of desire. But these interpretations are something that the theorist adds to the data, not something that he draws out of them. In the present state of our knowledge of human nature, such interpretations smack more of metaphysics than of science. Economists who practice quantitative analysis are likely to be chary of deserting the firm ground of measurable phenomena for excursions into the subjective.

That such excursions are not imperative is readily shown. The theoretical purpose of Jevon's calculus of pleasure and pain, of Marshall's opposing sets of motives, and of the simultaneous equations used by the mathematical writers was to lay a foundation in the behavior of individuals on which could be built an explanation of mass phenomena. Of course, the theorists have never supposed that any individual could really tell just how many units of one article he would give for successive units of another; but that mattered little

[5] See Book I, Chap. II, in the later editions of Marshall's *Principles of Economics*.

[25]

because the theorists have not been interested in the individuals as such. They presented the whole construction scrupulously as a conceptual device for getting insight into what happens in the real markets where the money incomes and costs of living of millions of men are fixed.

Now, the quantitative workers derive their data directly from these real markets. They start with the mass phenomena which the qualitative analysts approached indirectly through their hypothetical individuals. With the fuller reports they are obtaining and the more powerful technique they are developing, properly equipped investigators can study the relations between the actual responses of prices to changes in supply and of supply to changes in prices. They can work out demand schedules that hold empirically within the ranges and periods covered by experience. They can trace the changes in the consumption of commodities by whole communities or by large groups. They can investigate the relations between monetary changes and "real" incomes, between saving and spending, between different forms of economic organization and production.

With all these fascinating problems and numberless others before them in shape for attack, it seems unlikely that the quantitative workers will retain a keen interest in imaginary individuals coming to imaginary markets with ready-made scales of bid and offer prices. Their theories will probably be theories about the relationships among the variables that measure objective processes. There is little likelihood that the old explanations will be refuted by these investigators, but much likelihood that they will be disregarded.

III

If my forecast is valid, our whole apparatus of reasoning on the basis of utilities and disutilities, or motives, or choices, in the individual economy, will drop out of sight in the work of the quantitative analysts, going the way of the static state. The "psychological" element in the work of these men will consist mainly of objective analysis of the economic behavior of groups. Motives will not be disregarded, but they will be treated as problems requiring study, instead of being taken for granted as constituting explanations.

The obsolescence of the older type of reasoning in economics will be promoted by the change which is coming over our thinking about human nature. Psychologists are moving rapidly toward an objective conception and a quantitative treatment of their problems. Their emphasis upon stimulus and response sequences, upon conditioned reflexes; their eager efforts to develop performance tests, their attempts to build up a technique of experiment, favor the spread of the conception that all of the social sciences have a common aim—the understanding of human behavior; a common method—the quantitative analysis of behavior records, and a common aspiration—to devise ways of experimenting upon behavior.

This conception, that economics is one among a number of sciences all dealing with aspects of human behavior, need be no monopoly of the quantitative workers. But it will be especially congenial to their way of thinking. And it will put them in a better position than ever before to cooperate with quantitative analysts in other fields. What Jeremy Bentham's idea that all our actions are determined by pleasure and pain once did to provide a common program for jurists, economists, psychologists, penologists, and educators, may be done again by the idea that all these groups, together with the political scientists, sociologists, anthropologists, and historians, are engaged in the study of human behavior. On that basis the problems of each of these groups are significant for all the others, their technical methods are suggestive, their results pertinent.

The organizing influence of this conception will be felt inside of economics as strongly as in the whole program of the social sciences. Any objective study of economic behavior can find its place in this general scheme. In recent years many members of our Association have come to fear that economics may disintegrate into a number of specialties. This danger they combat by insisting that every young economist must receive "a thorough grounding in theory." The remedy seems inefficient, because the qualitative theory, in which we are commonly grounded, plays so small a role in our work as specialists in public finance and banking, in accountancy and transportation, in economic history and insurance, in business cycles, marketing, and labor problems. As economics becomes the study of objective behavior this breach between theory and the "practical" subjects will be narrowed. Specialization within economics will not be hampered, but it will become a process of "differentiation and integration" in Herbert Spencer's famous phrase, not a process of disintegration.

By this I do not mean that we can expect the rapid crystallization of a new system of economic theory built by quantitative analysis. Quite the contrary. The literature that the quantitative workers are due to produce will be characterized not by general treatises, but by numberless papers and monographs. Knowledge will grow by accretion as it grows in the natural sciences, rather than by the excogitation of new systems. Books will pass out of date more rapidly. The history of economic theory will receive less attention. Economists will be valued less on their erudition and more on their creative capacity. The advances will be achieved not only by conceiving new hypotheses, but also by compiling statistics from fresh fields, by inventing new technical methods, by refining upon old measures, and perhaps by devising experiments upon certain types of behavior. It will be harder for anyone to cover the whole field, perhaps quite impossible. From time to time someone will try to give a comprehensive survey of the results of quantitative research, but such books will not have the prestige won by the treatises by Adam Smith, Ricardo, Mill, and Marshall.

IV

Of the content of this quantitative economics we can form but uncertain surmises. One topic, however, is fairly sure to receive much attention—the topic defined twenty-four years ago at the thirteenth annual meeting of the American Economic Association by Dr. Veblen.[6] This is the relation between business and industry, between making money and making goods, between the pecuniary and the technological phases of economic life.

In qualitative analysis this problem has been sadly slurred over. The quantitative workers cannot so blink it. Much of their data will consist of two great groups of time series. One group shows variations in the output, stocks, shipment, or orders for economic goods expressed in physical units—bushels, pounds, yards, ton-miles, names on payrolls, hours of work, accident rates, labor turnover, and so on through a list that will grow with the growth of statistics. The second group of time series shows variations in quantities expressed in monetary units. The relations between these two groups of series will be an obvious problem of just the kind that quantitative workers enjoy attacking. They cannot content themselves by staying always on the money level of analysis, or always on the commodity level; and they cannot pass back

[6] "Industrial and Pecuniary Employments," 1901. Reprinted in *The Place of Science in Modern Civilisation*, pp. 279–323, New York, 1919.

and forth between the two levels without realizing what they are doing, as could the classical economists and their followers. Out of this technical characteristic of the statistical data we may expect to come a close scrutiny of the relations between our pecuniary institutions and our efficiency in producing and distributing goods. Such topics as the economic serviceability of advertising, the reactions of an unstable price level upon production, the effect of various systems of public regulation upon the services rendered by public utilities will be treated with incisive vigor as we become able to make the indispensable measurements. And investigations of this type will broaden out into a constructive criticism of that dominant complex of institutions known as the money economy—a constructive criticism which may guide the efforts of our children to make that marvelously flexible form of organization better fitted to their needs.

A bolder generalization may be hazarded. If our present beliefs are confirmed, that the human nature which men inherit remains substantially the same over millenniums, and that the changes in human life are due mainly to the evolution of culture, economists will concentrate their studies to an increasing degree upon economic institutions—the aspect of culture which concerns them. For whatever hopes we may cherish for the future of our race are bound up with the fortunes of the factor that certainly admits of change and perhaps admits of control. The quantitative workers will have a special predilection for institutional problems, because institutions standardize behavior, and thereby facilitate statistical procedure.

With the growing prominence of institutional problems, the fundamental issue of welfare is inextricably involved. What quantitative analysis promises here is to increase the range of objective criteria by which we judge welfare, and to study the variations of these criteria in relation to one another. The statistical worker is in no better position than any other student to specify what mankind should aim at; but in view of the multiplicity of our competing aims and the limitations of our social resources his help in measuring objective costs and objective results is indispensable to convert society's blind fumbling for happiness into an intelligent process of experimentation.

V

In speaking of experimentation, I do not forget the difficulty of making experiments in the social sciences. That difficulty seems to me almost insuperable, as long as we hold to the old conceptions of human nature. But the behavioristic concept promises to diminish this handicap under which economics and its sister sciences have labored. For we can try experiments upon group behavior. Indeed, we are already trying such experiments. We have experimental schools, in which the physical and social environments of the children are made to vary, with the aim of studying the relations between the stimuli offered by the schools and the learning response. So, too, we experiment with different systems of remunerating labor, different forms of publicity, different organizations for distributing products, different price policies, different methods of supervising public utilities, and the like.

Of course, these experiments upon group behavior lack the rigor of the experimenting done in physical laboratories. The limits within which human beings can be manipulated are narrow; the behavior processes under scrutiny cannot be isolated from complicating processes, except as one applies the method of partial correlation to statistical records. Hence the work of experimenting in the social sciences requires a technique different from that of the natural sciences. The experimenter must rely far more upon statistical considerations and precautions. The ideal of a single crucial experiment cannot be followed. The experiments must be repeated upon numerous individuals or groups; the varieties of reactions to the stimuli must be recorded and analyzed; the representative character of the samples must be known before generalizations can be established. This whole procedure may have more in common with the quantitative study of data drawn from common experience than with the procedure of the man who deals with electric currents passing through a vacuum tube. But whatever approaches are made toward controlling the conditions under which groups act will be eagerly seized upon and developed with results which we cannot yet foresee.

In collecting and analyzing such experimental data as they can obtain, the quantitative workers will find their finest, but most exacting, opportunities for developing statistical technique—opportunities even finer than are offered by the recurrent phenomena of business cycles. It is conceivable that the tentative experimenting of the present may develop into the most absorbing activity of economists in the future. If that does happen, the reflex influence upon economic theory will be more radical than any we can expect from the quantitative analysis of ordinary behavior records.[7] The most dazzling developments of the future may lie in this direction; but they are hardly more than a rosy glow upon the eastern horizon.

VI

So far my argument has run as follows: the increase of statistical data, the improvement of statistical technique,

[7] Compare Lawrence K. Frank, "The Emancipation of Economics," *American Economic Review*, vol. XIV, pp. 37, 38, March, 1924.

and the endowment of social research are enabling economists to make a larger use of quantitative analysis; in preparing for their work, the quantitative theorists usually find it necessary to formulate problems in a way different from that adopted by qualitative theorists; this technical necessity of restating problems promises to bring about radical changes in economic theory, in particular to make the treatment of behavior more objective, to emphasize the importance of institutions, and to promote the development of an experimental technique.

All this seems plausible as I reel it off; yet it runs counter to prevailing views. According to the classical concept of method, the business of the statistician is merely to verify conclusions established by deduction, and to discover disturbing causes that do not reveal themselves "to a reasoner engaged in the development of the more capital economic doctrines." Thus said Cairnes.[8] And even now some of the most distinguished statistical economists hold that their function is not to recast economic theory, but to provide a statistical complement for it. Professor Henry L. Moore, whose reformulation of Marshall's problem of the relations between demand and price I have cited, has taken this position.[9] What justification is there for a different opinion? Why should a freer use of quantitative analysis produce radical changes in economic theory?

I think there is a deeper-lying reason for my conclusion than is generally recognized. Our qualitative theory has followed the logic of Newtonian mechanics; our quantitative work rests on statistical conceptions. Between the mechanical

---

[8] J. E. Cairnes, *The Character and Logical Method of Political Economy*, Lecture III, section 5, 2d ed., London, 1875.

[9] See his paper "The Statistical Complement of Pure Economics," *Quarterly Journal of Economics*, vol. XXIII, pp. 1–33, November, 1908.

type of theory and the statistical type of theory there are differences that will force changes in our fundamental conceptions as we shift our emphasis from one type to the other.

Let me expand this statement. In the hedonistic calculus which Jevons followed, man is placed under the governance of two sovereign masters, pain and pleasure, which play the same role in controlling human behavior that Newton's laws of motion play in controlling the behavior of the heavenly bodies. Dr. Marshall's conception of economic behavior as controlled by two opposing sets of motives is scarcely less mechanical in its logic. Indeed, any theorist who works by ascribing motives to men and arguing what they will do under guidance of these forces will produce a mechanical type of explanation.

Intermixed with speculation of this type in economics, there has usually been an element of broad observation upon average behavior. Quantitative work with statistics means the expansion and systematization of this element of observation. It has its counterpart in physics, introduced by Clerk-Maxwell, just as speculation about the force of motives has its counterpart in Newtonian mechanics. Expounding the statistical view of nature, Clerk-Maxwell wrote:

. . . those uniformities of nature which we observe in our experiments with quantities of matter containing millions of millions of molecules are uniformities of the same kind as those explained by Laplace and wondered at by Buckle, arising from the slumping together of multitudes of cases, each of which is by no means uniform with others. . . . if the molecular theory of the constitution of bodies is true, all our knowledge of matter is of a statistical kind.[10]

The difference between the mechanical and the statistical conceptions of nature has been clearly worked out in physics.

[10] Quoted by J. T. Merz from Campbell and Garnett, "Life of Clerk-Maxwell," *History of European Thought in the Nineteenth Century*, vol. II, pp. 600, 601, 2d ed., London, 1912.

The mechanical view involves the notions of sameness, of certainty, of invariant laws; the statistical view involves the notions of variety, of probability, of approximations.[11] Yet Clerk-Maxwell's "new kind of uniformity" was found to yield results in many physical problems which corresponded closely to results attained on mechanical lines.

Such a close correspondence between the results based on speculation and the results based on statistical observation is not to be expected in economics, for three reasons. First, the cases summed up in our statistics seldom if ever approach in number the millions of millions of molecules, or atoms, or electrons of the physicist. Second, the units in economic aggregates are less similar than the molecules or atoms of a given element. Third, we cannot approach closely the isolation practices of the laboratory. For these reasons the elements of variety, of uncertainty, of imperfect approximation are more prominent in the statistical work of the social sciences than in the statistical work of the natural sciences. And because our statistical results are so marked by these imperfections they do not approach so closely to the results of our reasoning on the basis of assumed premises. Hence the development of statistical method may be expected to make more radical changes in economic than it makes in physical theory.

Of course, this lack of close agreement between the results attainable on the statistical and the mechanical views of nature in economics might be advanced as a reason for holding more strictly to the mechanical type of work. But that would be a wrong conclusion, provided our aim in economics is to understand the world of which we are a part. On this proviso, we seem bound to argue: the mechanical type of

[11] Compare the admirable paper "On Measurement in Economics," by Frederick C. Mills, in *The Trend of Economics*, edited by R. G. Tugwell, New York, 1924.

speculation works with the notions of sameness, of certainty, of invariant laws. In economics these notions do not fit the phenomena closely. Hence, we must put our ultimate trust in observation. And as fast as we can raise our observations to a scientific level we must drop the cruder, yet not wholly valueless, approximations attained by the mechanical type of work.

VII

The growth of quantitative analysis which I foresee in economics, with its reformulation of old problems and its redistribution of emphasis, does not promise a speedy ending of the types of theory to which we are accustomed. For an indefinite time we shall probably have theorists who keep strictly to qualitative analysis and draw upon quantitative work merely for occasional illustrations of their propositions. Others meanwhile will be extending the range of problems conceived and discussed in quantitative terms. But even in the work of the most statistically minded qualitative analysis will keep a place. Always our thinking will cover a field larger than our measurements; the preconceptions that shape our ends, our first glimpses of new problems, our widest generalizations will remain qualitative in form. Indeed, qualitative work itself will gain in power, scope, and interest as we make use of wider, more accurate, and more reliable measurements. And, to repeat what I said in the beginning, quantitative work cannot dispense with distinctions of quality. In the thinking of competent workers, the two types of analysis will cooperate with and complement each other as peacefully in economics as they do in chemistry.

Dr. Marshall's dicta, which I took as my text, hold out small hope of rapid progress in our science. If qualitative analysis has really "done the greater part of its work," and if the "growth of thorough realistic statistics" on which quantitative analysis "must wait" is slow, then Dr. Marshall's hope that his pupils will render his own work obsolete is not likely to be realized.[12] I cherish a livelier optimism. With more abundant and more reliable data, more powerful methods, and more liberal assistance, the men now entering upon careers of research may go far toward establishing economics as a quantitative science. In so far as they accomplish this aim, they will in transforming the subject make obsolete not only the qualitative work of Dr. Marshall and others, but also the crude beginnings of the quantitative work which their elders are now producing. All of us share in wishing them the fullest measure of success.

APPENDIX
THE PRESENT STATUS AND FUTURE PROSPECTS OF QUANTITATIVE ECONOMICS[13]

Writing in *Schmoller's Jahrbuch* for June, 1926, Joseph Schumpeter, whose sympathetic interest in the development of economic theory in this country is known to all of us, remarked that a new controversy over method seems to be latent in the United States. Not so latent, he added, on second thought. For a militant group of younger economists is criticizing orthodox economics in a fashion strikingly reminiscent of Gustav Schmoller in the eighties, and calling for a reorganization of the science such as Schmoller demanded. "Change the relative emphasis put upon statistical and his-

---

[12] Compare Dr. J. M. Keynes's charming memoir, "Alfred Marshall, 1842–1924," *Economic Journal*, vol. XXXIV, p. 366, September, 1924. Reprinted in *Memorials of Alfred Marshall*, edited by A. C. Pigou, p. 58; compare p. 499; London, 1925.

[13] Round Table discussion at American Economic Association meeting, Dec., 1927. Reprinted by permission from *American Economic Review*, vol. XVIII; supplement, pp. 39–41, March, 1928. Previous speakers were Professors Jacob Hollander, Jacob Viner, and E. B. Wilson.

torical materials in this picture," Schumpeter summed up, "and we have, even to details, the position that Schmoller held throughout his life."

I do not share Professor Schumpeter's impression that a controversy over method is impending among American economists. Perhaps my belief is colored by my wishes. For I see no need for controversy on the problem of how to work, and no useful result likely to come of discussions of method conducted in a controversial spirit. In economics we have tasks of many sorts to perform, and we have workers of many aptitudes. That each of us can increase his efficiency by noting how others set about their tasks is probable. That each of us should recommend to others methods that have served him well is proper. That we should pay critical attention to the merits and the defects of the methods utilized by one another is part of our duty as scientific workers. That we differ in our forecasts of what may be accomplished in the future by particular methods is a matter of interest, which we can discuss with pleasure, perhaps with profit. But that we shall let our different predilections and opinions involve us in a controversy upon methods at large seems to me almost as improbable as it would be deplorable.

If a spice of controversial spirit can be tasted in today's discussion, it is injected by those who have spoken as representatives of traditional economics. To my mind, they have overstated the claims that are made for quantitative economics, and have passed over in silence what spokesmen for this type of work have said about the role that distinctions of quality must play in the future development of our science. What the spokesmen in question have "really meant," I take to be what they have really said—not their remarks on the promise of quantitative analysis only, but also their remarks on the indispensability of qualitative analysis. I know no competent economist who would subscribe to the one-sided views that have been imputed this morning to persons unnamed. On the contrary, I agree that the man of straw merits the fate for which he has been set up. And if anyone should suggest that my notions about the service that quantitative analysis may render to economics are those of the straw man, I should still see no ground for controversy. All I need do in that contingency is to ask the critic to read what I have said before upon this topic.

But I attach slight importance to the fact that the case for quantitative analysis is often misconstrued. In scientific circles mere misconstructions have but a short life. The positive positions taken by the previous speakers are more significant than their criticisms of what they take to be opposing views. No one has denied the usefulness of quantitative analysis on the one side, or of qualitative analysis on the other. At most there are differences of emphasis. Indeed, the limitations of statistical procedure and the pitfalls it digs for the unwary have been emphasized mainly by a man eminent for his statistical accomplishments; while the speakers less addicted to statistical technique have noted the helpful part quantitative analysis may play in the gradual development of economic theory. That is as it should be; for the most competent critic of any method is the thoughtful worker who has learned its value and its limitations in the actual conduct of researches.

Certainly there is need of critical treatment of statistical procedure in economics. Everyone realizes that we should measure the phenomena which we treat whenever we can, and that increasing precision in measurement is a scientific gain. But there is danger that the seductions of statistical technique may blind enthusiasts to the imperfections and inadequacies of the data. One who elaborates statistical series in ingenious ways may get as far out of touch with reality as one who excogitates a set of speculative assumptions. Both types of work are prone to mislead inquirers who have less common sense than statistical technique or dialectical cleverness. If economists sometimes erred in the past because their reasoning rested upon assumptions that distorted reality in ways of which they were not clearly conscious, economists who rely upon statistics may often err because their samples misrepresent the facts in ways they fail to recognize. Happily, the one danger is as clear to competent workers as the other. Confidence in the fruitfulness of statistical analysis in economic theory should be increased by the precautions insisted upon by such statisticians as Professor Wilson, just as confidence in the use of qualitative reasoning should be increased by warnings such as Professor Schumpeter, for example, sprinkles over his *Wesen und Hauptinhalt der theoretischen Nationalökonomie.*

Doubtless such discussions as we are engaged in this morning have their value. Certainly I am not one to question the desirability of talking about the possibilities of quantitative economics. But I look forward to a day when a round table such as we are now holding will be an anachronism. Qualitative and quantitative analysis are becoming so interwoven in economics that it will soon seem pedantic to question the indispensability of either. It is obvious that the statistician works with distinctions of kind quite as much as with distinctions of number. And everyone who confines himself to qualitative discussions admits the desirability of pressing forward to quantitative determinations as rapidly as possible. If we may judge the future qualifications of economists by the courses offered them in our university departments at present, our successors will almost to a man be trained in statistical methods as carefully as they are trained to discriminate among concepts. Blessed with a wider range of data than we possess, accustomed to state their problems in ways that facilitate statistical attack, they will doubtless give economics a measure of precision we cannot attain. In proportion as our successors prosper in their undertakings they will make antiquated what this generation accomplishes. Qualitative distinctions must remain basic in all their work; but they may transform many of our qualitative notions as radically as they may transform much of our quantitative procedure. That is merely a surmise, born of hope and nourished by evidence that is open to question. If anyone thinks otherwise, all I can say is, "The future will tell."

3

STATISTICS AND GOVERNMENT[1]

SINCE the American Statistical Association was founded
in 1839 no year has brought such stirring changes in
American statistics as the year now closing. The war forced
a rapid expansion in the scope of federal statistics and the
creation of new statistical agencies. What is more significant,
the war led to the use of statistics, not only as a record of what
had happened, but also as a vital factor in planning what
should be done. The war also brought an unprecedentedly
large number of statisticians into government employ. Probably there are few professional societies that have had so
considerable a proportion of their membership engaged in
war work as this association.

Tonight we feel a just pride in the service our fellow members have rendered. We cherish the hope that what they have
helped to accomplish during the war toward the guidance of
public policy by quantitative knowledge of social fact may
not be lost in the period of reconstruction through which we
are passing, and in the indefinite period of peace upon which
we are about to enter. To forward that hope the Association
may seek a more active share in the work of federal statistics
in the future than it has ever taken in the past.

It is my pleasant task tonight to speak of these things—
our work in the year that has gone, our hopes for the years

[1] Presidential address at the eightieth Annual Meeting of the American Statistical
Association, Richmond, Virginia, December, 1918. Reprinted by permission from
Quarterly Publications of the American Statistical Association, vol. XVI, pp. 223–236,
March, 1919.

to come, and what we may do in the present toward achieving these hopes.

I

Dr. Cummings's review of "Federal Statistics" in our Memorial Volume shows that before the war there were more than a score of statistical bureaus in Washington publishing thousands of pages of figures each year. But there was no coordinating agency, no bureau whose duty it was to consider the statistical needs of the government as a whole and to formulate systematic plans for supplying these needs. Hence, there was duplication of work, no one knows exactly how much; many important fields were imperfectly covered, or not covered at all; the results of different bureaus could not be compared or combined readily because of differences in units used, in periods covered, and in classification; finally, the cost of federal statistics was needlessly high. To remedy these defects of organization Committees on Federal Statistics appointed by this Association and the Economic Association had endeavored to secure the appointment of a Central Statistical Commission; but they had met with little encouragement. As one member of these committees, I confess that our efforts had not been vigorously pushed.

The war revealed the defects of the federal machinery for collecting statistics with startling suddenness; for war imposes a strain upon statistical offices quite as much as upon steel mills or shipyards. As Professor Allyn A. Young said in his presidential address last year, "War has come to be a conflict of directed masses—of aggregates. Men, money, munitions, food, railways, shipping, raw materials, and manufactured products in great variety are impressed into the service of the nation. The problems of the effective control and use for war purposes of these varied national resources is intimately dependent upon a knowledge of their quantities, that is, upon statistics. . . . Just as this war is our largest national undertaking, so its statistical demands constitute, in the aggregate, the largest statistical problem with which we have had to deal."

We were not prepared to cope with this problem. It is not to be expected, of course, that the statistical output of peaceful years will include all the data required for waging war. But it is to be expected that a governmental organization for gathering statistics will grasp a new statistical problem promptly and prepare plans for treating that problem with vigor. This test our federal bureaus failed to meet.

The fault was emphatically a fault of organization rather than of individual officials. Whatever charges of incapacity are made against the officials themselves properly should be made against the system under which federal statisticians are chosen and rewarded. For they are not chosen with an eye single to technical skill and administrative capacity; they are not paid salaries sufficient to attract and retain men of uncommon ability and ambition; the inadequate salaries are not compensated by public recognition of efficient service. We had, indeed, many federal statisticians better than our treatment of them deserved—men who served the country with zeal and intelligence. But, scattered through numerous small bureaus, prescribed a set routine of departmental duties, granted scanty appropriations, these men had little chance to consider the vast new problems of the war. They certainly did not, perhaps they could not, come forward with an efficient war program.

For this shortcoming of our statistical organization we paid a heavy penalty. The time we spent in framing our war organization and getting it started might have been substantially shortened had anybody in Washington been able to put before the responsible authorities promptly the data they needed concerning men and commodities, ships and factories.

What did happen made an admirable exhibition of national energy and patriotism, but not a good exhibition of national intelligence. The War Boards which the government set up to supplement the regular departments faced stupendous tasks. They were led and manned for the most part by men inexperienced in public administration, and unacquainted with the duties and resources of the federal departments. While these men were in the throes of laying their plans, and forming their staffs, they had also to find out that they needed statistics, what statistics they needed, and how to get them. Although the federal government entered the war with twenty or more statistical agencies, the Council of National Defense, the Food Administration, the Fuel Administration, the Shipping Board, the War Trade Board, the Railway Administration, and the War Industries Board sooner or later set up each a new and independent statistical agency to meet its special needs. The War Department and the Navy Department followed suit. And these agencies, like the War Boards which created them, had to be manned with people inexperienced in government work and unfamiliar with Washington.

Although I was one of the raw recruits pressed into emergency work for the government, I cannot forbear speaking of the fine qualities which the new statistical staffs showed. Each group studied the particular needs of the board it served, and threw itself ardently into the task of collecting data. The new men worked with passionate intensity. They were appalled by no obstacles. Where they could not get definite data, they did not hesitate to estimate. The motto adopted by one of the leaders expressed the spirit of all: "It can't be done? But here it is."

Yet the statistical work of the War Boards as a whole showed precisely the same defect as the organization of the old statistical bureaus, and showed that fault in an aggravated degree. Each new agency worked by itself for a separate board. Hence there was much duplication of effort, and at the same time many important fields remained untilled; the results reached by different agencies could not be readily compared or combined: and the cost was needlessly great. Further, the energy of the new statistical agencies and the haste in which they worked magnified a minor fault of the old system to large proportions. These new agencies wanted to get their fundamental data from the original sources; so they sent out questionnaires to businessmen in a veritable flood. Many manufacturing plants got elaborate papers which they were asked to fill out and return by the next mail in tens and in dozens. Frequently, different questionnaires covered nearly the same ground, and usually they required not a little investigation within the plant to collect the data asked for. Considerable expense and serious irritation was caused throughout the country by this obvious failure of organization in Washington.

This questionnaire evil brought back a flood of complaints, echoes of which reached the responsible heads of the War Boards. The efficiency of economic mobilization seemed threatened; that was a more serious matter than the waste of public funds. The men who were most keenly aware of the lack of coordination in statistical work now had a strong talking point. Steps were presently taken to remedy a fault that had been patent for a generation or more on a peace basis. The head of the Division of Planning and Statistics of the Shipping Board, Edwin F. Gay, was put in charge of the Bureau of Research and Tabulation of Statistics of the War Trade Board, and then of the Division of Planning and Statistics of the War Industries Board. Thus three of the new statistical agencies were brought under a single direction. Later Dr. Gay became chairman of the Statistical Committee of the Department of Labor, and finally he was authorized to form a Central Bureau of Planning and Statistics. The Central Bureau set up a clearinghouse of statistical activities, appointed contact men to keep in touch with the statistical work of all the War Boards and certain of the old departments, and began to supervise the issuing of questionnaires. When the armistice was signed we were in a fair way to develop for the first time a systematic organization of federal statistics.

For the first few weeks after the fighting stopped, it seemed as if what had been gained in statistical organization might be lost almost at once. The rapid demobilization of the War Boards threatened to sweep with it their statistical bureaus, or to scatter the new statistical bureaus among the old departments and leave us again in statistical confusion—making figures in abundance but having no general statistical plan. But at a critical moment President Wilson approved a plan by which the Central Bureau of Planning and Statistics was made the single statistical agency to serve the American conferees at the Peace Table. Thus, the Central Bureau was granted a reprieve for some months. It still remains to be seen whether this bureau or some successor serving the same centralizing functions will be made permanent.[2]

[2] [The Central Bureau born of the war died in 1919; but another national emergency gave birth to the Central Statistical Board in 1933.]

II

In speaking next of our hopes for the future, I am speaking merely as one member of the American Statistical Association. Yet I believe that most members of our Association believe that the social sciences in general and social statistics in particular have a great service to render to government and through government to mankind.

The episode in statistical organization that I have sketched, the effect of the war upon our attitude toward the use of facts for the guidance of policy, links the present stage of civilization with man's savage past. Anthropologists have come to recognize that catastrophes have played a leading role in advancing culture. The savage and the barbarian are such conservative creatures that nothing short of a catastrophe can shake them out of their settled habits, make them critical of old taboos, drive them to use their intelligence freely. In physical science and in industrial technique, it is true, we have emancipated ourselves largely from the savage dependence upon catastrophes for progress. For in these fields of activity we have developed a habit of criticizing old formulations, of testing what our fathers accepted, of experimenting. We keep discarding the good for the better, even when not under pressure. The result is a fairly steady rate of advance—advance so regular that we count upon it in laying plans for the future. Today we are sure that ten years hence our present scientific ideas and our present industrial machinery will be antiquated in good part. In science and in industry we are radicals—radicals relying on a tested method. But in matters of social organization we retain a large part of the conservatism characteristic of the savage mind. A great catastrophe may force us for a little while to take the problems of social mobilization seriously. While under stress we make rapid progress. But when the stress is past we relapse gratefully into our comfortable faith in the thinking that has been done for us by our fathers.

I know that there are ardent folk who will challenge these contentions at least for the present. They trust that the outburst of patriotic fervor brought by the war will carry us triumphantly forward for a generation. They count on the generous self-sacrifice that all classes have shown, the fine discipline that our soldiers and war workers have maintained, to solve the problems of peace as they solved the problem of war. Certainly we shall never be again precisely what we were before the war. But just as certainly we shall not remain what we have been during the war. We are all subject to emotional reactions, and, as John Dewey has pointed out, the state of mind produced by the return of peace differs from that produced by the outbreak of war just as widely as peace itself differs from war. No, we cannot depend on any carry-over of "war psychology" to organize democracy in peace.

The "social reformer" we have always with us, it is true. Or rather most of us are "social reformers" of some kind. And we all admire the qualities that go to make the leaders in social reform—warm sympathy for the oppressed, courage to face ridicule, flaming zeal in the face of indifference, tact and energy in conducting crusades. But an indefinite succession of campaigns to secure this, that, and the other specific reform is what we have been having for a long, long time. Many of the reforms on which our grandfathers, our fathers, and our youthful selves have set their hearts have been achieved. Yet the story of the past in matters of social organization is not a story that we should like to have continued for a thousand and one years. Reform by agitation or class struggle is a jerky way of moving forward, uncomfortable and wasteful of energy. Are we not intelligent enough to devise a steadier and a more certain method of progress?

Most certainly, we could not keep social organization what it is even if we wanted to. We are not emerging from the hazards of war into a safe world. On the contrary, the world is a very dangerous place for a society framed as ours is, and I for one am glad of it. The dangers are increased by our very progress in industry and in democracy. Not long ago an English physicist reemphasized the fact that modern Christendom is using up at an ever-increasing pace the energy stored during long ages in the coal fields, and pictured the doubtful fate of humankind as hanging on the race between science and the atom. Has not the time come to apply our intelligence to taking stock of the resources that the earth still holds and to developing methods of utilization that will protect our future? As for democratic progress, we know that men who can read and vote make restless citizens in a state where their work is not interesting to them and where their rewards do not satisfy their sense of justice. And such is the present state of affairs with millions of aggressive Americans. They can be counted upon to change things by turmoil if things are not changed by method.

Taking us all together as one people in a group of mighty peoples, our first and foremost concern is to develop some way of carrying on the infinitely complicated processes of modern industry and interchange day by day, despite all tedium and fatigue, and yet to keep ourselves interested in our work and contented with the division of the product. That is a task of supreme difficulty—a task that calls for intelligent experimenting and detailed planning rather than for agitation or class struggle. What is lacking to achieve that end, indeed, is not so much good will as it is knowledge— above all, knowledge of human behavior.

STATISTICS AND GOVERNMENT

Our best hope for the future lies in the extension to social organization of the methods that we already employ in our most progressive fields of effort. In science and in industry, I have said, we do not wait for catastrophes to force new ways upon us. We do not rely upon the propelling power of great emotion. We rely, and with success, upon quantitative analysis to point the way; and we advance because we are constantly improving and applying such analysis.

While I think that the development of social science offers more hope for solving our social problems than any other line of endeavor, I do not claim that these sciences in their present state are very serviceable. They are immature, speculative, filled with controversies. Their most energetic exponents are still in the stage of developing new "viewpoints," beginning over again on a different plan instead of carrying further the analysis of their predecessors. In part the social sciences represent not what is so much as what their writers think ought to be. In short, the social sciences are still children. Nor have we any certain assurance that they will ever grow into robust manhood, no matter what care we lavish upon them. There are blind leads of speculation in which past generations have mined industriously for ages with little gain. Perhaps the social sciences will prove more like metaphysics than like mechanics, more like theology than like chemistry. The race may always shape its larger destinies by a confused struggle in which force and fraud, good intentions, fiery zeal, and rule of thumb are more potent factors than measurement and planning. Those of us who are concerned with the social sciences, then, are engaged in an uncertain enterprise; perhaps we shall win no great treasures for mankind. But certainly it is our task to work out this lead with all the intelligence and the energy we possess until its richness or sterility be demonstrated.

THE BACKWARD ART OF SPENDING MONEY

The social sciences, however, cover an immense field, and it is not probable that we shall encounter failure or success in all its parts. The parts where effort seems most promising just now are the parts in which this Association is particularly interested. Measurement is one of the outstanding characteristics of science at large, whether in the field of inorganic matter or that of life processes. Social statistics, which is concerned with the measurement of social phenomena, has many of the progressive features of the physical sciences. It shows forthright progress in knowledge of fact, in technique of analysis, and in refinement of results. It is amenable to mathematical formulation. It is capable of forecasting group phenomena. It is objective. A statistician is usually either right or wrong, and his successors can demonstrate which. Statisticians are not continually beginning their science all over again by developing new viewpoints. Where one investigator stops, the next investigator begins with larger collections of data, with extensions into fresh fields, or with more powerful methods of analysis. In all these respects, the position and prospects of social statistics are more like the position and prospects of the natural sciences than like those of the social sciences.

Above all, social statistics even in its present state is directly applicable over a wide range to the management of practical affairs, particularly the affairs of government. And this practical value of statistics is readily demonstrable even to a busy executive. Once secure a quantitative statement of the crucial elements in an official's problem, draw it up in concise form, illuminate the tables with a chart or two, bind the memorandum in an attractive cover tied with a neat bowknot, and it is the exceptional man who will reject your aid. Thereafter your trouble will be not to get your statistics used, but to meet the continual calls for more figures, and to prevent your convert from taking your estimates more literally than you take them yourself.

We may well cherish high hopes for the immediate future of social statistics. In contributing toward a quantitative knowledge of social facts, in putting this knowledge at the disposal of responsible officials, we are contributing a crucially important part toward achieving the gravest task that confronts mankind today—the task of developing a method by which we may make cumulative progress in social organization.

III

What can the American Statistical Association do toward realizing these hopes? Of course, that is for the Association to decide; but I venture to submit certain recommendations to the Association's judgment.

My plea is that the Association seek to play a more active role in public affairs than it has played in the past. We are holding our eightieth annual meeting—few learned societies in this country are so old. Through all these years we have been mainly a learned society, cherishing our particular subject, criticizing those who neglect or misuse it, occasionally proffering advice, summing up experience, but not participating aggressively in the rough-and-tumble of statistical practice. This kind of work has been serviceable. Certainly conditions in Washington and the state capitals have made participation by outsiders in official statistics exceedingly difficult. But conditions have changed somewhat and if we do our part with vigor they may change more.

Two changes seem to me especially promising. One is the active share that many members of the Association have taken in war work. These men will not entirely lose their interest in federal statistics when they leave Washington.

For the next few years at least we shall have a corps of workers who know a good deal about conditions under which government figures are compiled and used. These men will help to make the Association practical in any advice it may tender. Because of them we have greater capacity to do serviceable work now than we ever had before. The Association can be more helpful because it knows more and cares more about what the government bureaus do.

The second change is in the attitude of Washington officials toward the work of outsiders. Just as those of us who have been in government service temporarily have gained a sympathetic insight into the difficulties faced by the permanent statistical bureaus, so the members of the permanent bureaus have become better acquainted with the viewpoint of outside statisticians. They have listened to our criticisms; in turn, they have criticized many of our suggestions for improving their organization and practices. As a result, they know how to utilize our services better than they did before the war. And they are, I think, not unwilling to annul the divorce between working statistician and academic critic and enter into a new relationship of mutual understanding and cooperation.

One symptom of this new attitude is so gratifying that I cannot forbear calling especial attention to it. The Secretary of Commerce has asked the president of the American Economic Association and the president of the Statistical Association to appoint each a committee of three to advise with the Director of the Census on matters of statistical principle and on the selection of statistical experts. This arrangement, it is hoped, will be no formal affair; but a working plan by which the producers and the consumers of statistics can cooperate effectively to improve the products in which both parties are interested. To provide the two committees with

working facilities an office and a secretary have been fur-
nished them by the Director of the Census. If we do our part
toward making this arrangement a success, it may perhaps
lead to the establishment of other bonds between the associations which represent the statistical public and the offices in
which statistics are prepared.

There are several practical measures toward which we may
contribute if we like. For example, we may use our influence
whenever opportunity arises to secure more adequate salaries
for government statisticians. The scale of pay was too low
before the war; the increased cost of living has made it shock-
ingly inadequate. Unless increases are granted, many experienced men who would be glad to continue in public service
will be compelled in justice to their families to look for openings
elsewhere. Now that the war is over, we cannot justly ask
these men to stint their children for the rest of us. The profession of the statistician demands ability and training not
less than those needed by accountancy; yet, from what I can
learn, the average remuneration of statisticians is decidedly
lower than that of accountants. As representing the statistical
profession, it is certainly the right of this Association to urge
vigorously a higher scale of salaries.

We may also take a definite stand upon the continuation
of the new statistical activities begun during the war. The
War Boards found it necessary to obtain monthly figures of
stocks of certain commodities on hand, and monthly figures
of the production of other commodities. These figures were
collected in a variety of ways, by the Census Office, by trade
organizations like the Tanners' Council, or by sections of the
War Boards themselves. The results are of interest not only
to the industries concerned, but also to the government and
to the general public. The permanent maintenance of this
service, perhaps in a modified form, is a measure that prom-

ises to command increasing support from businessmen. If systematically extended this work might well develop into a continuing census of production, simple in form, inexpensive, but of great value in forecasting business conditions and directing public policy.

Once more, there is the question that I mentioned in the first section of this address, whether the Central Bureau of Planning and Statistics is to be continued or disbanded when the Peace Conference has finished its work. Some centralizing agency to consider the statistical needs of the government as a whole and to lay systematic plans for meeting these needs is our greatest statistical lack. On a question of this character, is it not the duty of the American Statistical Association to speak its mind?

In any action we take we shall do well to distinguish clearly between two types of statistics—the statistics that are used as a record of what has been and the statistics that are used as a basis for planning what shall be. Of these two types record statistics are the more familiar. They constitute the figures that go into annual reports, that are analyzed minutely by the student, that are quoted long after by the historian. Such figures have an influence in shaping public policies; but that influence is vague and intermittent. The average administrative official cares little about what happened day before yesterday—his thoughts are obsessed by what is happening today and what should happen tomorrow. Any one of us in his position would develop that frame of mind if he succeeded at all. What the administrator needs to guide public policy, what he will quickly learn to use if he gets them, is well organized planning statistics. Planning statistics to be of service must be strictly up to date. They must show the vital factors in the situation. They must be presented concisely, in standardized form, both in charts and in tables. The data must be simple enough to be sent by telegraph and compiled overnight. Rough approximations will serve the purpose. What we need practically at present is to develop statistical agencies for obtaining such planning statistics and putting them before the men whose decisions are important to the country, whether these men be administrators, legislators, or voters. As students, our concern will continue to be chiefly with record statistics—they must not be neglected; indeed, they must be extended and improved. But as men interested in future conditions, our emphasis must be put upon the development and the use of planning statistics.

The policy of active participation in shaping statistical work seems to me justified by the circumstances of the day. During the war we learned that many things that seemed impossible were easy of accomplishment if attacked with vigor. Doubtless, the situation has already crystallized in part; but many matters of governmental policy are still in a fluid state. Some changes will have to take place; the question is, What shall these changes be? If we put our technical knowledge and our practical experience at the disposal of the nation, we may increase our influence for years to come, and what is vastly more important, we may help to make quantitative knowledge of facts a potent factor in government.

4

INSTITUTES FOR RESEARCH IN THE SOCIAL SCIENCES[1]

THE establishment of institutes for research in the social sciences is a result of changes in the methods of work practiced by students of human behavior.

Not long ago one might have thought of the typical economist, for example, as a lone worker. A professorial chair in an academic cloister seemed his fitting station in life. He needed to be well grounded while young in the theories of his predecessors. When that training was finished, he might retire to his quiet alcove, where he could carry on a series of imaginary experiments undisturbed. It seemed futile to study the actual processes of economic life at first hand in all their bewildering complexities. So the theorist resorted to abstraction, setting up in his imagination a simplified world that he could shape and reshape at will. Including in this world as variables only such factors as he wished to consider, he speculated about what would happen under the simplified conditions. Later on, he might admit modifications into his original suppositions and consider what changes would follow in his first conclusions.

Needless to say, I am drawing a caricature to bring out essential features with the fewest possible lines. Imaginary experimentation has been used to excellent effect by men who knew the world of business intimately—Ricardo is the shin-

[1] Reprinted by permission from *Journal of Proceedings and Addresses of the Association of American Universities*, Thirty-First Annual Conference, pp. 62–70, Chicago, 1930.

ing example. The point is that, whether done by men who knew what they were leaving out or done by closet students, such work requires no equipment beyond pens, paper, and a few books. Economic theory of the speculative kind is as cheap and easy to produce as higher mathematics or poetry— provided one has the gift. And it has the same problematical relation to reality as do these products of imagination.

Not all economists have worked in this fashion in the past, however; and not all problems yield readily to this form of treatment. Adam Smith, though a college professor, was a realistically minded person who observed widely and carefully. But in his day the most earnest searcher for facts could collect little beyond descriptions of economic activities. By travel, by intercourse with men of affairs and statesmen, by reading official reports, an investigator could inform himself concerning the different styles of economic organization which prevailed in various countries. Yet his information did not lend itself to anything more than what Alfred Marshall, borrowing from chemistry, called "qualitative analysis." In such work analytic insight was so much the decisive factor that hardly anything else counted. Clerical assistance saved some time and labor, but economists of preceding generations seem to have prospered with very little.

Styles of work are changing with the times and what they bring. If Adam Smith were living today he would want a research staff such as Sidney and Beatrice Webb maintained for years. The present Lord Passfield and his wife are no more realistically minded than was their greatest predecessor in economic research; they have cherished no more revolutionary ideas about social reorganization than he had; they have labored no more strenuously than he to build upon facts. But they have needed far more assistance than Adam Smith had, because the range of social data to be handled expanded vastly during the years which lay between the *Wealth of Nations* and *Industrial Democracy*, or the nine volumes on *English Local Government*.

An increase in the amount of work to be done is a usual concomitant of scientific progress. The more we learn about any subject of human interest, the wider grows the circle of our known ignorance. The more powerful and precise our technique, the more exacting do we become in our demands for observations. The more penetrating our analysis, the more do we anatomize our problems. The questions we know enough to ask multiply faster than the answers we can give.

All this is a commonplace in the experience of the physical sciences. As their work has expanded, investigators have required ever more elaborate equipment and ever more personnel. Contrast Galileo's telescope with the 200-inch reflector now being designed; or Sir Isaac Newton, working in Cambridge, with the staff at Mount Wilson; or Sir Humphry Davy's laboratory, in which Faraday washed bottles as a youth, with the laboratories of the General Electric Company. As President Hoover remarked the other day at the Edison celebration:

In earlier times, mechanical invention had been the infrequent and haphazard product of genius in the woodshed. But science has become too sophisticated a being to be wooed in such surroundings. Nowadays a thousand applied science laboratories, supported by the industries of our country, yearly produce a host of new inventions. . . .

I may emphasize that both scientific discovery and its practical application are the products of long and arduous research. Discovery and invention do not spring full grown from the brains of men. The labor of a host of men, great laboratories, long, patient scientific experiment build up the structure of knowledge, not stone by stone, but particle by particle. This adding of fact to fact someday brings forth a revolutionary discovery, an illuminating hypothesis, a great generalization or a practical invention.[2]

[2] "Mr. Hoover's Tribute to Mr. Edison," *Science*, vol. LXX, p. 412, Nov. 1, 1929.

INSTITUTES FOR RESEARCH IN SOCIAL SCIENCES

The social sciences in our generation are just entering upon the stage of development which the President thus describes. From the stage of using observations that a single investigator can make with his own eyes and analyze by common logic, they are advancing to the stage of using mass observations made on a systematic plan by many men and calling for refined analytic technique. As they make progress in this direction, the social sciences are coming to require facilities for work more elaborate and more expensive than they have used hitherto. The establishment of institutes for research is a response to this need. So far, the requirements have been modest in comparison with those of astronomy, physics, chemistry, or biology. But if the present ventures in building upon observation prosper, the scale of demands for equipment and personnel will expand in proportion.

All this is very general; let me be more specific. The social sciences as a group deal with human behavior. They are concerned not with individuals, but with groups. Hence, the observations on which they build can rarely be made in a laboratory. While it is possible to persuade a few individuals to offer themselves as subjects for experimentation by physiologists or psychologists, it is not feasible to coop up groups of men to be experimented upon by economists or sociologists. And social groups in captivity would probably not reveal the phenomena characteristic of social groups in their wild state. Occasionally, however, life offers us an opportunity to observe something that can be called, without serious prevarication, a social experiment in the open. We cherish hopes that these opportunities will multiply, and that with increasing frequency investigators will be permitted to share in determining the setup of such experiments, so as to make them more significant for scientific

[61]

purposes. But as matters stand, our chief reliance for observations of social behavior is upon statistics.

In recent years the keeping of statistical records of what men do has expanded enormously—nowhere more so than in the United States. As society becomes more highly integrated, as one group of people becomes more dependent upon other groups for their livings, their amusements, their knowledge, their culture, and their children's opportunities, it becomes increasingly necessary to know about other groups. A modern large-scale business, for example, that sells to a national or international market draws its supplies from an area equally wide, gets its fixed capital from shifting thousands of stock- and bond-holders, borrows from banks in Wall Street and Lombard Street, and keeps abreast of the technical practice of competitors at home and abroad—such a business needs all sorts of statistical records relating to the commodities it buys and sells and to all the groups with which it deals, from its own employees to the potential customers for its products wherever they live. Some of these data a commercial enterprise can collect for itself; for a larger share it depends upon financial journals and trade associations. On a greater scale still, governments are becoming gatherers and disseminators of statistics. Municipalities need accurate information as a basis for imposing taxes, building schools, providing water systems, extending streets, and the like. States face the taxation problem, the highway problem, the employment problem, and I know not what else. The federal government has its departments, bureaus, and commissions dealing with agriculture, mining, fisheries, forestry, foreign and domestic commerce, railroads, shipping, labor, banking, business combinations, education, public lands, patents, law enforcement, child welfare, public health, weights and measures, income and corporation taxes, coinage, paper currency, and many other matters. Each department, bureau, or commission requires ever more elaborate statistical records for methodical administration. Our system of representation in Congress and our plan of electing presidents rests upon a population count, and on this foundation we have built up a most elaborate series of national censuses, which give periodical surveys of a wide range of social facts from marital conditions to the tenets of religious bodies. In addition to all this, Congress is continually calling for special investigations of the subjects pending before it. Then there is a long and miscellaneous list of private organizations with philanthropic or interested aims, which deem it needful to collect figures as a basis for the formulation of their policies or the propagation of their ideas. Probably the United States collects and publishes more square yards of statistics per capita than any other country in the world; but other nations are increasing their output as they become more civilized and have more money to spend.

Thus the students of social behavior have presented to them opportunities for getting far more extensive and far more reliable factual information than was available to their predecessors. Of course, the statistics now being gathered are designed primarily for administrative purposes. Hence, they are seldom perfectly adapted to the needs of scientific inquirers. For example, our peculiar way of counting the population of a given area on the basis of legal residence is imposed by the constitutional provisions regarding the election of representatives to Congress. A more accurate and significant count could be had if we located every individual at the point in space where he happened to be when the census is taken. But good use can ordinarily be made of the data as they stand. Moreover, scientific consumers of statistics are more and more often called into council by public

[63]

bureaus or employed by private agencies to advise concerning the collection and analysis of data. Their needs get a respectful hearing. For example, the Director of the Census has an Advisory Committee composed of men appointed by the American Economic and the American Statistical associations; the Department of Agriculture and the Federal Reserve Board have excellent research staffs of specialists trained in the social sciences. Thus the quality of the statistics for scientific purposes improves, while their quantity and variety increase.

As these observations became available, it was plain common sense to make the fullest possible use of them in efforts to understand human behavior. But to make use of statistical data was difficult, laborious, and expensive. Economists, sociologists, political scientists, anthropologists, and psychologists had to adapt statistical technique to the peculiar requirements of their several problems and invent new devices as they got deeper into the work. They needed compilers, copyists, and computers to handle masses of data; they needed mechanical equipment of varying kinds. They had to adjust their minds to a new approach, reformulate many of their problems, and learn to content themselves with conclusions of a tentative type.

When the possibilities of using statistical materials on a large scale began to impress the social scientists, most of the active workers were college or university teachers. Their institutions might arrange their teaching loads so as to leave them some leisure for research—particularly after a professor had attained years and dignity incompatible with laborious pioneering. But universities and colleges did not promptly see the propriety of adding considerable appropriations for clerical assistance and equipment. Laboratories were recognized as indispensable for physicists, chemists, biologists, and engineers. Even psychologists had an established claim. But laboratories were frightfully expensive, and the social sciences had got on fairly well in the past without more assistance than was called for by the departments of languages, philosophy, or mathematics. To talk of statistical laboratories seemed even a bit highfalutin, in view of the admitted inexactness of economics, not to mention sociology or political science. Moreover, a university president who was loyally defending his overtaxed budget could usually find men from the very departments concerned who questioned the importance of the new departure. All that was quite natural, but it meant that the first experimental institutes for research in the social sciences had to be set up outside the universities and prove their value before they could get university support.

I cannot give a history of these institutes: someday a candidate for a Doctor's degree will choose this subject for his dissertation and fill our crying need. Meanwhile Frederick A. Ogg's volume, *Research in the Humanistic and Social Sciences: Report of a Survey Conducted for the American Council of Learned Societies*, gives us an annotated list of American research agencies as of 1927. Ogg reports one research organization in history; 20 in economics; 12 in political science; 9 in sociology; 63 in miscellaneous social fields; 34 in business concerns of some sort, a number which it is hard to count rightly in federal government agencies; and 10 endowments more or less interested in conducting or supporting social science research. Were a new survey made today, the numbers would be larger. Many of the organizations in Ogg's list have slight claim to scientific standing; but there remains an impressive minority that are doing serious analytic work, and others that provide indispensable materials. Among the

[65]

oldest institutes of standing in their respective fields I may mention:

The Department of Historical Research, Carnegie Institution of Washington, organized in 1903

The Russell Sage Foundation, chartered in 1907

The Bureau of Municipal Research, chartered in 1907

The Bureau of Social Hygiene, chartered in 1911

The Ohio Institute, chartered in 1914

The Institute of Government, chartered in 1916

A much more rapid increase followed the war. Again I give examples only:

The National Bureau of Economic Research, 1920

The Pollak Foundation, 1920

The Institute for Research in Land Economics and Public Utilities, 1920

The Food Research Institute, 1921

The Personnel Research Federation, 1921

The Institute of Economics, 1922

The Scripps Foundation for Research in Population Problems, 1922

Most of these organizations had no direct relations with universities. Their rise, following upon the development of research staffs working on physical or chemical problems in great business corporations, excited some alarm in university circles. It was said that research was deserting the universities, that they would be left mere teaching bodies, and that both research and teaching would suffer when divorced from each other. The alarm was not wholly unfounded, and it had salutary effects upon university policy. Our larger institutions began providing better research facilities for the mentally enterprising members of their faculties. Sometimes this meant equipping statistical laboratories or providing research assistants; sometimes it meant setting up research organizations comparable in scope and character to the independent institutes. If one looks back at

[66]

Ogg's list, one finds that a larger proportion of the later entries have close university connections. To give examples once more:

The Industrial Relations Section, Department of Economics, Princeton University, endowed in 1922

The Local Community Research Committee of the University of Chicago, organized in 1923

The Social Research Society of the University of Southern California, organized in 1924

The Bureau of International Research of Harvard University and Radcliffe College, established in 1925

The Institute for Research in the Social Sciences of the University of North Carolina, set up in 1926

The Institute for Research in the Social Sciences of the University of Virginia, set up in 1926

The Institute of Human Relations of Yale University, established in 1929 (of course, later in date than Ogg's list)

In most, perhaps in all, of these cases the universities obtained special funds before they launched research institutes. Bringing in new money is a common prerequisite for entrance into a university budget. Even so, the readiness of university authorities to sponsor research programs in social science at present is in marked contrast to their attitude even five or six years ago. Perhaps pressure is now brought by the universities upon the social science faculties to engage in factual research almost as often as pressure is brought by these faculties upon the universities to provide research facilities.

All this concerns the recent past and present. What will happen in the near future depends upon three factors: first, what the realistic students of human behavior are able to accomplish by their study of objective observations; second, the policy university authorities develop toward their work; third, the attitude that donors take.

[67]

THE BACKWARD ART OF SPENDING MONEY

Of these three factors, I take the first to be of critical importance. The ground for this opinion is that the members of the Association of American Universities, your colleagues in positions of authority, the majority of people with money to give, and their advisers, are sensible men for the most part. Your policy and the attitude of donors toward research in the social sciences will be shaped primarily by what such research accomplishes. You will watch critically what the laboratories in your universities, the institutes you have set up or affiliated, and the independent research bureaus are attempting; and you will judge them by their fruits. There are fashions in philanthropy as much as in dress. Your opinion of the recent movement to support social science research will have deep influence upon the minds of donors. In turn, the technical advisers of the great foundations will follow closely the work of your organizations and the independents. Individual givers will catch echoes of the carefully considered verdicts and will follow suit. These outside opinions will have weight with you. Thus all will turn in the long run, as it should, upon the scientific fruitfulness of realistic research in human behavior.

What, then, are the prospects that the returns in knowledge gained will prove commensurate to the expenditure of time and money? No one can be sure in advance. Real research is always exploration of the unknown and therefore is an uncertain venture. Like geographical exploration, it attracts men of daring, imaginative minds, whose faith may leave them stranded in a wilderness. The fact that laboratory research has produced great results in dealing with the simple phenomena of physics, chemistry, and biology does not guarantee that it will yield similar results when applied to the complex phenomena of the social sciences. While many of us actively engaged in the work see much of significance in results already attained, and more of promise in what we are now attempting, we have few dramatic discoveries to display before critical laymen. We acknowledge that our measurements are rough estimates, like those of geologic time, and that the application to the future of our conclusions drawn from study of the past is attended by much uncertainty.

I might continue in this strain indefinitely. But the point is clear enough: we are still in the early stages of a great experiment. Intellectual curiosity and the grave importance of the issues at stake combine in urging an effort to solve social problems by taking systematic thought. That is the path by which mankind has won its long way up from the life of beasts; it is the most hopeful line of further progress. In the social sciences we have passed through an inevitable stage of speculative reconnaissance; now we are ready for a tamer and more painstaking type of work. Factual observations are accumulating for analysis; technical methods are being developed. The work must be pressed forward until we have established its fruitfulness or its barrenness.

While it is prudent to keep in mind this possibility that our current trial will prove to be an error, I can report that present indications seem highly favorable on the whole. In economics—the field with which I am most familiar—doctrinal controversy is on the decline; old problems are being broken down into their elements for more intensive scrutiny or being restated in a form that facilitates attack; new problems are being developed; through business enterprises, labor organizations, and government bureaus, investigators are getting into closer touch with the processes they study; the tools of analysis are being improved rapidly in design and efficiency; current publications show a drift away from dialectical essays and general treatises that present variations upon conventional themes toward papers and mono-graphs of a more scientific type. The institutes for economic research are playing a leading role in these developments. Men who can devote all their time and energy to investiga-tion for months on end get on faster than men who must divide their days between investigation and teaching. Favor-able working conditions appeal strongly to the ablest re-search men, so that the institutes have little difficulty in securing the personnel they wish. University authorities commonly recognize the benefits that will accrue to their faculties, and ultimately to their students, from participa-tion in the institute programs, and often grant leaves of absence to enable professors to spend a year or more in an independent institute, or even in a research organization connected with another university. The findings of the strictly scientific institutes command respect in technical circles and have prestige with the general public. Business en-terprises, philanthropic organizations, government agencies, even presidents of the United States, seek their aid in laying factual foundations for their planning. It is not surprising that the economists engaged in realistic investigation are developing a spirit of confidence, a vital interest in their work, which has scarcely been equaled since the generation of Malthus and Ricardo.

One other development must be noted: The several social sciences are gaining a clearer conception that they have a common task—the understanding of human behavior—and that they must pool their resources to attain the best results. The establishment of the Social Science Research Council in 1923 is one expression of this new spirit of cooperation among groups which hitherto have avoided entangling al-liances with one another.

INSTITUTES FOR RESEARCH IN SOCIAL SCIENCES

In fine, the study of social activities is entering upon a new phase, characterized by greater objectivity, greater realism, and greater exactness. This movement has proceeded far enough to justify considerable confidence in its future. Institutes for research, led by scientifically minded investigators, provided with adequate assistance, and equipped with proper materials and appliances, are the most effective instrumentalities for carrying on the work. Whether these institutes are physically situated on academic campuses or outside the walls, they belong spiritually to the circle of interests that your Association cherishes. They promise to become as authentic an agency for promoting human knowledge and human welfare as the laboratories from which physical science emerged to make over the world.

5

RESEARCH IN THE SOCIAL SCIENCES[1]

TO ALL concerned with the social sciences, or aware of what they promise to mankind's future, the dedication of a building to research in these fields is an occasion for thanksgiving. One of the ablest bands of inquirers into human behavior is here provided with technical equipment of unequaled excellence. Not less important, the university plans to give these investigators full opportunity to use the building. What mechanical facilities, clerical assistance, and time to think can do toward helping thought is here offered more abundantly than elsewhere. The fortunate workers who profit immediately by these opportunities will promote the efforts of their colleagues wherever research in the social sciences is going forward. In years to come, men may look back upon the ceremony in which we are now sharing with much the feeling we now cherish for the opening of Liebig's chemical laboratory at Giessen, 103 years ago—a brief interval in the history of human culture.

To one who was himself trained for research in a social science at the University of Chicago, the occasion has a heightened interest. When good fortune brought me here in the early nineties as an undergraduate student, Chicago was, I fondly believe, the most stimulating school of social science

[1] Address at the symposium on the occasion of the dedication of the Social Science Research Building at the University of Chicago, Dec. 16 and 17, 1929. Reprinted by permission of the University of Chicago Press, from *The New Social Science*, ed. by Leonard D. White, pp. 4–15, Chicago, 1930.

then to be found in any land. The apprentice in economics who could pass through Laurence Laughlin's hands without being provoked to think for himself was a flabby specimen. From Adolph Miller's balanced expositions he caught glimpses of the order that might reign in a rational world. If William Hill could not make him feel vital interests throbbing through the issues which economists discuss, no man could do so. Then there was the disturbing genius of Thorstein Veblen—that visitor from another world, who dissected the current commonplaces that the student had unconsciously acquired, as if the most familiar of his daily thoughts were curious products wrought in him by outside forces. No other such emancipator of the mind from the subtle tyranny of circumstance has been known in social science, and no other such enlarger of the realm of inquiry. From Veblen's philosophic view of social institutions and social theories a straight path led to John Dewey's lectures. There the student interested in any phase of human behavior heard a master of philosophy and psychology analyze the processes involved in activities, from dealing with a broken shoestring to constructing a system of metaphysics. Not less effectively than Veblen, though with a different emphasis, Dewey helped an economist to drag the psychological preconceptions lurking behind theories of value and distribution into consciousness, and to see how they stood the light of current knowledge. It was, indeed, a varied opportunity which these teachers offered, and a varied program of researches which they incited students to undertake.

For, widely as they differed in their approaches to the study of social behavior, all these men made one eager to share in the work of learning more. Professor Laughlin revered the body of economic doctrine expounded by Mill and revised by Cairnes; but year after year he gave a course upon "Unsettled Problems in Political Economy," and there was no more insatiable searcher after facts than he among the special students of monetary problems. On Veblen's showing, the social sciences must be rebuilt altogether in a different style of architecture, for which Darwinian biology supplied the model. And Dewey's analysis of thinking was scarcely less revolutionary when applied to economic behavior than Veblen's analysis of the cumulative growth of economic institutions. In this exciting atmosphere the students became ardent investigators and cross-fertilized one another. Henry Walgrave Stuart and H. Parker Willis, Robert Hoxie and Herbert Davenport, Harry Millis and Edwin Meade, Frederick Cleveland, S. J. McLean and Mackenzie King—to name only a few of my own contemporaries—these men covered a wide range, and even in their student years several of them made contributions to knowledge which became part of the working equipment of economics.

It is, then, quite in accord with her own tradition that the University of Chicago should become the seat of the first building dedicated wholly to research in the social sciences. For that tradition looked forward to fresh developments, rather than backward to the accomplishments of the past. To transcend what was then in the program was part of the program itself. In particular, two deficiencies in our equipment for research became clearer as the years passed. We had no adequate training in statistical technique in the nineties, and workers in the several departments of social science did not value one another aright. These weaknesses were common at that time; they did not then impress a student's mind as serious, though now it seems that the logic of what he was doing should have made them clear.

RESEARCH IN THE SOCIAL SCIENCES

I

Factual research was the breath of our nostrils in the department of economics. We speculated a great deal about what would happen under all sorts of hypothetical conditions. That was good sport. We took much more seriously the effort to find out how processes run in the actual world. In the course of these efforts we had often to deal with statistics. But we did not know how to get from our data any but obvious results. Our most ambitious ventures scarcely went beyond making index numbers of prices by very simple formulas. In the technique of statistical analysis we had virtually no instruction—a deficiency that I, for one, have never overcome. Yet this is the very tool which our interest in what we called, after the quaint fashion of that day, the "inductive verification" of economic theory should have led us to master. As far as I know, the other social science departments were no better equipped than economics in this respect.

Subsequent developments have shown how lacking in prescience we were. As society has become more highly organized, practical needs have forced business enterprises and governments of all grades to seek ever more varied and ever more precise information for the guidance of their policies. The wider the scope of an organization's activities, the less can its responsible officers know at first hand of the conditions it must meet, the less safe it is to depend upon native shrewdness, the more necessary it becomes to have definite reports as a basis for action. Hence, the collection of systematic information concerning social activities has grown apace in the last generation. Our old statistical data concerning prices, money, banking, foreign trade, transportation, production, population, migration, have

[75]

been greatly extended and improved. To them has been added much fresh information concerning topics about which we could do little but guess in my student days, such as retail trade, wage disbursements, employment, stocks of commodities, personal incomes, business profits, velocity of circulation, morbidity, and a long list of other matters.

Many of the data that practical needs have forced men to collect are published and so become available to scientific students of human behavior. Thus political scientists, sociologists, and economists have had opened to them opportunities for large-scale observation such as no earlier generation possessed. Where their predecessors had been able merely to speculate, present workers are able over an expanding range to observe with increasing accuracy. Like sensible men, they have seized this opportunity to advance their knowledge as rapidly as possible from the stage of speculations about hypothetical conditions to the higher stage of quantitative analysis of actual conditions.

To make the most of statistical data, however, the social science workers have had to master a new technique. A century earlier mathematicians had developed the theory of probability with many ingenious variations. Demographers, anthropologists, and biologists had adopted mathematical methods in the analysis of their own observations upon living objects, from plants to human bodies. It seemed a relatively simple matter to borrow the tools thus forged by others for use in the social sciences. But it was found, none too quickly, that social data often fail to meet the suppositions underlying the theory of probability and its biological applications. The problems of social behavior presented features peculiar to themselves, and it became necessary to adapt statistical procedure to these novel requirements. Therefore, attempts to use borrowed tools turned out to be but the first steps in a long process of developing a technical equipment especially suited to the varied tasks that sociologists, economists, and political scientists confront. Among all the efforts of the last quarter century in the social sciences, none has been pushed with more vigor and success than the excogitation of this statistical technique—a task still in full swing.

This development has produced a marked change in the conditions that our work requires. A political scientist concerned with the theory of the state or an economist dealing with problems of static equilibrium has little need of assistance. What he requires is a vigorous mind, a library, and leisure. The quantitative worker needs just as clear a mind, at least as much leisure, and as many books; in addition, he needs for many of his researches a great deal of help from statistical clerks and computers, and these assistants should be provided with machines. How genuine this need is has been shown by the establishment of numerous institutes for research in the social sciences—organizations which have grown up largely outside of university walls, because the universities have not been able, or ready, to provide the facilities that research men have come to require. Much of the most significant work of the last decade has been done in such institutes. They have been the only places where elaborate quantitative work could be done. Of late the universities have awakened to the need and begun to provide statistical laboratories, primarily for training students, but also in part for conducting research. Most of these laboratories, however, serve but a single department or a school of business. Chicago is now advancing farther, according to her wont. Not only is this building the most admirably equipped of social science laboratories; it is also reserved exclusively for research, and in the planning of the work to be done here all the social science departments are joining as in a common venture.

II

That remark recalls the second deficiency exhibited by the social science work of the nineties in Chicago—lack of a common understanding among the several departments concerned with "the proper study of mankind." Like our lack of statistical training, this deficiency also was a sin against the spirit of our program. Indeed, our two philosophers, Veblen and Dewey, were showing the error of our ways. More than that, they were building a platform on which the different departments might conduct a fusion campaign.

It was impossible to fit Veblen into a department pigeonhole—he seemed to be economist, anthropologist, sociologist, social psychologist, and political scientist by turns. For his problem—how cumulative changes come about in social habits of thinking—is one that admits of no such sharp divisions as administrative convenience and the progress of specialization had raised within our universities. And Veblen's learning was wide enough to embrace those parts of all the social sciences most pertinent to his problem. One cannot understand the evolution of social institutions if he confines himself to any single specialty.

With equal vigor John Dewey's philosophy called for cooperation among all the social sciences. In analyzing the processes involved in man's varied activities, he showed us how psychology illuminates the problem of social behavior. But his analysis made it clear that the psychologist alone cannot solve this problem. For, on Dewey's showing, the minds of the members of every social group are shaped by the environment in which they have developed, and the most potent environmental factors in shaping minds are other minds. One of Dewey's favorite sayings, "There is no psychology but social psychology," suggests how large and how active is the role that the social sciences must play in mankind's cumulative effort to know itself. The old notion that a science like economics can borrow a few ready-made conclusions about human motives from psychology, and on this foundation erect a towering theory of value and distribution, gave place to the realization that economics must recognize that it is a constructive study of human actions, making its own peculiar contributions to the knowledge of social behavior. The like holds true of all the social sciences. They have a common problem and a common working program.

How influential Dewey's teaching and Veblen's example have been in breaching the walls that separated the social sciences in the nineties I do not know. Perhaps these men merely glimpsed a little earlier than others views that soon dawned upon many. A historian of thought might even trace the recent reunion among the social sciences back to the great group of philosophical radicals who, in the lifetime of Jeremy Bentham, worked over the whole range from jurisprudence and psychology to economics and adult reeducation. Perhaps we should say that while the several disciplines drew apart from one another during a phase of intense specialization, it was inevitable that they should grow together again along their edges as specialization spread out from the original centers over wider areas. However we explain the process, there can be no doubt that recently the social sciences have become more aware of their common interests and their need for active cooperation.

Evidences of the *rapprochement* abound in this country at least. Half a dozen books have appeared in the last five

[79]

years designed to interpret the several social sciences to one another. It suffices to name one by way of example, *The Social Sciences and Their Interrelations*, written by thirty-three specialists running the gamut from philosophy to law, and edited by William F. Ogburn and A. A. Golden-weiser. Within a month or two there will be published the first volume of an *Encyclopaedia of the Social Sciences*, edited by Edwin Seligman and Alvin Johnson, to be followed at intervals by fourteen other volumes.[2] Equally significant is the active cultivation of borderlands between the several disciplines—work requiring a pair of names, like legal economics, human geography, cultural anthropology, social history, social psychology, social ethics. Several research agencies have been set up with staffs recruited from two or more of the social sciences—like the Brookings Institution in Washington, the Institute of Law at Johns Hopkins, the Institute of Human Relations at Yale, the Institutes for Research in the Social Sciences at the universities of North Carolina and Virginia. Finally, the professional associations of the United States representing seven social disciplines united in 1923 to form a national organization for promoting their common interests—the Social Science Research Council. In this council psychologists, anthropologists, sociologists, political scientists, economists, statisticians, and historians seek to combine the contributions which their several sciences may make to the understanding of social problems. Nor do they think that this combination is sufficiently comprehensive; for this year they have added to the Council members at large to represent jurisprudence, public health, and psychiatry.

Dewey and Veblen left Chicago years ago; but the ideas for which they stood remained. The Social Science Research

2 [The final volume was published in June, 1935.]

[80]

Council looks upon Charles E. Merriam as its father, and no man represents more authentically than he the Chicago viewpoint. This university was one of the first to set up an interdepartmental organization for treating social problems —the Local Community Research Committee, established in 1923. The building that we are now dedicating to research in the social sciences is but the physical embodiment of ideas that have flourished here since the nineties—ideas on which we did not then know how to act, and on which we find it very difficult to act even now.

For men of my generation were brought up as specialists. We have developed the limitations of outlook, technique, and information that specialization inflicts as an offset to its marked advantages. If you wish to see how hard we find the task of self reeducation, read the book mentioned a moment since, *The Social Sciences and Their Interrelations*. You will find that even the collaborators whom Ogburn and Goldenweiser chose for their open-mindedness do not really interpenetrate one another's minds very thoroughly. Great tasks can seldom be performed in short order, and the task of developing a common program for all the social sciences, without losing the efficiency that specialization brings, is not one that the present generation of adult workers can see through.

III

An old Chicago man can congratulate most warmly the Chicago men of today upon the fair prospects stretching before them in the field of social science. They will not be handicapped by inadequate training in statistical technique or cut off from one another by departmental walls. The points at which the university was once weak have become points at which it is exceptionally strong.

THE BACKWARD ART OF SPENDING MONEY

But with his congratulations upon these changes, an old student must combine the hope that the traits that made Chicago such a stimulating mother to his kind in the nineties may persist in the more elaborately equipped university of today and tomorrow. Statistics is a most efficient tool; we must use it with all the skill and energy we can muster. Cooperation among the social sciences is admirable; we must transform it from an aspiration into a working reality. Yet no one supposes that technical proficiency and a wide range of contacts suffice to make significant discoveries. There must be also the philosophic grasp and the ability to see with one's own eyes that distinguish men like the inspirers of research who shed luster upon Chicago in my day. What counts most of all in scientific work is that free play of ideas which we understand so little, but from which emerge at rare moments the flashes that keep reorienting our search for knowledge generation after generation. Such suggestions may come to one who is using a slide rule or sitting in a research council committee, quite as well as to one who is communing with himself in a closet. We know not how to produce such flashes, but we do know that they can scarcely occur in a mind that has not been dwelling upon scientific problems.

To him that hath much, much shall be given. You have excellent equipment. You have admirable organization. You have a philosophical tradition of conceiving human behavior in a way that lays it open to scientific attack. On this basis you can built up knowledge bit by bit, after the cumulative fashion of the elder sciences. So much is assured. May you who are privileged to use this building have also the flashes of insight that come to exploring minds duly prepared. May you thus open out ever fresh vistas of future work, that will keep research in social behavior always as enticing as it is today.

6

THE SOCIAL SCIENCES AND NATIONAL PLANNING[1]

AN IMPRESSION prevails in many minds that social science has made out a case against national planning, at least in economic matters. This impression is the vestigial remnant of what used to be a vigorous belief. English political economy arose as a destructive critique of the national planning done by mercantilist statesmen and as a constructive argument for a policy of *laissez faire*. But since Adam Smith published the *Wealth of Nations* in 1776, economic practice and economic theory have been evolving rapidly, each acting continuously upon the other. Present opinions upon national planning are the outcome up to date of these historical developments in the field of practice and of theory, which I shall sketch as briefly as I can.

I

The aim of mercantilist planning was to mobilize economic forces for national aggrandizement. The country should have a numerous population; the common people should be trained in husbandry and the crafts, inured to labor, and kept from the consumption of luxuries that are merely pleasant, such as sugar and tea. The necessaries of

[1] [This and the following essay on "Intelligence and the Guidance of Economic Evolution" cover much the same ground, but the differences seem to the editor sufficient to justify the inclusion of both.] Address as retiring chairman of the Section for Social and Economic Sciences, American Association for the Advancement of Science, Pittsburgh, Jan. 1, 1935. Reprinted by permission from *Science*, vol. LXXXI, pp. 55–62, Jan. 18, 1935.

life should be produced at home as a precaution against foreign attack; the mercantile marine should be fostered as an auxiliary of the navy; an abundant supply of the precious metals is desirable both for home trade and as the sinews of war. To guarantee this supply countries that have no mines of gold and silver must see that the balance of trade is "favorable." To that end, exports should be encouraged, and imports discouraged, except in the case of commodities destined for resale abroad or of raw materials for domestic manufactures. Private enterprise should be directed toward industries that the government is trying to develop on national grounds; colonies should get most of their manufactured goods from the home country and send raw materials in return; foreign commerce should be supervised to make sure that merchants comply with the national plan.

Of course this scheme of statecraft involves national economic planning of an elaborate, continuous sort, calling for eternal vigilance on the part of statesmen and tending to develop into detailed regimentation of economic life. The occupation a youth may chose, the apprenticeship he must undergo, the wages he may receive, the places in which he may live and work, the commodities he may consume, the products his master may make, the technical processes to be followed, the standards of materials and workmanship to be observed—these are but samples of the matters that mercantilism sought to control in its heyday.

This type of national planning grew up as centralized states emerged from the confusion of feudalism, and prevailed with numberless variations of detail over Central and Western Europe for two or three centuries.[2] At many

---

[2] Any brief sketch of mercantilist policies must be schematic to a degree. The present sketch is probably least misleading as a representation of the policies which Colbert sought to carry out in France.

points, the mercantilist regulations stood in the way of enterprising money-makers, or even created opportunities to make money by breaking the law—for example, by smuggling. Hence, the system tended to break down in detail whenever the administration of the laws grew lax for any reason. Certainly in England and her colonies private disregard of mercantilist regulations became a mass phenomenon in the eighteenth century. Nor did the authorities try hard to stop all infractions of the law. One may say that *laissez faire* was practiced on a considerable scale before it was preached as a formal doctrine.

Adam Smith was not the first, but he was the most effective, critic of mercantilist planning. His argument can be summed up in a syllogism: first, every individual desires to increase his own wealth; second, every individual in his local situation can judge better than a distant statesman what use of his labor and capital is most profitable; third, the wealth of the nation is the aggregate of the wealth of its citizens; therefore, the wealth of the nation will increase most rapidly if every individual is left free to conduct his own affairs as he sees fit. There need be no fear that consumers will be exploited under such a system; competition among producers is a sufficient safeguard against that danger. To make gains for himself each producer must offer goods that others want at prices set by competition. Thus, in pursuing his own gain, every producer is led to promote the public interest.

By formulating this argument with the authority of a moral philosopher, Adam Smith offered his contemporaries a justification of acts that thousands had been performing with a bad conscience. The "rationalization" lent new vigor to private disregard of hampering regulations and so contributed toward the breakdown of mercantilism. It is hard today to realize how Adam Smith clarified the minds of men and lifted their hearts with his ringing call to adopt "the simple and obvious system of natural liberty." His was a great service to blundering humanity during the difficult transition that lay so near at hand. And that service was accepted with a promptness having few parallels in the history of thought. Far more rapidly than he had supposed possible, Adam Smith's views were adopted by other thinkers, by businessmen, and by statesmen. Supplemented by the philosophical radicalism of Jeremy Bentham and his disciples, restated to fit changing conditions by later economists, *laissez faire* became the dominant maxim of British economic policy and exercised a powerful influence upon thought and action throughout the Western world. We may almost say that for two generations the British government planned to have no plan.

II

Economists no longer celebrate "the simple and obvious system of natural liberty" after the sweeping fashion of Adam Smith. Social organization has become vastly more complex than it was in the eighteenth century; business planning and governmental planning have become closely intertwined with each other; discussions of their roles in guiding economic activities now deal with the diversity of conditions produced by a century and a half of the industrial revolution.

Even while they were in process of assimilating the doctrine of *laissez faire*, the English people began using their government as an agency for correcting what they thought to be bad results of private enterprise. Some of these governmental controls could be defended by a shrewd interpretation of Adam Smith's logic. Thus laws to protect child workers and presently laws to limit the hours worked by "young persons" and women could be defended on the ground that minors and women of any age were not in fact the best judges of what is good for them. Public opinion came to believe that it was foolish to permit even grown men to take the risks of overloaded ships, unfenced machines, ill-ventilated mines, or occupational diseases, however accustomed they might be to doing so, and successive Parliaments passed laws to reduce industrial hazards of many sorts. If the mass of the wage earners were as blind to their economic interests as the Malthusian principle of population represented them to be, there was reason for tutelage in many matters. Compulsory education came to seem an obvious need. The industrial revolution called for operatives who could read blueprints and clerks who knew arithmetic. Democracy, the political complement of economic liberty, demanded literate citizens. Accordingly, the government went much further than Adam Smith recommended in providing education at public expense and forcing parents to accept it for their children. Adam Smith had justified state provision of public works; the list of such works grew with the density of population and scientific knowledge of public hygiene. The rise of the gas industry, of railroads, of tramways, of the telegraph, the telephone, electric lighting, and power transmission built up a great class of public utilities midway between the fields of private enterprise and public works. These utilities could not serve the public cheaply and efficiently under such competitive conditions as worked well in manufactures and trade; they were "natural monopolies," and as such they could be subjected to special regulation, or even owned and operated by governments that professed the doctrine of *laissez faire*. Presently it began to appear, though more strikingly in the

United States than in Great Britain, that in many industries competition was breeding combinations. The joint-stock company, which Adam Smith had thought of as limited by its own competitive inefficiency to a brief list of trades requiring vast capital rather than active enterprise, proved admirably adapted to the factory age with its heavy investments, once the principle of limited liability had been accepted. Incorporation made it easy to organize business enterprise in units large enough to dominate whole industries. Once more government intervention could be justified on familiar grounds. Adam Smith had taken it for granted that the consumer, for whom he felt tender solicitude, would be protected against exploitation by competition among numerous producers. If that was ceasing to be the case, it seemed logical that government should break up the monopolistic corporations and force the fragments to compete again.

So far I have mentioned governmental actions intended to remedy what were thought to be bad results of business planning or to supply social needs for which business planning made no adequate provision. I go on to list various shortcomings of business planning that are troubling our minds today, shortcomings that government is often called upon to correct or to supply.

A specter that has troubled men's minds more and more as the industrial revolution makes headway is the rapid depletion of natural resources. In 1865 W. Stanley Jevons pointed out that the fixed limits of coal deposits made it impossible that Great Britain should long maintain its current rate of increase in industrial output. Somewhat later Americans began to feel apprehensive about their supplies of lumber, natural gas, oil, and other minerals. Now we are becoming dimly fearful about the loss of soil fertility through reckless methods of cultivation and erosion. The appalling wastes of natural resources that are going on seem due largely to the policy of handing over the nation's heritage to individuals to be exploited as they see fit. It appears that business planning takes, and must take, a relatively short period of time into account—a period that is but as a day in the life of a nation. What is rational on the basis of this short-run private view may be exceedingly unwise on the basis of long-run public interest. We see now how vital a factor Adam Smith overlooked in assuming the nation's wealth to be the aggregate of the wealth of its individual citizens. And what can be said about the wasteful use of natural resources by private enterprise can be repeated with increased emphasis regarding the use of human resources. Private enterprise draws thousands of youths into "blind-alley" occupations from which they emerge little fitted to assume the responsibilities of mature life. The work it provides for millions of adults fails to make use of their full capacities and leaves many the victims of "balked dispositions." We have allowed our immediate economic interests to lead us into modes of living that fail to satisfy our emotional needs and our creative impulses.

Experience is showing also that, great as are its contributions to social welfare, business planning has a formidable array of technical limitations of which we are becoming increasingly conscious as the years pass and as our ideas of what is possible to mankind grow more daring.[3]

Business planning can secure effective coordination of effort only within the limits of each independent business enterprise; that is, each group of business activities subject

[3] In the following five paragraphs, I venture to reproduce with minor changes passages that I contributed to the *Report of the National Resources Board*, pp. 81, 82, Washington, 1934.

to a single financial control. It can not effectively coordinate the activities of independent enterprises.

> Coordination within an enterprise is the result of careful planning by experts; coordination among independent enterprises cannot be said to be planned at all—rather it is the unplanned result of natural selection in a struggle for business survival. Coordination within an enterprise has a definite aim—the making of profits; coordination among independent enterprises is limited by the conflicting aims of the several units. Coordination within an enterprise is maintained by a single authority possessed of power to carry its plans into effect; coordination among independent enterprises depends on many different authorities which have no power to enforce a common program, except so far as one can persuade or coerce others. As a result of these conditions, coordination within an enterprise is characterized by economy of effort, coordination among independent enterprises by waste.[4]

The planning of business enterprises aims at making money. If the ultimate test of economic efficiency is that of satisfying the most important social needs in the most economical manner, then business planning must be warped by inequality in the distribution of income. Where a few have money enough to gratify almost any whim and where many cannot buy things required to maintain their efficiency or to give proper training to their children, it can hardly be argued that the goods that pay best are the goods most needed.

From the viewpoint of business itself, planning to make money is a precarious undertaking which often ends in heavy losses or financial ruin. However skillfully the internal affairs of a corporation are managed, the whole venture may be wrecked by circumstances beyond the control and even beyond the knowledge of the managers. As markets grow wider, investments heavier, and financial interrelation-

[4] Wesley C. Mitchell, *Business Cycles: The Problem and Its Setting*, p. 172, New York, 1927.

ships more complicated, it becomes harder for the ablest management to anticipate the conditions that the next few years will bring forth. The movement toward business combinations is largely a businessman's remedy for uncertainty—his effort to extend the number of factors that he can control. But combination by one group of enterprises increases the hazards for other enterprises. It is not surprising that with growing frequency businessmen have turned to the government for aid, and demanded that it protect them against hazards they cannot control, including the hazard of combinations among other businessmen.

The frequent recurrence of economic crises and depressions is evidence that the automatic functioning of our business system is defective. In view of recent events, no one longer holds that the business cycle is being "ironed out." Instead, it appears that the difficulty of maintaining the necessary equilibrium among different factors in the enormously complicated mechanism is becoming greater rather than less. Aside from the widening of markets and the growth of combinations mentioned above, we face the fact that an increasing part of the annual output consists of semidurable goods which people can stop buying for a time if times are bad. The drift of population from farms to cities and the diminishing dependence of farm families upon what they can make for their own consumption, their increasing dependence upon selling farm produce to get the wherewithal for buying other goods, mean that general economic maladies afflict more people more seriously than they did in past generations. Business planning has found no effective means of preventing the growth of these factors that tend to make the business-cycle hazard more serious.

When a grave depression occurs, recovery is retarded by the divergence between the policies followed by powerful corporations in highly organized industries and the policies that are forced upon small producers in simply organized industries, of which farming is by far the most important. Formerly, when a depression came, prices fell in almost all markets. This decline proceeded until the resulting checks upon production and stimulations of purchasing produced a new equilibrium between the demand and supply of most commodities at prices lower than those prevailing during the preceding phase of expansion. Then business activity began to pick up again. The revival came about automatically: businessmen had merely to look after their individual interests, and government to remain a passive spectator, or at most to increase its allowances for the support of the poor. Of late this automatic process of recovery has become less prompt and effective. The managers of great corporations usually believe that the best way to minimize their losses during a depression is to maintain prices, despite the heavy falling off in sales and production that is likely to follow. This policy will at least cut down the heaviest items of current expense—cost of materials and wages. But farmers, who individually can exercise no control over the prices of their products, must continue to produce as much as they can and to sell for what they can get in a community where many consumers have lost their jobs. Because their incomes are cut by low prices, the farmers cannot buy freely from the corporations that are keeping their prices relatively high. Because farmers, other small producers in a similar position, and their former employees who are now out of work cannot buy freely, the rigid-price corporations have small inducement to increase output and put men back to work. Recovery under such conditions is a far slower and more halting process than it was when all prices were flexible in much the same degree.

If businessmen are justified in demanding that government take measures to protect them against the hazards of trade, how much stronger justification for such a demand have wage earners! The day when it was plausible to argue that steady work comes to steady workmen is past. Sobriety, industry, thrift will not enable a man to keep his job if the company that employs him shuts down. Nor is it his fault if he cannot get a new job promptly when there are ten applicants for every opening. Cyclical unemployment is the labor side of the business-cycle hazard, and, as said above, that hazard is not shrinking. Technological unemployment is the labor side of industrial progress and that hazard is growing. Economic security for wage earners, much the most numerous class of people in a commercial nation, certainly has not been provided by business planning.

Finally, we are often told nowadays that, even in the best of business years, our present economic organization prevents us from making full use of the technological skill we have attained and of the capital we have accumulated. As a rule, statements of this sort are vague and sweeping, better calculated to arouse interest than to convince a skeptic. But recently two efforts have been made to get more definite ideas about the margin by which actual production at the peak of prosperity falls short of what production might be if we could make full use of our facilities. In 1933 twenty-eight engineers of experience in various industries were persuaded to submit estimates of how much the aggregate output of all industries might be increased simultaneously with existing equipment and methods, provided a ready market could be assured for the products. More than half of the estimates ran above 25 per cent. Asked what increase might be expected if the equipment and management of all industries were "brought to the level of the best current practice," half of the engineers gave estimates of 60 per cent or more. Second, an elaborate statistical study of the proportion of the country's capacity for production that was utilized in 1925–1929 has yielded similar results. The conclusion drawn was that, taking the full gamut of operations from agriculture and mining, through manufactures and transportation to retail distribution, it would have been feasible to produce nearly 20 per cent more goods than we did by the methods then in use and with the equipment and labor we then possessed.[5] Thus the charge that our economic organization fails by a wide margin to secure the full use of our productive capacity even in years of business activity is sustained by both of these inquiries—neither of which, it must be admitted, pretends to be more than a preliminary treatment of an exceedingly important problem.

To draw up a list of errors and omissions under business planning is not to damn private enterprise. Few dispositions seem to me more misguided than the disposition to regard business as a monster that prevents suffering humanity from attaining its heart's desire. After all detractions are made, the historical fact remains that, in the countries that have given wide scope to private initiative since Adam Smith presented his momentous argument for *laissez faire*, the masses of mankind attained a higher degree of material comfort and a larger measure of liberty than at any earlier time of which we have knowledge, or under any other form of organization that mankind has tried out in practice. These blessings of relative abundance and freedom arise from the rapid application of scientific discoveries to the

---

[5] *Economic Reconstruction*, Report of the Columbia University Commission, pp. 87–104, New York, 1934; Edwin G. Nourse and Associates, *America's Capacity to Produce*, pp. 415–425, Washington, 1934.

humdrum work of the world, and that application has been effected mainly by men who were seeking profits. In societies organized on the basis of making money, *laissez faire* put the stupendous drive of private gain behind the industrial revolution. Further, the capital required for building machines, factories, railroads, steamships, electrical equipment, and the like was accumulated mainly from profits made by businessmen and investors and used, not to satisfy their own wants, but to provide new equipment for production. As Adam Smith argued, in pursuing their private gain businessmen were led to promote the public welfare.

III

Yet no class in the community has been satisfied with the workings of private initiative. From capitalists to farmers and workingmen, all of us have tried to use government as an agency for bettering economic organization. The way in which government should be used has been the central issue of our political struggles more often than the question whether government should be used at all. For few of us have been willing to trust what Adam Smith regarded as "natural" forces. Instead, we have cherished ambitious designs of harnessing social forces much as we have harnessed steam and electricity.

Nor have these attempts been fruitless. The familiar contrast between the rapid industrial progress since James Watt invented the separate condenser and the slow social progress since Watt's friend Adam Smith published the *Wealth of Nations* is often exaggerated. England today is a very different society from the England of 1776, and the difference is not limited to technology. For example, the working-class babies of this year will have educational opportunities that were closed to their ancestors; their choice of occupations will be wider; they will work fewer hours; their livings will be more secure; they will dwell in less hideous and more healthful towns; fewer of them will be maimed at work or will contract occupational diseases; their span of life will be longer; they will be free to unite with their fellows in promoting their common interests; they will have a share in governing their country. These advantages they will owe to the long series of social reforms which have been enacted one after another, and which these babies of today will have a better chance to extend in their turn than had the working-class babies of 1776.

But considerable as have been the advances effected in social organization during the last century and a half, the pace has been less rapid in this field of effort than in the field of industry. To explain this cultural lag is not difficult.

First, the social sciences, which are needed to guide efforts to control social forces, are less precise and dependable than the natural sciences, which guide efforts to control natural forces. That difference in the character of man's knowledge in these two fields is due to the vastly greater complexity of social phenomena, and to the conditions surrounding research in the two fields. In the one field experiments can be tried within the limits set by expense; in the other field experimentation is not wholly barred, but it is narrowly restricted.

Second, applications of social science to practical affairs rarely promise a personal profit to the innovator. At most he may dream of being honored by his fellow men.[6] Still

---

[6] Of course, this remark does not apply to all efforts to secure governmental action. The advocates of a tariff bill, for example, may expect and achieve substantial profits. But legislation promoted for private gain is seldom an application of social science to practical affairs.

more rarely can a second advance be financed from the proceeds of past successes. Thus the drive of profit, which gave such energy to the industrial revolution, has not pushed forward the social revolution. The *Communist Manifesto* told the workers of the world in 1848 that they had "a world to gain" by uniting; but this vague incentive to millions was a less effective spur to action than the concrete prospect of profits to individuals. And now that the workers of one country have captured the government and begun an experiment in communism, the workers of other countries seem inclined to wait for the gains to materialize before imitating the Russian example. Also the process of initiating industrial improvements is far simpler than the process of initiating social improvements. Any innovator who could command a modest capital might adopt what he believed to be an industrial improvement without more ado. If his faith proved justified, he could coerce his competitors to follow his example under penalty of commercial ruin. The innovator who wants to secure what he believes to be a social improvement must convince many men before he can secure a trial of his plan, and for convincing men he must rely upon persuasion. More commonly than not, the projected change threatens some vested interest, and the would-be reformer's campaign of education has to meet a well-financed countercampaign. The social innovator cannot coerce anybody until he has won government; the industrial innovator brings coercion to bear upon his competitors as soon as he begins to undersell them. Finally, experiment plays a role in the applications of science not less important than its role in scientific discovery. Again the advantage is all on the side of the natural as opposed to the social sciences, of industry as opposed to social organization. Social, like mechanical, inventions are usually crude at first;

both types need to be perfected in detail before they will work well. In industry this process of improving upon the original design is facilitated by practical trials on a small scale before large risks are taken. In social organization similar experimental runs are sometimes feasible; but often that is not the case. Nations must try many innovations upon a large scale or not at all; the crudities of the first plan must be discovered at heavy cost and eliminated by a process almost as halting as the process of inducing government to make the first venture.

IV

Beset by so many difficulties, social planning has run a most uncertain course during the last century and a half, while the industrial revolution has been marching forward. In England and the United States most of the attempts to use governmental agencies in new ways have been piecemeal efforts started by private citizens to remedy some single bad situation. Philanthropists have played the leading roles in many of these efforts; in others, groups that felt themselves aggrieved or oppressed have provided the spokesmen. To get what they wanted, these leaders have had to use the arts of propaganda and organization directed to the one specific aim in view. England has produced two great groups of thinkers who developed systematic programs of social reorganization—the philosophical radicals in the opening decades of the nineteenth century and the Fabian socialists in the closing decades; but in so far as their plans have been carried out, it has been on the empirical basis of one thing at a time and mainly through men who did not count themselves members of the groups in question. In this country it is hard to find even one group of systematic planners to set beside the Benthamites and the Fabians.

THE SOCIAL SCIENCES AND NATIONAL PLANNING

A less numerous but more imposing class of national plans are those that have been drawn by governments to meet grave emergencies. The most striking examples are the economic mobilizations effected during the World War and the efforts of President Roosevelt's administration to cope with the great depression. Other governments have been bolder in trying to change the social organizations of their peoples. Perhaps the most demonstrably successful case of systematic government planning which the world offers is that of Japan. When the shogunate was abolished and the Mikado was restored to power in 1867, the responsible statesmen of the country deliberately undertook to transform their feudal realm into a modern commercial state with the standard accompaniment of military power. How rapidly they have progressed toward this end within the short space of two generations everyone knows. Bismarck's plans for German development are the most notable European achievements of prewar days in constructive government planning. Of course, we can now add to the list the grandiose experiments of communism in Russia and of fascism in Italy.

Both types of planning that have prevailed in this country—efforts to solve one problem at a time and efforts to meet national emergencies by quick action—have grave defects. The piecemeal method overlooks the interdependence that is so important a characteristic of social processes. Change one feature of social organization and you are certain to change many other features also. Some of the changes you did not plan you will not like. For illustrations, recall the results that flowed from the Thirteenth Amendment to the Constitution abolishing slavery and from the Eighteenth Amendment that sought to abolish the liquor traffic. It is only by very careful study of the social situation as a whole that changes can be made with a maximum of beneficial and a minimum of harmful effects. As for emergency planning in the face of impending disaster, it is certain to be defective in many ways just because there is not time enough to use what wisdom we have.

Critics of both the piecemeal efforts of reformers and of the inspirational efforts of statesmen acting in a hurry can make out a strong case against much if not most of the national planning we have done in this country. But anyone who attempts to check the practice of national planning will argue in vain. As long as men have power to think, private citizens will go on devising plans for what they find amiss in social organization, and some of their plans will win general approval. Also, as long as we continue to encounter national emergencies from time to time our government will go on adopting hurried measures. The course of wisdom is not to oppose national planning, but to make that planning more intelligent. The more clearly any man grasps the enormous difficulties of the task, the more sharply he realizes the harm done by poor planning, the keener he should be to promote intelligent planning: for national planning of some sort, or rather of many sorts, we are certain to have.

The two great improvements needed in American planning are recognition of the interrelationships among social processes and preparedness to deal seriously with social problems before they have produced national emergencies. It is possible, of course, that our future reformers will have a wider field of vision than their single-eyed predecessors. It is possible, also, that our government in future will be more alert to coming troubles even when times are good. Let us hope so. But may we not also set ourselves to organize our intelligence for a systematic consideration of social problems and how they may best be solved?

An organization devoted to these aims we have never had; for no President and Cabinet can take time from their pressing executive duties for systematic long-range planning. Such planning is a task that demands the full time and energy of the ablest men in the country. And the abler these men, the more eager they would be to secure the services of a varied technical staff and the counsel of a wide circle of advisers. Indeed, a competent National Planning Board would conceive itself not as depending upon its own wisdom, but as an agency for focusing the intelligence of the nation upon certain issues, in the hope of formulating plans that would command sufficient confidence among their fellow citizens to be given trials. It is only as an advisory body that such a board would fit into the American scheme of institutions. A large part of its task would be to draw the line between cases in which government should seek to exercise control and cases in which private initiative should prevail. To preserve the effective liberty of the individual in the modern world requires national planning of as shrewd and elaborate a sort as the planning required to check abuses or to supply lacks. Indeed, it is only by preventing one group of citizens from exploiting other sets and by supplying those services which private enterprise cannot render that individual liberty can be secured.

How much a National Planning Board with advisory powers might improve upon our efforts to solve social problems by taking thought no one can tell in advance. What I have said about the difficulties that beset the social sciences warns us that success is not a foregone conclusion. To supply deficiencies in knowledge the board would doubtless have to undertake much research through its own staff or through other agencies. But after doing its best to lay a scientific foundation for its plans, the board would often have to advise proceeding in an experimental fashion on the basis of probabilities. It would be doing pioneer work; for it would be trying to better the social organization of one of the most advanced countries in the world—to do things that have not yet been done. Hence, it could not expect to achieve as brilliant a record as did the elder statesmen of Japan, who were seeking to pull abreast of other nations and so had models to imitate. And, of course, the usefulness of the board could be wrecked by the appointment of men chosen for partisan reasons. Or a board of men possessing technical competence but lacking in other qualities might antagonize the Executive, Congress, and the public, and lose its influence. Perhaps the idea of trying to mobilize the intelligence of the country for systematic and continuous study of social problems will be rejected by public opinion. But it would seem that we have had enough experience with reforms that produce almost as much harm as they remove to be willing to try a more scientific method of dealing with social problems.

7

INTELLIGENCE AND THE GUIDANCE OF ECONOMIC EVOLUTION[1]

IN THE confident days of its youth, political economy believed that it had solved the important and timely problem put before this session. It was ready to dispense advice on public policies, and its admonitions concerning the duties of the state toward economic enterprise were especially clear and urgent. Current economics, the offspring of this authoritative discipline, is a more cautious creature. When asked for practical advice it reveals an inferiority complex; but in compensation it claims to have a stricter scientific conscience than troubled its philosophic forebear. Economic theory now seldom forgets that its conclusions rest upon assumptions expressly designed to simplify its problems sufficiently to make them amenable to analysis. When asked for advice it answers primly: "That is not a proper request to make of a science. My task is merely to examine the functional relations among certain processes under a variety of carefully specified conditions. What I have to say is the truth and nothing but the truth; it is not the whole truth. In practical affairs," economics goes on, "it is necessary to take account of many factors that I purposely exclude. You should, indeed, pay heed to my findings; they are highly important. But you should not expect me to tell you what to do in this messy world, so unlike the orderly realm I create for scientific ends.

[1] Read at the Tercentenary Celebration of Harvard University, Sept. 8, 1936. Reprinted by permission of the President and Fellows of Harvard College in *Scientific Monthly*, vol. XLIII, pp. 450–465, November, 1936.

THE BACKWARD ART OF SPENDING MONEY

If some of my alleged representatives desire to dictate your policies, don't suppose that they speak with my authority. Of course, an economist is also a citizen, and like his fellows must reach decisions on current issues of all sorts; but if he remembers what I have taught him he won't try to pass off his notions about policy as my deliverances. You do well to seek scientific understanding as a basis for action; but please note that I have several sister sciences of human behavior whose business it is to study the numerous factors that I pass over. You should consult the whole family, though I am sorry to say that my younger sisters are so immature that you cannot expect much help from them." On which ungracious note economics resumes the irreproachable attitude it has learned to strike when asked to make itself useful.

Needless to say, the planners of this symposium on "Authority and the Individual" would not express themselves in this wise. They have proposed collaboration among the social sciences and humanities "with a view to breaking down traditionally specialized lines of approach to an important and timely problem and to make its solution the object of a common attack." My whimsical version of the methodological position of current economics indicates that its votaries are logically bound to accept this program. For us in particular collaboration should be a wholesome experience, for it should correct our attitude toward the other social sciences and put us in our proper place. The "purer" we make economics, the more generously must our findings be supplemented before they can be relied upon as a trustworthy guide, and the keener should we be to work with men of other disciplines.

But collaboration may take two courses. First, representatives of different disciplines may bring each his own contribution to the understanding of a problem in as perfect a form as his technique makes possible, leaving to others the responsibility of fitting together the several contributions. Conscientious specialists who realize how likely they are to go wrong when they wander outside their familiar boundaries may well prefer this course. But who can vouch that the several contributions worked out by independent specialists will make a whole? And what group is ready to assume the difficult and responsible task of putting the results together as far as they will fit? If there is no such group at present, can one be formed? That is a question for the future, and I shall come back to it later. But as matters now stand, cannot the representatives of the social sciences and humanities collaborate with one another in a more direct fashion? If we wish to break down our traditionally specialized lines of approach and join in a common attack upon social problems, must not each of us strive to effect some such change in his own thinking? This second mode of collaboration involves not merely following one another's work but also making use of one another's approaches to our own problems. It is a difficult course and beset by dangers; yet in so far as we can pursue it each of us can make his work as a specialist more interesting to himself, more valuable to his colleagues in other sciences, and more effective in a common attack upon the problems we hope to solve.

Believing that we should construe in this sense the invitation of Harvard University to collaborate with one another, I shall discuss the formidable topic assigned to me, "Intelligence and the Guidance of Economic Evolution," not as a problem in pure economics, but as realistically as I can, making use of what notions I possess about human behavior at large. Doubtless I shall make mistakes that economic historians, psychologists, sociologists, or political scientists would avoid. And I know that some men of my own craft will think my whole procedure ill-advised. But genuine efforts at collaboration involve such risks, and each of us is justified in running them.

I

Let me start with the solution of the problem set before me that was given by Adam Smith in 1776. His *Wealth of Nations* was devoted in large part to criticizing the mercantilist doctrine that it is the statesman's duty to regulate the economic activities of private people as much as it is his duty to provide for the common defense. Adam Smith's critique centered on the proposition that the wealth of a nation is the aggregate of the wealth of its citizens, and that each citizen in his local situation is a better judge of how to augment his wealth than a distant statesman can be. Restated in terms of my topic, this argument runs: Nations prosper more when they leave the guidance of their economic evolution to individuals than when governments attempt to guide. No distrust of intelligence as a guide is implied; the contention is that in the industrial army planning by a central staff is worse than futile; the planning should be done by the private soldiers, individually or in such companies as they voluntarily form under captains who rise from the ranks. All that the staff need do for industry is to see that the privates and officers treat one another fairly, and to perform a few necessary tasks that no private or company would find it profitable to undertake.

Had this symposium been held on the hundredth anniversary of the *Wealth of Nations*, I fancy that the economists invited to participate in it would have felt competent to treat this problem without the collaboration of authorities in the other social sciences. And they would have endorsed Adam Smith's solution of the problem, some with more, perhaps some with less reservations than the Father of Political Economy had made. It is true that the last of the great classical trinity, John Stuart Mill, had avowed himself a socialist; but he built his temperate hopes for the betterment of economic conditions not upon a recrudescence of governmental planning, but primarily upon the cumulative growth of producers' cooperation. Gradually the employees of business enterprises would take over the functions of ownership and management; for workers expecting a share in the profits would be more industrious and more intelligent than mere wage earners, and so cooperative concerns would prevail in the competitive struggle for survival. Of course, this speculation posits the continuance of what Adam Smith fondly called "the obvious and simple system of natural liberty." Since the most respected socialist of the time accepted the general principle of *laissez faire*, that doctrine seemed secure.

But 1876 marks as well as any date we could select the culmination of faith in the guidance of economic evolution by individual intelligence. Today the problem that Adam Smith thought he had solved is as timely as it was in 1776. I doubt whether any economist attending the present symposium feels as competent as Adam Smith did to tell governments just how far they should carry their intervention in economic activities. For within the past one hundred and sixty years economists have made progress toward grasping the complexities of social problems, if not toward agreement upon solutions. Numerous developments have combined to change their attitude toward governmental regulation of economic enterprise, of which the most important has been the world's experiences with different types of economic organization.

Great Britain was far better prepared than Adam Smith realized to accept his teaching. Private enterprise, often in defiance of mercantilist regulations, had become a mass phenomenon before the *Wealth of Nations* was published. The new doctrine was a philosopher's rationalization of practices engaged in by enterprising men because they were profitable. Negatively, it eased the consciences of technical lawbreakers by assuring them that their actions promoted the public welfare; constructively, it gave them a logical argument for demanding the repeal of hampering regulations. Of course, beneficiaries of the old system were not deterred by any theorizing from striving to maintain their legal rights. But technical developments that Adam Smith could not foresee kept weakening the defenders of the old order, swelling the number and increasing the power of those who profited by *laissez faire*. A growing volume of trade, domestic and foreign, stimulated men with initiative to try new forms of business organization, some of which proved highly efficient. The same factor created a lively interest in finding cheaper methods of producing, processing, and transporting materials in bulk. This alliance of mechanical invention and business enterprise proved irresistible. The classes that had vested interests in the old order could neither meet the commercial competition of their rivals who were introducing new methods nor make effective answer to Adam Smith's logic. Statesmen of a speculative turn of mind readily accepted the *Wealth of Nations* as their guide in commercial policy; statesmen who waited for the teachings of experience followed more hesitantly but in increasing number; politicians who accepted the dominant opinion of the day slowly fell into line. Partly by allowing mercantilist statutes to become dead letters, partly by formal action, the country dropped the policy of mercantilist planning and deemed the results good on the whole. By the sixties or seventies most Britons who thought about such matters believed that practical experience had demonstrated the soundness of Adam Smith's doctrine and that other countries would gradually learn the great lesson that theory and practice combined to teach. A glowing vision was cherished by liberal spirits of freedom for all men in their economic, political, and social relations, a vision of peace among the nations securely based upon recognition that peace is the best policy, a vision of cumulative progress in the conquest of nature assuring not merely a higher standard of comfort for all mankind, but also a nobler life. What Carlyle had dubbed the "dismal science" appeared to many as the brightest hope of the race.

II

But decades before this stage was reached, certain emendations had proved necessary in "the obvious and simple system of natural liberty" as presented by Adam Smith. The horrible treatment of "pauper apprentices" in some cotton mills and of climbing boys apprenticed to chimney sweeps early convinced the public that these unfortunate children were not able to judge or to defend their own interests. They seemed to need and they were granted the protection of the state. Later revelations of the exploitation of child workers at large, of young persons and also of women led to further protective legislation justified by the same argument. Only adult males were credited with knowing better than Parliament what was good for them and with being able to look out for themselves. But even that amended proposition was challenged with success. Seamen would sail on overloaded ships, colliers would go down ill-ventilated mines, factory hands would take foolish risks with unfenced machinery, men would expose themselves to occupational diseases. Indeed, the new industry, imperfectly controlling the powerful natural forces it was putting to work, was full of hazards that men underrated, and government felt constrained to exercise its superior intelligence for their benefit. It appeared also that many investors were quite incapable of judging where to place their capital safely, that consumers would buy impure foods and drugs, that town dwellers endangered one another by their ignorance of sanitation. In short, the assumption that the individual is a better judge of his own interests than a distant statesman was found to be subject to many exceptions. These exceptions became more numerous and more important as social organization became more complex. Hence, governmental intervention was gradually extended in many directions of which Adam Smith had not thought, but of which perhaps he would have approved could he have revisited Great Britain in 1876.

Interwoven with the problems presented by those who seemed not to know their own interests was a cognate problem presented by persons who claimed that they could not protect interests of which they were painfully conscious. The argument for *laissez faire* assumed that in pursuing his own interest every individual would be prevented from charging unduly high prices for his goods or services by the competition of rival sellers and also protected against having to accept unduly low prices by competition among buyers. This competitive regime promised to work out a rough sort of justice and also to stimulate efficiency in serving the public. Businessmen who did not measure up to current standards would be reduced to the status of workmen, taking orders from abler captains of industry. Thus inefficiency would be penalized, merit rewarded, and the country assured that its economic energies were directed by the ablest available leaders—the ablest because they were continually being subjected to the infallible test of ability to survive in a competitive struggle. It is no wonder that this view captivated many philosophic minds and suited successful men of affairs; nor is it any wonder that other classes were less satisfied. Wage earners in particular protested that the conditions of the labor market did not assure them a fair price for their services. For in this market the sellers were a crowd of individuals ill-informed about current conditions and future prospects, unskilled in bargaining, forced by pressing need to underbid one another. On the other side of the market stood the employers, each one a combination in himself, able to merge into larger combinations when they saw fit, the best judges of commercial conditions, keen bargainers, able to wait. How valid was this distressful picture of the workingman's plight in the early decades of the nineteenth century admitted of argument. The point that concerns us is that disciples of Adam Smith persuaded Parliaments that were moving toward *laissez faire* to repeal the Anti-Combination Acts and to legalize trade-unions. Some advocates of these measures believed that wage earners would learn that combinations were expensive and futile, but they were bad prophets. Trade-unions grew in strength after the fluctuating fashion of human institutions, and later Parliaments confirmed the policy of countenancing voluntary restriction of competition among sellers in the labor market.

Meanwhile cases were becoming prominent in which competition among business enterprises themselves seemed plainly detrimental to the public interest. The classic illustration was provided by the gas industry. If two competing companies sought to serve the same town each would have to lay mains and provide connections. The total investment would be needlessly large. If both companies received the going rate of return upon their capital the consumers would be overcharged. If neither company made money, or if one succeeded and the other failed, part of the country's precious capital would be wasted. Thus what were often called "natural monopolies" seemed to be exceptions to the rule that prices would be kept reasonable by competition. They were also recognized as exceptions to the rule that government should let business alone. For the only way to protect the customers of monopolies from extortion seemed to be governmental regulation of rates or governmental ownership. British municipalities that were strongholds of *laissez faire* became strongholds also of "municipal socialism," while the central government experimented with various plans for controlling the railways and took the telegraph and telephone systems into the post office.

The continued progress of the industrial revolution and the concomitant development of large-scale business kept raising new problems of this type. Were all public utilities best treated as monopolies and subjected to special controls? Should the production of electrical current, perhaps coal mining and even housing, be added to the list of public utilities? Was the progress of engineering with its trend toward more elaborate and specialized machinery threatening to put many industries into a position where cutthroat competition among independent concerns would be almost as wasteful as competition between two gas companies? And if business managers stopped short of cutthroat competition, how far short would they stop? Left to themselves, would they compete actively enough to protect consumers?

The theoretical difficulty underlying this practical danger had been pointed out by Adam Smith's younger contemporary, the Earl of Lauderdale, who challenged the assumption that the wealth of a nation is the aggregate of the wealth of its citizens. On the contrary, said Lauderdale, public wealth consists in an abundance of useful goods, while scarcity enhances the value of private property. The individual pursuing his own gain seeks to limit his output to the volume most profitable to himself, and that aim is antagonistic to the public's interest in abundance. Where active competition prevails, the individual who seeks to increase his profits by limiting the supply will lose customers to his rivals; there the pursuit of self-interest leads every producer to sell as much as he can so long as prices exceed his cost of production. But this "artificial harmony of interests" established by competition is precarious. For the pursuit of self-interest gives every man a strong incentive to escape from the pressure of competition into the ampler freedom of monopoly; that is, to destroy the one great safeguard of the public's interest in abundance. Every class engages in this destructive practice as far as it can, and blames other classes that succeed in so doing. Employers charge that labor unions limit the number of apprentices, working hours, and output per man-hour; that they seek to limit employment to union members, and limit admission to their own ranks by high initiation fees. Businessmen are popularly assumed to be the most successful sinners. Thorstein Veblen could picture the modern captain of industry as a strategist concerned mainly with the practice of "capitalistic sabotage"; that is, with the effort to limit the inordinate abundance of goods that modern engineering would provide to those modest supplies that will yield the maximum net revenues.

Another type of difficulty, business interference in government, had been pointed out by Adam Smith himself. In his eloquent plea for "the simple and obvious system of natural liberty," Smith tacitly assumed that government aimed to increase the wealth of the nation as a whole. But in a much earlier passage, not often recalled by his disciples, he had pointed out how unscrupulously clever are men of business in persuading the government that measures profitable only to their selfish interests will be advantageous to the public. A wise administration would be suspicious of advice from that quarter. Of course, the laboring classes were too ignorant to form opinions upon public policy; but the country gentlemen might be trusted, for, though often stupid about commercial matters, their interests coincided broadly with those of the nation. Ricardo reversed this dictum: the interests of the landlords were opposed to those of every other class in the community, and a government controlled by them was selfishly misused to restrict foreign competition in foodstuffs in order to keep up rents—a policy that made food dear and money wages high, thereby reducing profits and impeding the accumulation of capital, on which progress depended. Later generations found reason for believing both Smith and Ricardo, or rather for believing that every class, the wage earners included when they attain political influence, is eager to use the power of government for selfish ends. If any class has a bad eminence in this respect it is because circumstances enable that class to exercise more pressure upon government for the time being. And the more developments of one sort or another forced government to concern itself with economic affairs, the more private parties strove to control government. This development attracted more attention in the United States than in Great Britain; but it is naïve to think that in any country the problem of the state and economic enterprise can be treated realistically without considering economic enterprise in politics. We economists have been so prone to chide governments for interfering in business that we have often overlooked the extent to which these interferences are dictated by particular groups of businessmen. We usually think of government as Adam Smith did when he was expounding the policy of *laissez faire*, forgetting what we know of politics, just as Adam Smith for the moment forgot his warnings about the machinations of the commercial interest.

III

Not only did private enterprise produce various unfortunate results, it also failed to produce some good results that were expected by its champions. One bitter disappointment came in international relations. As noted before, during the heyday of *laissez faire* it was predicted that the mutual gains from free trade, demonstrated so convincingly by political economy, would bind the peoples of the world in an economic league of peace. Unhappily that was not the outcome. The volume of international trade did increase enormously as applications of science reduced the costs of transportation. But even the great commercial nations did not raise their foreign policies to the level of enlightened self-interest. They continued as in the age of mercantilism to waste their economic energies and to prostitute their intelligence in waging intermittent wars, though all sensible men knew that the chief outcome of wars is mutual impoverishment and frustration. Competition among the nations for economic gains kept degenerating into wrangles and wrangles into fights—as would competition among individuals if there were no authority in the background to enforce peace. The economic theorists of *laissez faire* had committed a sin of omission which John R. Commons is helping this generation tardily to repair. They had failed to realize the implications of the role played by courts in economic transactions. Where there is no court to decide disputes, backed by power to enforce its decisions, enlightened self-interest has but a feeble control over human passions.

Nor was that the whole or the worst of the psychological error. Even in individual dealings regulated by courts, enlightened self-interest did not dominate behavior so much as the logic of *laissez faire* required. The most disconcerting discovery, or rather rediscovery, made by the social sciences in the nineteenth century was that man is a less rational animal than he thinks himself. He is prone to commit the "intellectualist fallacy" in giving accounts of his own behavior; that is one of his subtle ways of maintaining his self-esteem. Systematic thinkers are especially subject to this fallacy because the easiest way to give an intelligible account of what men do is to suppose that they are guided by calculations that the theorizer can repeat and foretell. Thus, as Walter Bagehot happily remarked, Adam Smith tacitly assumed that "there is a Scotsman inside every man." The literal-minded closet philosopher, Jeremy Bentham, made the assumption explicit. He crystallized the conception of functional psychology current among British thinkers of his time in the "felicific calculus"—a scheme so congenial to minds formed by a money-making age that diluted versions of it still dominate many of our speculations about economic behavior. Even the Malthusian "principle of population," with its modern-sounding emphasis upon instincts and habits, could be interpreted in terms of the felicific calculus by disciples of Bentham. The working classes, like their betters, were controlled by the two sovereign masters, pain and pleasure: but their lamentably defective education prevented them from foreseeing the pains that large families would bring upon them. The obvious remedy was to teach these unfortunates to associate low wages with premature marriages. Thus political economy had a great civilizing mission to perform for the most wretched part of humanity as well as for the more fortunate; it should help all mankind to calculate correctly, that is, to find the real way of maximizing net pleasures. But Darwin's teaching that man is an animal fundamentally ruled by instincts changed the perspective in which the social sciences saw problems of human behavior. Psychologists revealed the artificiality of the hedonistic analysis. Thinking appeared to be at best an intermittent process, concerned with the humble task of finding ways toward ends set by more fundamental forces, and engaged in typically when routine modes of action encounter obstacles. Bentham's clarity gave way to confusion. Men are moved by fears and angers, vanity and curiosity, longings for adventure and longings for security, sympathy with others, and delight in making invidious comparisons to their own advantage, by obsessions, prejudices, visions, by forces conscious and unconscious to which we give a hundred names, but cannot delimit, describe, and classify in any way on which we can agree.

The rediscovery of man's irrationality helps us to understand why Adam Smith's "obvious and simple system of natural liberty" was never given a full trial. Perhaps a race evenly endowed with enlightened self-interest might have made an earthly paradise of the sort they would have liked by practicing *laissez faire*. Certainly the very unevenly endowed men who populate this planet, shortsighted, quarrelsome, sentimental, did not do so. When individual enterprise produced results they did not like, they would not wait for the evils to correct themselves in the long run. Each generation has realized the force of Mr. Keynes's remark that in the long run we shall all be dead. Nor do all economic evils tend to cure themselves; human nature being what it is, there are social processes of degeneration that work cumulatively. The actual outcome was a mixed system of control by the imperfect intelligence of individuals and control by the imperfect intelligence of governments. And toward the end of the nineteenth century the factor of governmental

control was gaining ground even in Great Britain. Just as
individual enterprise had become a mass phenomenon in a
nation that accepted mercantilism in principle, so governmental planning was becoming a mass phenomenon within
a nation that accepted the principle of *laissez faire*.

IV

While dwelling upon the difficulties encountered as the
system of free enterprise unfolded, we should not forget how
that form of economic organization stimulated men to apply
scientific discoveries to the work of the world, how industry
in turn aided scientific research, how standards of living rose,
death rates declined and population increased, how the
Europeans spread over the earth exploiting natural resources
and backward peoples, or how mightily the leading commercial nations gained in power and prestige. Those are high
lights in the dazzling picture of progress in the nineteenth
century, as seen by people of our culture. But the economic
progress, so powerfully promoted by individualism, produced
consequences that led the successful nations to tinker further
with their economic organization. If the earlier stages in the
resurgence of national economic planning were due primarily
to incidental defects in the workings of *laissez faire*, the later
stages were due primarily to results produced by the major
successes of that system.

The growing economic prosperity of the nineteenth century pushed men closer together while it also widened the
areas from which they drew supplies and over which they
marketed products. Increasing density of population makes
what one man does more important in numberless ways to
the health and happiness of his neighbors. Men feel the need
of more common rules concerning what no one shall do and
also concerning more things that everyone must do for the

commonweal. Government is the great agency for setting minimum standards of conduct that must be enforced upon the recalcitrant, and so finds its functions multiplying as the interdependence of individuals becomes more intimate and intricate. So also the wider geographic scope of economic organization exposes the modern man to more and more hazards that he cannot control, and he calls stridently upon his government for aid. Local regulations that served well enough in an earlier day are replaced by national rules, supplemented by international conventions.

This trend appears most clearly in American experience. "Rugged individualism" flourished on the frontier. Laws were of slight help to the trapper and the squatter; they wanted little from the government. But the farmers who followed soon began demanding that the government aid them in getting facilities for shipping their produce to market; when these facilities had been provided they demanded that government regulate railroad rates; that government provide "cheap money"; later that government make grants to improve roads, set up land banks, subsidize exports of surplus produce, extend protective duties to agriculture, and so on. When we tell the story of American prosperity we stress the westward expansion as one of the brightest episodes and celebrate the sturdy enterprise of the pioneers that made it possible. But when we study the record in detail, we find the conquerors of the continent full of complaints concerning their economic plight, and insistent with the full force of their rugged personalities that government come to their aid.

In other ways also the prosperity of the nineteenth century turned men's minds toward governmental planning. The extraordinary increase in the physical volume of production made unprecedented inroads upon the resources provided by nature. So far as I know Stanley Jevons was the first economist to call attention to this feature. In the sixties he showed that British industry and commerce rested on a foundation of cheap coal, and that if the extraction of coal continued to grow as rapidly in the future as it had been growing in the recent past the commercially accessible deposits would be exhausted in no long time. Mineral deposits were irreplaceable by man, and the race might wreck its career by looting Mother Nature's cupboard. Even abundantly endowed America took alarm over the destruction of its timber resources, the drain on its reserves of anthracite, the waste of its natural gas and petroleum, and, most menacing of all in the long run, the depletion of its soils through reckless cropping and erosion. The time span taken into account by individual enterprises was but as a day in the life of a nation. In manufacturing, transportation, commerce, and finance this difference might give rise to no grave troubles; but in the extractive industries a few generations of ruthless individuals might destroy the nation's heritage to get a mess of pottage for themselves. To prevent that irremediable disaster the conservationists saw no other remedy than governmental regulation based upon long-range planning.

Finally, the more completely any country organized its economic life on the basis of making and spending money incomes, the more effectively it developed its natural resources, but the more did it suffer from recurrent business depressions. It seemed that the equilibrium among economic activities directed toward the making of profits was essentially unstable. Periods of rapid expansion never lasted more than three or four years. Some parts of the economic mechanism always expanded faster than others, and when the resulting stresses exceeded the limit of tolerance prosperity ended in a crisis followed by a period of contraction, from which business recovered only to repeat the same disillusioning round. Men learned some devices for mitigating the violence of crises and alleviating the sufferings of depression; there were times when some nations fondly believed they had mastered the disease, but further experience corrected that optimistic error. And these rhythmical alternations in the fortunes of commercial nations produced cyclical fluctuations about the secular trends of *laissez faire* and of governmental planning. During the prosperous phases of business cycles men were minded to demand that government let business alone; during depressions they demanded governmental interventions of the most diverse kinds. In this way also governments have been led to assume heavier responsibilities for stimulating, repressing, and supplementing private enterprise.

Another concomitant of economic progress that caused grave apprehension in many minds was the increasing disparity in the size of individual fortunes and in the magnitude of business enterprises. The poor did not grow poorer, but the rich certainly grew richer. The one-man business did not disappear, but the billion-dollar corporation came into existence. Those who feared these trends invoked governmental action to moderate them. Inheritance taxes, steeply progressive income taxes, and antitrust legislation of numerous sorts were in large part efforts to check the inequalities in economic success which a system of individual enterprise breeds.

V

No other people had gone so far as the British toward accepting the doctrine of *laissez faire* and, to the best of my knowledge, in no other country was the reversal of the trend in the latter part of the nineteenth century as clear. But a change of the same type can be discerned in the economic speculation and the practical policy of various other nations, among them the United States.

From the outset, American policy had been an unstable mixture of national planning and reliance on the play of private enterprise. The severing of relations with Great Britain forced our ancestors to devise a formal plan for governing themselves. When their first plan, the Articles of Confederation, had proved itself inefficient, they drew a second plan providing for a stronger central government, and that worked better. The first Secretary of the Treasury under the Constitution plunged at once into national economic planning and scored a series of notable successes. Among other measures he induced Congress to adopt a mild protective tariff to stimulate domestic manufactures. After decades of acrimonious struggles over this issue, we built a high wall of tariffs around our borders, while practicing free trade within them. The more powerful our industries grew, the higher the duties rose; for this is one form of government planning that was guided substantially by private enterprise itself. Early in our history we sought to develop a national transportation system of highways and waterways; later we put our trust in privately owned railroads, to which we made lavish grants of public lands; later still we subjected the railroads to a complex set of state and federal regulations. We devised plans that promoted the settlement of the public domain by independent farmers, and allowed our timber and mineral lands to be plundered in wasteful fashion. First as farmers clearing fields for the plow, then as lumbermen supplying a market, we slaughtered our forests; now perhaps the most carefully devised of our national plans aims to conserve what remains of our timber resources. For decades we complacently watched the tide of immigration rise; then we began excluding those whom we held to be undesirable aliens;

recently we have adopted a systematic plan for limiting the number and supposedly improving the quality of those whom we admit. We lagged behind European countries in social legislation and in governmental ownership of public utilities, but we led in efforts to check the growth of monopolies and to compel businessmen to compete with one another. We have evinced a childlike faith in what we can accomplish by passing laws and a childlike vanity in our sturdy individualism. But more and more our individualism has expressed itself in efforts to use the government as an agency for attaining what we severally desire.

This secular trend toward bolder and more varied economic planning by governments that prevailed in the Western world during the closing decades of the nineteenth and the opening decade of the twentieth century was suddenly and enormously stimulated by the World War. Each of the belligerents felt compelled to mobilize its economic resources in order to maximize its military efficiency. Governments endeavored to control production and consumption, imports and exports, railroads and shipping, employment and investment, prices and finances. Vexatious as these schemes were felt to be, they were approved by the citizens at large as essential to success. No combatant dared trust to the free play of individual enterprise when threatened by invasion.

Though most of the governmental controls were released more or less promptly after the return of peace, there has been no such trend toward *laissez faire* as followed the Napoleonic wars. The collapse of the czarist regime in Russia under the stress of war made it possible for a Communist party to seize control and initiate the most ambitious experiment in national planning ever tried by a great country. Italy has accepted fascism and its plan of a "corporative state." Germany has entrusted her fortunes to a party that is trying to remold both the economic organization of the nation and its spirit. The new states set up in Europe by the Treaty of Versailles for the most part have followed a policy of extreme economic nationalism. For a time Great Britain and the United States seemed to be working back toward prewar conditions as rapidly as the unsettled state of world affairs allowed; but the grave economic errors perpetrated by private economic planning during the twenties combined with the aftereffects of the war to bring on the great depression of the early thirties, and with it a marked recrudescence of national planning. Great Britain gave up her historic gold standard for a managed currency and free trade for moderate protection. In the United States, discouraged by three years of ineffectual efforts to stem the growth of unemployment by an administration that believed in "rugged individualism," the electorate put in power a party whose leader promised a New Deal in economic affairs. Even France, which had withstood the earlier stages of the world depression most stubbornly, has installed a radical ministry pledged to sweeping economic reforms.

VI

To my mind, this cursory survey of the relations between the state and economic enterprise in the Western world since 1776 suggests that we are in for more rather than for less governmental planning in the calculable future. Economic forecasting is a notoriously hazardous enterprise, and political forecasting is perhaps even more risky. But the chances of forming approximately correct anticipations are best when we are dealing with a secular trend: when we can ascertain the more potent forces that have shaped this trend in the recent past, and when we have reason to believe that these forces will retain their character and their potency during the limited future of which we are thinking. We expect technological progress to continue, for it rests upon scientific discovery, which does not seem to be approaching a limit, and upon man's desire to get larger returns for his economic efforts, which shows no signs of failing. Presumably, technological progress will continue to throw men out of work, to depreciate old investments, to shift sources of supply, to introduce novel products. The growth of very large business enterprises has not been checked; the economic, political, and social problems to which their operations give rise have not been solved. In nations that retain a capitalistic organization these changes will bear heavily upon numerous individuals, while they benefit others largely. Economic life will continue to be full of uncertainties, and those who suffer mischances will follow the precedents our generation is setting and make even larger demands for government aid. Social security legislation is more likely to expand than to contract in the great democracies, and dictatorial governments will practice paternalism. Business enterprisers will increase their efforts to limit or suppress competition, for the more we mechanize industry and specialize machinery, the heavier will be overhead costs and the more dangerous competition will become to vested interests. The problems that the courts and the legislatures face in devising and enforcing rules of fair competition will grow more subtle and difficult. It will not be surprising if investors in great industries that are threatened with loss by technological progress organize campaigns for government purchase and operation. The draft upon exhaustible natural resources will grow greater and the movement for conservation through government regulation will wax stronger. Communities will become increasingly interdependent and the task of planning water supplies, sewage disposal, protection of streams against pollution, highway systems, power lines, and the like will be one in which the central governments will be forced to take a larger share. Nor can we leave out of account the probability of future wars and the practical certainty that, if they occur between great nations, each belligerent government will seek to effect a more drastic economic mobilization than was effected in the latest world war. It is most unlikely that this trend toward national economic planning will rise steadily. Its course will be diversified by accelerations and retardations, perhaps by some vigorous reactions toward *laissez faire*. But the indications seem to me fairly clear that in the long run men will try increasingly to use the power and resources of their governments to solve their economic problems even in those nations that escape social revolutions. And, if it should turn out that communism, or the corporative state, or some as yet unchristened form of economic organization makes a stronger appeal to the mass of people than does the complicated mixture of private enterprise and governmental regulation that is evolving in the capitalistic nations, then social revolutions may sweep the world, presumably carrying with them drastic governmental control over economic activities.

VII

Whether we fear or welcome these prospects of an evolutionary trend or a revolutionary shift toward governmental regulation, we must all agree that the relation of the state to private enterprise is a problem which the social sciences should join in attacking.

No scientifically minded man nowadays will assume that the immediate aim of this attack should be to pronounce a verdict that *laissez faire* is better than governmental regulation, or that governmental regulation is better than *laissez faire.* It is not the business of the social sciences to say what is good and what bad; all they can do is to trace functional relationships among social processes, and so elucidate the most effective means of attaining whatever ends we set ourselves. Nor should anyone expect a demonstration that private enterprise always begets one set of results, that governmental planning always begets a different set, and that as citizens we have merely to choose which of the two sets we prefer. The problem is not so simple as that. On the contrary, it is a problem of numerous variables that may combine with one another in an indefinite number of ways, and a given combination may produce very different results when applied to different processes. Our choice does not lie between two sharply contrasted systems—private enterprise and governmental regulation; the real choices that we shall be making more or less deliberately are choices among the indefinitely numerous possible mixtures of private enterprise and governmental regulation, as applied to this, that, or the other type of activity, under different conditions of time and place. Hence, the common attack of the social sciences upon this problem should aim, not at finding "a solution," but at finding methods by which communities can carry on intelligently the process of working out the endless series of detailed solutions with which they must keep experimenting.

In dealing with this problem the social sciences are not confined to speculation. They have before them for analysis the experience of several autocratic governments that are professing to guide the economic evolution of their nations according to some system and the experience of several democratic peoples that are fumbling with the problem in different ways. On paper, the methods of autocratic governments look the more imposing to an outsider; but how plans are really made in present-day Russia, Italy, and Germany I do not know. Perhaps the processes that go on behind the scenes are admirably organized to make use of the best intelligence available. Perhaps the critically important decisions are made on an inspirational basis by a leader whose genius is trusted as the guiding star of the state. Or the controlling group may believe that it is applying in practice rules deduced from a scientifically established body of principles. Or there may be a confused and shifting struggle among ambitious cliques, each seeking the favor of the powers that be. Probably a mixture of these various elements prevails in all autocratic governments, one element preponderating here, another there, one last year, another this year. Of course, it is part of the task of the social sciences to penetrate behind the stage sets painted by official propagandists, to find out as much as they can about how the national planning is actually done, and to trace its consequences, direct and indirect, immediate and delayed, in social and political as well as in economic affairs. The rapidly growing literature about these experiments will become increasingly instructive if they are continued long enough to let their cumulative effects mature. But anyone who glimpses the vastness and complexities of the researches called for will pardon me for considering only the processes of the democratic peoples, and primarily the people of this country.

As said before, American methods of applying intelligence to the guidance of economic evolution have run the gamut from a rather extreme reliance upon individual enterprise under some circumstances to a rather extreme reliance upon the federal government under other circumstances. However, one simple generalization may be ventured: we have seldom tried to work out national plans except when some considerable group among us has become seriously dissatisfied with the results of private enterprise, or of private enterprise as regulated by local or state governments. In the life of the nation, planning plays the role that thinking plays in individual life. Both processes are resorted to typically to find ways of surmounting difficulties that occur in the course of routine behavior. And just as our individual thinking is commonly directed toward an immediate, specific difficulty, so most of our efforts at national planning have dealt with some single need that has been keenly felt by groups sufficiently numerous or sufficiently powerful to command attention. Let me call this "piecemeal planning." Examples are campaigns for federal aid to develop turnpikes and canals in our early days, for protective duties on imports, for the abolition of slavery, for free silver, for reduction of railroad rates, for curbing the "trusts," for "prohibition," for old-age pensions, and so on almost without end. The groups pushing these plans have been animated at times by philanthropic zeal and at times by sordid interests; some groups have relied upon fervid appeals to the moral conscience, some upon frank presentation of economic claims, some have resorted to bribery. What they have in common is advocacy of a measure designed to accomplish some one change in social organization, with slight regard to its collateral and long-run effects upon other social interests.

Of course, piecemeal planning is defective in principle, however high its aims and however generous the spirit that inspires it. Each of the social sciences has its own way of demonstrating that all social processes are interrelated. When we alter the conditions under which one process operates we are certain to affect other processes. Many of these unplanned effects are negligible, but some are important; among the latter effects some may be pleasant surprises but others are likely to be unpleasant. Also, we know when we stop to think that the long-run effects of our reforms often differ widely from the immediate effects that we intended to produce. However heartily we approve the abolition of slavery, we must admit that emancipation as we effected it without regard to the cultural status of the slaves was attended by grievous results not only for the former masters, but also for the freedmen and for the relations between the Northern and the Southern states. No measure is so good in itself that its advocates are justified in thinking only of its direct and immediate effects. In short, we are not making the best use of what limited intelligence we possess when we plan on a piecemeal basis.

Though piecemeal planning is our common method of attempting to use the powers of government, on occasions we devise programs dealing with many matters at the same time. Every party platform makes pretensions to be a program of this sort; but we have learned not to take them seriously. Outstanding instances in our history are the adoption of the Articles of Confederation and the Constitution, the economic planning of Alexander Hamilton, the economic mobilization during the World War, and the attempt of our present administration to inaugurate a New Deal. In each instance the country faced a grave emergency—only under such pressure have we ever set ourselves vigorously to the task of thinking out and putting into practice a comprehensive scheme of national policies. Two of these emergencies were produced by war, one by the inefficiency of existing political organization, two by economic troubles. When times are good, we let well enough alone. As yet we have not risen to the point of continuous systematic efforts to think out coordinated policies that will make what we deem satisfactory better still.

Planning in the face of national emergencies is commonly handicapped by the need for quick action. There is not time enough to bring the nation's full intelligence to bear upon the problem. The more intense the pressure, the less the chance of doing a good job. The framers of the Constitution set an admirable precedent by taking time for deliberation; but our later emergency plans have been hastily concocted. Of course, the inspirations of a desperate moment are sometimes fortunate; but we do not trust to luck in our most rational activities. To design an efficient National Industrial Recovery Act is vastly more difficult than to design an efficient bridge across the Golden Gate. The one task we essayed in a fine frenzy of good intentions and rushed it through in short order; the other we performed deliberately after elaborate study of the geological as well as the mechanical factors involved.

One reason why we act less rationally in devising national plans than in building bridges is that the sciences of social behavior lag far behind the natural sciences in certainty. If economists, political scientists, and sociologists could tell us how certain proposals would work in practice with as much assurance as engineers can give, we would leave technical matters largely to them. The layman is naturally disinclined to trust professions whose members seem to be continually disagreeing with one another. That is a justifiable hesitation as matters stand. We might, however, if we chose, so alter the present status of affairs that we could make fuller use of the social sciences and, what is not less important, of the practical sagacity possessed by experienced citizens in many walks of life.

What I have in mind is an attempt to organize ourselves for deliberate and systematic study of social problems. Organization is often a critically important factor in determining the efficiency of group action. The same men who made a mess of national government under the Articles of Confederation made a success of national government under the Constitution. It is conceivable that we of the present generation who flounder so in public policy might reach a decidedly higher level of efficiency by following the example of reorganization set by the Fathers of the Republic.

Precisely what form an organization for the study of social problems should assume and how it should operate are delicate questions, but experience suggests some simple answers. First, the organization should be a continuing one, not like a constitutional convention that draws up a plan of government and adjourns *sine die;* for social problems are ever assuming new forms and the task of dealing with them is never finished. Second, to be effective the organization should center in a small board, responsible not for making technical studies and formulating plans—that task calls for more technical knowledge and more insight than any small group possesses—but for seeing that studies are made and that plans are formulated. It would be the board's task to make sure that in this work available knowledge is utilized to the full—not merely such contributions as social scientists could make, but also the contributions of experienced men of affairs, and the contributions of natural scientists, which are fundamental to many social problems. Also it would be the board's particular care to see that before measures were proposed for dealing with one issue the collateral effects, direct and indirect, immediate and delayed, were considered. The board should endeavor to take up problems before they reach the emergency stage, while there is time for full consideration before reaching a decision. To enable it thus to focus the intelligence of the nation upon social problems of a wide and shifting range, the board should have a technical staff including men of many qualifications, means for obtaining professional assistance from anyone whose counsel is needed, and close contacts with government agencies, federal, state, and local. It should foster the planning attitude toward public problems, cooperating with the state, regional, and municipal planning organizations in all parts of the country. Finally, it should give all the interests affected by the issues under consideration an opportunity to present their views before it formulates proposals.

Sharing in the staff work of a National Planning Board would give social scientists a continuing opportunity of the sort that this Tercentenary Conference seeks to provide for a few days. The most effective way to secure genuine co-operation among men of different disciplines is to get them to unite in attacking common problems. The specialists who participated in seeking solutions for the concrete problems taken up by a planning board would have facilities for thorough investigation, and they would have time to absorb in as large a measure as human limitations permit the significance of one another's contributions. While serving the board they would also be promoting the type of knowledge that the world most desperately needs—knowledge of human behavior.

An organization of this character would have the best chances of rendering service if it were accepted by public opinion as an agency of the federal government, but an agency empowered merely to draw up plans for consideration by the constituted authorities or the voters. No doubt the outcome of the deliberations upon many issues would be a recommendation to take no public action. In the many-faceted problem of how best to combine governmental regulation with private enterprise it might as often counsel a policy of *laissez faire* as a policy of intervention. If I am right in forecasting a multitude of demands that the federal government extend its activities vigorously in the future, I may be right also in thinking that a planning organization, charged to study the collateral and the long-run effects of public policies, would be the best safeguard against ill-considered measures. Only the careless will jump to the conclusion that systematic study of national problems by a federal agency would accelerate the trend toward governmental regulation. It might have the opposite effect.

Needless to say, the most wisely guided organization for national planning would encounter opposition. Every attempt to extend the role of intelligence over new areas seems to many persons presumptuous or silly. Despite the plainest explanations that the central board was merely a device for focusing the practical wisdom and scientific knowledge of the whole community upon problems that have to be dealt with in some fashion, there would be misunderstandings aplenty. Of course, interests that thought themselves threatene l would attack the organization with the weapons of prejudice, misrepresentation, and ridicule. Reformers in a hurry would wax indignant over the deliberate methods of a board that tried to foresee consequences before it recommended action. Early friends who expected the prompt formulation of sweeping plans embodying their own predilections might be turned by disappointment into enemies. Unless public opinion really believes that it is worth while to think carefully about social problems, no planning organization worthy of the name could last long in a democracy.

Even if given a fair trial, the organization would find its technical tasks exceedingly difficult. Experienced men of affairs and social scientists know how hard it is to foresee the indirect and cumulative consequences of public policies, to approximate social gains and social costs, to find the most efficient ways of accomplishing given ends. And the ends to be aimed at are not given; they must be chosen. There have been occasions in American history when public opinion accepted a definite end as paramount, but these occasions have been rare and of brief duration. They vastly simplify the problem of national planning. For example, economic mobilization during the World War was facilitated by the fact that a large majority of the people were ready to sacrifice comfort, property, and life for military success. But seldom is the national scale of values thus crystallized in a single dominant pattern. As a rule numerous limited ends command wide support, but no one end is predominant. To make matters more puzzling, the widely popular ends are likely to conflict with one another. I suppose that at present most people think it desirable to balance the federal budget, to reduce taxation, to increase employment, and to keep the unemployed from suffering hunger and cold. Most of the time a national planning organization would have to work amidst confusion of this sort. That condition makes planning difficult, but not impossible. It is the condition that most individuals habitually face in their private planning. Somehow they manage to reach decisions despite the incompatibility among their desires. Presumably a wisely conducted planning organization could achieve a similar qualified success. In a democratic country national planners would have to serve as an agency for accomplishing what the majority desired. But by throwing light upon the consequences that different lines of action would produce they could contribute much toward making social valuations more rational. Perhaps in the long run the chief gain from trying to plan national policies in the light of their probable consequences would be the attainment of a more valid scale of social values than now prevails among us.

Whether this country is ready to organize its intelligence, practical and scientific, in an effort to guide the evolution of its institutions more wisely, I do not know. But a bill creating a National Planning Board along the lines that I have followed is now pending in Congress. We may prefer to continue for years our past policy of piecemeal planning, supplemented in grave emergencies by sweeping changes made in a hurry. Or we may follow the example of those nations that have made a sudden plunge into fascism or communism. Our best chance of avoiding a dictatorship of some sort, with its compulsory regimentation of our lives, lies in infusing a larger measure of intelligence into our public policy.

8

MAKING GOODS AND MAKING MONEY[1]

BOTH engineering and economics have been concerned with the production of wealth since their beginnings. But they approached the problem from such different angles and with such different aims that at the outset they scarcely came into touch. Adam Smith and James Watt were friends at the University of Glasgow, when Smith was delivering the lectures that grew into the *Wealth of Nations* and when Watt was making his experiments upon Newcomen's engine. Both of these Scotsmen had a plan for increasing the efficiency of production; but one plan centered in freedom for individual initiative, and the other in a separate condenser. It was not at all apparent at the time that this economist and this mechanical engineer could contribute to each other's work.

One hundred and sixty-odd years have passed since Adam Smith and James Watt started their careers in Glasgow. In this interval the industrial revolution, which was getting under headway in the 1750's, has produced a new world. Looking backward, it is now clear that this new world is a joint product of engineering and economics. Adam Smith's ideas could not have influenced the reorganization of economic policy as they did without the development of steam

[1] Address at a joint session with the American Economic Association at the Annual Meeting, New York, Dec. 4 to 7, 1922, of The American Society of Mechanical Engineers. Reprinted by permission of the American Society of Mechanical Engineers from *Proceedings of the Joint Session Held on Dec. 6, 1922 by the American Economic Association* and *the American Society of American Engineers*, pp. 1-8, New York, 1923.

power. James Watt's engine could not have run its conquering career as it did without an opportunity for individual initiative. The mathematical instrument maker of the University of Glasgow and its professor of moral philosophy have been more intimate coworkers than either dreamed.

Meanwhile engineering and economics themselves have been growing. The engineer has begun to busy himself with other things than machine designing. He sees his problem as one that takes in all phases of the process of producing goods. He is interested not merely in his mechanical equipment, but also in the choice and training of the personnel, in the planning and routing of work, in the purchasing and storing of materials, in the distributing agencies handling the product, in the methods for winning markets, even in questions of financing. Thus the engineer has begun to attack many of the problems that concern the economist.

Although it must be admitted that the progress of the economist has been less rapid, he is to be credited with trying to practice the quantitative methods characteristic of engineering. Adam Smith had "no great faith in political arithmetic." His successors, blessed with better data and knowing more mathematics, are coming to have great faith in statistics. By the development of this technique they hope gradually to establish their science upon a quantitative basis.

This expansion of the engineer's problems and this improvement in the economist's methods are bringing the two sets of workers into closer touch. Today they are conscious of their common interests, as Adam Smith and James Watt were not. They wait no longer for a later generation to perceive that they are coworkers.

Fundamentally their common problem is still what it was when Smith was lecturing and Watt experimenting. The industrial revolution which was beginning then is continuing still. Every decade since 1750 has witnessed important advances in engineering and important changes in economic problems, if not in economic solutions. The need for further progress in the technical arts of production is not one whit abated by all the marvels of electricity and automatic machinery. Nor is the need for further progress in the arts of economic organization less pressing than it was in the generations of Adam Smith, Ricardo, and John Stuart Mill. The common task is to carry forward the industrial revolution through this generation—to carry it forward in such fashion as to make it yield our race still greater benefits.

It is not likely that economists can contribute to the further perfecting of machine design, though they may render help in problems of industrial organization. On the other hand, engineers no doubt can and will contribute greatly to the solution of economic problems. To those problems they bring a special type of training, an organized method of attack, which should enable them to see many things wanting or awry in the economists' conceptions. By constructive criticism they may make the economists' contribution more efficient, and in working with economists they may learn some things of advantage to themselves.

I

All that I have said so far is exceedingly general in character. May I go on to matters somewhat more definite? My aim is to set our common problem of production in a perspective useful alike to engineers and economists.

The process of producing goods has been viewed in three ways. Subjectively it has been treated as a process of seeking to gratify wants. Industrially it is a process of making goods. From the business viewpoint it is a process of making money.

Corresponding to these three ways of viewing one and the same process of production, there are three levels of economic analysis: the level of satisfactions, the level of goods, and the level of prices.

Economic theory long cherished the ambitious design of penetrating to the satisfactions level of analysis. It sought to explain most economic phenomena in terms of a balancing of subjective sacrifices against subjective satisfactions. In so doing it became itself subjective. As long as it followed that tack it was not possible for economists to use quantitative methods. For, despite much searching, no satisfactory units have been found in which to reckon either men's sacrifices or their satisfactions. And without units, of course, one cannot cast up totals or strike averages. At best this level of analysis yields but a dubious explanation of why men behave in certain ways—"dubious" because modern psychologists have discarded for the most part the notion that our conduct is a calculated pursuit of satisfactions.

Gradually dropping this inefficient type of speculation, economists have recently begun to develop a more objective type of work—a descriptive analysis of economic behavior, as opposed to a subjective explanation of choices. It is this shift that enables them to use quantitative methods in their theoretical inquiries. We cannot measure sacrifices and satisfactions, but we can count goods and reckon in money. Within a limited range of problems we can also go behind commodities and prices to something more fundamental and yet susceptible of measurement—not sacrifices or satisfactions, but some objective index of physiological conditions or some objective record of behavior. For example, it is possible to investigate fatigue, to grade men by intelligence tests, to study the reaction of certain occupations upon health, and so on. It is true that these efforts to carry quantitative analysis into the realm of physiology and psychology are still in the pioneering stage, but does not the success already attained suffice at least to justify faith in future progress in this direction—progress to which not only engineers and economists, but also physiologists and psychologists, must contribute? For convenient reference, let us say that this type of work runs on the welfare level of analysis.

The quantitative economist, then, and the engineer who attacks economic problems are concerned with money values, with goods, or with some objective index of welfare. As between these three levels of analysis there is no question but that the welfare level is the most significant and that the money level is the least significant. Indeed, money and goods get whatever significance they possess only in so far as they represent a contribution to welfare. We rate the goods level of analysis as more significant than the money level because a bushel of wheat has a more direct and unambiguous relation to welfare than has $1.25, which may be the price of wheat on some given day.

To illustrate the practical importance of these distinctions, let us refer to the national income. We should like to reckon this income in terms of common welfare, but we cannot conceive of welfare as a magnitude. So we do the next best thing and think of the national income as an aggregate of commodities and services obtained by the nation within a year. Such an aggregate we can conceive in bushels of wheat, tons of coal, board feet of lumber, ton-miles of transportation, months of schooling, and so on. When we come to measure this magnitude, however, we are forced to express the different classes of goods in terms of money values. That is, we make our computations on the most superficial level of analysis and state the national income in billions of dollars.

THE BACKWARD ART OF SPENDING MONEY

We are not forced, however, to stop short with so superficial a result, for we can work back again from money to goods. Thus, when our money estimates of the income of the American people show an increase from 33 billions of dollars in 1914 to 45 billions in 1916 we can analyze this nominal gain of 37 per cent into the part due to the rise of prices and the part due to the increase of physical output between a year of severe depression and a year of great activity. By applying appropriate index numbers of prices to the various sections of the data we can get revised estimates of the national income in "dollars of constant purchasing power." These revised figures come out 33 billions in 1914 and 40.7 billions in 1916. That is, the estimate of the two-year gain in national income is cut down from 37 to 23 per cent.[2]

For most purposes this lower estimate of the increase in the national income in which the fluctuations of prices have been canceled as accurately as may be, strikes us as more significant than the unrevised estimate. It is easy to increase the national income to any limit by monetary inflation—easy, and harmful to welfare.

Where, then, do we stand in our efforts to treat economic problems by quantitative methods? What we seek to promote is welfare, but welfare we cannot measure except in certain details where objective indexes of physiological or psychological conditions are available. So we work on the assumption that an increase in commodities and services generally brings with it an increase of welfare. It is on that assumption that we seek to promote efficiency in producing goods. But we have to measure the progress of efficiency in money values whenever we are including goods of many different kinds. While we can afterward correct our figures

[2]*Income in the United States.* By the Staff of the National Bureau of Economic Research, vol. I, pp. 64 and 72, New York, 1921.

for changes in the price level, they still remain in money terms—a hypothetical money of constant purchasing power. And the meaning of these monetary aggregates is exceedingly difficult to interpret except when we are comparing one such aggregate with another.

II

The various levels of analysis in economic investigation are matters of profound and practical concern to the engineer as well as to the economist.

In considering the national income it is obvious, as previously stated, that money is important because it represents goods, and that goods in turn are important because they contribute to welfare. But in the process of production as now organized these relations are reversed in large measure. Production is carried on more and more by business enterprises, and business enterprises must make money if they are to keep going. The men in charge of a business enterprise may be filled with zeal for public service, but they must make enough to pay expenses and something over or they will have to find some other way of serving the public than running a business. The men in charge of another enterprise may be engineers interested primarily in perfecting their processes and products; but they must keep their passion for technical perfection within the limits set by money profit or they will be eliminated from the ranks of business managers.

It is no disparagement of businessmen to say that in business they subordinate the making of goods to the making of money. They are compelled to do so by the system of which we all are parts. If they fail to get their profits they cannot go on making goods. And it is to the interest of all of us that businessmen should get their profits, as every period of business depression proves. For when business promises losses instead of profits, production falls off and the national income is diminished, in extreme cases perhaps by 25 per cent.[3]

But while it is silly to blame anyone for this situation, it nevertheless bristles with economic contradictions. From the national viewpoint money-making is a means toward making goods; from the individual viewpoint making goods is a means toward making money. From the national viewpoint the engineer is the central figure in production; in practice he takes orders from the businessman. A community is well off in proportion to its efficiency in producing a current supply of the necessities, comforts, and amenities of life; an individual is well off in proportion to his efficiency in getting a money income.

This practical subordination of our common interest in making goods to our individual interest in making money produces grave consequences. But before enumerating them it should be emphatically stated that the money economy is doubtless the best form of economic organization for promoting the common welfare that men have yet devised. This opinion is based on the fact that the money economy has developed out of simpler forms of economic organization in all the most progressive nations of the world, and that, broadly speaking, this development has been spontaneous. No one forced our forefathers in America to give up raising their own food, making their own clothing, and cutting their own fuel. They changed from the practice of making goods for their own families to the practice of making money incomes and buying goods made by others because they liked the results of the more elaborate plan better. In medieval times the King of England traveled around the realm with his court subsisting on the produce of the royal manors. When

[3] [In 1929–1932 the decline in "real" income seems to have been about one-quarter. In terms of money the drop was much larger than that.]

the king began to commute the labor services of his villeins and their dues in kind into money payments, the villeins shared with the king in the advantages of a better arrangement. So almost all the elaborate machinery of the money economy has grown up by slow degrees because men thought they got more goods or better goods when they worked for money than when they produced for themselves. The villeins have been converted into wage earners, the craft guilds have given way to the merchant and the factory, the weekly markets where neighbors met to barter have been superseded by retail shops, banking has evolved from small beginnings into a ubiquitous business, the joint-stock company has become the dominant form of business organization, all because on the whole these changes recommended themselves on trial to large and growing sections of the population. Of course, most of these changes were accompanied by grievous hardships to many individuals, but if the new organizations had not filled demands numerous enough to make them pay they could not have broken through "the cake of custom."

It must also be set down to the credit of the money economy that it is a marvelously flexible institution. It has been developed in a dozen ways undreamed of by the medieval moneylender. Its capacity for further development and adaptation to human needs has no visible limits except the limits of man's capacity for invention. With that thought in mind, let us consider some ways in which the money economy serves us ill, in the hope that the engineers and economists may invent practicable devices for bettering its operation.

III

To begin with an obvious point, our dollar is not a stable unit. It is subject to continuous and wide variations in purchasing power, and these variations introduce uncertainty into business plans, cause undeserved losses to some, and confer undeserved gains upon others. Various plans for stabilizing the dollar have been proposed—plans that merit critical study. But this whole topic is so familiar and its challenge to our inventive power so clear that this mere mention is sufficient.

Scarcely less obvious is the probem of controlling business cycles. Economic history shows that when any nation develops the money economy to such a point that a large part of its people get their livings by making and spending money incomes, its industry becomes subject to more or less regular alternations of feverish activity, financial crisis, and industrial depression. Of late years these business cycles have been the subject of quantitative investigation, so that our knowledge of the phenomena, while still far from complete, is yet sufficient to suggest various methods of exercising control over the cycle—methods such as the systematic scheduling of business operations with reference to anticipated changes in demand, the long-range planning of construction work, the launching of new products and increase of advertising when business is dull, more circumspect granting of credit in periods of activity, the improvement and wider use of business barometers, various schemes of unemployment insurance to reduce labor turnover and sustain the purchasing power of wage earners in periods of depression, and the like. Most of these plans emphasize the policy of "prevention rather than cure"; that is, they seek to diminish the wasteful excesses of booms as the best means of diminishing the severity of crises and depressions. All these plans are in the experimental stage. Engineers by virtue of their scientific training and their intimate relations with businessmen are likely to take an active share in testing these schemes and perfecting the best among them.

Another problem presented by the money economy is the clash between our desire for efficient production and our fear of being exploited by very large corporations. At present the work of production is systematically planned and controlled within the limits of each independent business enterprise. But we have no systematic plan for industry as a whole. Our industrial army is like a collection of military units of different sizes, each efficiently led—squads under sergeants, companies under captains, regiments under colonels, a few brigades under generals—but an army without a general staff and without a general plan of campaign. However well the separate units are disciplined and led, there is loss of efficiency through lack of cooperation among the units. Under such circumstances every increase in the size of the independent units extends the area within which careful organization exists and lessens the area in which no planning is possible. But as the companies combine into regiments and the regiments into brigades, we are afraid that the larger units will levy upon us a tribute that exceeds the savings from heightened efficiency. How, then, can we unite the efficiency of large-scale production with safety to the consumer? To that vexed issue of economic policy the organizing genius of the engineering profession may address itself with excellent results.

Other problems might be discussed—the possibility of cutting down the overhead that business needs impose upon industry, the possibility of raising the efficiency of government service, the elimination of all methods of making money that are detrimental to public welfare, the advantages of investment in improving the personnel of industry as compared with the advantages of investment in plant, conflicts in interest arising from the long life of nations and the short span of individual lives, what constitutes waste and how it may be minimized, the effect of changes in the standard of living upon production, the relations between the distribution of income and the production of income—all matters of concern to engineers and economists alike. But enough has already been said to illustrate the main contentions, and illustration is all that is possible in treating so wide a topic in a brief paper.

To sum up, the industrial revolution has been marked by changes in economic organization as well as by changes in engineering technique. To keep this beneficent revolution going will require further changes of both types, economic and engineering. We should not be less alert to note the imperfections of economic organization than to note those of mechanical methods. In one field as in the other our best hope of constructive accomplishment lies in developing scientific analysis in quantitative terms.

How to make production for profit turn out a larger supply of useful goods under conditions more conducive to welfare is a problem that gives scope for the most diverse abilities and training. It is a problem that can be broken down into manageable parts that can be attacked by quantitative methods, and the advances made by one discoverer can be made the starting point of his successor.

9

THE ROLE OF MONEY IN ECONOMIC THEORY[1]

AMONG recent tendencies in economic theory none seems to me more promising than the tendency to make the use of money the central feature of economic analysis. What forms, tacit and explicit, this tendency assumes and what future work it suggests are my chief themes. But the significance of recent developments will stand out more clearly if I recall the curious role played by money in the parent stock from which our current types of economic theory are descended.

I

"The science of Political Economy as we have it in England," wrote Bagehot, "may be defined as the science of business, such as business is in large productive and trading communities. . . . It assumes the principal facts which make that commerce possible . . .": free laborers working for money wages, capitalist employers in quest of money profits, a highly developed monetary system with a loan fund and a speculation fund—in short, the whole set of pecuniary institutions under which the "general art of money-making has grown up." "It assumes that every man who makes anything, makes it for money. . . ." Finally, it assumes the sort of human nature appropriate to money-makers. "Dealing with matters of 'business,' it assumes that

[1] Reprinted from *American Economic Review*, vol. VI, supplement, pp. 140–161, March, 1916.

man is animated only by motives of business."[2] Or, as Dr. Marshall phrased it, the classical economists worked out "their theories on the tacit supposition that the world was made up of city men."[3]

There are no better accredited interpreters of classical political economy than Bagehot and Marshall. Yet these tacit assumptions which they impute to the classical writers seem at variance with the explicit statements about money found in the classical texts. Mill puts the matter most clearly. He holds the use of money to be a superficial phenomenon, one that often "obscures, to an unpracticed apprehension, the true character of" economic processes.[4] He discusses production, distribution, and even exchange, "without introducing the idea of Money (except occasionally for illustration)." When he does "superadd that idea," he admits that without "a Circulating Medium" we should suffer two great inconveniences: "the want of a common measure for values" and inability to carry the division of labor to any considerable extent.[5] But, "Great as the difference would be between a country with money, and a country wholly without it, it would be only one of convenience."[6] For, "The introduction of money does not interfere with the operation of any of the Laws of Value laid down in the . . . chapters" written before the idea of money was superadded.[7] And the like holds of distribution. Money makes no difference in the

[2] "The Postulates of English Political Economy," 1876, reprinted in *Economic Studies*, edited by R. H. Hutton, especially pp. 6, 7, London, 1879.

[3] *Principles of Economics*, 1st ed., p. 62, London, 1890.

[4] *Principles of Political Economy*, Ashley's ed., p. 72, London and New York, 1909.

[5] *Ibid.*, pp. 483, 484. It would be going too far to credit Mill with a full appreciation of all that lies latent in his admission that without money we should lack "a common measure for values."

[6] *Ibid.*, p. 6.

[7] *Ibid.*, p. 488.

law of wages or the law of rent. "Wages and Rent being thus regulated by the same principles, when paid in money, as they would be if apportioned in kind, it follows that Profits are so likewise."[8] "There cannot, in short, be intrinsically a more insignificant thing, in the economy of society, than money, except in the character of a contrivance for sparing time and labour."[9]

Political economy, then, is the science of business, and economic men are money-makers; nevertheless, the use of money is a fact of no importance for economic theory. This seeming contradiction between the letter of the economic law and its spirit as interpreted by loyal commentators long passed without notice.[10] It was part of the classical tradition to accept both views, and not to think of them at the same time.[11]

[8] *Ibid.*, pp. 688, 691.

[9] *Ibid.*, p. 488.

[10] I have not scrupled to set Mill's clear statements about the insignificance of money against Bagehot's and Marshall's interpretations of classical economics, although both the latter were probably thinking of Ricardo rather than of Mill. As Mr. J. M. Keynes remarks, "Bagehot kicked morally and intellectually against the Mill despotism, just as Jevons did. The same feeling, far less intense, is to be found in some of the criticisms of Dr. Marshall." ("The Works of Walter Bagehot," *Economic Journal*, vol. XXV, p. 375, September, 1915.) In the point at issue, however, it seems to me that Mill was merely formulating lucidly the tacit views of his predecessors.

[11] As far as I know, the first writer to raise the issue in any form was Professor F. von Wieser. In the preface to his *Natural Value* (1888, English translation, 1893, pp. xxvii-xxix) he pointed out the confusion between the "philosophical" theory of value and the "empirical" theory of price in Adam Smith and Ricardo. Professor A. C. Whitaker has worked out this theme fully in his *History and Criticism of the Labor Theory of Value in English Political Economy* (Columbia Studies in History, Economics and Public Law, vol. XIX, no. 2, New York, 1904). The result of these inquiries is a detailed demonstration that the classical writers from Adam Smith to Cairnes did not succeed in resolving all items of "entrepreneur's cost" into "labor costs"—that is, they did not really get rid of pecuniary factors in their theory of exchange.

It has indeed become more difficult to understand than to criticize the classical attitude toward the use of money. One clue to it is given by Professor Thorstein

II

When Jevons "shunted the car of Economic science" to another track, he pushed the use of money farther into the background. This result followed from his explicit avowal of hedonism as the basis of economic theory. The "ultimate quantities which we treat in Economics," he holds, "are Pleasures and Pains."[12] "But it is convenient to transfer our attention as soon as possible to the physical objects or actions which are the source to us of pleasures and pains."[13] Accordingly, he develops his theory of exchange without consciously introducing the use of money.[14] His "trading bodies" are engaged in barter—swapping corn for beef. Few men of his generation knew more about money and the mechanism of exchange than Jevons, and no man contributed

---

Veblen ("The Preconceptions of Economic Science, II," *Quarterly Journal of Economics*, vol. XIII, pp. 411–426, July, 1899 [reprinted in *The Place of Science in Modern Civilisation*, pp. 129–145, New York, 1919]). Veblen lays stress upon the hedonistic conception of human nature which the classical writers held tacitly, either as professed disciples of Bentham or as sharers in the common sense of their day. This preconception shifted the center of interest in economics away from Adam Smith's concern with the bearings of industry upon the community's material welfare to Ricardo's problem of value and distribution. To conceive economic behavior as concerned primarily with buying and selling commodities, or with getting wages, rent, and profits, was to emphasize the pecuniary side of life. Hence, the legitimacy of Bagehot's interpretation of "English Political Economy" as "the science of business." But on the hedonistic basis money was a mere symbol: nothing really counted in controlling behavior but pleasures and pains. Hence, Mill's confident assertions about the insignificance of money. A hedonist could admit no fundamental inconsistency between the hedonic and the pecuniary calculus, though he might admit that the pain cost of a day's labor to a skilled man stood for more money than the corresponding pain cost to an unskilled man, and so need to supplement his "philosophy" of value by an "empirical" theory of prices.

[12] *Theory of Political Economy*, p. 65, 4th ed., London, 1911.

[13] *Ibid.*, p. 37.

[14] That his exposition does logically involve the existence of a general medium of exchange has been shown by Professor Allyn A. Young. "Jevons' 'Theory of Political Economy,'" *American Economic Review*, vol. II, p. 584, September, 1912.

more to our knowledge of price fluctuations. But he believed heartily in the subdivision of economic studies.[15] Among the fundamentals of economic theory—that is, in "the mechanics of utility"—he saw no place for money. It belonged among "the higher complications of the subject," into which his great treatise did not enter.[16]

For the "motives of business" which Bagehot found dominating classical economics then, Jevons substituted the striving for pleasure. Granted the validity of Hedonism, his way of conceiving economic behavior was a great advance. Economic theory became more profound in that it dealt directly with ultimate motives, or with the physical objects and actions that evoked them. Human nature itself became simple enough to let the economist use the powerful methods of analysis provided by mathematics. The hypothesis "that Pleasure is the concomitant of Energy" and the "conception of Man as a pleasure Machine" promised to elevate social mechanics to a throne beside celestial mechanics.[17] Further, the economist's explanation of why things happen, his statements of what does happen, and his criterion of what ought to happen, were all established upon a single harmonious basis. Economics led directly to ethics; no radical shifting of the viewpoint was required.[18] To this admirable simplicity the conception added admirable practicality. On the hedonistic basis, "the materials with which exact social science is concerned are no metaphysical shadows, but the very substance of modern civilization, destined, doubtless ere long to become embodied in practical politics and morals."[19]

[15] Preface to the 2d ed. of the *Theory of Political Economy*, London, 1879; pp. xvi–xviii of the 4th ed.

[16] See the last paragraph of the program sketched by Jevons in 1862, published in 1866, and republished in the 4th ed. of his *Theory*, p. 314.

[17] Professor F. Y. Edgeworth, *Mathematical Psychics*, pp. 9–15, London, 1881.

[18] *Ibid.*, p. 56.

[19] *Ibid.*, p. 97.

It is curious that this splendid vision, set forth with such precision and such eloquence by Professor Edgeworth, induced few of the economists who followed Jevons's line of attack to accept his explicit hedonism. Most of them worked with the concept of marginal utility—a notion less adapted to mathematical analysis than final degree of utility, but better adapted to popular exposition.[20] That is, they built, usually at the first remove, upon Menger, and Menger did not build upon Bentham. Likewise, those who were especially influenced by Professor John B. Clark did not find the word "hedonism" in *The Philosophy of Wealth*. As for the mathematical economists, they found in Walras a better master than Jevons, one who formulated the problem of exchange in all its generality, and Walras had no more to say of hedonism than Menger or Clark. Hedonistic preconceptions may have been tacitly held by these masters; they were not explicitly avowed.

To the example of reticence concerning the basis of choice set by Menger, Walras, and Clark, there was added in the late eighties and the early nineties a series of warnings from men who cultivated the borderland between economics and philosophy. Professors James Bonar, J. S. Mackenzie, and, most thoroughly, H. W. Stuart called the attention of economists to the passing of hedonism in psychology, and raised the question whether the whole utility analysis fell with it.[21] That ticklish question was little debated by mere economists

[20] Compare Professor Allyn A. Young, *op. cit.*, p. 583.

[21] James Bonar, "The Austrian Economists and Their View of Value," *Quarterly Journal of Economics*, vol. III, pp. 24, 25, October, 1888; extract from a paper on the "Relations of Carlyle to Political Economy" (Dec., 1890) published in *Philosophy and Political Economy*, p. 236, 2d ed., 1893; John S. Mackenzie, *An Introduction to Social Philosophy*, pp. 267, 268, 2d ed., Glasgow, 1895; Henry W. Stuart, "Hedonistic Interpretation of Subjective Value" and "Subjective and Exchange Value," *Journal of Political Economy*, vol. III, pp. 64–84, December, 1895; vol. IV, pp. 208–239, March, 1896; pp. 352–385, June, 1896.

for the next decade,[22] but they did seek anxiously to free their terminology from hedonistic implications. In 1892 Professor Irving Fisher protested against the foisting of (hedonistic) psychology upon economics by Gossen, Jevons, and Edgeworth as inappropriate and vicious, and held that utility might be derived from desire, whether the antecedent of desire was pleasure, duty, fear, or any other state of consciousness.[23] In the later editions of his *Principles*, Dr. Marshall changed utility "or pleasure" to utility "or benefit," defined consumer's rent as "surplus satisfaction" instead of "surplus pleasure," dropped his reference to Bentham's treatment of the propinquity and certainty of pleasures, and inserted a note contesting "the belief that economists are adherents of the philosophical system of Hedonism or of Utilitarianism."[24] Such efforts to free economics from its entangling alliance were spurred on by critics—above all, Professor Veblen—who urged that the substance of hedonism remains in marginal theory even after its semblance is dropped.[25] Though scant public notice

[22] Professor H. J. Davenport was among the first to take up this issue. See his "Proposed Modifications in Austrian Theory and Terminology," *Quarterly Journal of Economics*, vol. XVI, pp. 355–358, May, 1902; *Value and Distribution*, pp. 303–311, Chicago, 1908; *Economics of Enterprise*, pp. 97–102, New York, 1913. See also Professor A. C. Pigou, "Some Remarks on Utility," *Economic Journal*, vol. XIII, pp. 66–68, March, 1903.

[23] Irving Fisher, "Mathematical Investigations in the Theory of Value and Prices," *Transactions of the Connecticut Academy of Arts and Sciences*, IX, 5, 11, 23, 1892.

[24] As examples of such modifications in his phraseology, compare the following parallel passages in the 1st and 6th eds. (1890 and 1910), pp. 83, 84 note with p. 17 note; pp. 187, 188 with p. 141; pp. 153, 154 with pp. 119, 120; p. 175 with p. 124; p. 156 with pp. 117, 118; similarly in the 2d (1891) and 6th eds., compare p. 150 with p. 93, and p. 153 with p. 95.

[25] Thorstein Veblen, "Why Is Economics Not an Evolutionary Science?", "The Preconceptions of Economic Science," 1899, and 1900; "Professor Clark's Economics," *Quarterly Journal of Economics*, July, 1898, Jan. and July, 1899, February, 1900, [reprinted in *The Place of Science in Modern Civilisation*, 1919]; "Fisher's Capital and Income," "Fisher's Rate of Interest," *Political Science*

was taken of these criticisms,[26] they contributed toward the feeling of uneasiness about the psychological basis of economics that is so marked at present. If hedonism is dropped what shall take its place? Or can economics dispense with psychology altogether?

III

Since the ostensible dropping of hedonism began, three fairly distinct types of orthodox economic theory have been developed by the psychological school, the pure theorists, and the neoclassicists.

The name "American Psychological School" was invented, I believe, by Professor Fetter. His *Principles of Economics* (1904) is the best example of this type of theory for present purposes, because it surveys "the whole range of economic inquiry" in brief compass;[27] and because it has such aesthetic simplicity. This simplicity is attained by resolving all branches of economic theory into. problems of value. The value of material things,—present goods and durable goods,— the value of human services, and the social aspects of value include the whole field. Further, all these value problems are treated in terms of a single unit, "the simplest, immediate, temporary gratification."[28] Since "the attainment of pleasurable conditions in mind or soul . . . is the aim of all economic activity,"[29] the economist must carry all his

---

Quarterly, March 1908, June, 1909 [reprinted in *Essays in Our Changing Order*, 1934]; "The Limitations of Marginal Utility," *Journal of Political Economy*, November, 1909, [reprinted in *The Place of Science in Modern Civilisation*, 1919].

[26] By way of exception, see Professor Irving Fisher's reply to Professor Veblen, "Capital and Interest," *Political Science Quarterly*, Sept., 1909; and Böhm-Bawerk's note on the subject, *Positiv Theorie des Kapitals*, pp. 310–321, 3d ed., 2d half volume.

[27] *Principles of Economics*, p. 413, New York, 1904.

[28] *Ibid.*, pp. xiv, 73, 413. Cost, of course, even psychic cost, is not recognized as coordinate in importance with gratification in determining value. See pp. 273, 274.

[29] *Ibid.*, p. 43.

analyses back from money to goods, and from goods to the psychic income that goods yield. "All things at last become comparable in terms of psychic income in each individual's judgment."[30]

Now this "consistently subjective analysis of the relations of goods to wants,"[31] which Professor Fetter manages so deftly, has received two interpretations. First, it has been taken as what it purports to be—a psychological theory of economic behavior. The gist of the criticism on this reading is that the theory misrepresents the process of valuation. The assumption that men value goods as instruments for arousing certain feelings logically involves the following steps: the kind and magnitude of the feelings that given goods in given quantities presumably will arouse in a given person must be separated in his mind from other elements in his ideas of the goods; then these feelings must be valued and discounted according to their presumed futurities; finally the values set on the feelings must be passed back again to the goods. A generation that has lost faith in hedonism cannot accept such an analysis as psychologically valid. Men do not practice psychic bookkeeping in terms of "the simplest, immediate, temporary gratification." They value goods, not feelings.[32]

The second interpretation is that the American psychological school has turned political economy into "business economics," "a system of economic accounting," "pecuniary logic."[33] It has taken the habit of mind developed by business

[30] *Ibid.*, p. 225.

[31] *Ibid.*, p. xiv.

[32] For examples of such criticisms of the psychological school see Professor Veblen's reviews of Professor Fisher's *Capital and Income* and *The Rate of Interest*, in *Political Science Quarterly*, March, 1908, and June, 1909 [reprinted *in Essays in Our Changing Order*, 1934]; Alvin S. Johnson's review of the last edition of Böhm-Bawerk's *Kapital und Kapitalzins*, in *American Economic Review*, March, 1914.

[33] John R. Commons, "Political Economy and Business Economy: Comments on Fisher's Capital and Income," *Quarterly Journal of Economics*, November,

traffic and imputed it to mankind at large in their dealings with goods in general. It has used the refined concepts of wealth, service, property, capital, and income—concepts that are slowly elaborated products of the money economy— to frame an account of how men might behave if they were faultless products of the countinghouse. "In short, for system's sake," the psychological school has recast "the whole material equipment of human living . . . in molds fashioned after the notions of catallactics," as Professor Young puts it.[34] And in so doing the school has rendered a notable service, for the use of money and the pecuniary way of thinking it begets is a most important factor in the modern situation. To isolate this factor, to show what economic life would be if it dominated human nature, is to clarify our understanding of economic processes. It is regrettable only that these writers have not emphasized the monographic character of their work.

Of these two interpretations the second accords better with the trend of development within the school. Even in 1904 Professor Fetter put three excellent chapters on the evolution of the money economy into his textbook. He pointed out "that the problem of time value was first clearly recognized in connection with money and a formally expressed capital sum." He admitted that the practical men who are "fixing the 'capital value' of goods are usually only dimly conscious of the logical nature of the process."[35] Indeed, he seemed on the verge of saying that the pecuniary

---

1907; Alvin S. Johnson's review of Fisher's *Elementary Principles of Economics*, in *Journal of Political Economy*, Nov., 1913; W. C. Mitchell's review of Davenport's *Economics of Enterprise*, in *American Economic Review*, September, 1914.

[34] Allyn A. Young, "Some Limitations of the Value Concept," *Quarterly Journal of Economics*, vol. XXV, p. 424, May, 1911.

[35] The chapters are numbered 13, 14, 15. The quotations are from pp. 142 and 126.

logic which he was expounding was something that men have learned from business experience and carry back from that objective realm a little way into their psychic life. Professor Fisher, in 1909, granted to Professor Commons that his *Capital and Income* dealt only with one side of economic life,[36] and then in his textbook in 1912 he gave a more uncompromising pecuniary version of economic behavior than Professor Fetter had done.[37] Finally, in 1913, Professor Davenport carried this line of work through to its logical outcome by defining economics as "the science that treats phenomena from the standpoint of price," by accepting completely the "private and acquisitive point of view" in his search for explanations, and by distinguishing sharply between that scientific task of explaining and the larger task of passing judgment upon the economic situation as a whole.[38]

Professor Fetter, indeed, has refused to accept Davenport's "price conception of economics."[39] But his new book, published since this paper was drafted, shows that he has shifted his own ground since 1904.[40] According to the preface, "he presents here a quite new statement of the theory of value, one in accord with the modern volitional psychology, thus eliminating entirely the old utilitarianism and hedonism

[36] "A Reply to Critics," *Quarterly Journal of Economics*, May, 1909.

[37] *Elementary Principles of Economics.*

[38] *Economics of Enterprise*, pp. 25, 517, New York, 1913. Professor Fetter claims Davenport as a (wayward) member of the American psychological school. See his review, "Davenport's Competitive Economics," *Journal of Political Economy*, June, 1914. Of course, Davenport's desire to divorce economics from psychology (see pp. 97–102, 230–232) is no reason for counting him out of the school. Professor Fisher is a member of unquestioned standing, and, as noted above, he protested from the start against "the foisting of psychology upon economics." Similarly, Professor F. von Wieser ranks himself in the psychological school, though he disclaims dependence upon psychology proper. See his new *Theorie der gesellschaftlichen Wirtschaft*, in *Grundriss der Sozialökonomik*, vol. I, p. 132, Tubingen, 1914.

[39] See his article referred to in the preceding note.

[40] *Economics*, vol. I, New York, 1915.

which have tainted the terms and conceptions of value ever since the days of Bentham. The basis of value is conceived to be the simple act of choice, and not a calculation of utility. Even the phrase 'marginal utility' is definitely abandoned."[41] As this change is a concession to critics who have charged the psychological school with hedonism, so another change is designed to meet critics who have charged the school with turning political economy into business economics. Without altering substantially his theories of prices and distribution, Professor Fetter now emphasizes the fact that these theories deal not with economic behavior as such, but with elements logically implicit in economic behavior. And he shows that these logical implications are brought out by the use of money. Hence, the pecuniary aspects of economic life get clearer recognition than in Professor Fetter's earlier work. But they are not permitted to cover the whole field. To his analysis of the process by which business incomes are fixed, Fetter adds a brief discussion of the social aspects of value.[42]

The "psychological" type of theory, then, has brought money back into the very center of economics. From the use of money is derived not only the whole set of pecuniary concepts which the theorist and his subjects employ, but also the whole countinghouse attitude toward economic activities. In its use are found the molds of economic rationality and the clues to economic explanations.

[41] *Ibid.*, p. ix.

[42] With reference to the place of this topic in economics, the difference between Davenport and Fetter seems to be important only from the terminological viewpoint. Both treat social value, and treat it apart from the main body of their theories; one calls this addendum economic theory, the other doesn't.

It may be added that Professor Fetter's new book brings the psychological type of economics distinctly nearer to recent pure theory in the discussion of value, and nearer to neoclassical theory in certain other respects, *e.g.*, the relation of cost to value and prices.

IV

While the psychological school has been developing its pecuniary logic, certain pure theorists have sought another way of emancipating themselves from hedonism. The leader of this diversion is Professor Vilfredo Pareto.

As his disciple, M. Zawadzki, says, Pareto employed the hedonistic hypothesis in his earlier work. But since 1900 he has developed "a new theory, which he calls the theory of choice, a theory which may replace the hedonistic hypothesis with advantage."[43] Adopting a device invented by Professor Edgeworth in 1881,[44] he deduces everything necessary for his theory of equilibrium from "curves of indifference." Pareto's innovation consists in this: while Edgeworth derived indifference curves from the concept of utility, Pareto treats them as factual data.[45] Thanks to this procedure, "The theory of economic science . . . acquires the rigor of rational mechanics: it deduces its results from experience, without requiring the intervention of any metaphysical entity."[46]

This apparatus of indifference curves or surfaces in hyperspace presents difficulties to "the literary economists," whom Pareto scorns. But fundamentally the same procedure has been brought within the nonmathematical comprehension by one who is free both of the mathematical and of the literary guild. Mr. Wicksteed conceives "of a general 'scale of

[43] M. Zawadzki, *Les Mathématiques appliquées à l'economie politique*, pp. 142, 143, 1914.

[44] *Mathematical Psychics*, pp. 22, 29, London, 1881.

[45] *Manuel d'economie politique*, p. 169, note, Paris, 1909.

[46] *Ibid.*, p. 160. Pareto does not, however, wholly discard the concept of utility, or ophelimity. Concerning the role which it continued to play in his new theory, see Zawadzki, *op. cit.*, pp. 151–156. Compare the comments by Professor Edgeworth, "Recent Contributions to Mathematical Economics," *Economic Journal*, vol. XXV, pp. 57–62, March, 1915.

preferences' . . . on which all objects of desire or pursuit (positive or negative) find their place, and which registers the terms on which they would be accepted as equivalents or preferred one to the other." This construction gives him "a system of ideal prices," upon which he can erect his whole edifice of theory, without inquiring into the grounds on which men's preferences rest.[47] Similarly, Professor Schumpeter, following Walras, assumes as data for his general theory m individuals, their respective value functions for each of n goods, and the quantity of each good in the possession of each individual, denying that the economist has any business with the psychological processes from which the value functions are derived.[48]

It is clear, at once, that this type of theory eliminates the problem of valuation from economics. That is, it does not concern itself with the way in which men find out what relative importance different goods have for their purposes. Instead, it assumes that this process of valuation has been completed before they come to market by each of the men with reference to each of the goods, and furthermore that the process has yielded in each man's mind definite quantitative results. Not until that stage has been reached does the pure theorist begin his work. His first step is to cast the finished individual valuations into the form of indifference curves, scales of preference, objective expressions of choice, or value functions. That gives him a set of what Mr. Wicksteed terms "ideal prices" as data for analysis. Then the theorist develops a logical scheme of conceiving the process by which mutually interdependent market prices result from the

[47] P. H. Wicksteed, *The Common Sense of Political Economy*, pp. 32, 33, London, 1910.
[48] Joseph Schumpeter, *Das Wesen und der Hauptinhalt der theoretischen National-ökonomie*, pp. 64–68, 77–79, 85–87, 154, 155, 261, 541–547, Leipsig, 1908.

"ideal prices." He does not, of course, profess to show what the market prices will be;[49] but he does demonstrate more adequately than any other type of economist the complex interrelationships logically involved in the determination of prices in modern markets.

Even more strictly than the writings of the psychological school, pure economics is a generalized statement of the businessman's problem, a countinghouse view of economic life. The problem concerns the complex mutual adjustments among a host of possible prices, on the one hand, and the possible quantities of different goods that might be bought and sold at these prices, on the other hand. Just as businessmen think in the same terms of investments in commerce and in industry, so the pure theorists carry their argument forward from exchange to production, treating their subjects as exchanging goods and efforts with nature for new products on the same principles that rule their exchanges among themselves. Perhaps the chief difference between the viewpoints of business and pure theory is that the businessman is less indifferent toward the grounds of choice than the theorist. He wants to know why people value goods in order that he may spend his advertising money wisely. To drop the theory of valuation from economics, therefore, reduces its significance for him. But in drawing narrow limits round their work the pure theorists know exactly what they are doing, and seldom fail to give their readers adequate warning of the modest pretensions of their results. These are merits which cannot be claimed so confidently for the psychological school at large.

[49] For (1) the "value functions" are as yet arbitrarily assumed, (2) the whole discussion presupposes static conditions, and (3) when many men and many goods are involved the number of equations to be handled becomes too great for solution.

THE BACKWARD ART OF SPENDING MONEY

V

Neoclassical economics, as represented by Dr. Marshall's *Principles*, puts money conspicuously into the foreground from the start. Indeed, Dr. Marshall declares that money "is the center around which economic science clusters."[50] But he hastens to add: " . . . this is so, not because money . . . is . . . the main aim of human effort . . .; but because . . . it is the one convenient means of measuring human motive on a large scale."[51]

Why is the measurement of motive so important as to make money "the center around which economic science clusters"? The full answer to that naïve question runs as follows: Economics is a science of human behavior.[52] Behavior is determined by motives. Motives differ widely in kind, and are continually conflicting with one another. Yet the economist may not exclude "the influence of any motive the action of which is regular."[53] What he does is to arrange motives in "two opposing sets of forces, those which impel man to economic efforts and sacrifices, and those which hold him back."[54] To know what economic actions men normally will take, then, the theorist must know the relative strength of these opposing sets of motives. But motives are mental states; and mental states are not directly commensurable unless they are similar in kind, and "unless they occur to the same person at the same time." "If then we wish to compare even physical gratifications, we must do it not directly, but indirectly by the incentives which they afford to action. . . .

[50] *Principles of Economics*, 6th ed., p. 22, London, 1910.
[51] *Loc. cit.*, cf. p. 782.
[52] Cf. pp. 1, 14, 33, 49.
[53] *Ibid.*, p. xiii, compare p. 24. For the great variety of motives which Marshall takes into account, see pp. 23–25, 86–89, 120–121, 141, etc.
[54] *Ibid.*, p. 324.

the force of a person's motives—*not* the motives themselves—can be approximately measured by the sum of money which he will just give up in order to secure a desired satisfaction; or again by the sum which is just required to induce him to undergo a certain fatigue."[55]

To explain and to predict economic behavior, then, the economist needs a measure of the strength of the opposing sets of regularly acting motives. Such a measure money gives him. Indeed, in the whole task of explaining the phenomena of exchange and distribution, the money measures are more than mere measures of the forces at work—they are themselves these forces. For the intensities of a man's desires and aversions do not affect the market, except as they become embodied in demand or supply prices. It is the magnitude of these pecuniary embodiments of motives, not the strength of the motives as such, that determines the results.[56]

To explain how prices are determined and how wealth is distributed, however, is but one-half of Dr. Marshall's task. He is equally interested in stating what results these processes produce. These results are subjective matters—magnitudes of satisfaction achieved and of sacrifice endured. Here again he uses his money measure, albeit with greater reservations. He is forced to assume that in general satisfactions correspond fairly well to anticipations. On this basis he makes the money measure of the strength of motives "serve, with all its faults, *both* for the desires which prompt activities and for the satisfactions that result from them."[57] There is, however, an important difference between the use of money measures to explain economic processes and to state

[55] *Ibid.*, pp. 15, 16.

[56] That Dr. Marshall does not dwell upon this rather patent feature of his theory arises from his practice of discussing homogeneous groups to which equal money measures stand presumably for equally intense motives.

[57] *Principles*, p. 92, and note.

their results. As demand prices the rich man's shilling and the poor man's shilling are equal in the market; as measures of satisfaction they are not equal to the economist.

Thus Dr. Marshall makes money an instrument of economic research. What Mill spoke of as obscuring the true character of economic processes, what Professor Fisher calls "the chief stumblingblock in economic theory,"[58] becomes in his hands the "economist's balance," which "has made economics more exact than any other branch of social science."[59] He even questions whether there could be a science of economics in a community that did not use money, unless there existed some substitute that would "serve to measure the strength of motives just as conveniently and exactly as money does with us."[60]

Not only does Marshall use money for his own theoretical purposes; he also represents men as using money for their practical purposes—buying and selling at money prices, making and spending money incomes. Instead of brushing these pecuniary phenomena aside as superficial, he treats them as serious problems to be solved in their own right, and as making a real difference in economic behavior that is not to be explained away. This it is that gives his treatise its realistic atmosphere.[61] But it is not merely to gain a real-

[58] "Capital and Interest," *Political Science Quarterly*, vol. XXIV, p. 513, September, 1909.

[59] *Principles*, p. 14.

[60] *Ibid.*, p. 782.

[61] Professor Allyn A. Young remarks that Marshall's "theory is cast more consistently in terms of price than that of any other writer since Cournot." ("Some Limitations of the Value Concept," *Quarterly Journal of Economics*, vol. XXV, p. 412 note, May, 1911.) But he also reminds us that Marshall takes the price of anything "as representative of its exchange value relatively to things in general, or in other words as representative of its general purchasing power" (*Principles* p. 62). This distinction means in practice that Marshall follows the businessman in neglecting changes in the purchasing power of money, except when he is dealing with long periods. And on these latter occasions he allows for changes in the price

istic effect that Marshall pictures men as using money; he has a deeper reason. As no other theorist he sees how the use of money clarifies obscure relations and simplifies economic thinking, both for the man in the street and for the economist in the study. For example, he shows how the use of money facilitates the task of distributing a person's resources in such fashion that the marginal utilities of a given outlay may be approximately equal in all branches of expenditure.[62] He demonstrates that buying and selling for money is a *simpler* problem than barter, both for the participants and for the theorist.[63] He points out that while "the distinction between prime and supplementary costs operates in every phase of civilization," still "it is not likely to attract much attention except in a capitalistic phase."[64] He recognizes that his whole theory of normal value applies with more precision of detail to the actions of "city men," who are thoroughly disciplined in the use of money, than to the actions of the unbusinesslike classes.[65] Finally, he argues that the commutation of labor dues into money payments increased economic freedom, and that economic freedom has given "a new precision and a new prominence" to the causes that govern value.[66] Specifically, money rents brought it about that "the line of division between the tenant's and the landlord's share coincides with the deepest and most important line of cleavage in economic theory": namely, "the distinction between the quasi-rents which do not, and

---

level much in the businessman's fashion. For example, see pp. 109, 132, 237, 238, 355, note, 362, 593–595, 709.

[62] *Principles*, p. 118.

[63] *Ibid.*, p. 336 and Appendix F.

[64] *Ibid.*, p. 362.

[65] *Ibid.*, p. xiv.

[66] *Ibid.*, pp. 5, 741.

the profits which do, enter into the normal supply price of produce for periods of moderate length."[67]

VI

Economics has advanced far since Mill declared, "there cannot . . . be intrinsically a more insignificant thing, in the economy of society, than money, except in the character of a contrivance for sparing time and labor." In one way or another, tacitly or explicitly, the types of theory current at present all make money in Dr. Marshall's words "the center around which economic science clusters." The psychological school started by representing economic life as guided by psychic bookkeeping, and has developed economics into "the science that treats phenomena from the standpoint of price." Pure theory in its severer forms drops the subject of valuation altogether and confines itself mainly to the inter-relations among "ideal prices." Neoclassical theory makes money the "economist's balance," and shows how the use of money simplifies economic problems both practical and theoretical.

In thus singling out the use of money as bringing system into economic behavior, as providing the basis for exact analysis, current theory is returning to the starting point from which Cournot set out on his researches in 1838. What we call price, what Cournot calls the "abstract idea of *wealth* or of *value of exchange*," he explains in his first chapter, is "suited for the foundation of a scientific theory," because it is "a definite idea, and consequently susceptible of rigorous treatment in combinations." This abstract idea of wealth "could not have been grasped by men of Teutonic stock, either at the epoch of the Conquest, or even at much later periods, when the feudal law existed in full vigor. . . . Such

[67] *Ibid.*, p. 636 and note.

an idea of wealth as we draw from our advanced state of civilization, and such as is necessary to give rise to a theory, can only be slowly developed as a consequence of the progress of commercial relations." A remarkable anticipation of the outcome of two generations of hard thinking! And Cournot applies his insight: as a first problem he chooses not barter, but foreign exchange—the kind of transaction in which nothing but pecuniary factors are involved.[68]

In singling out the influence of an institutional factor as the basis of rationality, current economics is also in line with current psychology. Psychologists hold that man starts with an immense number of inborn reflexes, instincts, and capacities, inherited generation after generation with numberless differences as between individuals, but with slight changes as regards the species. The behavior these propensities produce is at first quite unreasoning. But among the inborn capacities is the capacity to learn; that is, the capacity to form innumerable *combinations* among the innumerable original propensities. Practically every activity of mature life is the expression not of any single instinct, but of some combination into which several or many propensities have entered. It is these changing combinations among substantially unchanging elements that differentiate the behavior of the civilized man from that of the savage. And these combinations are formed afresh in every child, primarily in his intercourse with other human beings. Thus intelligence is a social product developed in the individual through the exercise of his inherited propensities, and its special character depends

[68] A. Cournot, *Researches into the Mathematical Principles of the Theory of Wealth*, 1838, translation by N. T. Bacon, New York and London, 1897, Chaps. I and III. Professor Henry L. Moore has pointed out to me two later passages in Cournot's writings in which he seems to lose the vision of these early pages. One occurs on p. 164 of the translation cited, the other on p. 4 of his *Revue sommaire des doctrines économiques*, Paris, 1877.

upon the society into which the individual is born. The great social institutions, such as speech, writing, the practical arts, and religion, which are passed on with cumulative changes from one generation to another, play the leading role in this nurture of intelligence. They are standard behavior habits—habits of feeling, thinking, and acting in the face of frequently recurring situations—that have approved themselves to the community. These institutions include among their other elements the abstract concepts that are the most precious products of intelligence because they are the indispensable tools of further thought. By learning to use such concepts in dealing with the situations that confront him, the individual standardizes and rationalizes his own behavior. To find the basis of rationality, then, we must not look inside the individual at his capacity to abstract from the totality of experience the feeling elements, to assess their pleasant or unpleasant characters, and to compare their magnitudes. Rather must we look outside the individual to the habits of behavior slowly evolved by society and painfully learned by himself.[69]

Of course, the use of money is one of these great rationalizing habits. It gives society the technical machinery of ex-

[69] This statement does not mean that the exercise of intelligence is a prominent feature in all habitual action, any more than it means that all institutions are rational. But, as our pure theorists insist, those actions which are most frequently repeated get most thoroughly organized, because they give the fullest scope to learning by trial and error. The more thorough such a piece of organization becomes, however, the less it calls for supervision by intelligence. Hence arises the possibility of contrasting routine with intelligent action. But the successful routine of today remains a triumph of yesterday's creative intelligence, and if today's hard thinking prove equally successful it may organize the routine of tomorrow. Of course, the growing individual must master the past achievements of intelligence before he can participate in work upon present problems. And these past achievements are embodied primarily in social institutions. The more intelligently these institutions have been adapted to current social needs, the more can a learner get from them and the more will creative intelligence seek new worlds to conquer.

change, the opportunity to combine personal freedom with orderly cooperation on a grand scale, and the basis of that system of accountancy which Sombart appropriately calls "economic rationalism." It is the foundation of that complex system of prices to which the individual must adjust his behavior in getting a living. Since it molds his objective behavior, it becomes part of his subjective life, giving him a method and an instrument for the difficult task of assessing the relative importance of dissimilar goods in varying quantities, and affecting the interests in terms of which he makes his valuations. Because it thus rationalizes economic life itself, the use of money lays the foundation for a rational theory of that life.[70] Money may not be the root of *all* evil, but it is the root of economic science.

That economists are coming to accept this view is no more due to their study of psychology than it is due to their study

[70] Of course, an economic theory might be worked out concerning the way in which a species of animals or a tribe of lower hunters get their livings. But such a theory would be a descriptive analysis of behavior written by an outsider. Our economic theory is less an account of what men actually do than a statement of what it is rational for them to do, as seen by a shrewd fellow citizen. Ricardo expressed this difference clearly in the remarkable letter to Malthus written Oct. 22, 1811, concerning international shipments of money. "I assume," he says, "that nations . . . are so alive to their advantage and profit . . . that in point of fact money never does move but when it is advantageous . . . that it should do so. The first point to be considered is, what is the interest of countries in the case supposed? The second, what is their practice? Now it is obvious that I need not be greatly solicitous about this latter point; it is sufficient for my purpose if I can demonstrate that the interest of the public is as I have stated it. It would be no answer to me to say that men were ignorant of the best and cheapest mode of conducting their business . . . because that is a question of fact not of science and might be urged against almost every proposition in Political Economy." (*Letters of Ricardo to Malthus*, ed. by J. Bonar, p. 18, Oxford, 1887.) As long as economists follow this practice of explaining what is rational conduct under the conditions assumed, and depend upon an assumption that men are rational to make the theory a tolerably accurate account of the "facts," it is particularly desirable for them to keep their rational explanations on the same basis as men's rational economic choices.

of Cournot.[71] It is the result of learning by trial and error. They have tried treating money as a superficial phenomenon: they have tried using hedonism as the basis of economic rationality. But in working out, in treatise after treatise, a reasoned account of how men behave, they have come, without foreseeing what they were doing, to the basis on which Cournot built in 1838. That a serious and long-sustained effort to explain their phase of human behavior has brought economists unwittingly to much the same viewpoint as psychologists have attained by other routes may well raise their confidence.

VII

If it is good to celebrate this achievement, it is better to consider how we may turn what has been won for us by others to best account in our own future work. Are we to confine our theorizing consciously to the pecuniary aspect of life? Are we to devote our energies wholly to elaborating the theory of prices, to refining the logic of economic accounting? I think not. Clear recognition of the role which money does play in economic life is more likely to broaden than to narrow the scope of economic theory. It should help us to design, what we sorely need, a framework within which all sorts of contributions may find their proper places. I see the situation thus:

Economic life may be regarded as a continuous process of providing and using commodities and services. This industrial process includes the work of the farm, the mine, the railway, the warehouse, the store, the engineering office, etc., as well as the work of the factory. It has its elaborately differ-

[71] Dr. Marshall does indeed acknowledge his indebtedness to Cournot, but with reference to certain mathematical features of his work, not with reference to the use he makes of money. See preface to the first edition of the *Principles*, London and New York, 1890; p. xv, 6th ed., 1910.

entiated techniques, resting primarily upon the physical sciences and mathematics, in less measure upon certain branches of biology. It has its technical experts, its organized labor force, and its capital in the shape of material equipment.

Economic life may be regarded also as a process of making and spending money. This business process is shared in by everyone who is getting a money income in any way or laying out money for any purpose. Its technique rises from the simple planning of family budgets, through "the exact science of making change,"[72] the arts of bargaining and sales-manship, bookkeeping and accountancy, to the large tasks of financial administration. Its technical experts are business enterprisers, chartered accountants, bankers, brokers, busi-ness agents of trade-unions, etc. Its special labor force in-cludes bookkeepers, cashiers, advertising clerks, and the like. Its material equipment is meager; but all capital be-longs here in the guise of pecuniary funds.

Making goods and making money are both objective pro-cesses: at some points quite distinct from or even opposed to each other; at most points running side by side, concerned with the same objects and supervised by the same men. We habitually interpret these two objective processes in terms of personal and social interest. These interpretations give us two other ways of looking at economics. To be specific:

Economic life may be regarded also as a process of making efforts and gaining satisfactions; or better, the activities of getting and using goods, of making and spending money, have a subjective aspect upon which attention may be focused. In this dim inner realm of consciousness it is difficult to make out the technique; there are no technical experts, no labor forces, no material appliances, and no capital in any sense, except by virtue of fanciful analogies.

[72] The phrase is borrowed from Thorstein Veblen's *Instinct of Workmanship*, New York, 1914.

THE BACKWARD ART OF SPENDING MONEY

Economic life may be regarded finally as the process by which a community seeks its material welfare. On this view every person is a contributor to, a burden upon, or a detractor from the commonweal. Such technical experts as there are must be sought among the people in public or private life who seek to promote social welfare by constructive thinking, by agitation, by philanthropic effort, or by doing their daily work with an eye to its serviceability to the community rather than its profit to themselves. Such accounting as is possible runs in terms of heightening or lowering the community's vitality. The concept of capital merges into the broader concept of resources—soil and climate, mines and forests, industrial equipment, public health, intelligence and general education, the sciences that confer control over nature, the sciences that aid in developing body and mind, and the sciences that bear upon social organization.

Now our interest in economics centers in its bearing upon social welfare in the present and the proximate future. As Professor Pigou and Mr. Hobson have shown,[73] it is feasible even now to set up a tentative criterion of economic welfare, and make investigations into the relations between various features of economic activity as now conducted and welfare as thus conceived. Such work may have as keen theoretical interest, as genuine scientific standing, as work that professes to maintain a serene indifference to the fate of humankind.[74]

[73] A. C. Pigou, *Wealth and Welfare*, London, 1912; J. A. Hobson, *Work and Wealth; a Human Valuation*, London and New York, 1914.

[74] The "socioethical" element in the work of many German economists, on the contrary, does not seem to me to be economic theory, or to have a scientific character—however excellent it may be in other respects. For these writers are concerned to inculcate their own ideals of social welfare, and to show by what specific changes they may be approximated more closely. They exercise the functions of preachers and statesmen rather than the functions of investigators. It is interesting to notice that the scientific sterility of this type of work has recently been the subject of numerous complaints in Germany itself.

But its successful prosecution on a scientific basis presupposes considerable knowledge of how economic processes actually work at present. While the understanding of these processes has been the chief aim of economic investigation for a century, no one fancies that this fundamental task has yet been adequately performed. In the interests of social welfare itself we need clearer insight into the industrial process of making goods, the business process of making money, and the way in which both sets of activities are related to each other and to the individual's inner life.

Into our conjoint attack upon these problems a clear recognition of the role played by money promises to bring more definite order and more effective cooperation. It helps us to formulate our tasks in ways that suggest definite things to try next. For example, to find the basis of economic rationality in the development of a social institution directs our attention away from that dark subjective realm, where so many economists have groped, to an objective realm, where behavior can be studied in the light of common day. It shows the high promise of that effort to frame an "institutional theory" of value which certain of our colleagues have begun.[75] It helps us to keep in mind the fateful distinction between those elements in human nature that are inherited and hence presumably unchanging, and those other elements that are acquired and hence presumably susceptible of modification—a distinction around which turns so much of our thinking concerning days to come. To realize that our theoretical inquiries cluster about the workings of an institution bridges the gulf that has existed to the detriment of both

[75] See the various papers of Professor C. H. Cooley, referred to in the latest of his series, "The Progress of Pecuniary Valuation," *Quarterly Journal of Economics*, Nov., 1915; and the discussion of "The Concept of Value" by Professors B. M. Anderson, Jr., and J. M. Clark in *Quarterly Journal of Economics*, Aug., 1915, especially Professor Clark's remarks on p. 715.

between economic theory and economic history. It establishes upon a common plane the work of those who seek to know how economic organization has developed in the past, of those who seek to know how it functions in the present, and of those who seek to know what changes it promises to undergo in the future. To differentiate sharply between making money and making goods brings into its proper prominence the problem of the relations between business management and industrial efficiency. It prepares us to face that subtler problem of the dissimilar habits of thought drilled into men by the daily work of the countinghouse and of the factory.[76] By going in for a realistic treatment of business life we may hope to arouse a keener interest and a wider cooperation in economic theory. For we shall be analyzing the actual processes with which men of affairs are concerned; we shall be treating problems that have meaning to legislators, administrators, and judges; we shall be stating our hypotheses in ways that facilitate their practical testing; and we shall be reaching conclusions that have a clearer bearing upon our hopes and fears for the future.

The current tendency to make money "the center around which economic science clusters," then, is a tendency to be fostered. For that course promises (1) to clarify economic theory by giving it a better framework, (2) to render economic theory more useful by directing attention to those actual processes with which all serious proposals for governmental regulation and social reorganization must deal, (3) to make economics more realistic and therefore more interesting intellectually as well as practically, and, finally, (4) to make economic theory more profound by orienting the economist for a fruitful study of his aspect of human behavior.

[76] See Thorstein Veblen "Industrial and Pecuniary Employments," *Publications of the American Economic Association*, Series 3, 1901 [reprinted in *The Place of Science in Modern Civilisation*, 1919].

10

BENTHAM'S FELICIFIC CALCULUS[1]

JEREMY BENTHAM has one service yet to perform for students of the social sciences. He can help them to work free from that misconception of human nature which he helped their predecessors to formulate. This role of emancipator he plays in the following paper.

In the social sciences we are suffering from a curious mental derangement. We have become aware that the orthodox doctrines of economics, politics, and law rest upon a tacit assumption that man's behavior is dominated by rational calculation. We have learned further that this is an assumption contrary to fact. But we find it hard to avoid the old mistake, not to speak of using the new knowledge. In our prefaces and introductory chapters some of us repudiate hedonism and profess volitional psychology or behaviorism. Others among us assert that economics at least can have no legitimate relations with psychology in any of its warring forms. In the body of our books, however, we relapse into reasonings about behavior that apply only to creatures essentially reasonable.

Bentham cannot help toward making the social sciences valid accounts of social behavior. But better than anyone else he can help us to see the absurdity of the intellectualist fallacy we abjure and practice. For Bentham has no rival as an exponent of the delusions that haunt the backs of our heads, and gain control over our speculations when we are

[1] Reprinted by permission from *Political Science Quarterly*, vol. XXXIII, pp. 161–183, June, 1918.

not thinking of psychology. The way to free ourselves from these delusions is to drag them into the light of full consciousness and make them face our other thoughts about behavior. We can perform this psychoanalytic operation upon our own minds best by assembling in orderly sequence the pertinent passages scattered through Bentham's writings.

I

Bentham dealt not only with many branches of jurisprudence,—criminal law, evidence, procedure, codification, international law, constitutional law,—but also with economics, psychology, penology, pedagogy, ethics, religion, logic, and metaphysics. Yet all his books read as one. They work out a single idea in diverse materials. They apply the sacred principle of utility whether the subject matter be colonies or Christianity, usury or the classification of the sciences, the crimes of judges or the reformation of criminals.

But utilitarianism as such is not the differentiating characteristic of Bentham. A line of English philosophers running back at least to Richard Cumberland in 1672 had expounded that doctrine before him. About these predecessors Bentham knew little; but "Utilitarianism had been so distinctly in the air for more than a generation before he published his *Principles of Morals and Legislation* that he could not possibly have failed very substantially to profit by the fact."[2] Indeed, Bentham was conscious of doctrinal indebtedness to Hume, Hartley, and Priestley in England, Helvetius in France, and Beccaria in Italy.[3] Among his own contemporaries utilitari-

---

[2] Ernest Albee, *A History of English Utilitarianism*, p. 167, London and New York, 1902.

[3] For Bentham's numerous references to these writers see the index of the *Works of Jeremy Bentham*, published under the superintendence of his executor, John Bowring, 11 vols., Edinburgh, 1843.

anism prevailed widely outside the circle of professed philosophers. The regnant theologian of the day, William Paley, was
as grim an exponent of the sacred principle as Bentham himself.[4] In the English controversy about the French Revoul-
tion all parties agreed tacitly or explicitly in accepting utility
as the final test of political institutions—Burke as well as
Godwin, the respectable Whig Mackintosh as well as the
agitator Tom Paine. And when Malthus, a clergyman, answered Godwin on the population issue he showed himself
as good a utilitarian as his atheistical opponent.[5] No one has
studied currents of English thinking in these times so thoroughly as Elie Halévy, and he remarks: "Towards the end
of the eighteenth century, it is not only the thinkers, it is
all the English who are speaking the language of utility."[6]
"It was plain," he adds in another volume, "that the doctrine of utility was becoming the universal philosophy in
England, and that the reformers must speak the language of
utility if they wished their opinions to be understood—let
alone accepted—by the public they were addressing."[7] This

[4] Compare Paley's famous definition of virtue: "the doing good to mankind, in
obedience to the will of God, and for the sake of everlasting happiness." *Principles
of Moral and Political Philosophy*, Book I, Chap. VII (21 st. ed., London, 1818, vol. I,
p. 42). Further see Paley's remarks upon population in Book VI, Chap. XI. "The
final view of all rational politics is, to produce the greatest quantity of happiness
in a given tract of country . . . The quantity of happiness in a given district,
although it is possible it may be increased, the number of inhabitants remaining the
same, is chiefly and most naturally affected by alteration of the numbers: . . .
consequently, the decay of population is the greatest evil that a state can suffer;
and the improvement of it the object which ought, in all countries, to be aimed at
in preference to every other political purpose whatsoever." Vol. II, pp. 345–347.

[5] See particularly Book IV, Chap. III, of the second and later editions of the
Essay on the Principle of Population. For example, "I do not see how it is possible
for any person, who acknowledges the principle of utility as the great foundation of
morals, to escape the conclusion that moral restraint, till we are in a condition to
support a family, is the strict line of duty." p. 504, 2d ed., 1803.

[6] *La Formation du radicalisme philosophique*, vol. I, p. 231, Paris, 1901.

[7] *Ibid.*, vol. II, pp. ii, iii.

view certainly accords with Bentham's own impression as recorded in his commonplace book: "The opinion of the world (I am speaking of the people in this country) is commonly in favor of the principle of utility."[8]

What did distinguish Bentham from other utilitarians, what made him the leader of a school, what keeps his work instructive to this day, was his effort to introduce exact method into all discussions of utility. He sought to make legislation, economics, ethics into genuine sciences. His contemporaries were content to talk about utility at large; Bentham insisted upon measuring particular utilities—or rather, the net pleasures on which utilities rest.

The ideal of science which men then held was represented by celestial mechanics; its hero was Newton, whose system had been popularized by Voltaire; its living exemplars were the great mathematicians of the French Academy. Bentham hoped to become "the Newton of the Moral World." Among the mass of his papers left to University College, Halévy has found this passage:

> The present work as well as any other work of mine that has been or will be published on the subject of legislation or any other branch of moral science is an attempt to extend the experimental method of reasoning from the physical branch to the moral. What Bacon was to the physical world, Helvetius was to the moral. The moral world has therefore had its Bacon, but its Newton is yet to come.[9]

II

Bentham's way of becoming the Newton of the moral world was to develop the "felicific calculus." There are

---

[8] *Works*, vol. X, p. 141. Written sometime between Bentham's thirty-third and thirty-seventh years.

[9] Halévy, *op. cit.*, vol. I, pp. 289, 290.

several expositions of this calculus in his *Works;* but the first and most famous version remains the best to quote.[10]

> Nature has placed mankind under the governance of two sovereign masters, *pain* and *pleasure*. It is for them alone to point out what we ought to do, as well as to determine what we shall do. On the one hand the standard of right and wrong, on the other chain of causes and effects, are fastened to their throne.

Hence, to know what men will do, to tell what they should do, or to value what they have done, one must be able to measure varying "lots" of pleasure or pain. How are such measurements to be made?

> To a person considered *by himself,* the value of a pleasure or pain considered *by itself,* will be greater or less, according to the four following circumstances: 1 Its *intensity.* 2 Its *duration.* 3 Its *certainty* . . . 4 Its *propinquity* . . . But when the value of any pleasure or pain is considered for the purpose of estimating the tendency of any *act* by which it is produced, there are two other circumstances to be taken into the account; these are, 5 Its *fecundity* . . . 6 Its *purity* . . . [When a community is considered, it is also necessary to take account of] 7 Its *extent;* that is, the number of persons to whom it *extends*.

The unit of intensity is the faintest sensation that can be distinguished to be pleasure or pain; the unit of duration is a moment of time. Degrees of intensity and duration are to be counted in whole numbers, as multiples of these units. Certainty and propinquity are reckoned as fractions whose

[10] "Introduction to the Principles of Morals and Legislation," *Works*, vol. I, pp. 1, 16. The exposition in "Logical Arrangements, or Instruments of Discovery and Invention employed by Jeremy Bentham," *Works*, vol. III, pp. 286, 287, is a convenient summary. Another brief statement is given in "A Table of the Springs of Action," *Works*, vol. I, p. 206. The value of the calculus is best stated in the curious "Codification Proposal," *Works*, vol. IV, pp. 540–542. A more discursive version appears in ch. iv, of *Deontology*, vol. I (not included in the *Works*). As will appear below, several of the most important points are best explained in passages which remained unpublished until Halévy's day—see the notes and appendices of his first and third volume.

limit is immediate actual sensation; from this limit the fractions fall away. In applying the calculus, one begins with the first distinguishable pleasure or pain which appears to be produced by an act, multiplies the number of its intensity units by the number of duration units, and then multiplies this product by the two fractions expressing certainty and proximity. To bring in fecundity, one computes by the preceding method the value of each pleasure or each pain which appears to be produced after the first one; the resulting values are to be added to the value previously obtained. To bring in purity, one computes the values of all pains that attend a given series of pleasures, or of pleasures that attend a given series of pains; these values are to be subtracted from the preceding sums. That is, pleasure is a positive, pain a negative, quantity. Since the unit of extent is an individual, one completes the computation by multiplying the net resultant pain or pleasure ascertained as above by the number of individuals affected. Usually, however, this last step is more complicated: not all the people affected are affected in the same way. In that case one does not multiply by the number of individuals, but makes a separate computation for each individual and then strikes the algebraic sum of the resultants.[11]

III

If these technical directions for measuring "lots" of pleasure and pain be taken seriously, the felicific calculus is a complicated affair at best. In addition, it is beset by subtler and graver difficulties, some that Bentham saw clearly, others that he barely glimpsed. Unfortunately the disciples who pieced his manuscripts together into books did not think fit to publish his sharpest bits of insight into the haze, so that

[11] "Introduction to the Principles of Morals and Legislation," *Works*, vol. I, p. 16, and extracts from Bentham's mss. published by Halévy, *op. cit.*, vol. I, p. 398 *et seq.*

later writers had to rediscover much that their master had descried. The type of social science on which Bentham worked might have been completed and superseded much sooner than it was had his difficulties been made known in his own lifetime.

That all comparisons of the feelings of different men are questionable Bentham was perfectly aware. In his *Principles of Morals and Legislation*, indeed, he enlarged upon this topic by discussing thirty-two "circumstances influencing sensibility" to pleasure and pain.[12] Since these thirty-two circumstances exist in an indefinite number of combinations, it would seem that the felicific calculus can scarcely be applied except individual by individual—a serious limitation. As long as he was thinking only of the problem of punishments Bentham accepted this conclusion. The legislator and the judge ought each to have before him a list of the several circumstances by which sensibility may be influenced: the legislator ought to consider those circumstances which apply uniformly to whole classes, for example, insanity, sex, rank, climate, and religious profession; the judge ought to consider the circumstances that apply in varying degrees to each individual, for example, health, strength, habitual occupation, pecuniary circumstances, etc.[13]

But as Bentham's problems widened he concluded that his calculus must apply to men at large, if it was to yield scientific generalizations, although he still thought that this application rested upon an assumption contrary to fact. One manuscript found by Halévy runs:

[12] Ch. vi. The list includes health, strength, firmness of mind, habitual occupations, pecuniary circumstances, sex, age, rank, education, climate, lineage, government, religious profession, etc.

[13] *Works*, vol. I, pp. 31, 32. Compare the discussion of this theme in Bentham's essay "Of the Influence of Time and Place in Matters of Legislation," *Works*, vol. I, pp. 172, 173, 180, 181.

'Tis in vain to talk of adding quantities which after the addition will continue distinct as they were before, one man's happiness will never be another man's happiness: a gain to one man is no gain to another: you might as well pretend to add 20 apples to 20 pears . . . This addibility of the happiness of different subjects, however when considered rigorously it may appear fictitious, is a postulatum without the allowance of which all political reasoning is at a stand: nor is it more fictitious than that of the equality of chances to reality, on which that whole branch of the Mathematics which is called the doctrine of chances is established.[14]

Of course, this postulate of the "addibility" of the happiness of different men tacitly assumes that numerical values can be set on the feelings of each individual. But is that really true? Indeed, can any individual put a definite figure upon his own pleasures and pains, let alone compare them with the pleasures and pains of other men? The more Bentham dwelt upon this aspect of his calculus, the more difficulties he developed and the more assumptions he found necessary to his type of social science.

One fundamental doubt he sometimes overlooked, and sometimes admitted. Intensity is the first "element" in which feelings differ. Can any man count the intensity units in any one of his pleasures or pains, as he counts the duration units? Bentham usually assumes that he can, without telling how.

. . . the degree of intensity possessed by that pleasure which is the faintest of any that can be distinguished to be pleasure, may be represented by unity. Such a degree of intensity is in every day's experience: according as any pleasures are perceived to be more and more intense, they may be represented by higher and higher numbers.[15]

In his *Codification Proposal*, however, Bentham frankly grants that intensity is not "susceptible of measurement."[16]

[14] Halévy, *op. cit.*, vol. III, p. 481.
[15] *Ibid.*, vol. I, p. 398.
[16] *Works*, vol. IV, p. 542.

With a closely related problem, Bentham wrestled frequently: can a man make quantitative comparisons among his qualitatively unlike pleasures or pains?

The difficulty here was aggravated by one of Bentham's favorite ideas. He held that most of our feelings are complexes made up of simple elements. One of the tasks that he essayed was to enumerate exhaustively the "simple" pleasures and the "simple" pains, which, like the elements in chemistry, cannot be decomposed themselves, but which can combine with one another in the most diverse ways. In his *Principles of Morals and Legislation* he listed fourteen simple pleasures (counting nine alleged pleasures of the senses as one) and twelve simple pains.[17] In his *Table of the Springs of Action* he, or his editor, James Mill, modified the lists somewhat, but kept the general idea that in the last analysis our pleasures and pains are compounded of qualitatively unlike elements.[18] Now, if that be literally true, how can one apply the felicific calculus even in the case of a single individual? Some common denominator seems needed for the two dozen or more elements; but if there exists a common denominator, are not the elements themselves homogeneous?

When he wrote his *Principles of Morals and Legislation* Bentham did not discuss, perhaps did not think of these questions. Despite all the trouble he took to describe "the several sorts of pains and pleasures," he referred to pain and pleasure as "names of homogeneous real entities."[19] Throughout the book he assumed tacitly not only that different pains and different pleasures, but also that pains and pleasures are commensurable. Yet the one passage most to the present purpose shows that his method of comparing quantities was strictly limited. He says:

[17] *Works*, vol. I, pp. 17–21.
[18] *Ibid.*, pp. 195–219.
[19] *Ibid.*, p. 22, footnote.

The only certain and universal means of making two lots of punishment perfectly commensurable, is by making the lesser an ingredient in the composition of the greater. This may be done in either of two ways. 1. By adding to the lesser punishment another quantity of punishment of the same kind. 2. By adding to it another quantity of a different kind.[20]

Indeed, in this whole treatise Bentham relies upon classification, and not upon calculation.[21] He splits everything he discusses—pleasures, pains, motives, dispositions, offenses, "cases unmeet for punishment," etc.—into kinds, limits his quantitative comparisons to relations of greater and less, and makes even these comparisons chiefly among phenomena belonging to the same kind. He does, indeed, bid the authorities do things which imply bolder comparisons, as when he rules that "the value of the punishment must not be less in any case than . . . the profit of the offense;"[22] but he does not make such comparisons himself.

And yet Bentham did find a way of reducing qualitatively unlike pleasures and pains to a common denominator, and so of putting figures on felicity. There are traces of this method in his published works,[23] but much the best exposition remained in manuscript until Halévy's day. The following passages have peculiar interest as anticipations of Edgeworth's use of "indifference" and more definitely of Marshall's "money measures."

If of two pleasures a man, knowing what they are, would as lief enjoy the one as the other, they must be reputed equal. . . . If of two pains a man had as lief escape the one as the other, such two pains must be reputed equal. If of two sensations, a pain and a pleasure, a man had as lief enjoy the pleasure and suffer the pain, as not enjoy the first and not suffer the

[20] *Works*, vol. I, p. 92.

[21] Compare Halévy, *op. cit.*, vol. I, pp. 47, 48.

[22] *Works*, vol. I, p. 87.

[23] For example, "Codification Proposal," *Works*, vol. IV, pp. 540–542; *Deontology*, vol. I, pp. 76, 131, 192.

latter, such pleasure and pain must be reputed *equal*, or, as we may say in this case, *equivalent.*

If then between two pleasures the one produced by the possession of money, the other not, a man had as lief enjoy the one as the other, such pleasures are to be reputed equal. But the pleasure produced by the possession of money, is *as* the quantity of money that produces it: money is therefore the measure of this pleasure. But the other pleasure is equal to this; the other pleasure therefore is as the money that produces this; therefore money is also the measure of that other pleasure. It is the same between pain and pain; as also between pain and pleasure.

. . . If then, speaking of the respective quantities of various pains and pleasures and agreeing in the same propositions concerning them, we would annex the same ideas to those propositions, that is, if we would understand one another, we must make use of some common measure. The only common measure the nature of things affords is money. . . .

I beg a truce here of our man of sentiment and feeling while from necessity, and it is only from necessity, I speak and prompt mankind to speak a mercenary language. . . . Money is the instrument for measuring the quantity of pain or pleasure. Those who are not satisfied with the accuracy of this instrument must find out some other that shall be more accurate, or bid adieu to Politics and Morals.[24]

That Bentham did not follow up this promising lead was due to a further difficulty. Every time he began thinking about money measures of feeling he was checked by the diminishing utility of wealth. The "quantity of happiness produced by a particle of wealth (each particle being of the same magnitude) will be less and less at every particle; the second will produce less than the first, the third than the second, and so on."[25] " . . . for by high dozes of the exciting matter applied to the organ, its sensibility is in a manner worn out."[26] Consider the monarch with a million a year and the laborer with twenty pounds:

[24] Halévy, *op. cit.*, vol. I, pp. 410, 412, 414.
[25] "Pannomial Fragments," *Works*, vol. III, p. 229.
[26] "Constitutional Code," *Works*, vol. IX, p. 15.

> The quantity of pleasure in the breast of the monarch will naturally be greater than the quantity in the breast of the laborer: . . . But . . . by how many times greater? Fifty thousand times? This is assuredly more than any man would take upon himself to say. A thousand times, then?— a hundred?—ten times?—five times?—twice?—which of all these shall be the number? . . . For the monarch's, taking all purposes together, *five times* the labourer's seems a very large, not to say an excessive allowance: even *twice*, a liberal one.[27]

Quite apart from differences in the sensibility of different men to pleasure, then, equal sums of money can by no means be supposed to represent equal quantities of feeling.

Once, at least, Bentham thought he had found a solution of this difficulty. In the manuscript last quoted he argues:

> Money being the current instrument of pleasure, it is plain by uncontrovertible experience that the quantity of actual pleasure follows in every instance in some proportion or other the quantity of money. As to the law of that proportion nothing can be more indeterminate. . . . For all this it is true enough for practice with respect to such proportions as ordinarily occur (var.: small quantities), that *caeteris paribus* the proportion between pleasure and pleasure is the same as that between sum and sum. So much is strictly true that the ratios between the two pairs of quantities are nearer to that of equality than to any other ratio that can be assigned. Men will therefore stand a better chance of being right by supposing them equal than by supposing them to be any otherwise than equal. . . .
>
> Speaking then in general, we may therefore truly say, that in small quantities the pleasures produced by two sums are *as* the sums producing them.[28]

This passage lies on the frontier of Bentham's realm of thought. It shows that the idea of dealing with small increments of feeling occurred to him, as a method of avoiding the embarrassment caused by diminishing utility and still using

[27] "Codification Proposal," *Works*, vol. IV, p. 541.
[28] Halévy, *op. cit.*, vol. I, pp. 406, 408, 410.

money as a common denominator. But all this was rather dim; the idea did not develop vigorously in his mind. He missed, indeed, two notions that his disciples were to exploit later on: Bernoulli's suggestion that, after bare subsistence is provided, a man's pleasure increases by equal amounts with each equal successive percentage added to his income; and the plan of concentrating attention upon the increments of pleasure or pain at the margin.

The net resultant of all these reflections upon the felicific calculus collected from Bentham's books and papers might be put thus: (1) The intensity of feelings cannot be measured at all; (2) even in the case of a single subject, qualitatively unlike feelings cannot be compared except indirectly through their pecuniary equivalents; (3) the assumption that equal sums of money represent equal sums of pleasure is unsafe except in the case of small quantities; (4) all attempts to compare the feelings of different men involve an assumption contrary to fact. That is a critic's version of admissions wrung from Bentham's text; a disciple's version of his master's triumphs might run: (1) The felicific calculus attains a tolerable degree of precision since all the dimensions of feeling save one can be measured;[29] (2) the calculus can handle the most dissimilar feelings by expressing them in terms of their monetary equivalents; (3) in the cases which are important by virtue of their frequency, the pleasures produced by two sums of money are as the sums producing them; (4) taken by and large for scientific purposes men are comparable in feeling as in other respects. Heat these two versions in the fire of controversy and one has the substantial content of much polemic since Bentham's day.

[29] This is substantially Bentham's own language. "Codification Proposal," *Works*, vol. IV, p. 542.

THE BACKWARD ART OF SPENDING MONEY

IV

The quintessence of Bentham's social science is the double
role played by the felicific calculus. On the one hand, this
calculus shows how the legislator, judge, and moralist ought
to proceed in valuing conduct; on the other hand, it shows
how all men do proceed in guiding conduct. That is, Bentham
blends utilitarian ethics with a definite theory of functional
psychology. The ethical system has been more discussed, but
the psychological notions are more important to students of
the social sciences.

1. Human nature is hedonistic. It is for pain and pleasure
alone "to determine what we shall do . . . They govern us
in all we do, in all we say, in all we think." These words from
the first paragraph of *Principles of Morals and Legislation*
put simply the leading idea. "Nothing—" Bentham remarks
in *A Table of the Springs of Action*—"nothing but the expectation of the eventual enjoyment of pleasure in some shape,
or of exemption from pain in some shape, can operate in the
character of a *motive*."[30]

The psychological processes by which pleasure incites to
action are more fully described in later passages. "Every
operation of the mind, and thence every operation of the
body," says the *Essay on Logic*, "is the result of an exercise
of the will, or volitional faculty."[31] The relations between
will and intellect are explained by the *Table of the Springs
of Action:*

To the *will* it is that the idea of a pleasure or an exemption [from pain]
applies itself in the *first* instance; in *that* stage its effect, if not conclusive,
is *velleity:* by velleity, reference is made to the *understanding*, viz. 1. For
striking a *balance* between the *value* of this *good*, and that of the *pain* or
loss, if any, which present themselves as eventually about to stand asso-

[30] *Works*, vol. I, p. 215.
[31] *Ibid.*, vol. VIII, p. 279.

[190]

ciated with it: 2. Then, if the balance appear to be in its favor for the choice of *means:* thereupon, if *action* be the result, *velleity* is perfected into *volition,* of which the correspondent *action* is the immediate consequence. For the process that has place, this description may serve alike in *all* cases: *time* occupied by it may be of any length; from a minute fraction of *a second,* as in ordinary cases, to any number of years.[32]

2. Human nature is rational. There is nothing in the felicific calculus "but what the practice of mankind, wheresoever they have a clear view of their own interest, is perfectly conformable to." This passage from Chapter IV of the *Principles*[33] is supported in Chapter XVI by an answer to the objection that "passion does not calculate." But, says Bentham:

When matters of such importance as pain and pleasure are at stake, and these in the highest degree (the only matters, in short, that can be of importance) who is there that does not calculate? Men calculate, some with less exactness, indeed, some with more: but all men calculate. I would not say, that even a madman does not calculate. Passion calculates, more or less, in every man: in different men, according to the warmth or coolness of their dispositions: according to the firmness or irritability of their minds: according to the nature of the motives by which they are acted upon. Happily, of all passions, that is the most given to calculation, from the excesses of which, by reason of its strength, constancy, and universality, society has most to apprehend: I mean that which corresponds to the motive of pecuniary interest.[34]

3. Human nature is essentially passive. Men do not have propensities to act, but are pushed and pulled about by the pleasure-pain forces of their environments.

On every occasion, *conduct*—the *course* taken by a man's conduct—is at the absolute command of—is the never failing result of—the *motives,*—

[32] *Ibid.,* vol. I, p. 209.
[33] *Ibid.,* vol. I, p. 17.
[34] *Works,* vol. I, pp. 90, 91. Compare the similar passage in "Principles of Penal Law," *Works,* vol. I, p. 402.

and thence, in so far as the corresponding interests are perceived and under-stood, of the corresponding *interests*,—to the action of which, his mind—his will—has, on that same occasion, stood exposed.[35]

Of course, this view of human nature as a passive element in the situation greatly simplifies the task of social science. Whenever one can make out what it is to men's interest to do, one can deduce what they will do. The only uncertainty arises from the actor's imperfect comprehension of his interest, of which more in a moment.

Human nature is also passive in the sense that men are averse to work. In his *Table of the Springs of Action*, Bentham includes both pleasures and pains of the palate, of sex, of wealth, of amity, of reputation, and so on through eleven heads until he comes to labor—under that head he recognizes nothing but pains. If any pleasure in activity is to be found in this table we must read it into the pleasures of power or of curiosity.[36] Enlarging upon this point, Bentham says, "*Aversion*—not *desire*—is the emotion—the only emotion—which *labor*, taken by itself, is qualified to produce: of any such emotion as *love* or *desire*, *ease*, which is the *negative* or *absence* of labor—*ease*, not *labor*—is the object."[37]

4. Since men ought to follow the course which will secure them the greatest balance of pleasure, and since they do follow that course so far as they understand their own in-

---

[35] "A Table of the Springs of Action," *Works*, vol. I, p. 218.

[36] This omission of pleasure in labor is clearly no oversight; indeed, it must represent a deliberate change of opinion; for in his "Introduction to the Principles of Morals and Legislation" Bentham had included "The pleasures of skill, as exercised upon particular objects." *Works*, vol. I, p. 18.

[37] *Works*, vol. I, p. 214. In "Chrestomathia" Bentham discusses the "pain of ennui." "Ennui is the state of uneasiness, felt by him whose mind unoccupied, but without reproach, is on the look out for pleasure . . . and beholds at the time no source which promises to afford it . . . the pain of ennui soon succeeds to the pleasure of repose." *Works*, vol. VIII, p. 8.

terests, the only defects in human nature must be defects of understanding.

> *Indigenous* intellectual weakness—*adoptive* intellectual weakness—or, in one word, *prejudice*—*sinister interest* (understand self-conscious sinister interest)—lastly, *interest-begotten* (though not self-conscious) *prejudice*—by one or other of these denominations, may be designated (it is believed) the cause of whatever is on any occasion amiss, in the opinions or conduct of mankind.[38]

There is no such thing as a bad motive—or a disinterested action—but men may blunder.

Similarly, whatever lack of uniformity in human nature we find must be due to differences in men's intellectual machinery for calculating pleasures and pains. Such is the sole reason for the gulf that separates civilized men from savages. In "the variety and extent of the ideas with which they have been impressed . . . may be seen the only cause of whatsoever difference there is between the mind of a well educated youth under the existing systems of education, and the mind of the Esquimaux, or the New Zealand savage at the same age."[39] Men do vary in sensibility, as we have seen; but the thirty-two "circumstances influencing sensibility"[40] act by associating the motor ideas of pleasure and pain with the ideas of different objects or actions. So Bentham asserts, "Legislators who, having freed themselves from the shackles of authority, have learnt to soar above the mists of prejudice, know as well how to make laws for one country as for another." They must master the peculiar local circumstances affecting sensibility—that is all.[41] In the *Codification Proposal addressed by Jeremy Bentham to all Nations professing Liberal*

[38] "Springs of Action," *Works*, vol. I, p. 217.
[39] "Chrestomathia," *Works*, vol. VIII, p. 11.
[40] "Introduction to the Principles of Morals and Legislation," *Works*, vol. I, p. 22.
[41] "Influence of Time and Place in Matters of Legislation," *Works*, vol. I, pp. 180, 181.

Opinions he even argues that a foreigner is in a better position to draft a general code of laws than a native.[42]

The understanding, it will be noted, is conceived as a matter of associations among ideas. As hedonism explains the functioning of mind, so the "association principle" explains the structure of mind. Bentham derived this principle from Hartley, and left its working out to James Mill.[43]

5. Since whatever is amiss in the opinions or conduct of mankind is due to "intellectual weakness, indigenous or adoptive," education must be the one great agency of reform. And since the understanding is made up of associations among ideas, the forming and strengthening of proper associations must be the one great aim of education.

In the possibility of establishing almost any desired associations in a child's mind, and even in the possibility of dissolving old and forming new associations in an adult mind, Bentham had considerable faith. "As respects pleasures, the mind of man possesses a happy flexibility. One source of amusement being cut off, it endeavors to open up another, and always succeeds: a new habit is easily formed."[44] Hence, Bentham's interest in the educational experiments of the day, hence the time he spent in planning a "chrestomathic school . . . for the use of the middling and higher ranks in life"; hence, his financial support of Robert Owen's scheme of industrial education at New Lanark; hence, his claims for the Panopticon Penitentiary as "a mill for grinding rogues honest, and idle men industrious."[45]

---

[42] *Works*, vol. IV, pp. 561–563.

[43] *Works*, vol. X, p. 561; Mill's *Analysis of the Phenomena of the Human Mind* appeared in 1829, three years before Bentham's death.

[44] "Principles of Penal Law," *Works*, vol. I, p. 436.

[45] See "Chrestomathia," *Works*, vol. VIII, and the following passages in Bowring's life of Bentham—*Works*, vol. X, pp. 476, 477, 226.

Bentham once suggested—not more than half in jest—that "metaphysics"

BENTHAM'S FELICIFIC CALCULUS

In a larger sense, Bentham conceived all his work on law as part of an educational program. "The influence of government," says one of Dumont's treatises, "touches almost everything, or rather includes everything, except temperament, race, and climate. . . . The manner of directing education, of arranging employments, rewards, and punishments determines the physical and moral qualities of a people."[46] A sharper point and a graver meaning were given to this task by Bentham's slow discovery that men do not all spontaneously desire "the greatest happiness of the greatest number."[47] Thereafter the "self-preference principle" was a regular component of human nature as Bentham saw it, and the great task of statecraft was to contrive cunning devices by which necessarily selfish individuals must serve the pleasure of others to get pleasure for themselves. While Adam Smith and his disciples assumed that a natural identity

---

might be made an experimental science by applying his "inspection-house principle" to the training of children. That plan would enable the instructor to determine what sensible objects, conversation, books should have part in forming the child's mind. Then, "The genealogy of each observable idea might be traced through all its degrees with the utmost nicety: the parent stocks being all known and numbered." "Panopticon," *Works*, vol. IV, p. 65.

Mr. C. E. Ayres has just propounded a modern version of this suggestion. Epistemology, he argues, is becoming a science. "Whence comes the mental content of every man's mind, and what are the limitations that are imposed upon that mental content by its sources? The solution of this problem lies along the path of the investigation of the social sources of all mental content and of the limitations which are imposed upon the human mind by the fact that it is always the product of some particular environment and so must always receive an environmental bias. This investigation is the business of social psychology." "The Epistemological Significance of Social Psychology," *Journal of Philosophy, Psychology and Scientific Methods*, vol. XV, p. 43, Jan. 17, 1918.

[46] Quoted by Halévy, *op. cit.*, vol. I, p. 139.

[47] In his earlier period Bentham had tacitly assumed that the authorities would spontaneously adopt any plan that promised to increase social happiness. It took him sixty years to learn that the authorities were seeking their own happiness, not that of the nation. See his own account of how his eyes were opened, *Works*, vol. X, pp. 79, 80 and vol. I, pp. 240–259.

of interests bound men together in economic affairs, Bentham thought it necessary to establish an artificial identity of interests in law and politics.[48] The ruler himself was to be kept in tutelage his whole life long.

But robust as was Bentham's faith in the potency of schools and government to improve man's character and lot, it was modest in comparison with the expectations cherished by certain among his masters and his contemporaries. Helvetius and Priestley, Condorcet, William Godwin, and Robert Owen believed in the "perfectibility" of man. Bentham put his views in opposition to Priestley's:

Perfect happiness belongs to the imaginary regions of philosophy, and must be classed with the universal elixir and the philosopher's stone. In the age of greatest perfection, fire will burn, tempests will rage, man will be subject to infirmity, to accidents, and to death. It may be possible to diminish the influence of, but not to destroy, the sad and mischievous passions. The unequal gifts of nature and of fortune will always create jealousies: there will always be opposition of interests; and, consequently, rivalries and hatred. Pleasures will be purchased by pains; enjoyments by privations. Painful labor, daily subjection, a condition nearly allied to indigence, will always be the lot of numbers. Among the higher as well as the lower classes, there will be desires which cannot be satisfied; inclinations which must be subdued: reciprocal security can only be established by the forcible renunciation by each one, of every thing which might wound the legitimate rights of others.[49]

V

Social science nowadays aims to give an intelligible account of social processes, to promote the understanding of social facts. While we may value such "science" mainly for

[48] The contrast between these two views of the relations between society and the individual is one of the chief points developed fully by Halévy in the course of his three volumes. See particularly his first and last chapters.

[49] "Of the Influence of Time and Place in Matters of Legislation," *Works*, vol. I, pp. 193, 194.

its practical serviceability, we profess to distinguish sharply between our explanations of what is and our schemes of what ought to be.

In Bentham's world, on the contrary, the felicific calculus yields a social science that is both an account of what is and an account of what ought to be. For, on the one hand, "the chain of causes and effects" and, on the other hand, "the standard of right and wrong" are fastened to the throne of our two sovereign masters—whose books the felicific calculus keeps.[50] Indeed, of the two aspects of the science the more reliable, and therefore the more scientific, is the account of what ought to be. The account of what is holds only in so far as men understand their own interests—that is, associate the ideas of pleasure and pain with the ideas of the proper objects and acts. Really to account for what is, on Bentham's basis, one would have either to observe with elaborate care what men do, or to work out their defects of understanding and deduce the consequences for conduct. Needless to say, Bentham spent little time on such procedures.

Bentham plumed himself, indeed, upon assigning priority to normative science—in strict accordance with his philosophy. He writes:

When I came out with the principle of utility, it was in the *Fragment*, I took it from Hume's *Essays*, Hume was in all his glory, the phrase was consequently familiar to every body. The difference between Hume and me is this: the use he made of it, was—to account for that which *is*, I to show what *ought to be*.[51]

[50] "Introduction to the Principles of Morals and Legislation," *Works*, vol. I, p. 1.
[51] Letter to Dumont, Sept. 6, 1822, in Halévy, *op. cit.*, vol. I, p. 282. Compare the "History of the Greatest-happiness Principle" given in *Deontology*, vol I, pp. 293–294.
Like many a modern, Bentham held that the value of science consists in its subserviency to art—though he admits that in so far as science pleases it is an end in

Practical conclusions regarding what ought to be done, then, were the chief product of Bentham's science. That, indeed, was what made Bentham the leader of the utilitarians, or philosophical radicals, who were first and foremost reformers. But it must be admitted that Bentham's attitude upon the crucial problem of reform was not derived strictly from his science. The felicific calculus turned out to be a singularly versatile instrument. Men could make it prove what they liked by choosing certain assumptions concerning the relative importance of various imponderable factors, or concerning the relative sensitiveness to pleasure of different classes of people. Some assumptions have to be made on these heads before the argument can proceed far, and the assumptions which seem natural to the utility theorist are those which yield the conclusions in which he happens to believe on other than scientific grounds. "All history proves" anything that a writer has at heart. The felicific calculus is equally obliging.

Now, Bentham and his school believed firmly in the institution of private property. They might have proved that property, despite its resulting inequalities of wealth, is necessary to produce the greatest amount of happiness if they had been willing to assume that the propertied classes are more sensitive to pleasure than the poor. For, if some men are better pleasure machines than others, then to maximize happiness more wealth—the most important raw material of pleasure—should be fed to the better machines than to the poorer ones. Such is the course Professor Edgeworth was

---

itself. ("Chrestomathia," *Works*, vol. VIII, p. 27; "Manual of Political Economy," *Works*, vol. III, p. 33.) That is as true of his science of what ought to be as of his science of what is. The peculiarity of his position from the modern viewpoint is in conceiving his account of what ought to be as itself a science—not in taking a pragmatic view of science.

to take many years later.[52] Bentham did not like that course: to make social science possible, he felt obliged to assume that men are substantially alike in their capacity for turning commodities into pleasure. But he had another shift, just as effective, just as little needing proof to those who agreed with him and just as unconvincing to a doubter.

Every code of laws that is to promote the greatest happiness, he argues, must do so by promoting "the four most comprehensive particular and subordinate *ends*, viz. *subsistence, abundance, security,* and *equality.*"[53] "Equality is not itself, as security, subsistence, and abundance are, an immediate instrument of felicity."[54] It gets its claim upon us from the diminishing utility of wealth—other things being the same, a given quantity of wealth will produce more pleasure if distributed equally among a given population than if distributed unequally. But other things are not the same. Unless people had security in the possession of their wealth, they would not produce it, and so there would be nothing to distribute—equally or otherwise. Thus from the viewpoint of maximum happiness security is more important than equality. And granted security in enjoying the fruits of labor a certain inequality results. The conclusion is "that, so far as is consistent with security, the nearer to equality the distribution is, which the law makes of the matter of property among the members of the community, the greater is the happiness of the greatest number."[55]

Equality . . . finds . . . in security and subsistence, rivals and antagonists, of which the claims are of a superior order, and to which, on pain of universal destruction, in which itself will be involved, it must be obliged

[52] See his *Mathematical Psychics*, especially pp. 77–82.
[53] "Codification Proposal," *Works*, vol. IV, p. 561.
[54] "Constitutional Code," *Works*, vol. IX, p. 14.
[55] *Ibid.*, p. 18.

to yield. In a word, it is not equality itself, but only a tendency towards equality, after all the others are provided for, that, on the part of the ruling and other members of the community, is the proper object of endeavor.[56]

VI

We have seen that Bentham relied upon the felicific calculus to make himself the Newton of the moral world—the felicific calculus, which was to treat the forces pain and pleasure as Newton's laws treated gravitation. But he did not really frame a quantitative science of the Newtonian type. His calculus, indeed, bore little resemblance to the mathematical conceptions by which in his own day chemistry and crystallography were being placed upon a secure foundation. No man could apply Bentham's calculus in sober earnest, because no man could tell how many intensity units were included in any one of his pleasures—to go no further. And, indeed, Bentham did not use the calculus as an instrument of calculation; he used it as a basis of classification. It pointed out to him what elements should be considered in a given situation, and among these elements *seriatim* he was often able to make comparisons in terms of greater and less— comparisons that few men would challenge, though Bentham might not be able to prove them against a skeptic. So his science as he elaborated it turned out to be much more like the systematic botany than like the celestial mechanics of his day. Bentham himself was a classifier rather than a calculator; he came nearer being the Linnaeus than the Newton of the moral world.[57]

[56] "Logical Arrangements," *Works*, vol. III, p. 294. For still other expositions than the three cited above, see "Pannomial Fragments," *Works*, vol. III, pp. 228–230; "Leading Principles of a Constitutional Code for Any State," *Works*, vol. II, pp. 271–272.

[57] Compare Bentham's own reference to Linnaeus in *Deontology*, vol. I, p. 202; his discussion of his own "natural method" of classification by bipartition— including the reference to botany in a footnote in "Introduction to the Principles

BENTHAM'S FELICIFIC CALCULUS

Far as he fell short of his dream, Bentham's line of attack on social problems represented a marked advance upon the type of discussion common in his day—or in ours. Though he could not literally work out the value of any "lot" of pain or pleasure, he had a systematic plan for canvassing the probable effects of rival institutions upon the happiness of populations. By pinning debates conducted in "vague generalities" down to fairly definite issues he was often able to find a convincing solution for practical problems. The defects of the rival method if not the merits of his own stand sharply outlined in what Bentham says about the dispute between England and her American colonies:

I . . . placed the question . . . on the ground of the greatest happiness of the greatest number, meaning always in both countries taken together. With me it was a matter of calculation: pains and pleasures, the elements of it. . . . No party had any stomach for calculation: none, perhaps, would have known very well how to go about it, if they had. The battle was fought by assertion. *Right* was the weapon employed on both sides. "We have a *right* to be as we now choose to be," said people on the American side. "We have a right to continue to make you what we choose you should be," said rulers on the English side. "We have a right to legislate over them, but we have no *right* to tax them," said Lord Camden, by way of settling the matter.[58]

What he claimed for his results in his *Codification Proposal* may well be granted:

How far short soever this degree of precision may be, of the conceivable point of perfection . . . at any rate, in every rational and candid eye, unspeakable will be the advantage it will have, over every form

---

of Morals and Legislation," *Works*, vol. I, p. 139; and certain other references to the merits of classification in botany, *Works*, vol. VI, p. 442; vol. VIII, pp. 121–126, 254, 255.

[58] Historical Preface to the 2d ed. of "A Fragment on Government," *Works*, vol. I, p. 248.

of argumentation, in which every idea is afloat, no degree of precision being ever attained, because none is ever so much as aimed at.[59]

Probably every reader of this article will share the impression that Bentham's conception of human behavior is artificial to an extreme degree. That impression is not due, I think, to any trick in my exposition. Nor is it due to any quirk in Bentham's mind. He can hardly be charged with doing violence to the common-sense notions of his day, unless it be violence to develop and accept their full consequences. The real reason why we find the conception artificial is that we have another stock of ideas about behavior with which Bentham's ideas are incompatible. Our business is to be consistent as he was, and to use the set of ideas in which we believe as fully as he used the set in which he believed. Then if our ideas prove wrong, as is not unlikely, we may at least give later comers the same kind of help that Bentham now gives us.

[59] *Works*, vol. IV, p. 542.

POSTULATES AND PRECONCEPTIONS OF RICARDIAN ECONOMICS[1]

WHEN English political economy became sophisticated, in the generation following Ricardo, the practice began of asking what conditions the orthodox theories of value and distribution took for granted. The subtler critics of still later years have looked less for logical postulates than for preconceptions—convictions that shape the general trend of a man's thinking without being themselves submitted to critical scrutiny.[2]

The search for postulates was a lead that yielded large returns at the beginning, but soon ran out. It suffers two limitations. First, one can no more list all the postulates of an economic doctrine than one can list all the causes of a physical phenomenon. Where to stop in the one case as in the other is a matter of the particular purpose in hand, and the purposes for which we discuss economic doctrines are varied, indeed. Ricardo, for example, was satisfied by saying that the payment of rent presupposes (1) that land is limited in quantity and variable in quality, (2) that the most fertile land is comparatively scarce.[3] Malthus insisted on going

---

[1] Reprinted by permission of Open Court Publishing Co., Chicago, from *Essays in Philosophy*, edited by T. V. Smith and W. J. Wright, pp. 27–60, 1929.

[2] The best examples of such inquiries are Walter Bagehot's "Postulates of English Political Economy," 1876; reprinted in *Economic Studies*, edited by R. H. Hutton, London, 1879; and Thorstein Veblen's "Preconceptions of Economic Science," 1899 and 1900; reprinted in *The Place of Science in Modern Civilisation*, 1919.

[3] *Principles of Political Economy* edited by E. C. K. Gonner, pp. 47, 397, London, 1891; *Letters of Ricardo to Malthus*, ed. by James Bonar, p. 127, London, 1887.

further back; rent could not be paid unless land yielded sustenance exceeding that necessary to maintain the cultivators.[4] To Senior the important postulate was that agriculture "obeys the law of diminishing returns";[5] while to Richard Jones the Ricardian theory presupposes a definite set of legal and social institutions found only in two corners of the earth.[6] Bagehot suggested incidentally and Marx brought out explicitly the fact that "the state of the productivity of labor . . . is as much an element in the so-called natural fertility of the soil as its chemical composition."[7] Quite clearly occasion might arise for stressing any one of these alleged postulates; quite clearly the list might be elaborated indefinitely;[8] and quite clearly such elaboration would be of little service without some guiding end in view.

The second difficulty in listing postulates is that the logical implications of an economic doctrine depend upon the strictness with which it is taken, and the degree of precision attributed to these doctrines varies with the doctrine, the expositor, and his purpose, not to say his mood. For illustration we may take the celebrated Ricardian proposition: "A tax on wages is wholly a tax on profits."[9] To make that

[4] He also postulated, "That quality peculiar to the necessaries of life of being able . . . to raise up a number of demanders in proportion to the quantity of necessaries produced." In answer Ricardo pointed out that farmers are not wont to produce the necessaries in advance of demand, and wait for this supply to raise up demanders. See *The Nature and Progress of Rent*, p. 8, London, 1815 (p. 15 of Hollander's reprint, Baltimore, 1903); Ricardo's *Principles*, p. 399.

[5] See the last of Senior's "four elementary propositions of the science." *Political Economy*, 4th ed., p. 26, London, 1858.

[6] *Essay on the Distribution of Wealth*, pp. vi, vii, and Chap. VII, London, 1831.

[7] *Capital*, translated by E. Untermann, vol. III, p. 763, Chicago, 1909; W. Bagehot, "The Preliminaries of Political Economy," *Economic Studies*, p. 113.

[8] For example, in the Ricardo Centenary discussion of 1910, Professor H. C. Taylor pointed out that the Ricardian theory of rent assumes "that all men of the class in competition for the land under consideration possess essentially the same degree of economic productivity." *Bulletin of the American Economic Association*, April 1911, Fourth Series, pp. 103–105.

[9] *Principles*, p. 198.

proposition literally true we must posit an incompressible standard of living, a human nature of extraordinary rigidity, a commercial organization of not less extraordinary elasticity, etc., etc. We may refuse to force this strict construction upon Ricardo's words; but just as soon as we introduce a convenient vagueness into the interpretation of the theory we become uncertain what the postulates may be.

Preconceptions are more intriguing. We take postulates up, play with them, and drop them for others. They are external to us and we feel no affection for them. But preconceptions are parts of us. They grow up in our minds. We are but dimly aware of the role they play in shaping our conclusions about the matters on which we focus attention. They shade off from common-sense opinions about things in general, opinions which we share with many of our contemporaries, to personal prejudices and wishes dressed up as convictions. Even in our most rigorous work we are influenced by them. If critically inclined, we may recognize certain of our own preconceptions and form deliberate judgments concerning their validity, whereupon they cease to be preconceptions. Scientific progress consists largely in this process of taking thought about what had theretofore been taken for granted. As any science grows it keeps turning back upon itself in this fashion, and thus becoming conscious of more and more elements in its structure. The present paper essays to perform a service of this sort for economic theory.

There is no more possibility of cataloguing all Ricardo's preconceptions than of listing all the postulates of his theory of rent. Nor is there point in discussing any thinker's preconceptions, unless we can make some advance in knowledge of fact, of technique, or of the curious ways of the mind. All that I shall attempt is to consider three of Ricardo's most significant preconceptions, and the levels on which his analysis runs.

Ricardo took for granted (1) the physical environment in which he lived; (2) the social organization, including the industrial technique, of his day and people; and (3) the human nature of his contemporaries as he understood them. He did not analyze this familiar world beyond explaining a few technical points in the mechanism of the money market, which lay readers could not be expected to know. Still less did he consider the problem of how social organization or human nature had reached their current patterns. But in his common-sense acceptance of nature, society, and man there were features anything but obvious to the common sense of our generation. And these features played a large role in shaping some of his most characteristic conclusions.

I

The physical world entered into Ricardo's economics in the guise of natural resources. The important fact was that in future the nation must find it ever harder to wring from the soil a living for its growing numbers. The accumulation of capital, the progress of invention, the importation of food from abroad cannot be expected to do more than wage a losing fight against "the law of diminishing returns." Hence, a larger and larger part of human energy will be absorbed by the work of providing merely food. Needless to say, Ricardo assigned no reasoned ground for this expectation; but it shaped the conclusions of his "science" just as effectually as if it had been conclusively demonstrated. Living in the early days of the industrial revolution, he might have expected much more than he did from "the progress of invention." Had he done so, the orientation of classical political economy would have been appreciably different.

On the other hand, Ricardo was not troubled by the specter of soil exhaustion, by the wasting of coal measures, by the destruction of forests, or by the idea that climates change. All the large theories that hang thereby were beyond his horizon. His physical world was eminently stable, a constant in the theory. He could speak of rent as paid "for the use of the original and indestructible powers of the soil"; a modern man's common sense is at once offended by the phrase— "indestructible," indeed![10]

II

Ricardo thought of social organization as something that had changed materially in the past, but had reached maturity and would not change materially in the future. With Adam Smith, he looked back to "that early and rude state of society which precedes both the accumulation of stock and the appropriation of land."[11] Of course, this state of affairs was known to him as a logical abstraction, not as that varied reality of many cultures revealed by ethnology. It was by the light of a capitalist's reason that Ricardo saw how savages behave; a more deceptive light he could not have had. But even the professed anthropologists in his day innocently read their own thoughts into the savage mind; so Ricardo was in good contemporary company when he spoke of "the weapon necessary to kill a beaver" as capital; when he tacitly implied that savages keep account of the average time required by various processes; and when he pictured them as carrying on trade for commercial advantage. With so capitalistic a con-

[10] Professor Taussig suggests that Ricardo be credited with glimpsing the notion that what is permanent and indestructible about land is not the original powers of the soil, but the differences among soils. "Exhaustion of the Soil and the Theory of Rent," *Quarterly Journal of Economics*, vol. XXXI, pp. 345–348, February, 1917.

[11] *Principles*, p. 7; *Wealth of Nations*, Cannan's ed., Book I, Chap. VI, p. 49, London, 1904.

ception of precapitalistic life, of course he did not see that
the rise of capitalism is itself an economic problem of the
first importance.

As for the future, Ricardo expected "the progressive
state" in which he lived to run down like a clock into "the
stationary state"; that is, the state in which population will
cease to grow and capital cease to accumulate. The changes
involved in this transition are primarily changes in the shares
of produce that go respectively to landlords, capitalists, and
laborers: for there will be a denser population and more intensive cultivation. But he contemplates no great change in
the organization of society. In the stationary state there will
be the same three classes of men dividing the fruits of industry; the same system of private property, investment for
profit, and production for the market; the same dependence
of the mass of mankind upon wage labor, and the same
government maintaining "security." Various minor reforms
are feasible; but the institutional framework of society will
remain as it is. Men like Robert Owen who cherish hopes of
an economic revolution are "visionaries."[12]

It was not that Ricardo had a high opinion of the existing
social order. Besides minor faults that he strove manfully
to mend,[13] he saw fundamental defects that would abide.
On his showing, the existing order presents an irreconcilable
conflict of interests. It is not only that "the interest of the
landlord is always opposed to that of the consumer and
manufacturer";[14] but also that "there is no way of keeping

[12] *Letters of Ricardo to Trower,* ed. by James Bonar and J. H. Hollander, p. 47,
Oxford, 1899. "Is not the experience of ages against him?" asked Ricardo after his
examination of Owen's schemes. *Ibid.*, pp. 79, 80.

[13] Ricardo testifies that in Parliament he was "treated as an ultra reformer and
a visionary on commercial subjects by both agriculturalists and manufacturers."
Letters of Ricardo to McCulloch, ed. by J. H. Hollander, p. 75, New York, 1895.

[14] *Principles*, p. 321.

profits up but by keeping wages down."[15] And there is nothing to be done about these class conflicts; they are as much
a part of the natural order as is the scarcity of fertile lands.[16]
Furthermore: "Nothing contributes so much to the prosperity and happiness of a country as high profits,"[17] yet the
inevitable drift of prosperity is to stimulate the accumulation
of capital, to reduce profits, and so to destroy itself.[18]

The reason why we must acquiesce in the present order
despite its fundamental defects is found in "that principle
which should ever be held sacred, the security of property."[19]

[15] "On Protection of Agriculture," *Works*, p. 476, London, 1846. It is sometimes
argued that Ricardo's doctrine that profits vary inversely as wages, does not pre-
clude the possibility of such an increase in the joint product that the amount of
necessaries and comforts received by both capitalists and laborers may increase.
Quite true; but it is also true that Ricardo expected a diminution, not an increase,
in this joint product per man and per pound sterling (after the deduction of rent) as
the pressure of population forced resort to poorer soils and intenser agriculture.
Compare the following note.

[16] Compare, "High rents and low profits, for they invariably accompany each
other, ought never to be the subject of complaint, if they are the effect of the
natural course of things," "Essay on the Influence of a Low Price of Corn," *Works*,
p. 378. Even a check upon the increase of population would not remove the conflicts. It would mean that wage earners would get higher wages and retard the rise
of rents—an improvement in Ricardo's eyes, for laborers are "by far the most important class in society." (*Principles*, p. 416.) Still, the gain of the laborers would
be made at the expense of landlords and capitalists.

Of course, the possibility mentioned in the preceding note might be realized
in fact. That is, were a check upon population imposed by voluntary restraint,
continuing improvements in the arts might so raise the joint product (always after
deduction of rent) as to make the smaller share of the capitalists a larger sum. But
as far as I know, Ricardo did not discuss this possibility; he did not look for a
restriction of numbers except under pressure from the approaching stationary state.

[17] "On Protection to Agriculture," *Works*, p. 474.

[18] Compare Marx. "It is here demonstrated in a purely economic way, that is,
from a bourgeois point of view, within the confines of capitalist understanding,
from the standpoint of capitalist production itself, that it has a barrier, that it is
relative, that it is not an absolute but only a historical mode of production corresponding to a definite and limited epoch in the development of the material conditions of production." *Capital*, Untermann's translation, vol. III, pp. 304, 305;
compare pp. 384, 923, 1022.

[19] Ricardo is opposing the suggestion which Adam Smith made, and to which his
own analysis seemed to point, that rent was a peculiarly fit income for heavy

This principle is sacred for no mysterious reason; it has its ground in ordinary human nature. Even the laborers whose prospects are so drab would find any disturbance of the present order a catastrophe:

> . . . for the quantity of employment in the country must depend not only on the quantity of capital, but upon its advantageous distribution, and, above all, on the conviction of each capitalist that he will be allowed to enjoy unmolested the fruits of his capital, his skill, and his enterprise. To take from him this conviction is at once to annihilate half the productive industry of this country, and would be more fatal to the poor laborer than to the rich capitalist himself. This is so self-evident, that men very little advanced beyond the very lowest stations in the country cannot be ignorant of it.[20]

Here, of course, we are in the dignified presence of another unreasoned conviction, one that has not wholly lost its grip with the passing of time. It may have been self-evident even to the ignorant in Ricardo's day; it is now self-evident only to the ignorant, but they are many. To the more alert, the proposition is one to be critically analyzed, not to be accepted or rejected *in toto*. That is because the whole conception of human nature has altered with the generations.

III

Like Bentham, his guide, philosopher, and friend, Ricardo conceived behavior as a calculating pursuit of self-interest.[21]

---

taxation. "Rent often belongs to those who, after many years of toil, have realised their gains, and expended their fortunes in the purchase of land, or houses; and it certainly would be an infringement of . . . the security of property, to subject it to unequal taxation." *Principles*, p. 184.

[20] "Observations on Parliamentary Reform," *Works*, p. 555. Compare Bentham's more systematic treatment of this issue in "Constitutional Code," *Works* (edited by Bowring), vol. IX, pp. 14, 18, and corresponding passages in "Logical Arrangements" and "Pannomial Fragments," *Works*, vol. III, pp. 294, 228–230.

[21] Compare the present writer's essay on "Bentham's Felicific Calculus," *Political Science Quarterly*, vol. XXXIII, pp. 161–183 [reprinted in this volume as essay 10] June, 1918.

It is self-interest which regulates all the speculations of trade, and where that can be clearly and satisfactorily ascertained, we should not know where to stop if we admitted any other rule of action.[22]

Self-interest also regulates politics. "Let me know what the state of [the electors'] interest is, and I will tell you what measures they will recommend."[23] The same proposition holds in morals:

To keep men good you must as much as possible withdraw from them all temptations to be otherwise. The sanctions of religion, of public opinion, and of law, all proceed on this principle, and that State is most perfect in which all these sanctions concur to make it the interest of all men to be virtuous, which is the same thing as to say, to use their best endeavor to promote the general happiness.[24]

Hence our concern in all social matters should be not with individuals, but with those large impersonal factors which shape men's conception of self-interest:

I have long been convinced that our security for good government must rest on the institutions themselves, and the influence under which those who govern us act, and not on the more or less virtue in the characters of our government. The conduct of two different sets of men educated nearly in the same manner, acting under the same checks, and with the same object in view, as far as their own personal interest is concerned, cannot be materially different.[25]

While agreeing with Bentham in this fundamental conception of behavior, Ricardo differed from him in several significant details. Ricardo's men are rather less rational in understanding their own interest than Bentham's men. For example: "the chances of a reverse of fortune are always

[22] "The High Price of Bullion," *Works*, p. 292. Compare p. 268, and *Letters of Ricardo to Malthus*, pp. 17, 18.
[23] "Observations on Parliamentary Reform," *Works*, p. 554.
[24] *Ibid.*
[25] *Letters Ricardo to McCulloch*, p. 89.

considerably undervalued by all of us;"[26] even statesmen are subject to such delusions as that of the sinking fund;[27] investors habitually underrate the capital value of annuities;[28] "prejudices and obstinacy" make businessmen persevere too long "in their old employments; they expect daily a change for the better, and therefore continue to produce commodities for which there is no adequate demand;"[29] worst and most important, there is "the improvidence of the lower classes."[30]

In particular, Ricardo lays more stress upon habit as a factor in controlling behavior than does Bentham. The "natural price of labor . . . essentially depends on the habits and customs of the people."[31] Nor are the business classes exempt from such trammels:

. . . the fancied or real insecurity of capital, when not under the immediate control of its owner, together with the natural disinclination which every man has to quit the country of his birth and connections, and entrust himself, with all his habits fixed, to a strange government and new laws, checks the emigration of capital.[32]

Even in their home country most men are disinclined "to abandon that employment of their capital to which they have long been accustomed."[33] So, too,

[26] *Letters of Ricardo to Trower*, p. 28.

[27] "Essay on the Funding System," *Works*, pp. 538–546.

[28] *Ibid.*, p. 539.

[29] *Letters of Ricardo to Malthus*, p. 174; compare *Letters of Ricardo to McCulloch*, p. 88.

[30] See especially Ricardo's letters to Maria Edgeworth, *Economic Journal*, vol. XVII, pp. 440, 441, September, 1907.

[31] *Principles*, p. 74.

[32] *Ibid.*, p. 117. Later Ricardo argues that this "natural reluctance which every man feels to quit the place of his birth" may be overcome by excessive taxation in his home country. *Ibid.*, p. 232.

[33] *Ibid.*, p. 250.

The desire which every man has to keep his station in life, and to maintain his wealth at the height which it has once attained, occasions most taxes, whether laid on capital or on income, to be paid from income.[34]

Again,

Whatever habit has rendered delightful, will be relinquished with reluctance, and will continue to be consumed notwithstanding a very heavy tax.[35]

The only instinct upon which Ricardo lays stress is that of sex. But even this instinct figures in his system with a difference. It is not sexual passion, but "the delights of domestic society" of which Ricardo speaks.[36] And this phrase is more than a prudish euphemism. What concerned Ricardo as an economist was not the sexual instinct itself, but "the propensity to a too abundant population, the great source from whence all the miseries of the poor flow in so profuse a stream."[37] Certain among his friends and acquaintances were beginning to preach "birth control." Francis Place and Robert Owen vigorously espoused that cause; James Mill hinted at the same remedy in the *Encyclopaedia Britannica*, of all places; Jeremy Bentham lent his tacit approval. Other friends, Malthus and McCulloch, disapproved the new propaganda. Ricardo died before the issue had become one on which men must take sides, and we do not know where he stood.[38] When he wrote his *Principles*, at all events, it was still taken for granted that marriage meant children, and

[34] *Ibid.*, p. 133; but see the next page.
[35] *Ibid.*, p. 225.
[36] *Ibid.*, p. 400.
[37] *Letters of Ricardo to Trower*, p. 18.
[38] See James A. Field, "The Early Propagandist Movement in English Population Theory," *Bulletin of the American Economic Association*, April, 1911, Fourth Series, pp. 207–236. [Reprinted in *Essays on Population and other Papers*, ed. by H. F. Hohman, pp. 91–129, Chicago, 1931.]

that many children were not to be expected outside of wed-lock. So what Ricardo feared really was, "the delights of domestic society."

It should be particularly noted that these aberrations from perfect rationality which Ricardo takes into account are so thoroughly standardized as not to interfere with the work of making theories. Thus the accustomed standard of living and the seductions of domestic society together kept real wages a constant or a slowly shrinking variable in Ricardo's reasoning, a quantity easy to manipulate. Similarly, the patriotic prejudices of capitalists enabled him to draw a hard and fast line between his two problems of domestic and in-ternational trade. Once more, while Ricardo allowed that the "real or fancied" advantages which some employments have over others produce inequalities in both wages and profits, he at once assigned these notions the fixity of habits. The resulting inequalities thereby became constants in his problem: constants to be mentioned and then set aside.[39] It did not occur to him that a constant required analysis. To say that some factor is fixed by habit was a happy ending of the story in Ricardo's mind. What fixed the habit and whether it remains fixed are modern questions.

With this conception of human nature, Ricardo had no occasion to set up a distinct species of economic men. The whole race was fit raw material for theorizing. But he did recognize substantial differences among people from the viewpoint both of a practical man and of a theorist.

As a legislator, Ricardo felt that his Irish constituents presented an inferior brand of human nature; they did not

take a commonly enlightened view of their own interest . . . An English landlord knows that it is not his interest to make his tenant a beggar by

[39] *Principles*, pp. 15-17, 67.

exacting the very hardest terms from him if he had the power of dictating the rent, not so the Irish landlords.[40]

As for the common people of Ireland, what they need

is a taste for other objects besides mere food. Any stimulus which should rouse the Irish to activity, which should induce them to dispose of their surplus time in procuring luxuries for themselves, instead of employing it in the most brutal pursuits, would tend more to the civilization and prosperity of their country than any other measures which could be recommended.[41]

More important are the varieties of human nature that Ricardo implicitly assumes in framing his principles of political economy. The role he assigns to each of the three great economic classes requires an actor of special qualifications. In this sense, if not by native endowment, the capitalist is a different man from the laborer, and the laborer from the landlord. Ricardo's capitalists are animated chiefly by a "restless desire" to find the most profitable investments, modified by a conventional eye for the nonpecuniary disadvantages of certain trades, and a not insuperable preference for home over foreign investments. His laborers are creatures ruled by habit and a tropismatic longing to marry. His landlords are Olympians raised above economic strife, reaping their double gains in idleness and honor. "Their rent is the effect of circumstances over which they have no control, excepting indeed, as they are the law makers, and lay restrictions on the importation of corn."[42]

[40] *Letters of Ricardo to Trower*, p. 207. Ricardo concludes: "Ireland is an oppressed country—not oppressed by England, but by the aristocracy which rules with a rod of iron within it; England could redress many of her wrongs, but stands itself in awe of the faction which governs." *Ibid.*, p. 208.

[41] *Ibid.*, pp. 21, 22. Compare *Principles*, p. 77.

[42] *Letters of Ricardo to McCulloch*, p. 67. Compare *Principles*, pp. 52, 268.

IV

In his social science Bentham dealt with the "real forces" of pleasure and pain from the outset. To money and commodities he assigned minor roles as media for giving pain or pleasure. Welfare he treated as a net balance of pleasurable feeling experienced by the community in the long run. By this procedure he attained a formal simplicity and a seeming profundity.

Simplifier though he was by temperament, Ricardo made no effort to imitate this example in economics. There are, indeed, three distinct levels in his analysis, interrelated, but each treated as having its independent interest. Ricardo turns from one level to the other, as naturally as the man in the street thinks of himself in successive moments, as making money, making commodities, and making sacrifices. Having been himself a man in the street for years before he became an economist, Ricardo acquired this habit of thinking as other businessmen acquire it. When he came later on to reflect upon the problem he found an insuperable obstacle in the way of doing as Bentham had done.

Ricardo was acutely sensitive to the one great complication that the use of money introduces into economic problems. His first essays were devoted to demonstrating that the English currency was a variable, not a constant, factor in business dealings. Not only the fact, but also the changing degree of depreciation, was a problem to which he kept reverting.[43] How should he deal with this complication?

---

[43] See *The High Price of Bullion* (first edition, 1810); *Reply to Mr. Bosanquet* (1811); *Proposals for an Economical and Secure Currency* (1816); the chapters on money in the *Principles* (1817); *On Protection to Agriculture* (1822), especially pp. 30–35 (*Works*, pp. 470–472); *Plan for the Establishment of a National Bank* (1824); and the frequent references in all three collections of his letters.

In the first sketch of his system he tried the device that has recommended itself to so many later economists. He put money quite aside at the outset, and cast his discussion in terms of wheat. Not until everything had been made clear on that level of analysis did he bring money back and inquire what difference was made by its use.[44] But when Ricardo came to restate his system on an ampler scale, he discarded this device for a better. He did not abstract from the use of money, but, as long as he was focusing his attention upon other subjects, he supposed that money was invariable in value, that all changes in prices came from the commodity side of the equation.[45] By this shift he kept his problems simple enough to be managed, and yet let his capitalists, laborers, and landlords behave like real men and calculate in money.

A very large portion of Ricardo's general theory runs thus on the pecuniary level. "What all producers look steadily at is market price and its relation to natural price."[46] With their "restless desire . . . to quit a less profitable for a more advantageous business," capitalists are alert to withdraw "funds" from trades where the price margin is narrow and invest them where the margin is wide. Ricardo explains briefly the financial mechanism by which this constant redistribution of capital is effected.[47] Even the growth of population is governed proximately by a similar process; when the market price of labor is higher than the natural price, men multiply rapidly; when the market price is lower, the increase

[44] See Ricardo's "Essay on the Influence of a Low Price of Corn on the Profits of Stock," *Works*, especially pp. 371–379.

[45] *Principles*, p. 38. With unwonted care, Ricardo several times recalled this supposition to the attention of his readers. For example, see p. 87 and p. 188, note.

[46] *Letters of Ricardo to Trower*, p. 125. Compare the similar but less concise statements in *Principles*, p. 408.

[47] *Principles*, pp. 65–67, 282–284, 408, 409.

is checked.[48] In short, Ricardo treated "the money surface of things" not as a distorting veil to be pushed aside, but as part of the subject to be investigated.

He did not, however, stop with pecuniary analysis, but went through money to what it represented. "Productions are always bought by productions, or by services; money is only the medium by which the exchange is effected."[49] Indeed, computations of money value may be "very deceptious," as when a short crop sells for more money than an abundant one.[50] Distribution, accordingly, is concerned not with money income, but with "the produce of the earth."[51] In one sense, of course, capital consists of funds; but it is defined as "that part of the wealth of a country which is employed in production"; it "consists of food, clothing, tools, raw materials, machinery, etc., necessary to give effect to labor."[52] It is capital in this sense which limits the volume of business a community can carry on. Even the mobility of capital funds depends upon the physical character and uses of the commodities in which they have been invested.[53] So, too, with wages: the substantial factor is "the food, necessaries, and conveniences required for the support of the laborer and his family."[54]

[48] *Ibid.*, pp. 71, 72.

[49] *Ibid.*, p. 275. Compare *Works*, pp. 378, 389.

[50] "On Protection to Agriculture," *Works*, pp. 465, 466. Compare Ricardo's letter of Jan. 11, 1823, to Maria Edgeworth, *Economic Journal*, vol. XVII, p. 440, September, 1907.

[51] *Principles*, preface, p. 1.

[52] *Ibid.*, p. 72.

[53] *Ibid.*, pp. 171, 172, 251, 254.

[54] *Ibid.*, p. 70. One might add: the money metals are distributed among commercial nations in such proportions "as may be necessary to regulate a profitable trade by *barter*" (p. 120). Gold is perhaps the one staple commodity in the abundance of which the world is least concerned: half or double the quantity would perform the same money work, though at different levels of prices (p. 173).

In the dim subjective realm of feeling, Ricardo felt less at ease than in the tangible realm of commodities or the rational realm of money. He admitted the fundamental importance of desires as the basis of demand. "Give men but the means of purchasing, and their wants are insatiable . . . We all wish to add to our enjoyments or to our power. Consumption adds to our enjoyments, accumulation to our power, and they equally promote demand."[55] But there Ricardo dropped the subject. He was stopped from following out this line of analysis by an obstacle encountered by Bentham and set aside.

Bentham admitted to himself in a manuscript which remained unpublished until 1904:

> 'Tis in vain to talk of adding quantities which, after the addition, will continue distinct as they were before, one man's happiness will never be another man's happiness; a gain to one man is no gain to another: you might as well pretend to add 20 apples to 20 years.[56]

That was precisely where Ricardo stuck. As he put it: "Every man has some standard in his own mind by which he estimates the value of his enjoyments, but that standard is as various as the human character." From the same commodity "two persons may derive very different degrees of enjoyment." "One set of necessaries and conveniences admits of no comparison with another set; value in use cannot be measured by any known standard; it is differently estimated by different persons."[57]

---

[55] *Letters of Ricardo to Malthus*, pp. 45, 49. See also *ibid.*, p. 43, and *Principles*, pp. 273, 277, 280, 378, 379. Are the Irish an exception to the insatiability of wants, or is the desire to be idle counted in? See Ricardo's reference to the Irish quoted in the preceding section and his reference to the inhabitants of New Spain quoted below.

[56] See the paper on "Bentham's Felicific Calculus," *Political Science Quarterly*, vol. XXXIII [reprinted in this volume as essay 10].

[57] *Principles*, pp. 225–226, 420; *Works*, p. 401.

Bentham had gone on:

> This addibility of the happiness of different subjects, however when considered rigorously it may appear fictitious, is a postulatum without the allowance of which all political reasoning is at a stand.

Not so Ricardo: he could carry on, he had carried on, economic reasoning without that fiction. He had found a basis for economic science where the businessman finds a basis for rational practice—in money prices. One may assuredly compare the shilling of one man with the shilling of another. Why pretend to compare their feelings? After all, it is the shillings and not the feelings that count in business. And whenever there is occasion to go back of prices, are not wants standardized and made dependable for business purposes by "habits and customs"? Why not accept this obviously relevant explanation of wants, instead of going into the problematical weighing of one enjoyment against another, even by a single person? Ricardo does not elaborate this argument, but he does adopt this practice and so steers clear of Bentham's subjective tangle, except in one particular. That particular, however, was nothing less than his treatment of value.

The inquiry in this field to which Ricardo wishes

> to draw the reader's attention relates to the effect of the variations in the relative value of commodities, and not in their absolute value.[58]

Now, "relative value" lies on the commodity level of analysis, just as price lies on the pecuniary level. But Ricardo cannot account for variations in relative value without dipping deeper into "absolute," or "real," or "positive," or "natural" value; for "exchangeable value is regulated by positive value."[59]

---

[58] *Ibid.*, p. 16.

[59] *Letters of Ricardo to Trower*, p. 151. For examples of the various aliases under which "real" value passes in Ricardo, see *Principles*, pp. 14, 16, 36, 376. For the

Unfortunately, Ricardo never defined "real value." It does not mean "value in use"; it "essentially differs from riches"; Say "certainly has not a correct notion of what is meant by value when he contends that a commodity is valuable in proportion to its utility";[60] "there is not and cannot be an accurate measure of value."[61] But all this is negative. The nearest approach to a positive definition is a statement that value depends

on the difficulty or facility of production. The labor of a million men in manufactures, will always produce the same value, but will not always produce the same riches . . . That commodity is alone invariable, which at all times requires the same sacrifice of toil and labor to produce it. Of such a commodity we have no knowledge, but we may hypothetically argue and speak about it, as if we had.[62]

In this sense, labor is "the foundation of all value."[63]

Still, value does not result from labor except under certain conditions: the products must have utility, they must be relatively scarce,[64] the amount of labor that counts is the socially necessary amount.

To interpret: The real value of any given quantity of any good is the practical importance that attaches to it in our

---

way in which the problem of prices led Ricardo on to the problem of value, see "High Price of Bullion," *Works*, pp. 267, 268.

[60] *Principles*, pp. 258, 265; *Letters of Ricardo to Malthus*, p. 173.

[61] *Letters of Ricardo to McCulloch*, p. 173. This was Ricardo's conclusion after spending a great deal of energy in search of an invariable measure of value—a search in which his whole generation of economists seems to have joined with the exception of McCulloch. *Letters of Ricardo to Trower*, pp. 211, 212.

[62] *Principles*, pp. 258, 260. Compare the carelessly phrased statement about the "real value" of wages, p. 42.

[63] *Ibid.*, p. 15. Ricardo explained to Trower in 1821, "I do not, I think, say that the labour expended on a community is a measure of its exchangeable value, but of its positive value. I then add that exchangeable value is regulated by positive value and therefore is regulated by the quantity of labour expended." *Letters of Ricardo to Trower*, p. 151.

[64] Compare "On Protection to Agriculture," *Works*, p. 466.

economic planning. In the case of freely reproducible goods—and they make the vast majority of commodities—this practical importance lies in the sacrifice which production imposes. For, as current supplies are used up, we keep turning out new supplies; the difference which loss of goods makes to us is not that we stop consuming, but that we undergo fresh "toil and trouble."[65] This sacrifice is, therefore, what we have to consider in most of our dealings with goods; notably, it is what we consider in exchanging goods. Riches, not value, is what we desire; but to pursue riches effectively, the thing we have to think about is not the utility of goods, that is obvious enough, but the varying amounts of painful effort by which we wring them from nature.

In a sense, of course, this means that Ricardo rested his theory upon a foundation of feeling. But the strong objective element in his conception of human nature counts even here. On Ricardo's showing, feelings exercise no practical influence until they are embodied in money costs, and he makes no effort to show that money costs can be resolved into feeling without residuum. Moreover, the feelings that he has in mind are widely prevalent, conventionalized feelings, such, for instance, as the social deference paid to certain professions in England, "the comparative degree of estimation in which the different kinds of human labor are held," the recognized preference of "most men of property" for home investments, etc.[66] Even the "toil and trouble" upon which real value depends is the socially necessary "toil and trouble," and how

---

[65] Ricardo himself suggests the test of deprivation: "If I am obliged to devote one month's labour to make me a coat, and only one week's labour to make a hat, although I should never exchange either of them, the coat would be four times the value of the hat; and if a robber were to break into my house and take part of my property, I would rather that he took three hats than one coat." *Letters of Ricardo to Trower*, pp. 151, 152.

[66] "Essay on the Funding System," *Works*, p. 541; *Principles*, pp. 16, 117.

much "toil and trouble" is socially necessary depends upon such matters as the fertility and extent of the land, the number of the people, their knowledge of the arts, their willingness and ability to profit by foreign trade, and the like. Ricardo's economic psychology, in short, is the broad observation of a businessman rather than the introspection of a philosopher. Its legitimate descendants are found among the "social value" theorists, rather than within the so-called "psychological school." It smacks of behaviorism as well as of hedonism.[67]

While Ricardo did not confine himself within the formal bounds of hedonistic psychology, he definitely accepted the utilitarian criterion of welfare. He wrote to Maria Edgeworth, "My motto, after Mr. Bentham, is: 'The greatest happiness to the greatest number.'"[68] The "general happiness" is the final test applied by him to economic policy.[69] To this view he remained faithful in the face of provocation hard for an economist to bear. Alexander Humboldt, in his account of New Spain, tells how idle are the people, whose land with little labor yields abundance. Ricardo reflects upon this situation, and concludes loyally:

[67] I used certain extracts from a manuscript of which part is published in this essay in a chapter contributed to the volume, *The Trend of Economics*, edited by Rexford G. Tugwell, New York, 1924 [reprinted in this volume as essay 16]. In reviewing that book, Professor Allyn A. Young predicted that I "will ultimately be compelled" to admit that economics "always *has been* a study of human behavior" (*Quarterly Journal of Economics*, vol. XXXIX, p. 178, February, 1925). That has long been one of my favorite remarks, though I like to add, "whether economists recognize the fact or not." But economics should advance with surer steps when economists see clearly what they are really discussing. It is therefore pleasant to have Professor Young's assent, guarded though it is by reservations in a footnote.

The above passage concerning Ricardo's psychological assumptions is printed just as it was written some dozen years ago.

[68] *Economic Journal*, vol. XVII, p. 434, September, 1907.

[69] *Principles*, p. 257. Compare *Letters of Ricardo to Trower*, p. 67.

Happiness is the object to be desired, and we cannot be quite sure that, provided he is equally well fed, a man may not be happier in the enjoyment of the luxury of idleness than in the enjoyment of the luxuries of a neat cottage and good clothes. And after all we do not know if these would fall to his share. His labor might only increase the enjoyments of his employer.[70]

Although, in a real sense, welfare was Ricardo's chief concern, it receives much less attention in the *Principles* than money, commodities, or feelings. He dealt, as an economist must, not with ends, but with ways and means. When fairly started upon an investigation, Ricardo would get so interested in the "truth" of his propositions that he would let their "utility" go.[71] Also he would have said, I think, that the best service he could render to public welfare was to explain the economic processes on which welfare largely depends. Welfare in the sense of "the general happiness" is not a principle of explanation, but of appraisal. It explains the behavior even of philanthropists and statesmen only on the supposition that they are guided by such advice as the economist can give, after he has studied what men do. That study must treat men frankly as aiming at money, goods, or pleasure, rather than at welfare.

[70] *Letters of Ricardo to Malthus*, p. 138.
[71] Compare the often-quoted passage from *Letters of Ricardo to Malthus*, p. 53.

12

WIESER'S THEORY OF SOCIAL ECONOMICS[1]

THE *Grundriss der Sozialökonomik*, in which this treatise appears,[2] is planned as a cooperative venture in nine volumes to take the place once held by Schönberg's *Handbuch*. It is edited by as distinguished a list of five and forty economists as could be chosen from the generation of Germans younger than Wagner and von Schmoller. That these editors turned to von Wieser for their fundamental section upon economic theory and to Schumpeter for their history of economic doctrines is a piquant triumph for the Austrian school, whose methods, as Schumpeter ventures to remind us, were once bitterly contested in Germany, and whose disciples were long barred from German professorships.[3]

Wieser's *Social Economics*, however, owes none of its prestige to the company it keeps. In the literature of the Austrian school it merits the place held by Mill's *Political Economy* in the literature of the classical school. It sums up, systematizes, and extends the doctrines previously worked out by the author, his master, and his fellow disciples. Like Mill's great book, it is distinguished by admirable exposition—elegant in proportions, mature in expression, and authoritative in source. The parallel runs on into the future.

---

[1] Reprinted by permission of *Political Science Quarterly* vol. XXXII, pp. 95–118 March, 1915.

[2] *Theorie der gesellschaftlichen Wirtschaft*, by Friedrich Freiherr von Wieser. (*Grundriss der Sozialökonomik*, vol. I, pp. 125–444.) Tübingen, 1914. [An English translation has been published by A. Ford Hinrichs, with a preface by the reviewer, under the title *Social Economics*, by Friedrich von Wieser, pp. xxii +470, New York, 1927.]

[3] *Ibid.*, p. 115.

In making classical theory so clear Mill revealed to others defects in his system that he did not see. Wieser's work promises to render a similar service.

In two respects, however, a comparison with Mill does less than justice to Wieser. This is the first systematic treatise upon economic theory at large produced by the Austrians proper, whereas several attempts at covering the whole ground of classical economics had been made before Mill wrote.[4] Wieser's economic work is also more original than Mill's. His own early writings rank higher among the constructive contributions which he weaves into a balanced exposition than do Mill's *Essays upon Some Unsettled Questions of Political Economy*. More than that, in extending the discussion beyond the limits of his earlier work, Wieser shows again the vigor and independence for which he has always been notable. Mill was much more than an economist; he wrote his *Principles* at high speed to round out his system of social philosophy. There was more of his style than of his thinking in many chapters. Wieser, on the contrary, has lived a concentrated intellectual life, if one may judge by his writings, and has brought his full power to bear upon every section of this treatise. It is the fruition of a lifetime's reflection as well as the crowning achievement of a famous school.

Although two years and a half have passed since the volume containing Wieser's contribution was published, I have not been able to find any review of it in the economic journals, American or foreign.[5] This neglect is a loss to other

[4] Böhm-Bawerk's *Kapital und Kapitalzins* in its final form touches on most problems of theory; but the whole discussion is organized on monographic lines. Philippovich's *Grundriss*, on the other hand, is eminently systematic—no book more so; but it is more accurate to say that he took the Austrian analysis into his system, than to say that he based his system on the Austrian analysis.

[5] The recent numbers of the German and Austrian journals, however, are not available.

economists even more than it is an injustice to the author. Under the circumstances a rather full account of the book is called for.

I

The ground plan of *Social Economics* is a projection of lines which Wieser sketched in 1884. In writing *Über den Ursprung und die Hauptgesetze des wirtschaftlichen Werthes* he analyzed a valuation made apart from others by a single subject (page 41). Four years later he built *Natural Value* on the foundations laid in the *Ursprung des Werthes*, and attempted "to exhaust the entire sphere of the phenomena of value without any exception."[6] His aim was "to find what, among our forms of value, would continue in a perfect or communist state, and so to find the permanent basis of all economic life."[7] Accordingly, he imagined "a completely organic and most highly rational community" (page 61) as the valuing subject.

Twenty-six years have passed, and the field to be treated has expanded again. Now he does first in logical order what he once did first in chronological order. Book I is "The Theory of the Single Economy." The valuing subject of this economy is a single person (as in the *Ursprung des Werthes*) who represents the million-headed population of a nation with modern methods of production (as in *Natural Value*). Again the theoretical problem is to find the laws of value under these conditions (of course, there is no exchange and no price); again the valuer is a paragon of economic virtue, making no blunders, having no weakness, swayed by no

---

[6] Preface, p. xxv, of Mrs. C. A. Malloch's translation.

[7] Preface, p. xxxix. The words are Professor William Smart's, but are published with Wieser's approval.

passions; again the results are conceived to be pure theory, destined when perfected to constitute a core of doctrine common to all schools of the future. Book I might still be an independent volume, like *Natural Value*. As part of a general treatise its relationship to the other parts is that of a foundation upon which everything else rests.

Books II, III, and IV differ from Book I in the conditions under which and the persons by whom valuations are supposed to be made. One by one the assumptions contrary to fact, employed to make the "single economy" simple, are dropped, and by corresponding stages the pure theory of Book I is elaborated into a theory measurably applicable to real conditions. Thus in Book II (*Theorie der Volkswirtschaft*) the assumption of a single valuing subject gives place to the assumption of many different valuing subjects, each following his economic interests in a world where social classes exist and competition and monopoly divide the field. It is still assumed, however, that government does not interfere with the pursuit of self-interest. In Book III (*Theorie der Staatswirtschaft*) this last assumption is dropped; it is now assumed that the individual citizens are subordinated to a state, which follows an economic policy for the promotion of the commonweal. Finally, in Book IV (*Theorie der Weltwirtschaft*) the single state discussed in Book III is supposed to be surrounded by similar states, and the economic problems arising from their interrelations are faced.

Mill's *Political Economy* diverges widely from the narrow path marked out twelve years earlier in his essay "On the Definition of Political Economy." Wieser, on the other hand, has scarcely shifted his position in thirty years. Since he received Menger's stamp only one man seems to have changed his thinking—Böhm-Bawerk—and, needless to say, that man changed nothing fundamental. The changes Wieser has made himself are extensions rather than revisions. *Einfache Wirtschaft, Volkswirtschaft, Staatswirtschaft, Weltwirtschaft*—the main divisions of his theoretical system—grow in due order out of the basic conceptions that he formulated in 1884.

II

Since Wieser is so consistent with himself, and since Book I covers the ground all economists have traversed with him, there is no need to detail the doctrines there propounded. A brief statement supplemented by comment upon two important points will suffice.

The theory of the single economy begins with a brief consideration of the subjective elements in economic processes— man's aims and activities, his wants, satisfactions, and attitude toward future wants. Then the discussion turns to goods as means of satisfaction, the fundamental principle of man's economic dealings with goods, the process of production, and the three great factors of production—labor, capital, and land. Later comes the analysis of the interrelations among these various elements within the economic process, and at the very end a new definition of value.

In the course of these chapters Wieser expounds again the various doctrines for which he is known. The term "marginal utility," which he invented, still satisfies him; the view that costs are merely a disguise assumed by the protean law of utility—Wieser's most important addition to Menger's theory—reappears; more emphatically than ever Wieser denies that as a rule men discount future in comparison with present wants (page 155); he still insists that capital and land are fundamentally distinct categories (pages 172–173); he holds fast to the doctrine that the value of a stock of similar goods is obtained by multiplying the number of units by the marginal utility (pages 192–194); and he restates his theory of imputation—with a difference.

Technically the most important modification of his earlier work is the widening of the distinction between "monopoly goods" and "cost goods," into a distinction between "specific means of production" and "cost means of production" (pages 185–187). The specific means of production in the strict sense are limited by physical scarcity or by peculiar quality to a single use, whereas cost means are sufficiently abundant and sufficiently adaptable to be used in many ways. A corresponding distinction is drawn between specific products and cost products. In general, lands are specific means, while most kinds of labor and capital goods are cost means.

Now, cost means in production and cost products in household management are subject to accurate adjustments which fit them into the general scheme of economic activity according to the marginal law. The only irregularity here arises from the fact that each different want has its own peculiar scale of satiation, so that men cannot achieve precisely the same marginal utility in each branch of consumption, but merely draw "a wavering marginal line" through all branches. In production greater precision is attainable. The numerous combinations in which cost means are used in various industries yield equations sufficient in number to determine what proportion of the utility produced should be imputed to each, and from this productive contribution, in conjunction with the marginal utility of the marginal product, is derived the value at which each unit in each cost good is held in all its manifold uses (pages 201, 213). And this systematization on the basis of costs is carried back into the field of consumption. A steel bridge which as a unit possesses great utility is, nevertheless, valued only at the moderate rating derived from the marginal utility of the cost goods—iron, coal, labor, etc., required to produce it.

Specific products and specific means of production are more refractory. The proportion of the utility produced imputable to a good serving a single use cannot be worked out directly by means of equations drawn from different branches of industry. But it can be worked out indirectly when the other means of production used in cooperation with it are cost goods. For then in the single equation in which it appears it is the only unknown. Subtract from the marginal utility of the product the utilities of the cost means employed, and credit whatever utility remains to the specific means of production in question. In effect, this is the rule that Ricardo applied to land and that men really apply to all specific means of production. Of course, this procedure supposes the marginal utility of the specific *product* to be known. In fact, however, this item in the economic calculus often lacks definiteness. The marginal utility of a good which serves a single use in the household may be either above or below the general level of marginal utilities in most lines of consumption, depending upon its scarcity or abundance in comparison with the amount required to satisfy the want, the initial intensity of that want, and its rate of satiation. But whatever that somewhat indefinite rating may be, it is handed on by imputation to the specific means of production after the standard deductions have been made for the cost means.

To this modification of his earlier exposition Wieser attaches great importance. The distinction between specific means of production and cost means, he says, together with the corresponding distinction between specific and cost products, gives "the exhaustive objective basis for all the chief problems of the economic calculus" (page 188). He thinks that its application in the problems of imputation meets what is valid in Böhm-Bawerk's criticisms of the exposition given in *Natural Value*.[8]

III

Theoretically the most interesting feature of Book I is Wieser's conception of economic calculus. The gist of economic activity and therefore the central problem of economic theory is rational control over the process of meeting wants. The aim of this rational control is to secure the maximum utility possible under the circumstances. This aim implies that the calculations shall be made in "utility units"—*Nutzeinheiten*—a term freely employed by Wieser. But what are these utility units? The primary values are the values attached to the satisfaction of wants (page 151). "Primary want-values, however, are not subject to numerical computation, since they cannot be reduced to a common denominator" (page 215). They have not numerical magnitudes, but merely intensity magnitudes. How, then, can there be an economic calculus in terms of utility units, even in the single economy where there is no question concerning comparisons among the feelings of different men?

This is the difficulty that so many economists have felt in developing what Jevons called the "mechanics of utility." Professor Edgeworth faced it squarely in 1881, and proposed to use "a unit of pleasure" which has three dimensions—intensity, time, number.[9] Marshall adopted another solution. He dealt not with utility units but with the "money measures" of desires and satisfactions, and assumed, whenever the problem required, that equal sums of money represent on the average equal feelings to groups in similar

[8] *Positive Theorie des Kapitales*, 3d ed., Excursus VII.
[9] *Mathematical Psychics*, Appendix III.

economic circumstances. Pareto, combining suggestions made by Irving Fisher and Edgeworth, has tried to avoid the whole difficulty, to cast all metaphysical entities out of his system by developing a "theory of choice." Wicksteed's plan of dealing with "preferences," Davenport's conclusion that economics is merely the "science of prices," and Fetter's effort to restate the theory of value without using marginal utility are variants of Pareto's scheme. All these recent emendations betray distrust of the "hedonism" which is said to lurk in marginal analysis.

In the midst of these latter-day doubts, Wieser stands firmly for the old Austrian doctrine carefully interpreted. He denies that "the economic principle of maximum utility" is "bound up with a hedonistic view of life" (page 152); and yet justifies himself in using "utility units" as the basis of his economic calculus. After admitting that our primary want values have not numerical, but merely intensity magnitudes, he argues as follows: While the intensities of different wants cannot be measured, they can be compared. The results of such comparisons, it is true, do not go beyond statements of equality or difference. Thus one cannot say how many times greater is intense hunger than a simple aesthetic longing; but one knows there is a wide difference between them, and one can even give this difference a somewhat more definite expression by naming a whole list of desires less intense than the first and more intense than the second. Now, he asserts—and this is the gist of his position, ability to discriminate equal, greater, and less intensity magnitudes among our desires, limited as it is, yet suffices to solve the practical problems of controlling economic activity. How so?

To maximize the utility derived from goods is the aim of economic effort. With a single good this aim requires the application of the article to the most intense want it is capable of satisfying. That want can be found by anyone who is able to tell the more from the less intense. The same equipment suffices to apportion properly the different units in a stock of similar goods; it is necessary only to make sure that no unit is applied to the satisfaction of a less intense want when it might have been used to satisfy a more intense rival. And when the stock is valued as a whole one merely multiplies the number of units by the marginal utility. "The units of quantity are at the same time units of utility, and when one computes them as units of mass one is also computing their utility." Estimates made in this way, of course, tell nothing about amount of satisfaction gained; but that is not "the task of the economic utility calculus, which has merely to find the margin up to which one dare carry his gratifications." The whole "surplus utility" above the margin is neglected.

This marginal law, applicable to all divisible stocks, attains its full significance through the law of cost and the law of imputation. The first permits one to analyze all cost products—Wieser's new term referred to above—into multiples of cost units, and the cost units are made comparable with one another by the law of imputation which expresses them in the common utility units of their marginal products. Thus the whole mass of varied cost products and cost means which a people possesses is converted into a single vast supply, the magnitude of which can be reckoned in cost units of any kind desired—for example, labor units—and by means of these cost units translated finally into any kind of utility units desired. Here we have the basis for a general scheme both of household management and of production that marks out accurately the margin up to which consumption and production should be carried in all branches and beyond which they should cease.

The specific products make more trouble; for their marginal utilities deviate from the general margin, being a little higher or a little lower. A numerical magnitude cannot be set upon these deviations; for that is a matter of primary want values, which as has been said cannot be computed. But even in this case mankind has discovered a way of assigning numerical values. Practice derives these numerical values from the quantities of the products that balance each other on the general marginal line. One cannot make a quantitative comparison between the gratification derived from wearing sable and that derived from eating bread; but one can find the quantity of bread that has utility equal to that of a sable skin, for the relationship of equality can be established between different intensity magnitudes. In this way even the specific products are brought into the general economic calculus. One can tell what costs can properly be incurred for a sable skin as accurately as for a sack of flour.

Wieser admits that the practical serviceability of this calculus is subject to three qualifications: (1) Changes in methods of production disturb the accurate adjustments between costs and products; while these disturbances continue, the cost goods affected must be treated as specific goods. (2) Comparisons between periods far apart as well as between different "economies" are not feasible because the utility units have not the same meaning. (3) The calculus becomes positively misleading whenever the decline in marginal utility outruns the increase in the supply, so that the total utility of the stock reckoned by multiplication falls off. In such cases production must be guided not by marginal utility, but by a vaguer estimate of total utility (§ 22).

So far von Wieser. His argument is that of his *Ursprung des Werthes*, modified by his new distinction between specific and cost goods. The whole discussion, it will be noticed,

[235]

purports to be a descriptive analysis of economic activity reduced to essentials. Does it really imply that men do their economic thinking in "utility units"? Certainly not in the sense that any man has a unit of feeling, equipped with which he goes about measuring gratifications of different kinds. In dealing with goods of different kinds men are supposed to measure them by the physical units appropriate to each kind, units of length, of weight, of cubic content, etc. Utility does come into the problem in the sense that every physical unit of every kind of goods gets its significance for every individual from the marginal contribution that unit makes to the gratification of his wants. To repeat, physical units are at the same time utility units, and whenever we reckon by yards, or pounds, or bushels our quantities have economic meaning, because these units of the good in question are likewise units of utility. There is no more one unit of utility than there is one unit of quantity. But one can determine whether he prefers a pound of tea or a dozen eggs, and when he answers that question he is comparing utilities whether he knows it or not. We have no common denominator of feelings; but merely a balance telling that one of two different things is weightier in importance, or that the two are equal. That balance, however, suffices to enable us to make rational choices.

IV

All this leads up to a new definition of economic value: "the effectiveness for economic purposes associated with the portions of goods and portions of labor that are used." Wieser contrasts this definition with Menger's famous one: "the importance that concrete goods, or quantities of goods, receive for us from the fact that we are conscious of being dependent on our disposal over them for the satisfaction of

our wants."[10] His own definition is wider than Menger's in
that it includes labor as well as commodities, but narrower in
that it refers only to economic value proper, while Menger
defines our fondness for *things* at large (*Sachliebe überhaupt*).
The subjective origin of economic value, Wieser adds in
explanation, does not in practice stand out so clearly in consciousness as Menger's definition suggests. The new definition
with its more objective phrasing better describes what men
are actually conscious of in their economic activity. "The
effectiveness for economic purposes, of which we speak, has
reference primarily to external relationships within economic activity." As Wieser remarked near the beginning,
economics is immediately concerned not with satisfying
wants, but with providing the means of satisfaction (page
143).

V

Having shown how a single subject controls his economic
activity, Wieser turns in Book II to the problem of how a
number of persons following their economic interests under
a regime of private property meet in exchange, and constitute
a social economy upon the basis of prices. So far as competition with equal opportunities for all prevails in such a
society, he holds that the pursuit of self-interest will promote
public welfare (page 138). If that were the whole truth, society might be regarded after the classical fashion as an aggregate of simple economies. But that conception of society
is clearly inadequate today. The problem of monopoly is

---

[10] In the original, "die Geltung, die beim Wirtschaften den verwendeten Teil-
gütern und Teilarbeiten assoziiert wird"; "die Bedeutung, welche konkrete Güter
oder Güterquantitäten für uns dadurch erlangen, dass wir in der Befriedigung
unserer Bedürfnisse von der Verfügung über dieselben abhängig zu sein uns bewusst
sind" (pp. 230–231).

practically more pressing than the problem of free competition; instead of equal opportunity for all, there is a struggle between the strong and the weak. What is the nature and the origin of this inequality in power? Where lies the unity of society? An economic sociology is needed to answer these questions. Wieser supplies it with all possible brevity.

Men are by nature social beings, he says, held together by two kinds of social forces—the forces of freedom and the forces of compulsion. United action requires leadership, and the mass of men show their independence chiefly in choosing what leader they shall obey, or how faithfully they shall follow the examples set them. In the last resort, however, acceptance or rejection by the masses is the decisive factor; the leaders must follow their followers. Within the realm of private life, indeed, the leaders have little coercive authority; they come and go rapidly; they are so numerous as to become anonymous; to the masses they stand for freedom rather than compulsion. This anonymous leadership in detail does no more than conserve what society has attained, or make slow advances along lines clearly marked out. Greater changes require greater leaders, who become personally conspicuous and focus the forces of compulsion.

Now, leadership, which is necessary to progress, rests upon social inequality. The relations of ruler and subject grow into a stratification of classes; on the economic side the "Have-and-Holders" confront the "Have-Nots." No theory of exchange that neglects differences in power between these classes explains what happens in the market place. For the social stratification is not merely an objective fact; it molds men according to its image. Their wants, their impulses, their very egoisms are dominated by social forces; subordination becomes comfortable. The economic principle of least cost and highest utility does not rule men's actions in the way assumed in the theory of the simple economy; rather it assumes this form: "Be as good an economic man as your fellows." Moreover, through the initiative of leaders and through imitative acceptance by the masses, society develops certain institutions serving the common needs so well as to seem like the creation of an organized social will. Money, markets, division of labor, the social economy itself are such creations. They make an essential part of the historical situation into which the individual is born, bonds which unite him to his fellows and establish conditions to which his individual efforts are subjected.

VI

Upon this theory of economic society and his theory of the single economy, Wieser builds his theory of exchange. He starts with barter, then turns to markets, and money prices under competitive, monopolistic, and "monopoloidal" conditions, when business is normal, and in times of panic when "the marginal law loses its effectiveness" (page 264). The various forms of money, credit, the general level of prices, money capital and its formation, the money and investment markets are all treated with point and brevity.

Perhaps the most unusual feature of the whole discussion is that it really does rest upon its alleged foundations. Personal valuations and personal adjustments among costs and utilities continue to play the fundamental role assigned them in the theory of the single economy. But not for a moment does Wieser forget that the whole process is twisted into new shape by the inequalities emphasized in his theory of economic society. For example, price is a social product, not by virtue of a valuation made by society, but as the result of a social conflict for the possession of goods waged between men who differ radically in their valuations and their power as demanders. Therefore price is fixed not by marginal utility as such, but by a socially stratified marginal utility (pages 259–260). Again, in an exchange economy marginal costs do not tend to coincide with marginal utilities as they do in the single economy (page 271). Once more, in our stratified society even competition no longer results in a natural selection of the ablest enterprisers; large capital may outweigh superior ability (page 274). And besides, the field is largely occupied by concerns with monopolistic and monopoloidal advantages; the "excessive competition" of the strong and the "excessive competition" of the weak are to be reckoned with (page 273).

Exchange value is "the efficiency which the object and the medium of exchange have by virtue of their exchange relations within the economic process." Of the two forms it assumes, subjective, or better, personal exchange value is the more fundamental. This is the mediated or indirect use value in mind when one thinks of the efficiency for his purposes of that which a good will command in exchange (page 287). The objective, or better, the economic exchange value of a commodity—its "efficiency in the social economic process"—is its money price, society's rating which controls the expenditure of costs in producing it, and which controls likewise the uses to which it may be put (page 291). In modern communities the economic calculus is made in terms of money; but this reckoning in money is at the same time a reckoning in utility units, which, of course, differ from household to household. If incomes, needs, and values were alike for all households, the money calculus would correspond exactly with the calculus of the simple economy; but, as matters stand, the richer classes can extend their utility margins much farther down the scale of satiation than the poorer classes (pages 340–341).

Exchange and its mechanism lead on to social production and distribution of income. Wieser's theory of distribution is, on the one hand, a continuation of his theory of prices and, on the other hand, a continuation of his theory of imputation applied to the factors of production where economic classes have been differentiated (page 359). There is an economic rent, interest, profit, and wage ascertainable by imputation, and a contract rent, interest, and wage, though, of course, not a contract profit, determined on the basis of the first in the form of prices. Wieser gives us in substance a Ricardian theory of rent, a productivity theory of interest with a time-discount appendage to take care of consumer's loans, and a residual-claimant theory of profits. Perhaps the last phrase has misleading implications. Enterprisers' incomes include wages for labor of management, interest on invested capital, and profits proper—what remains. This remainder, when there is one, enters into the calculus by virtue of specific imputation as the product of the enterpriser's function (page 374). As for wages, they are fixed in the last resort by the marginal contribution imputed to labor (page 384).

VII

Wieser cannot leave distribution without dilating upon the errors inherent in the capitalistic calculus of exchange values. On this head he winds up:

The judgment of history upon the present condition of labor under capitalism cannot be rendered until its trend has been made clear by future developments. If our times show themselves to have been a transition historically necessary for providing a secure and human existence for elements of the population left in want by earlier times, then it will finally merit that wondering praise heaped today upon its technical inventions. But if society splits into a small class of exceedingly rich and a proletarian mass, while the middle classes nearly disappear; or even if the status of today becomes fixed and unchanging, then the much-admired era of capitalistic technique and organization will be condemned as the ending of civilization. For the time being the saying of . . . . Förster applies: "Morally and spiritually modern society is unequal to the task of using the enormous material power harnessed by its science and technique" [page 397].

Most of us are ready to stop with some such safe verdict of the either-or variety. Not so Wieser. The meaning of social economy is not made clear in his eyes until the question is answered whether private property itself is compatible with what social economy stands for. As he phrases the question for purposes of attack, "Is private property imposed by the strong, or is it maintained by the community's common sense?"

In answering this question Wieser takes up the historical development of private property in medieval and modern times. The transition from the manorial and guild systems to capitalism was accompanied by, and in large part consisted in, removing restrictions upon economic freedom. Organization based upon individual initiative and private property won a complete victory over feudalism; and this victory was due to no external force but to the inherent economic superiority of the new system. In part this revolution was sanctioned by changes in the written law; but the essential content of economic individualism has sustained itself by its own strength; it has remained unwritten law. Neither the fact that the social process of industrial production is segregated into parts under individual control, and that the national wealth is divided up among private citizens, nor the fact that the state and other governmental agencies play a secondary role in economic life is ordained by statutes. Yet these facts are the foundation that determines the character of modern economic organization; they even lend the written economic law its wide importance. Institutions of such crucial significance could develop without legal enactment only because of the strong appeal they made to men's economic judgment. Historically the older system of constraint was justified; it was necessary to subordinate personal interest to the commonweal. But economic freedom through the cumulative social training it gave to individuals won an ever greater security, and the time came when compulsion could be dispensed with. The superiority of the new system consists at bottom in this: it bends the colossal energy of egoism to the service of public welfare.

Thus capitalism in its earlier stages was one of the forces of freedom and with its definitive victory came in the *laissez-faire* doctrine of the classical economists. But the new system of freedom promptly developed a despotism of its own. Profits obtained from the sheer financial control over markets without the exercise of social leadership, the creation of a laboring proletariat, the reduction of work to a mechanical routine, the physical and moral degradation of the lower classes—these phenomena of capitalism are socially irrational, anti-economic.

Hence, the chief problem of domestic politics today is to protect the commonweal against the despotic might of capital. The classical doctrine of nonintervention assures the maximum of social utility only when there is general equality of power. Where that condition fails, the state must protect the weak against exploitation. There can be no doubt, Wieser believes, that the modern theory of utility when thoroughly worked out will afford the basis for guiding economic policy toward this end. The controlling aim must be the highest attainable social utility; the utility theory will show under what conditions this end can and under what it can not be attained. Even in the present state of the theory certain fundamental principles can be laid down for the guidance of economic policy.

(1) The intervention of the state to prevent economic freedom from breeding economic oppression is in complete harmony with economic rationality. (2) Outside the field occupied by the greater capitalism economic individualism still maintains its historical success. An alteration of fundamental economic institutions is therefore unreasonable. (3) Such a reorganization of large-scale productive enterprises is desirable as will split the difference between industrial despotism and industrial democracy, somewhat as constitutional monarchy splits the difference between absolutism and republicanism. (4) With reference to organizations both of capital and of labor, the state must discriminate those that promote industrial peace and efficiency from those others that merely secure monopolistic advantages to their members. (5) In general, private exchange value plays a wholesome role even in our capitalistic times. But where the state seeks to complement or correct the economic process as it works in private hands, it must make its own independent valuations (pages 412–414). The theoretical basis of these valuations requires a special investigation, which occupies the next book.

VIII

Book III (*Theorie der Staatswirtschaft*) aims to describe the ways in which the economy of the state differs from private economy. The state aims less at the immediate gratification of wants than at the protection and development of gratifications; and less at turning out tangible goods than at furthering social production as a whole. Also, it provides the income necessary to pay for its services to the commonweal by compulsory levies such as no individual can impose.

These peculiarities of the economy of the state express themselves in the state's valuations. As far as it engages in strictly business undertakings, the state reckons like any enterpriser in terms of exchange value. In the various branches of public administration also, the post office, state railways, etc., it must base its calculus upon exchange value, but not upon that alone. It takes social utility into account, as when it sells workingmen's railway tickets at unprofitably low rates. In still other departments where the service rendered is not sold, for example, in building and maintaining roads, these considerations of social, or more accurately, state utility become the controlling factor.

Whenever the goods or services it buys are divisible into parts, the state can follow the trouble-saving marginal law in its use of exchange value or utility. But in many cases it must value things that cannot be divided, that must be taken or rejected as wholes, for example, a railway line needed for national defense though not economically self-supporting. Here the state must fall back upon the total utility of the thing in question. Even then, however, the state treats the particular commodities and services it requires as divisible goods. But in its valuations of labor it diverges from the businessman's attitude. To the state, labor is not a mere commodity to be bought at the market price; the laborer is a citizen whose welfare is of concern to it.

All these seeming inconsistencies in the modes of valuation followed by the state are reconciled when one remembers that they are merely the roads through different districts to a single goal—the maximizing of utility. The vagueness of total utility, its incalculable character as opposed to marginal utility, is responsible for much of the uncertainty and for many of the differences of opinion concerning state policies.

The principle of greatest utility determines not only what the state should undertake, but also how it should distribute the cost. The concept of subjective or personal value affords the theoretical basis for taxation according to faculty with its progressive rates. But, Wieser adds with characteristic caution, the state is not justified in using progressive taxes to equalize the distribution of incomes and property; for it has been shown that the individualistic organization of economic life is to be respected as an historically sanctioned form of society, and with that organization goes its legitimate consequence, inequality in wealth.

IX

The brief fourth book, with which the treatise closes, is devoted primarily to showing how the *Weltwirtschaft* differs from the *Volkswirtschaft*. The former possesses no such unity as the latter in political organization, historical development, or social culture. Hence, the tendency to establish an equilibrium in economic affairs is much less marked in the world at large than within the several nations. This difference appears clearly in the matter of prices; the number of goods that really have a world market is relatively small. Even interest on capital is not reduced to the same level in different countries. That means that the purchasing power of money is not equalized. The classical theory that gold flows away from the places where its value is low to places where its value is high does not hold true. The international balance of payments is simply a result of the fact that each family within a nation must maintain a balance of payments. Nor were the classical economists right in proclaiming free trade advantageous for all countries. Friedrich List's policy of protective tariffs to develop home industries is sound. Nations are debarred from entering upon a diversified industrial development less by lack of natural resources, as the classicists implied, than by lack of technical knowledge, business experience, and capital. These requisites do not flow freely across international boundaries as they do to different sections of a single country; but they can be developed at home if protected for a time.

For a nation menaced by superior foreign competition, a well-considered system of protective duties assures in the long run the furthest attainable stretching of the economic utility margins, and in the last resort it assures this same desideratum to the whole world economy, since it brings about the greatest attainable equality of development [p. 444].

X

In the preceding pages, I have tried to give an accurate sketch of Wieser's system of theory—to indicate its scope, its articulation, and its main conclusions. But to me the most interesting feature of the book is the writer's attitude toward his own work.

When von Wieser published his treatise, Menger's *Volkswirtschaftslehre* lay more years behind him than Ricardo's *Political Economy* lay behind Mill when Mill published his *Principles*. In the meantime the utility theory has been as much discussed, as variously judged, and as thoroughly tried out as classical political economy in its day. It has passed through a time of cold neglect, a time of hot controversy, and a time of temperate acceptance. It has been extolled as a revolutionary discovery, and depreciated as a minor variant of classical doctrine; adopted as a substitute for Marxism by one set of socialists,[11] and decried as a covert defence of the established order by another set; buried as a corpse infected with hedonism and resurrected as an innocuous theory

[11] See Bernard Shaw, "On the History of Fabian Economics," in *History of the Fabian Society*, by Edward R. Pease, Appendix I, London, 1916.

of choice. The three original strains of the theory, English, Austrian, and French, have been cultivated independently, crossed upon each other, blended with other types, and fertilized by new ideas, giving rise in this process of experimentation to a bewildering variety of doctrines.

Wieser has seen all this happen since he sat at Menger's feet. He can read his own contributions in every history of modern economics, and meet his critics in every economic journal. He has had years for reflection. We know that he holds fast to the fundamentals of his youth; but how does he justify that attitude? How is his version of the Austrian doctrine related to other types of economic theory? Above all, what service does he render toward an understanding of economic behavior?

XI

At the very outset Wieser ranks himself in the psychological school. "The following investigation," runs his first sentence, "employs that method which people have been wont of late to designate as 'psychological.'" This term is appropriate in that the theory starts with the subjective aspect of economic activity and works outward to account for objective facts, but inappropriate in that it suggests that economics is based upon the science of psychology, which is by no means the case. "The observations of man's inner life developed by 'psychological' economics are independently made, and will remain quite unaffected by whatever conclusion scientific psychology may reach regarding the fundamental character of consciousness."

The task of economic theory is to exploit scientifically and interpret the content of common economic experience. . . . In this work it need not follow connections in the individual's mind farther than is necessary to make clear the sense of his behavior; from more penetrating psychological analysis it should refrain. The consciousness of economic men offers a mine of experiences, possessed by everyone practically engaged in economic activity—experiences that every theorist therefore finds ready within himself, so that he needs no scientific apparatus to assemble them. There are experiences of outer facts, for example the existence of goods and their kinds; there are experiences of inner facts, for example human needs and their laws; there are experiences of how the economic activity of the mass of men arises and runs on. . . . The scope of economic theory is just as wide as these common experiences. The theorist's task always ends when common experience ends, and where science must assemble its observations by historical or statistical work, or, in some other supposedly reliable way [page 133].

This "psychological method" is "empirical; it rests upon observation and has no other aim than to describe reality." But while the historian strives to present a given situation in its full idiosyncrasy, while the statistician tries to count all pertinent cases, the theorist limits himself to what is typical, neglecting the secondary, the accidental, the peculiar. To this end he avails himself of the devices of isolating and idealizing.

The complex presented by experience cannot be explained in its totality, one must isolate and split it up into its elements in order to comprehend their working; further, one must keep these elements in thought free from all disturbances, in order to comprehend their unmixed effects, and if in thought one finally admits disturbances one must take these very disturbances in their typical course, omitting everything accidental. . . . Besides the isolating assumptions that contain less than the full truth, the theoretical economist makes many idealizing assumptions that contain more than the truth. In them he elevates the empirical case in thought to the highest conceivable degree of completeness, because the completest situation is at the same time the simplest and therefore the most comprehensible. Thus, for example, the theorist assumes a model economic man such as never has existed and never can exist in fact.

The theorist begins his work "with isolating and idealizing assumptions of the highest degree of abstraction, in which he includes the pure elements of reality." Then step by step he introduces assumptions of greater concreteness and so approximates a description of experience, though without ever attempting to reach the limit of the full detail (pages 134, 135).

XII

Such is the writer's preliminary statement regarding the scope and method of his work. What are the reader's final impressions of Wieser's results?

He may sum up the treatise as follows: Economic activity is the exercise of rational control over the process of providing for wants; its aim is to secure the maximum satisfaction possible under the circumstances; its instrument is the utility calculus. The theory is an elaborate analysis of this calculus: first, as it would be conducted by a single, perfect economic man; next, as it is conducted by many men living under a regime of nominally free contract and private property unequally distributed; then, as it should be conducted by a single state aiming at the welfare of its citizens; finally, as it should be conducted by one among several states.

"Psychological" is certainly a misleading term to apply to such theory, not merely for Wieser's reason, that it implies the dependence of economics upon psychology, but because it implies an intention to explain how men's minds actually work in economic behavior. "Logical" would be a more accurate adjective. For, even more than most members of his school, Wieser deals not with economic activity as it is, but with economic activity as it logically ought to be. His work is not a positive, but a normative theory.

There is no mistaking that conclusion in Books I, III, and IV. We are not left to inference; Wieser declares his position explicitly:

The way in which economic theory presents its description of the laws of economic valuing and economic acting, differs strikingly from the way in which the natural sciences present their laws of nature. The natural sciences show us a necessary connection between cause and effect—what must be; economic theory shows us a connection that follows under the pressure of economic duty—what ought to be; economic valuation is the valuation that economic duty demands, economic action is the economically requisite action [p. 152].

And so, on page after page, one finds the discussion concerned with what a good economic subject, whether an individual or a state, must do to attain his end of maximizing satisfaction.

Even Book II (*Theorie der Volkswirtschaft*) deals less with how men do behave than with why their behavior diverges from what it ought logically to be. Wieser's theory of economic society shows how inequality arises; his theory of prices and of distribution shows the struggle between the effects of inequality and the demands of "economic duty"; his program of economic reform shows how far the state should go in reducing inequality.[12] The "pure elements of reality" (page 135) presented in the theory of the single economy are to Wieser's mind not only the fundamental economic truth, but also the standard by which to try the imperfect world of business dealings, and the guide by which to mend what is there amiss.

XIII

Both in his normative conception of economics and in his program of moderate reform, Wieser stands close to the classical economists. For their work he expresses the warmest admiration. The classical theory, says his preface, is "one of the most splendid and practically significant achievements of the scientific spirit, and despite all opposition it will not

[12] See Sections V, VI, and VII above.

wholly lose its influence upon theory and practice so long as its place is not filled by a maturer doctrine." For this maturer doctrine he hopes a practical success like that which the elder English economists attained.

> As the times of the classicists needed a theory of economic freedom, so our times need a modern theory that represents the practical tendencies of the present in their true meaning; that sees both lights and shadows, guarding against optimism and pessimism alike; that recognizes not only the community of interests but also the existence of force, struggle, and economic evil; that provides a theoretical basis for economic freedom, and also for the necessary limitations upon it [page 136].

Concretely, this turns out to mean the maintenance of private property and such inequalities of wealth as do not arise from unfair competition.[13] So Bentham and Ricardo might have advised had they lived long enough to see free competition begetting monopoly and requiring state intervention to undo its work.

For the mathematical economists and their theory of static equilibrium, on the contrary, Wieser has little use. He will not allow his system of logic to be turned into a system of mechanics. To him the central element in economics is man's planning, and he becomes uneasy when a mathematician replaces human nature by a set of equations. Besides, he argues, nature yields some goods abundantly, some moderately, some scantily; while this fact remains it is vain to talk about establishing an equilibrium in all branches of production. Similarly, the differences between the satiation scales of various wants prevent our reaching an equilibrium in all branches of consumption. Marginal boundaries, not equilibria, represent the facts and should therefore be represented by the theory (pages 164, 165).

[13] See Section VII above.

XIV

The advantages of Wieser's type of economic theory are evident. To show what economic men logically ought to do is far easier than to show what they actually do. For this purpose, as Wieser says, the theorist needs no historical or statistical apparatus; he has simply to analyze that treasure of common experiences that he finds ready within himself. Besides being easy to make, such theory meets the human appeal for guidance toward reform. One has only to accept economic duty as moral duty; then, whenever facts diverge from the theory, the facts are wrong, though none the less facts, and wrong in ways that the theory shows how to correct. Another shift fits the theory to pass as scientific. Grant that men are essentially rational; then the theory reveals substantial economic truth. Discrepancies between this substantial truth and the literal truth are accounted for by showing that existing inequalities imply subordination and that subordination weakens the economic judgment as well as reduces economic power. These three advantages, indeed, are not peculiar to Austrian theory; they are shared by classical economics. But for the Austrians a fourth advantage may be claimed: they seem to be more profound than the classical masters in that they base their whole analysis upon man's ultimate economic interest, the gratification of wants. Finally, as opposed to much modern work, Austrian theory in general and Wieser's version in particular is agreeably realistic; it deals with human planning, not with mathematical abstractions.

To make the defects of the theory as clear as its merits, one must take the psychological viewpoint in sober earnest—far more seriously than Wieser takes it. Seen from this viewpoint, economics is one among several sciences dealing with different aspects of human behavior. It is, of course, a social science; that is, it deals with the behavior of men in organized communities. Its special province is the behavior of social groups in providing the means for attaining their various ends.

Now, human behavior can be studied either from outside or from inside the human being. An economist may observe and record what men do in business, as a meteorologist observes and records the weather. An economic historian may study the recorded observations of others on human behavior, as a geologist studies evidences of former conditions of the earth's crust. And these objective students may try to frame illuminating generalizations about human behavior, without the aid of suppositions concerning human aims. Such work is as truly part of economic theory from the psychological viewpoint as is the Austrian analysis. Contemporary observation, indeed, is that part of economic theory in which the most rigorous standards can be applied, the most refined analysis developed, and the best-grounded hopes entertained for improvements in data and results. But work of this objective kind cannot be done without the statistical and historical apparatus that Wieser rejects.

Most economic theorists, however, elect to study behavior from inside the individual. Introspection of their own feelings and common observation provide the data; common sense decides what items in the array are typical; common logic weaves these items into a theory. This is the most intimately human and the most treacherous of all professedly scientific methods. The classical economists employed it in the early stages of theorizing with more justification than any writer of today can claim; yet they admitted the need of a safeguard, "inductive verification." Wieser, however, will not let a theorist use the statistical and historical apparatus which such verification requires; when anyone does use these aids he ceases to be a theorist.[14] Another safeguard has been invented by the mathematical economists. After making an (imaginary) photograph of each individual's "curves of indifference," they throw away the rest of human nature, and demonstrate mathematically that one composite and only one can be made from a given set of negatives. But neither will Wieser join this company. He will not limit his theorizing to the simplest problems or put his reasoning into the severest form. Still a third way of guarding against errors and omissions remains. The economist who works from inside the human mind might seek all the aid possible from psychology. Wieser will have no such aid.

Yet if he had been willing to utilize psychology, Wieser might have made out a better case for his own theory. The behavior that concerns the economist is directed chiefly by certain social institutions, that is, by certain widely shared habits of feeling, thinking, and acting in frequently recurring situations. These habits, like our space perceptions, have elaborate implications that are not immediately apparent. It is useful to think out these implications carefully, as it is useful to excogitate geometry. Such elaboration is by no means the whole task of economic theory, but it is part of the task. Wieser expounds the Austrian contribution to this

---

[14] Although Wieser occasionally refers to history, for example in discussing the rise of the money economy (pp. 327–329), the differentiation of economic classes from antiquity to modern times (pp. 348–351), and the development of large business enterprise (pp. 355–356), his references are so general in their terms as hardly to justify the charge of inconsistency. The only case in which his theory really bases its validity upon historical data occurs when he discusses the problem whether private property is compatible with true social economy. The answer to this question, he admits, cannot be deduced from the psychology of the model economic man (p. 403). But the historical sketch by which he justifies his faith in private property as a proper economic institution is, as he points out (p. 400), very much a theorist's version of history.

logic of economic institutions better than any of his com-
patriots; but his work would have been more effective if he
had seen the place his contribution occupies in the study of
behavior.

A man who realizes that he is studying an institution keeps
his work in historical perspective, even when he confines
himself to analyzing the form that the institution has assumed at a particular stage of its evolution. By so doing he
opens vistas enticing to future exploration, instead of suggesting a closed system of knowledge. He does not delude
himself into believing that anyone's personal experience is an
adequate basis for theorizing about how men behave; rather
is he eager to profit by any light shed upon his problem
by any branch of learning—history, statistics, ethnology,
psychology.

More particularly, a student of economic institutions
recognizes that business accounting is much more thoroughly
rationalized than household accounting, that the money calculus is better thought out than the utility calculus. Hence
he does not picture economic logic as having its stronghold
in the single economy, without money and without price. To
him money is a powerful instrument of theoretical analysis
because money is the most effective practical instrument for
systematizing economic control, and because its use enforces
the strictest discipline upon vague and careless human nature. As Wieser remarks, the most perfect cases are the
simplest and easiest to analyze. It follows that economic
theory should begin with the most thoroughly organized
money prices, instead of postponing money to a late stage
of the investigation. When the definite and objective interrelations among money prices have been analyzed it is time
enough to penetrate into the dim mysteries of our feelings
about utilities, and to inquire how the logical system of con-

trol men learn in business dealings is related to their subjective valuations.

When the latter problem is approached, the economist who still remembers that he is a student of institutions finds more work and more materials on hand than Wieser dreams. It is an old and valid criticism that the Austrian theory of value throws little light on the process of valuation. It supposes men to come to market with their minds definitely made up regarding the prices they will pay. The demand schedules it presents are purely imaginary and are used only as illustrations. Everything that happens in the market—and that means substantially the whole content of economic theory—is supposed to be predetermined in an almost mechanical way by such schedules. Nevertheless, a serious study of them has been no part of orthodox theory. It is, however, a vital part of the study of economic behavior. We all know that our wants are standardized by certain social habits, that these habits present remarkable uniformities, and that they have a long recorded history. Hence, they can be investigated with excellent prospects of success, as the widely different studies of Professors Veblen and Henry L. Moore may prove to all doubters. But in this field again the investigators must employ the aids that Wieser bans, psychological analysis, historical research, and statistical measurement.

Wieser's greatest service is that by rounding out Austrian theory he has shown the limitations of what can be accomplished along that line. More emphatically than any criticism, his finished construction calls for a fresh start. The task before us is to attack the problem of economic behavior, equipped with the fullest knowledge and the most powerful instruments of analysis that the day affords.

13

SOMBART'S HOCHKAPITALISMUS[1]

Der moderne Kapitalismus made its first appearance in
1902. The work then consisted of two stout volumes, some
1,350 pages, tracing the rise of capitalism from its tentative
beginnings in the Middle Ages to its full development in the
nineteenth century. At once this vigorous study of economic
behavior excited keen interest. The wide scope of the investigation, the full documentation, the constructive power
revealed in organizing a vast mass of materials elicited admiration. Werner Sombart seemed to recapture that blend
of history and theory which had lent intellectual distinction
to Marx's *Kapital*—that blend which Schmoller had striven
after with less success. But in detail the work was uneven. A

[1] Reprinted by permission from *Quarterly Journal of Economics*, vol. XLIII,
a review of pp. 303–323, February, 1929. *Der moderne Kapitalismus.* Dritter
Band. *Das Wirtschaftsleben im Zeitalter des Hochkapitalismus.* Munich and Leipzig,
1928.

All three volumes of *Der moderne Kapitalismus* (bound as six), in their several
latest editions, may now be had from the publishers in uniform style. As the work
now stands, the titles may be rendered thus: *Modern Capitalism—An historical and
systematic exposition of Europe's economic life from its beginning to the present day.*
    Vol. I. Precapitalism.
        Part i. Introduction, The Precapitalistic Economy. Pp. xxiv + 462.
        Part ii. The Historical Foundations of Modern Capitalism. Pp. ix + 463–919.
    Vol. II. Early Capitalism.
        Parts i and ii. Economic Life of Europe in the Age of Early Capitalism, chiefly
            the sixteenth, seventeenth, and eighteenth centuries. Pp. xii + 585
            and xi + 587–1229.
    Vol. III. High Capitalism.
        Part i. Foundations and Structure. Pp. xxii + 514.
        Part ii. Economic Processes of High Capitalism. Economic Organization as a
            Whole. Pp. x + 517–1063.

succession of critics cast doubt upon several of the writer's fondest contentions. Fortunately for the rest of us, Sombart was driven by the demoniac energy of one of those capitalist enterprisers at whose irrational self-exploitation he marvels. Spurred on by praise and blame, he set himself to rework the whole field more intensively.

In 1916 the first volume of the expanded treatise came out in two parts. A second volume, also in two parts, followed in 1917. Ten years later "the third and provisionally the last" volume appeared—another set of twins.

Closely related to various parts of this imposing structure are Sombart's other books: *War and Capitalism, Luxury and Capitalism, The Jews and Economic Life, The Future of the Jews, The Bourgeois, Traders and Heroes, Proletarian Socialism, The Nineteenth Century in Germany.* Truly a prodigious pile to come from one pen!

The quality of this output is as intriguing as its quantity is impressive. Werner Sombart puts his own stamp upon everything he writes. From its metaphysical foundations to its literary finish, his work is highly individualized. He has brought to light buried treasures of daily life in the Middle Ages. He has found new meanings in familiar materials. He has challenged conclusions that pass muster in our economic histories and concepts accepted in our theoretical treatises. In view of the seeming collapse of the German "historical school," his method of work has an interest approaching the dramatic. Every serious student of economics should acquaint himself with Sombart's contribution.

Yet that contribution seems not to be well known outside the writer's land. No one has ventured to translate the three thousand pages of *Der moderne Kapitalismus* into English. The books that have been translated are less impressive than the *magnum opus.* And German is a glass through which most

English-speaking economists see but darkly. The competent scholar who presents us with a full-length sketch of Sombart's work and its bearing upon other approaches to economics will merit our thanks. Meanwhile, the best service a reviewer of the volume on *Hochkapitalismus* can render is to tell what the book contains.

I

The age of high capitalism began in the 1760's and ended in August, 1914. A series of great inventions, among which the coke process of smelting iron was decisive, ushered in the age. Signs of its approaching end appeared before 1914— the intrusion of normative ideas into business practice, the disestablishment of profit seeking as the sole guide of economic activity, declining flexibility, the steadier course of evolution, the substitution of agreements for free competition, the standardizing of industrial organization. Capitalism was growing old—its spirit was suffering change. The war made this change manifest.

To Sombart, capitalism is a "historical individual," "a peculiar episode in the history of mankind." At bottom, money-making has no relation with the economic life that matters. Yet because a handful of men were smitten with a passion to make money, hundreds of millions of human beings have been called into existence, and human culture has been made over. The revolutionary changes spread at extraordinary speed from England, their cultural center, over Western Europe and Eastern North America. From these strongholds high capitalism turned to its uses the rest of the earth.

It is an idea that has wrought these wonders. But—and here Sombart's metaphysics gets in his way—idea and actuality cannot be causally related. How comes it, then, that the actual world has been stamped with the pattern of the capitalist idea? Sombart surmounts this artificial difficulty by a most characteristic argument. (1) We must accept certain fundamental facts of economic evolution as historical accidents. In recent times the fundamental economic facts happened to fit well with the premises of capitalism—that is the basic reason why evolution followed the line marked out by the capitalistic idea. The facts in question are three: a new type of man assumed the direction of economic activities; a new type of state developed; a new technique came to dominate industry. The business enterpriser, the modern state, the machine process are "the foundations" upon which high capitalism is built. (2) The conditions under which high capitalism was erected upon these foundations might have been such as to hinder the work. What capitalism needed for full development was capital, labor, markets. These needs were met in optimal fashion. Again accident played a role, as in the discovery of great gold deposits, the rapid increase of population, the existence of virgin resources awaiting exploitation. But other favorable factors—increased productivity, the credit system, the "mobilizing of commodities"—were evoked by the primary forces themselves. (3) The capitalistic process, as it unfolded, forced developments in the direction that suited its spirit, by rationalizing economic activity.

This curious argument in the preface controls the whole discussion of *High Capitalism*. Book I, "The Foundations," deals successively with the capitalist enterpriser, the modern state, and modern technique. Book II, "The Building," deals with capital, labor, and markets. Book III, "The Process," deals with the rationalizing of wants, of marketing, of production. There follows a brief section upon noncapitalistic forms of organization which have lasted over from an earlier age, or which appear as harbingers of an age to come. The last chapter of all dips into the future. Whatever doubts one may feel about the professed origin of this scheme of organization, the outline is neat.

II

Sombart assigns the leading role in the drama of high capitalism to the business organizer. It is he and he alone who furnishes the driving power. Whether primarily a captain of industry, a merchant, a financier, the business leader assigns all minor functions to others. He can buy routine intelligence and install it in his enterprise like a master clock. His operations are not bound by the limits of his own property, for he uses mainly the property of others. He is not hampered like his predecessors by regard for tradition or regard for religion. Desire of gain, a will to power, a drive toward activity inspire his restlessness. These dynamic impulses are disciplined by a sublime economic rationality. Hand in hand passion and reason have produced an unprecedented outburst of human efficiency, which is blind to but one thing—the end of all this teeming activity.

The modern state represents the union of two incompatible principles—liberalism and the policy of power. Domestic policy is liberal in the sense that economic affairs are left mainly to individual initiative. Foreign policy also was affected by the liberal ideology for a time, particularly in England. But the free-trade movement never cut very deep, and the last quarter of the nineteenth century brought a reaction toward "Realpolitik," of which Bismarck was the prophet. Neomercantilism now dominates the field, with its high tariffs, militarism, and imperialism.

What Sombart has to say about the third cornerstone of high capital may be reported a bit more fully, to give at least one example of his characteristic mode of elaboration.

Industrial technique is twin sister to natural science. Scientific discoveries give rise to invention; inventions often lead to discoveries; frequently discoveries are inventions. Hence, the stages in technical progress derive from the stages of scientific advance. The theoretical work of Galileo and Newton, of Euler, Maclaurin and Lagrange, of Poinsot and Robert Mayer provided the basis for three successive stages of applied mechanics. In chemistry, Lavoisier and Priestley laid the foundations; Wöhler and Liebig pushed into the organic field; Kekule and van't Hoff founded stereochemistry. Similarly in the electric field: Faraday and Ampère established the basic conceptions; Gauss and Weber developed the theory of conduction, Clerk-Maxwell and Hertz that of electrical waves. Our dynamos, telegraphs, and radios grew out of these successive achievements. Cosmical theory in the age of early capitalism was content with the traditional view of a craftsman God who made the world in six days, pronounced it good, and rested on the seventh day. Modern science conceives the universe as a system of relationships among electrical charges. Industrial technique likewise has moved out of the craftsman stage, trying (as Andrew Ure said a century ago) "to substitute mechanical science for hand skill." Science thinks the world a physico-chemical mechanism; industrial technique makes a world on this scientific model. Trade secrets jealously guarded give place to scientific publications; rules based upon experience give place to scientific laws that are demonstrated; as far as possible all operations are transferred from the variable personal factor to automatic mechanisms.

Granted all this, the crucial question remains: How can we explain the extraordinary number of inventions made in our epoch? Sombart answers, "By observing both the objective and the subjective conditions which have stimulated invention." I shall save space by listing these conditions in quasi-tabular form:

Objective Conditions

1. The scientific basis of modern technique.
   (*a*) The objective recording of technical knowledge guarantees its preservation and facilitates its spread.
   (*b*) The systematizing of technical knowledge binds one problem to another, so that one invention leads to other inventions.
   (*c*) The mathematical form in which technical knowledge is cast tends to produce a quasi-automatic extension of a solution found for one problem to other problems.
2. The favorable reception accorded to inventions.
   (*a*) The hostility toward inventors and their works, violent in the Middle Ages, still strong in the early capitalistic era, has turned into a spirit of admiring welcome.
   (*b*) The striving after material progress, so characteristic of our time, creates an eager demand for inventions.
   (*c*) Capitalism favors inventions for the profits hoped from them.
3. The active stimulation of inventions in three ways:
   (*a*) Technical schools with research laboratories.
   (*b*) Research bureaus set up by great corporations.
   (*c*) The subvention of inventing by

   A. paying for patents,
   B. granting subsidies,
   C. offering prizes.

Subjective Conditions

In former times the finer spirits paid scant attention to vulgar matters of technique. As for the hewers of wood and the drawers of water, they did things as they had been taught. Not until the dawn of modern times did an interest in invention appear. At first this interest was irrational, romantic, baroque. Gradually it grew into the many-sided interest of our time.

In the epoch of high capitalism we have three types of inventors:
(*a*) The genius, like Bessemer or Solvay, who invents new processes despite his lack of technical training. Such cases are exceptional.

[264]

(*b*) The lay inventor, who happens upon one, perhaps upon several, ingenious contrivances. But more important, and peculiar to our age, is

(*c*) The professional inventor, who may be a man working on his own account like Edison, but is usually a highly trained employee in some research laboratory.

The motives that stimulate modern invention may be classified as follows:

1. Pleasure in inventing.
2. Interest in the results of an invention arising from philanthropy, enthusiasm for progress, military considerations, ambition, and so on.
3. Desire for gain, which doubtless remains the most powerful incentive.

Finally, we should ask: What inventions are made? The answer is: The business organizer decides whether an invention is "good," that is, profitable. Only inventions that promise a profit are put to use. Thus invention in the era of high capitalism serves business, and business alone. Other interests of mankind are not cared for, save in so far as service is good business.

Sombart's volumes run a thousand pages apiece because nearly every topic is drawn out after this fashion. I have condensed on the scale of one to twelve. Despite the author's gusto, despite his gift for phrasemaking, the reader's interest flags as he descends the ladder from numerals to Roman and then to Greek letters. But ever and again an arresting idea springs from its formal setting and grips his attention. From this point forward I shall note only the intriguing parts.

One such is Sombart's favorite idea that modern technique seeks emancipation from the hobbles of living nature. As far as possible, it chooses inorganic materials in place of organic—metals replace wood, coal-tar dyes replace vegetable dyes, mineral lubricants replace animal oils, and so on. Similarly with prime movers: man power and animal power are replaced by steam, electricity, and the internal combustion engine. Working processes undergo a like transformation. For the ordinary processes of nature, modern technique substitutes artfully arranged chemical or mechanical processes, designed to convert standardized materials into standardized products, through a continuous series of operations on a quantity basis. And, of course, human labor is one of the erratic natural agents of which the technician is most eager to be rid.

III

Book II, as said above, deals with capital, labor, and markets.

Sombart defines capital as "those sums of exchange value that serve as the material basis for a capitalist enterprise." Capital comes into existence whenever money is used to establish or enlarge a business. The most conspicuous characteristic of our era is that it presented optimal conditions for the growth of capital. Large "savings" were made possible by the increase in production, by the exceedingly uneven distribution of wealth, and by the prevalent interest in accumulating. There were also strong inducements to invest these accumulations in business, thus converting potential into actual capital. Credit has contributed enormously to the growth of capital by the facilities it provides for making business use of scattered savings, by enabling the able businessman to expand his operations far beyond the limits of his own fortune, by bringing "into commerce the present value of future profits," and by giving the whole business structure an extraordinary combination of intricate organization and flexibility.

Capital goods consist of the commodities in which capital "clothes itself" for a time. The problem concerning their origins is the problem of production. There are three ways in which production can be heightened, and high capitalism has made use of all three: more effective use of given resources, exploitation of new areas, drawing upon the past accumulations of nature. Sombart dwells at length upon the many methods of making labor more effective, and upon the spread of capitalist exploitation into the crannies of Western Europe, thence eastward across Russia into Asia, westward across the Atlantic to the Americas, and southward to Australia and Africa. Most of all he emphasizes the extent to which high capitalism has flourished by robbing the soil, felling the forests, and drawing lavishly upon irreplaceable mineral resources. The greater part of capital goods, at least in manufactures and transportation, represents not annual income but the consumption of man's natural patrimony.

Passing from capital to labor, Sombart attacks a similar problem: Whence came the labor power that high capitalism needed to handle the enormous flow of capital goods? Several sources were drawn upon. Capitalists stole savages and worked them as slaves. But that proved a dwindling resource. Far more important was the dissolution of the old rural and craft organizations in which and by which a large part of the European populations still lived in the age of early capitalism. These organizations could not withstand the direct competition of rationalized technique and its influence upon legislation and administration. Deprived of their old methods of livelihood, a large part of the peasantry and the handicraftsmen had to seek capitalist employment. But the richest source of labor power was the spontaneous growth in population. Never had the world known such an increase as appeared in the nineteenth century. The increase came not from a rise in birth rates, but from a fall in death rates. Hygiene and medicine made remarkable progress, but the chief credit must be assigned to the more abundant means of livelihood. In the last resort, capitalism itself produced the labor power it needed by filling the bellies of the multitude that had hungered.

The production of abundant labor power, however, merely provided a raw material, which high capitalism had to adapt to its exacting needs.

First, population had to be shifted about from the places where it was produced to the places where goods were to be handled. The dissolution of the old forms of organization and the growth of numbers left the rural districts and small towns with far more hands than could be used there. The redistribution of these local surpluses produced the greatest migrations of history. By the millions, families were shifted from country to city, from one country and from one continent to another. And beside these quasi-permanent shiftings, capitalism established a seasonal flow, which carried laborers hundreds or thousands of miles from winter tasks to summer tasks and back again.

Second, the workers had to be adapted to the technical requirements of capitalism. Sombart recalls the difficulties experienced by the early factory managers in teaching refractory human beings, accustomed to irregular paroxysms of labor, the sustained regularity of effort demanded by machine tending—difficulties half forgotten in Europe, but experienced afresh in each backward land invaded by the machine process. To induce steady habits, the workers had further to be inspired with the desire to get on in the world after the capitalist ideal. "It is one of the strangest stupidities of current theory to represent the desire for gain as an inborn trait of human nature." At first it seemed necessary to keep wages down to a minimum, so that men must work steadily or go hungry. But when some measure of steadiness was attained, it appeared that intense application could not be sustained on minimum wages. So employers adopted various schemes intended to stimulate effort. While Sombart questions Max Weber's thesis that Puritanism had a large share in forming the capitalist spirit of businessmen, he thinks it did help to discipline workers in the new way of life. But more important in his eyes was the direct influence of the new environment. As capitalism produced its own labor force, so it shaped its products after its own image. With characteristic rationality, it facilitated the task of adapting the workers to its needs by adapting its needs to the workers. Splitting up its processes into numberless successive steps, it produced mass jobs of the simplest that required scarcely any training, and confined its demand for intelligence within limits that could be met. Recently it has begun to grade its human material, seeking to put every man into a job that suits his peculiar capacities. In this way capitalism can get the most out of its employees, and provide the most for them.

Third, capitalism had to adjust labor to its economic needs—that is, to establish such a relationship between the total value of the product and total wage disbursements as meets its primary requirement of profits. The only real "law" of wages is the law of supply and demand. As shown above, capitalism produced an enormous supply of labor in Europe; it made use of children, women, and the rural surplus; at need it drew also upon the population of backward lands. On the other hand, its demand for labor mounted ever higher, threatening to raise the price of labor to levels that would encroach upon profits. But high capitalism provided safeguards against this danger. At recurrent intervals it reduced its demand for labor well below the current supply. The existence of the famous "reserve army" is an indisputable fact. Changes in technique kept throwing men out of employment, and the quasi-rhythmical fluctuations of capitalist activity reduced the demand whenever profit margins shrank.

There remained as final safeguard increases of physical output. Hence, though earnings per capita rose in the nineteenth century, the cost of labor per unit of product declined. The net resultant of the complicated forces is best shown by the American Census of Manufactures. Labor's share in the product is reported directly. One can approximate capital's share by subtracting costs of materials plus wage disbursements from the value of products. Thus analyzed, the American figures show an average annual rise of 2.52 per cent in wages during the 65 years from 1850 to 1915. But profits rose faster still—3.08 per cent per annum. Others may doubt this use of the census data; it convinces Sombart that high capitalism has succeeded in adapting labor to its needs economically, as well as technically.

It remains to show how the third requirement of high capitalism—markets—has been met. Who bought the products turned out in such masses?

Two sources of demand must be distinguished: the exogenous and the endogenous—the demand from outside the capitalist system proper, and from inside the system.

Of the two, the exogenous demand is the older. Nascent capitalism sold its products mainly to people who were neither business enterprisers nor employees of business enterprises. And this demand has continued large. It includes landed proprietors, the world of high finance (brokers and speculators), governments of all grades, the population of the Balkan States, Russia, Asia, Africa, and Latin America. In this class, too, Sombart reckons the agricultural and handicraft workers, whose practice of producing for themselves capitalism has broken down in large measure. Finally, he mentions the monetary demand arising from the production of gold, the issue of uncovered paper currency, and credits.

Endogenous demand embraces both the buying of consumers' goods by capitalist enterprisers and their employees, and the buying of industrial equipment by business concerns. High capitalism can really thrive on itself: as the classical economists claimed, each unit of its output constitutes a demand for other goods. It is forever creating a demand for its own products by altering its methods. Machines, factories, railways, ships, mines, electric installations—it needs such things without number. And its own personnel are fed, clothed, lodged, amused more and more by what it makes and transports with its varied equipment. British, French, and American statistics show that real wages have doubled within the period of high capitalism. This finding confirms and is confirmed by an estimate that the productivity of labor has about doubled within the same time. If profits have grown faster still, as seems to be true, it must be that capitalists have got the better of their exchanges with the non-capitalist classes and countries.

IV

Book III, "The Process," is as long as Books I and II put together. It deals with the activities characteristic of high capitalism. The end of these activities is to gain profits. The means employed to this end are contracts in terms of money concerning services to be rendered and received. Paradoxically, this scheme of organization, which does not aim at satisfying wants, nevertheless does provide for human wants incomparably better on the whole than any other scheme that men have tried. The reconciliation between making money and satisfying wants is effected by market prices. A price shows when a need is felt; it also shows the chance of profit and determines the capitalist enterpriser to make his contribution to the satisfying of needs. Hence, there are three "elements" in the capitalistic process: the need, the market, the business enterprise. To these elements correspond three sets of activities: consumption, circulation, and production.

After expounding abstractly the pure concepts of needs, markets, and industry, Sombart turns to the types of motion characteristic of high capitalism. Competition is one type. It is treated with pregnant brevity.

Second come "conjunctures." Whereas crises occurred frequently in precapitalistic and early-capitalistic times, business booms are peculiar to the later period. Sombart still holds to the hypothesis he advanced in 1903—the decisive factor in bringing on a crisis is the disproportionate increase during the boom in the output of inorganic products. Agriculture and the industries that fabricate organic materials have but a small share in expansion, and so disturb the balance of the business world.

Third, high capitalism is characterized by a tendency toward increasing uniformity of its phenomena. It drills us all in a school that inculcates its own peculiar rationality. Absorbing the spirit of our institutions and coerced by the conditions these institutions create, we devote ourselves ever more uniformly to the one great aim of money-making. In this preoccupation we make ever more rational use of ever more standardized means. We live in an economic environment of money prices and our survival depends upon our capacity to adjust our behavior to its demands. So we get rationalized and standardized ourselves—the farmer and the handicraftsman less than the machine tender and the businessman, but all of us in increasing degree.

The business enterprise itself is becoming more and more rationalized and standardized in form and functioning. While individual ventures still constitute the majority of enterprises in every country, corporate organizations do most of the business. A network of varied relationships binds these legally separate entities to one another, making it possible to organize large, intricate, and rapidly shifting undertakings in a fashion that combines close supervision in detail with centralized planning. On the industrial side, there has been achieved a remarkably varied adaptation of organization to the conditions of money-making presented by different trades—specialization here, combination there, each in a bewildering array of forms, and each susceptible of union with the other. With the important exception of agriculture, almost every branch of trade shows a tendency toward increase in the size of the business enterprise. In a few fields, concentration has actually reduced the number of independent enterprises. More commonly, concentration has brought merely an increase in the share of business obtained by the giants. Certainly there has occurred no such sweeping concentration of business control as Karl Marx forecast. As for the internal organization of business enterprises, Sombart points out three closely related developments: business administration becomes more scientific; it becomes more objective and less personal; it becomes more intensive, speeding up the whole set of operations, utilizing more perfectly the materials, equipment, and personnel at its disposal.

V

Having concluded his survey of capitalism "from Charlemagne to Stinnes or Pierpont Morgan," Sombart takes a bird's-eye view of modern economic organization as a whole.

At its apogee just before the war, capitalism did not employ more than a quarter or a third of the breadwinners in Western and Central Europe. This proportion rose to two-fifths in the United States, but it sank to a tenth in Russia. Doubtless capitalism's share in the output is larger than its share in the labor force; yet two older forms of organization dispute its primacy even on this basis.

Handicraft shops with less than six employees provided a living for half of all German workers outside of agriculture, according to the occupational census of 1907. Similar data are not available for all branches of trade in other countries; but common observation, eked out by such figures as can be had, shows that in all capitalistic countries many types of work are still carried on prevailingly or exclusively by small personal enterprises, which retain much of the old-time handicraft spirit.

By far the most important form of economic organization in the world, however, is small-scale agriculture. Europe's peasantry did not decline during the nineteenth century. When the war broke out, there must have been 27 or 28 million peasant enterprises from Poland westward, and 22 million more in Russia. To this number must be added 6 or 7 million farms in North America. Altogether, perhaps two-thirds of the world's population lives in this noncapitalistic fashion.

Cooperative enterprises have made considerable progress in retail trade, wholesale trade, manufacturing, agriculture, and finance—though they are far from rivaling any of the older forms of organization in extent of operations. Their importance lies rather in their promise for the future. The like can be said about communal enterprises. Governments, national and local, do a much larger volume of economic work than is commonly realized, and this share promises to grow.

VI

One of the most interesting chapters in the three volumes of *Modern Capitalism* is the last chapter of all, wherein Sombart dips discreetly into the future.

Certain expectations he is sure will not be realized. No single form of economic organization will prevail to the exclusion of all other forms. For an indefinite time to come capitalism, cooperation, communal enterprises, individuals in business by themselves, handicraft shops, and small-scale agriculture will continue operating side by side. Also everyone who anticipates a violent change in economic organization is mistaken. The recent adventures of Soviet Russia should convince the most skeptical that the past will live on in the future. Nor can mankind turn back to the simpler life of precapitalistic days. The hopes, or fears, that modern technique will end its career by exhausting the natural resources, which it is exploiting so recklessly, overlook one seemingly inexhaustible resource—the inventive ingenuity of that technique itself.

On the positive side, Sombart expects capitalism to endure indefinitely, but to continue changing in the future as it has changed in the past. It will gradually lose its position as the dominating form of economic organization; it will suffer an increasing measure of public control; it will pursue a steadier course, as befits its advancing years. The forms of organization that will gain ground at the cost of capitalism will be those that represent more conscious planning—planning aimed not at making money, but at satisfying needs. We shall find that there is little difference between stabilized and regulated capitalism and a technically developed, rationalized socialism. But this highly organized form of organization will not gather all workers into its fold. The small craftsman and the shopkeeper will continue to exist, perhaps to flourish. The peasant and his American counterpart, the farmer, will grow stronger; for agriculture's share in satisfying needs will mount with the growth of the world's population. Doubtless changes will come over the cultivators—they will acquire a more scientific technique and more businesslike habits; but they will not be enslaved by the spirit of capitalism.

Not, says Sombart in conclusion, so artistic a sketch of the future as Marx drew. But we must resign ourselves to the facts of science, and expect the world to remain a jumble of the old, the changing, and the new.

VII

If economic theory aspires to explain economic behavior, then Sombart's *High Capitalism* is a theoretical contribution. It differs from ordinary expositions of economic theory primarily in respect to the problems it attacks. About the problems that bulk largest in our books on "principles," it says something, but not much. Sombart now and then touches upon value and distribution; but he is chiefly concerned to find what features differentiate high capitalism from other forms of economic organization, how these features got their present form, and how they function. And about these problems our books on economic "principles" say something, but not much. Yet if economics is to give us understanding of economic behavior, treatment of the one set of problems is as indispensable as treatment of the other set. The two approaches complement each other, and an economist needs intimate acquaintance with both.

Sombart's methods differ from the methods employed by a writer like Marshall much as Marshall's methods in *Industry and Trade* differ from Marshall's methods in the *Principles of Economics*. In the superficial jargon we ought to banish, "induction" plays the stellar role that is usually assigned by theorists to "deduction." But no one can read Sombart critically without realizing that speculative notions control the whole course of his investigation. The materials he chooses are those which fit into a more or less fixed scheme of ideas. Indeed, I get the impression that Sombart's chief weakness as a scientific inquirer is that he does not keep restudying and enriching his preconceived notions as he gathers and assimilates his data. His framework is too hard and fast. It does not grow out of his subject matter so much as his subject matter grows out of it. One telltale bit of evidence is the frequency with which he finds three factors in his problems. Do economic phenomena really occur so commonly in triplets?

Sombart is not the only economic theorist whose interest centers in the problems of economic evolution. Karl Marx had that orientation in his scientific moods. So, too, has Thorstein Veblen when he is not indulging his satiric vein. For that matter, is not every economic historian who tries to make the materials he presents fit into a pattern, contributing, in so far as he succeeds, to our understanding of economic behavior?

That theories of the evolution of our current scheme of institutions differ appreciably is disturbing—just as disturbing as are the differences among theories of distribution. Every original inquirer finds his eminent critics. Sombart offers a particularly broad target for attack. He has organized an enormous mass of materials, and few things are easier than to pick flaws in his details. Also, one who does not share his metaphysical and psychological preconceptions must feel doubts of a more searching character. To take but a single point: Can we accept Sombart's contention that the rise of businessmen to power, the transformation of the state, and the development of modern technique were "historical accidents"? I should think it possible to give an account of the development of capitalism in which these phenomena appear as inevitable and closely related products in the process of cumulative change.

[277]

Both by what its readers will take to be defects and by what they will hail as merits, Sombart's work promises to stimulate further inquiry. That is the greatest service a scientific investigation can perform. Certainly *High Capitalism* will give a direct impetus to research in the evolution of institutions. Perhaps it will render a wider service by helping all of us to see how much an economic historian needs to be a theorist, and how limited is the theoretical grasp of an economist who neglects history.

14

THORSTEIN VEBLEN[1]

"TO EXPLAIN the characteristic animus for which Hume stands, on grounds that might appeal to Hume, we should have to inquire into the peculiar circumstances—ultimately material circumstances—that have gone to shape the habitual view of things within the British community."[2] Thus Thorstein Veblen formulates the problem of accounting for the preconceptions of another "placid unbeliever."

To explain the characteristic animus for which Veblen stands, on grounds that might appeal to Veblen, we need a similar inquiry into the peculiar circumstances that have gone to shape the habitual view of things within the American community of his own day. That need is readily met—Veblen has made the inquiry for us. By logical implication, his explanation of the preconceptions of modern science is an explanation of his own characteristic animus. Though there is scarcely a word about himself in all his writings, we can piece together from various books and essays his account of those elements in his thinking which he deems it feasible and interesting to explain.

But this explanation will not satisfy our "idle curiosity" about Thorstein Veblen. There are other elements in the make-up of a thinker besides the habitual view of things that

---

[1] Reprinted by permission of Viking Press, New York, from *What Veblen Taught*, ed. by W. C. Mitchell, pp. vii–xlix, 1936.

[2] "The Preconceptions of Economic Science," 1899. Reprinted in *The Place of Science in Modern Civilisation and Other Essays*, p. 96, New York, 1919.

prevails in the community from which he springs. For example, note what further Veblen says about Hume:

Hume was not gifted with a facile acceptance of the group inheritance that made the habit of mind of his generation. Indeed, he was gifted with an alert, though somewhat histrionic, skepticism touching everything that was well received. . . .

There is in Hume . . . an insistence on the prosy, not to say the seamy, side of human affairs. . . . He insists, in season and out of season, on an exhibition of the efficient causes engaged in any sequence of phenomena; and he is skeptical—irreverently skeptical—as to the need or the use of any formulation of knowledge that outruns the reach of his own matter-of-fact, step-by-step argument from cause to effect.

In short, he is too modern to be wholly intelligible to those of his contemporaries who are most neatly abreast of their time. He out-Britishes the British; and, in his footsore quest for a perfectly tame explanation of things, he finds little comfort, and indeed scant courtesy, at the hands of his own generation. He is not in sufficiently naïve accord with the range of preconceptions then in vogue.

These comments have a double interest. If one knows Veblen, what jumps to mind is that his characterization of Hume might pass as a characterization of himself. Veblen, too, is unable to accept his group inheritance; he is skeptical, he has a histrionic bent, he insists on the seamy side of life, he practices an irreverent neglect of all theories not cast in the matter-of-fact mold. Hence, like Hume, he has not been wholly intelligible to his contemporaries, and he has received scant courtesy at their hands.

A second impression is that Veblen seems to contradict himself. Hume was and was not the child of his time. He was more British than the British, yet he did not accept the habit of mind of his generation. Of course, the contradiction is one in seeming only. Human culture is a crazy quilt of durable patches from the spiritual garments man has worn at successive ages in the past, pieced out by a few patches sewed on recently. Hence, the quilt has many patterns; which one a thinker will prefer depends upon his taste. Hume's contemporaries who treated him with scant courtesy were likewise legitimate children of their time. They liked the older patterns in the crazy quilt—the relics of their ancestors' clothing. Yet a man in advance of the age, repudiated by his generation, may appear in historical perspective to have been the most authentic spokesman for what that generation was adding to culture. He may be typical, for all that he is unique.

This solution of the seeming contradiction throws the problem of the thinker's personality into higher relief. To explain Hume's work, we need not only an inquiry into the peculiar circumstances that shaped the habitual view of things within the British community, but also an inquiry into the circumstances that shaped David Hume into the individual he became, and set him in opposition to his age.

These two inquiries run on different lines and encounter different hazards. One is a venture in cultural history, the other is a venture in psychological biography. It is hard enough to demonstrate an explanation of cultural developments. It is impossible to demonstrate an explanation of personal idiosyncrasies. Veblen, who dealt so confidently with mass habits of thought, left the individual out, or took him for granted. The part of prudence is to follow his example. But Veblen's personality is too intriguing a problem for my prudence. I shall sketch the circumstances of his early years and add a few conjectures, wrested from his own writings, concerning the way in which these circumstances contributed to his characteristics. All of which will do but little to dispel the mystery.

THE BACKWARD ART OF SPENDING MONEY

I

The son of Norwegian immigrants, Veblen was born on a Wisconsin farm, July 30, 1857. When he was eight years old, his parents moved to a larger farm in Minnesota. There he grew up in a frontier settlement with eight brothers and sisters who continued to speak Norwegian at home while they learned English in school. The Veblens prospered as efficient farmers may, and gave their children better educational opportunities than most native American farmers have thought worth while. An intellectual drive seems to characterize the family. An elder brother of Thorstein's became a professor of physics and one of his nephews is a distinguished mathematician.

At seventeen Veblen entered the academy of Carleton College; at twenty he entered the college, and at twenty-three he graduated with the class of 1880. Carleton was then a small Congregational school that gave a youth predisposed to skepticism abundant provocation to amuse himself with the infirmities of traditional wisdom. By all accounts, the undergraduate impressed his college circle much as the adult was to impress the reading public. But however gravely folk might reprobate his views, everyone acknowledged his extraordinary capacity for assimilating knowledge and putting it to strange uses.

John Bates Clark, later to win fame as one of the foremost economic theoreticians of his generation, was teaching in Carleton in the late seventies. Thus Veblen was introduced early to the subject about which he finally organized his interests. But for the time being he was engrossed by classical philology, natural history, and philosophy. When he went to Johns Hopkins University in 1881, philosophy was his major subject and economics his minor. Not finding what he wanted, Veblen transferred to Yale, where he took a Doctor's degree in philosophy in 1884, with a dissertation entitled "Ethical Grounds of a Doctrine of Retribution." In that same year he published a paper on "Kant's Critique of Judgment"[3] in the *Journal of Speculative Philosophy*.

All this looked like the fair beginning of an academic career. But in those days there were not many openings for young philosophers whose preconceptions resembled Hume's. Veblen was never one who could "sell himself," as advertisers have taught us to say. So he returned to Minnesota, presently married a classmate of literary gifts, and entered on a desultory course of life with wide reading, some writing, and a bit of nondescript office work. This period of incubation lasted some six or seven years. Doubtless the difficulty of obtaining an academic appointment reinforced Veblen's critical attitude toward American "seminaries of the higher learning." Hope deferred is a bitter diet. But the lack of regular occupation and of intellectual companions other than his wife gave Veblen long hours to follow his own thoughts wherever they led. He became more detached than ever from conventional viewpoints and more firmly rooted in his own habit of mind.

A new phase of Veblen's life began in 1891, when he entered Cornell as a graduate student of the social sciences. While there he published a paper called "Some Neglected Points in the Theory of Socialism."[4] It was "offered in the spirit of the disciple" to Herbert Spencer—in the spirit of the disciple who demonstrated that his master misconceived the grounds of popular dissatisfaction with economic "free-

[3] Reprinted in *Essays in Our Changing Order*, New York, 1934.

[4] *The Annals of the American Academy of Political and Social Science*, November 1891; reprinted in *The Place of Science in Modern Civilisation*, New York, 1919.

dom." Professor J. Laurence Laughlin, then at Cornell, appreciated the quality of this essay. When asked to take charge of the department of economics at the newly founded University of Chicago, Laughlin invited Veblen to go with him. Thus Veblen became one of that extraordinary faculty which President Harper gathered about him—perhaps the most stimulating group of scholars in the country, certainly the group with the most varied traditions.

Teaching courses on agricultural economics, socialism, and the history of economic theory, plus managing the *Journal of Political Economy*, was a heavy load for one of Veblen's physique and temperament. But he seems to have worked best under pressure. In 1898 he published his first critique of economic theory, "Why Is Economics Not an Evolutionary Science?"[5] and in 1899 brought out his first book, *The Theory of the Leisure Class*. From that year he was a man of mark, known as widely to the intelligentsia as to his professional brethren.[6]

II

The essence of Veblen's critical work and the type of his constructive efforts, as we have known them since, are revealed in the article of 1898 (which was elaborated in "The Preconceptions of Economic Science," 1899–1900) and the book of 1899. It is time to see what account we can make his writings yield of their author's viewpoint.

In that effort my bald sketch of his early life gives a hint. It suggests that as an observer of social behaviour in the American field, Veblen had the initial advantage of coming

[5] *The Quarterly Journal of Economics*; reprinted in *The Place of Science in Modern Civilisation*, New York, 1919.

[6] Dr. Joseph Dorfman has given a full account of Veblen's life and an admirable analysis of his work in *Thorstein Veblen and His America*, New York, 1934.

from a different culture. In his essay on "The Intellectual Pre-eminence of Jews in Modern Europe,"[7] Veblen explains how such an experience fits a youth for scientific inquiry.

The first requisite for constructive work in modern science, and indeed for any work of inquiry that shall bring enduring results, is a skeptical frame of mind. . . .

The young Jew who is at all gifted with a taste for knowledge will unavoidably go afield into that domain of learning where the gentile interests dominate and the gentile orientation gives the outcome. There is nowhere else to go on this quest. . . .

Now it happens that the home-bred Jewish scheme of things, human and divine . . . all bears the datemark, "B.C." . . . it runs on a logic of personal and spiritual traits, qualities and relations, a class of imponderables which are no longer of the substance of those things that are inquired into by men to whom the ever increasingly mechanistic orientation of the modern times becomes habitual.

When the gifted young Jew, still flexible in respect of his mental habits, is set loose among the iron pots of this mechanistic orientation, the clay vessel of Jewish archaism suffers that fortune which is due and coming to clay vessels among the iron pots. . . . He is divested of those archaic conventional preconceptions which will not comport with the intellectual environment in which he finds himself. But he is not thereby invested with the gentile's peculiar heritage of conventional preconceptions which have stood over, by inertia of habit, out of the gentile past, which go, on the one hand, to make the safe and sane gentile conservative and complacent, and which conduce also, on the other hand, to blur the safe and sane gentile's intellectual vision, and to leave him intellectually sessile. . . .

By consequence [the young Jew] is in a peculiar degree exposed to the unmediated facts of the current situation; and in a peculiar degree, therefore, he takes his orientation from the run of the facts as he finds them, rather than from the traditional interpretation of analogous facts in the past. In short, he is a skeptic by force of circumstances over which he has no control. Which comes to saying that he is in line to become a guide and leader of men in that intellectual enterprise out of which comes the

[7] *Political Science Quarterly*, vol. XXXIV, March, 1919; reprinted in *Essays in Our Changing Order*, pp. 226–230, New York, 1934.

increase and diffusion of knowledge among men, provided always that he is by native gift endowed with that net modicum of intelligence which takes effect in the play of the idle curiosity.

Now, a Norwegian family of farmer folk is like an orthodox Jewish family at least in one respect: it also has a culture that differs widely from the culture of modern America. The Norwegian brand is not date-marked "B.C.," but it savors of the sagas. There is less of business in the Norwegian than in the Jewish heritage, and the former is by so much the more remote in spirit from today. A boy brought up in such a family, largely sufficient unto itself, acquires an outlook upon life unlike that of the son of thoroughly acclimated parents. As he ventures into the world, he finds much strange which those to the manner born take for granted. If endowed with curiosity, he wonders both about the notions that his parents cherish and about the notions that his mates accept. That was Thorstein Veblen's case. And he was insatiably curious about everything he encountered—minerals, plants, and animals, the tongues men speak, the arts they practice, the faiths they venerate, and the proofs they find convincing. He had no collection of established truths to check his questioning; for the truths taken for granted at home and the truths taken for granted in school raised doubts about one another. Thus he, like the Jewish boy of his analysis, became "a skeptic by force of circumstances over which he had no control." On some such lines, the creature of these circumstances might explain his own preparation for scientific inquiry.

But scientific inquiry does not exhaust itself in asking questions; it seeks also to find answers. Veblen's constructive bent is not less marked than his skepticism, though of course it is more specialized. An inquisitive youth may come to doubt all things on principle; but when he begins to contrive explanations, he must limit himself within a range that he can study intensively. What fixed Veblen's choice of problems?

All I can say in answer is that, given his temperament, Veblen's final choice seems a natural outcome of his circumstances. A son of immigrant farmers must wonder about differences among people. That theme is both obvious and subtle; it is beset by prejudices, difficult to treat objectively, fascinating, and slippery. Veblen found its dangers, open and concealed, alluring; for in the realm of thought he was bold as a Viking, and as fond of wiles. Yet differences among people are manifold; no one can explore and explain them all. Veblen might have held fast to his early philological interest, fed by his bilingual upbringing. He might have stuck to his first "major," philosophy. Perhaps he would have done so, had he secured a position in that department of learning. He might have pushed deeper into biology, which in the days of Darwinian speculation seemed neatly fitted to his talents. In the end he found for himself a field more attractive than any one of these. He could fuse his leading interests by studying human cultures. That large venture gave scope to his double heritage from home and school, to his linguistic equipment and facility, to his inveterate skepticism, to his liking for organized systems of thought, to his interest in biology. Also it gave free play to another set of impulses that were as much a part of him as curiosity.

Veblen loved to play with the feelings of people not less than he loved to play with ideas. Now, there are few objects of scientific scrutiny more exciting to our feelings than cultural differences. These differences touch our dear selves. Recall how fond we are of making invidious comparisons between people of our own kind and others. We feel magnanimous if we let the comparisons turn to our disadvantage; we feel resentful if others point out inferiorities in us. However objectively our traits are analyzed, we react emotionally. The delicate nature of this subject must repel men who dislike complex and ambiguous situations; it attracted Veblen. He usually wrote with one eye on the scientific merits of his analysis, and his other eye fixed on the squirming reader. To him, this reader is the creature of cultural circumstances that have produced standard habits of feeling as well as norms of thinking. Veblen practices vivisection upon his contemporaries; he uses no anaesthetic; he has his notions about what emotional reactions each type will exhibit. Instead of seeking to facilitate the reception of his analysis by minimizing the reader's emotions, he artfully stimulates them for his own delectation.

Of course, most critics of modern culture have strong feelings of their own, which they strive to impart to their readers. Moral indignation is the commonest note, and the one to which we respond most readily. We get a certain satisfaction from being preached at; even when we think the preacher bears down rather hard upon our amiable weaknesses, we respect his zeal. Also we are used to the open satirist who seeks to laugh us out of our follies. Veblen repudiates preaching. As an evolutionist, his office is to understand, not to praise, or blame, or lead us into righteousness. From his point of view, any notions he may entertain concerning what is right and wrong are vestiges of the cultural environment to which he has been exposed. They have no authority, and it would be a futile impertinence to try to impose them upon others. There is much of the satirist in him; but it is satire of an unfamiliar and a disconcerting kind. Professedly, he seeks merely to describe and to explain our cultural traits in plain terms. But he likes to put his explanations in a form that will make the commonplaces of our daily lives startling and ridiculous to us. It is this histrionic foible which gives his writing its peculiar flavor.

Veblen is an inveterate phrasemaker, and he designs his phrases to get under our skins. "Conspicuous waste" fits our habits of consumption like a whiplash. Our philanthropies are "essays in pragmatic romance." Modern industry is so "inordinately productive" that prosperity requires "a conscientious withdrawal of efficiency" by the businessmen in control—their chief service to production is to practice "capitalistic sabotage." The common stock of trusts formed by combining companies that had competed with one another represents "defunct good-will." As individuals, we find our places either in the "kept classes" or among the "underlying population"—and either ranking makes us wince. His wit spares nothing and no one. If the pulpit is "the accredited vent for the exudation of effete matter from the cultural organism," the scientist is a "finikin skeptic," an "animated slide-rule," "machine made."

To explain this quirk in Veblen's humor would require the assurance of an amateur psychoanalyst. One who lacks that qualification must take the trait for granted, and merely register its consequences. I think Veblen's fondness for quizzing folk helped to determine his choice of problems and to shape the course of his analysis. I am sure it has been largely responsible for the reactions of readers, both professional and lay, to his work. One must be highly sophisticated to enjoy his books.

Within the field of human culture, an investigator must make a more definite choice of themes. Anthropology, history, sociology, economics, political science, social psychology, all deal with culture. A worker in that field must know something of all these disciplines, and Veblen knew much. In the end he organized his inquiries about economics. Perhaps his early contact with an original, though widely different, thinker in that line had some influence upon his choice. But there is an explanation in terms of logic that carries more conviction than psychological conjectures.

Darwin tells what stimulation he received from reflecting upon Malthus's theory of population when he was groping after his own theory of natural selection. An installment upon this debt of biology to economics was paid by the stimulation that Darwin's doctrines gave to Veblen's theory of cultures. Cultures are complexes of "prevalent habits of thought with respect to particular relations and particular functions of the individual and of the community."[8] The significant question about these habits is the question that Darwin asked about animal species: How did they develop into the forms that we observe?

The biological view of man's evolution suggests that habits of thought are formed by the activities in which individuals engage. The activities that occupy most hours are likely to exercise most influence in making the mind. The task of getting a living has busied incomparably more men and women for more time than any other task. Hence, economic factors have had and still have a major share in shaping mass habits of thought; that is, in making human culture what it has been under varying circumstances in the past, and what it is today. Other types of activity get whatever time and attention the peremptory job of finding food and shelter leaves free. Where the economic activities themselves are efficient, this margin for indulging such human propensities as emulation, propitiation, predation, and idle curiosity becomes appreciable. A good many individuals can spend most of

---

[8] *The Theory of the Leisure Class*, p. 190, New York, 1899.

their time in other tasks than making a living, and so can build up a considerable body of habits not drilled in by the exigencies of humdrum work. Yet there is perforce a certain congruence among all the mental habits formed in any single brain, and even among the habits prevalent in any community at a given time. So the emancipation even of our religious, aesthetic, and scientific notions from economic determination is but partial.

Only one other factor can conceivably rival the influence of getting a living in shaping culture. That is the strictly biological factor of breeding. Veblen thinks, however, that the evidence is all against supposing that *homo sapiens* has undergone any substantial change in anatomy or physiology for thousands of years. Our brains are about as efficient organs as were the brains of neolithic men. Selective breeding under stress of changing circumstances doubtless tends to lower the reproduction rate of individuals whose propensities run toward violence in exceptional degree. Perhaps other generalizations of that type may be made. But the effects of the breeding factor are slight and dubious in comparison with the effects of cumulative changes in habits of thinking under the discipline of cumulative changes in modes of getting a living. That the lives we live today are so vastly different from the lives lived by our ancestors who left their sketches on the walls of caves and lost their stone implements in the kitchen middens is due in but minor measure to bodily modifications. The theory of evolution begun by biologists must be continued by students of culture, and primarily by economists.

III

Needless to say, economists found this a novel conception of their office when Veblen began writing. The "science of wealth," as they commonly defined their subject, dealt with production, exchange, and distribution, as these processes run in modern times. About the way in which the modern scheme of institutions has evolved, the professed theorists knew little and cared little, for they did not see that such knowledge would help to solve what they took to be their central problem—how prices are determined now, particularly the prices that effect the distribution of income.

Veblen does not claim that genetic studies will answer the questions that economists have posed in the form they have chosen. His fundamental criticism is that economists have asked the wrong questions. Their conception of science and its problems is antiquated, pre-Darwinian.

> The sciences which are in any peculiar sense modern take as an (unavowed) postulate the fact of consecutive change. Their inquiry always centers upon some manner of process. This notion of process about which the researches of modern science cluster, is a notion of a sequence, or complex, of consecutive change in which the nexus of the sequence, that by virtue of which the change inquired into is consecutive, is the relation of cause and effect.[9]

Neither the theory of value and distribution as worked out by Ricardo nor the refined form of this theory presented by Veblen's teacher, J. B. Clark, deals with consecutive change in any sustained fashion. The more classical political economy was purified, the more strictly was it limited to what happens in an imaginary "static state." Hence, orthodox economics belongs to the "taxonomic" stage of inquiry represented, say, by the pre-Darwinian botany of Asa Gray. Therefore, it possesses but meager scientific interest. If

[9] "The Evolution of the Scientific Point of View." Read before the Kosmos Club, at the University of California, May 4, 1908; first published in *University of California Chronicle*, vol. X, no. 4; reprinted in *The Place of Science in Modern Civilisation*, p. 32, New York, 1919.

political economy is to modernize itself, it must become "an evolutionary science," and it can become an evolutionary science only by addressing itself to the problem: How do economic institutions evolve?

In so far as modern science inquires into the phenomena of life, whether inanimate, brute, or human, it is occupied about questions of genesis and cumulative change, and it converges upon a theoretical formulation in the shape of a life-history drawn in causal terms. In so far as it is a science in the current sense of the term, any science, such as economics, which has to do with human conduct, becomes a genetic inquiry into the human scheme of life; and where, as in economics, the subject of inquiry is the conduct of man in his dealings with the material means of life, the science is necessarily an inquiry into the life-history of material civilization, on a more or less extended or restricted plan. . . . Like all human culture this material civilization is a scheme of institutions—institutional fabric and institutional growth.[10]

Associated with this fundamental charge, that economists have mistaken their chief problem, is a second criticism, that they have worked with an antiquated conception of human nature.

In all the received formulations of economic theory . . . the human material with which the inquiry is concerned is conceived in hedonistic terms; that is to say, in terms of a passive and substantially inert and immutably given human nature. The psychological and anthropological preconceptions of the economists have been those which were accepted by the psychological and social sciences some generations ago. The hedonistic conception of man is that of a lightning calculator of pleasures and pains, who oscillates like a homogeneous globule of desire of happiness under the impulse of stimuli that shift him about the area, but leave him intact.[11]

[10] "The Limitations of Marginal Utility," 1909. Reprinted in *The Place of Science in Modern Civilisation*, pp. 240–241, New York, 1919.

[11] "Why Is Economics Not an Evolutionary Science?" 1898. Reprinted in *The Place of Science in Modern Civilisation*, p. 73, New York, 1919.

Veblen molded his own notions of human nature on Darwin, William James, and anthropological records. To the biologist and the open-eyed observer, man is essentially active. He is not placed "under the governance of two sovereign masters, pain and pleasure," as Jeremy Bentham held; on the contrary, he is forever doing something on his own initiative. Instead of studying pleasures and pains, or satisfactions and sacrifices, on the supposition that these "real forces" determine what men do, economists should study the processes of human behavior at first hand. For this purpose, the important psychological categories are not the felicific calculus and the association of ideas, but propensities and habits. The human individual is born with a vaguely known equipment of tropisms and instincts. Instincts differ from tropisms in that they involve an element of intelligence; in other words, they are susceptible of modification by experience. What modifications instincts will undergo, into what habits they will develop, depends upon the nature of the experience encountered, and that depends in turn upon the environment, especially the human environment, in which the individual grows up. The human environment is of critical importance because through tradition, training, and education "the young acquire what the old have learned."

Cumulatively, therefore, habit creates usages, customs, conventions, preconceptions, composite principles of conduct that run back only indirectly to the native predispositions of the race, but that may affect the working out of any given line of endeavor in much the same way as if these habitual elements were of the nature of a native bias. Along with this body of derivative standards and canons of conduct, and handed on by the same discipline of habituation, goes a cumulative body of knowledge, made up in part of matter-of-fact acquaintance with phenomena and in greater part of conventional wisdom embodying certain acquired predilections and preconceptions current in the community.[12]

[12] *The Instinct of Workmanship*, p. 39, New York, 1914.

This emphasis upon the cumulative character of cultural changes takes us back to Veblen's conception of what constitutes the problems of science and to his fundamental criticism of economics. The distinctively modern sciences, we have found him contending, deal with consecutive change. He might have added, though I do not recall his doing so, that the consecutive changes studied by different sciences appear to be cumulative in varying degree. Even physics and chemistry, when applied to the history of the cosmos, are concerned with a situation that develops from millennium to millennium. Biology has its branches that deal with processes conceived to repeat themselves over and over without marked alteration in the total situation to be accounted for; but the problems in which cumulative change is prominent bulk larger in biological than in physicochemical theory. Cumulation rises to its highest pitch, however, in the social sciences, because the behavior of men changes in the course of experience far more rapidly than does the behavior of stars and infra-human species. For that reason, the major explanation of human behavior at any point in the life-history of our race must be sought in the preceding installments of the story. As Veblen put it: "Each new situation is a variation of what has gone before it and embodies as causal factors all that has been effected by what went before."[13] To take economic institutions as they stand at a given moment for granted, and merely to inquire into their working, cuts out of economics that behavior trait which differentiates human activities most clearly from all other subjects of scientific inquiry.

Yet Veblen might have admitted that the quasi-mechanical economics, which takes existing institutions for granted

[13] "The Limitations of Marginal Utility," 1909. Reprinted in *The Place of Science in Modern Civilisation*, p. 242, New York, 1919.

and inquires how they work, has a certain value. This type of inquiry may be regarded as elaborating the logic implicit in the institutions of which it takes cognizance, usually without recognizing their transient character in the life-history of mankind. For example, pecuniary institutions are a prominent feature of current life in the Western world. Most of us make money incomes and buy what we want at money prices. To some extent all of us are drilled by experience into the habit of thinking in dollars; all of us acquire some skill in "the exact science of making change"; all of us accept in part "the private and acquisitive point of view." Now, a theory such as Veblen's warm admirer, Herbert J. Davenport, developed on the express assumption that all men are animated by the desire for gain throws light on our economic behavior just to the extent that men are perfect products of the countinghouse. The logician who excogitates this mechanical system is prone to exaggerate its adequacy as an account of contemporary behavior. But Veblen would be the last to deny the importance of pecuniary institutions in modern culture. He does not, in fact, hold that work such as Davenport has done is wrong, or wholly futile. Yet he inclines to take what is valuable in it for granted, much as Davenport takes for granted the existing scheme of institutions. For Veblen is impatient of the well known and eager to develop aspects of the modern situation about which more orthodox types of economic theory have little to say. Men whose conception of what is "scientific" has been molded by mechanics, criticize his precipitate neglect of their problems, much as Veblen, who builds upon Darwinian biology, criticizes them for their precipitate neglect of evolutionary problems.

One more characteristic of Veblen's procedure must be noted. Representatives of the "exact" sciences stress the importance of measurement. There are those, indeed, who go so far as to claim that the outstanding characteristic of scientific thought is its quantitative precision. Now, Darwinian biology was not an exact science; it made but slight use of measurements in any form; it confined itself mainly to "qualitative analysis," supplemented by a recognition that certain factors have played major and other factors minor roles in the development of species. In comparison with Darwin's method, Mendel's experiments in heredity seem precise, and we all know what an impetus the rediscovery of Mendel's work gave to biological research.[14]

Veblen was a good Darwinian in this respect also. His native bent was toward speculation of a philosophical sort. No one had keener insight or nicer subtlety in dealing with ideas, and like all efficient inquirers, he used the tools of which he was master. Further, the statistical invasion of the biological and social sciences was but just starting in Veblen's youth. Galton was not then recognized as a figure of the first magnitude; Pearson's and Edgeworth's work on quantitative methods lay in the future. It was easy for one who had little liking for mathematical procedures to overlook the promise

[14] That Veblen grasped the significance of Mendel's work and of the experiments to which it led is shown by his paper on "The Mutation Theory and the Blond Race," reprinted in *The Place of Science in Modern Civilisation*, pp. 457–476, New York, 1919. See also his references to "the Mendelian rules of hybridization" in *The Instinct of Workmanship*, pp. 21–25, New York, 1914, and in *Imperial Germany and the Industrial Revolution*, pp. 277–278, New York, 1915. But this appreciation, supplemented by his admiration for the experiments of Jacques Loeb, did not induce him to attempt close quantitative work of his own. Two early articles on the price of wheat and "A Schedule of Prices for the Staple Foodstuffs" drawn up for the Food Administration in 1918 are the only papers I recall in which Veblen made detailed statistical inquiries. The articles appeared in *Journal of Political Economy*, vol. I, pp. 68–103, 156–161, December, 1892, and 365–379, June, 1893; the memorandum for the Food Administration was unearthed by Dr. Dorfman and may be found, minus the statistics, in *Essays in Our Changing Order*, pp. 347–354, New York, 1934.

of statistics. Finally and most important, problems of cumulative change in "life-history" are exceedingly difficult to treat by any method of measurement. Each change is by hypothesis a unique event, begotten by an indefinite number of causes. To disentangle the tangled skein is impossible. Without the aid of an elaborate technique it is hard to do more with such problems than what Darwin and Veblen have done—that is, to study the evidence and select for particular attention what seem to be the salient factors. That might go without saying concerning all parts of man's history before social statistics were collected on a liberal scale and preserved for analysis. It is only when he comes to recent changes that an investigator has tolerably accurate data. These materials Veblen did not reject; but he made no great effort to exploit them. In this respect, at least, his practice resembled that of most orthodox economists.

While not addicted to the quantitative method, Veblen was a keen observer. Having climbed to Darwin's mountain peak, his eyes ranged over a vast stretch of human experience. About many matters quite invisible to economists immersed in the nineteenth century he thought intensively. The Neolithic age in Europe, the feudal system in Japan, the lives of the Australian blackfellows, and a thousand things equally remote in time or space from present-day America seemed strictly pertinent to his problem. Even what he saw of his immediate surroundings differed from what was patent to his contemporaries.

"All perception," said William James, "is apperception." Every scientific inquirer sees what his mind is prepared to see, and preparation of the mind is a compound of previous experiences and the thoughts to which they have given rise. Recall how Darwin's vision was clarified when, after long fumbling with a mass of observations, he hit upon the idea of natural selection.

What Veblen saw when he looked at man's activities differed from what other economists saw because his mind was equipped with later psychological notions. How widely Veblen's conception of human nature departed from that which he imputed to his predecessors has been remarked. It remains to show how his ideas upon "original nature" and "culture" controlled the larger issues of his theorizing, just as notions concerning man's substantial rationality controlled the larger issues of earlier speculation.

There are two ways of studying behavior. One may observe men "objectively," as an experimental psychologist observes animals, and try to form generalizations concerning their activities without pretending to know what goes on inside their heads. Or one may take his stand inside human consciousness and think how that organ works. If the latter method is chosen, the results arrived at depend upon the thinker's notions about consciousness. Logically, these notions form one premise—usually tacit—in a syllogism. The procedure at this stage is "deductive," though it may have been preceded by an "inductive" derivation of the psychological premise, and it may be followed by an "inductive" testing of the conclusions.

Veblen adhered to the standard practice of the classical masters—he chose to reason out human behavior. But he sought to explain actual behavior, not what men will "normally" do; his conclusions are supposed to conform to "facts" and to be open to testing by observation in a directer fashion than are most expositions of "economic laws." Also Veblen gave closer attention than his predecessors to the character of his psychological premise and made it explicit. Profiting by two generations of active research in biology and anthropology as well as in psychology, he could reach what is certainly a later, and presumably a juster, conception of human nature. In so far as his economic theories rest upon psychological premises, they may be rated a more "scientific" account of human behavior than theories which rest upon what latter-day writers call the "intellectualist fallacy of the nineteenth century." Yet in so far as any theories of behavior are conclusions deduced from some conception of human nature, they must be subject to change as knowledge of human nature grows.

Veblen's dealings with psychology, however, are not confined to borrowing ideas from other sciences for use as premises in economics. Anyone who gives an enlightening account of any phase of human behavior is himself contributing toward our understanding of ourselves. By working with psychological conceptions, he develops them and makes their value and limitations clearer. Thus Jevons contributed to the breakdown of hedonism by applying Bentham's felicific calculus in good faith to explain how exchange value is determined. His literal exposition helped economists to realize the artificiality of ideas which seem plausible so long as they remain vague. The more clearly a social scientist sees that he is dealing with human behavior, and the more explicit he is about the conceptions of human nature with which he works, the larger the service which he can render to our self-knowledge. Veblen's service in this direction is that he has applied the instinct-habit psychology of Darwin and William James to explain a wide range of human activities. The nascent science of social psychology owes him a heavy debt of gratitude for this accomplishment—a debt which will be all the heavier if his work helps future investigators to do something better than he accomplished.

One of the ways to press forward along Veblen's path is to turn back and test for conformity to "fact" our plausible reasonings about how men behave—that is, to see how our theories about what men do agree with what we can observe. Of course, what we can observe is not wholly objective. As recalled above, it depends upon what we are mentally prepared to see, and also upon our techniques. Yet when we can apply them, factual tests of ideas are one of our most effective ways of promoting knowledge. The men who laid the foundations of economics recognized this point, and in their writings upon method admitted the desirability of "inductive verification." But in practice they spent little effort upon this desideratum—it seemed too hopeless a task as matters stood. The notion that inquiries should be framed from the start in such a way as to permit of testing the hypothetical conclusions was not common property in their time. Unless such plans are laid in advance, and laid with skill, it is more than likely that the results attained by reasoning will be in such form that no inquirer can either confirm or refute them by an appeal to facts. Observing this run of affairs, the classical methodologists spoke disparagingly of induction in general and of statistical induction in particular: it seemed to them a tool limited to a narrow range of uses in economics.

Veblen's case is not so very different, except that he deals with actual as distinguished from "normal" behavior. He does not plan in advance for testing his conclusions. Of course, he is bound to be skeptical about them—that attitude is not merely logical in him, but also congenial to his temperament. There is always an aura of playfulness about his attitude toward his own work in marked contrast to the deadly seriousness of most economists. Yet, when the opportunity offers, he will cite evidence to support a contention. Usually it is evidence of a sweeping sort which those who do not agree with his viewpoint can interpret in a different sense. Sometimes the evidence is an illustrative case, and the question remains open how representative the case may be. Rarely does he undertake a factual survey. Many of his propositions are not of the type that can be tested objectively with the means now at our disposal. His work as a whole is like Darwin's—a speculative system uniting a vast range of observations in a highly organized whole, extraordinarily stimulating both to the layman and to the investigator, but waiting for its ultimate validation upon more intensive and tamer inquiries.

IV

All this about the man, his problems, his viewpoint, and his methods of work. What constructive results did he reach?

Veblen's studies in the life-history of mankind range over the whole interval between "the origin of the blond type" and the future prospects of business enterprise. Into this range he has dipped at will, preferring always the little-known features of the story. He has never written a systematic treatise upon economics; instead, he has produced numerous essays and ten monographs. An adequate summary of the ideas he has contributed to the social sciences would fill another volume as large as *Absentee Ownership*. All that is feasible here is to select topics illustrative of his conclusions. The whole body of writing is so much of one piece that almost any of his disquisitions would serve as an introduction to the whole. Doubtless it is best to take discussions of matters with which everyone is familiar.

Looking over the modern world, Veblen marked a difference between industrial and pecuniary employments; that is, between the work of making goods and the work of making money; in still other terms, between the machine process and business enterprise. No fact of daily life is more commonplace than this difference; neither men on the street nor economic theorists see in it anything exciting or novel. What comments it seems to call for have been made long since. Adam Smith pointed out in the *Wealth of Nations* that division of labor requires exchange of products and that exchange is greatly facilitated by money. But money is merely an intermediary; we must not exaggerate its importance, as the mercantilists did. Bentham's psychology reinforced this view. Pleasures and pains are the only things that really matter to men; commodities and services are important as instruments of pleasures and pains; money stands at a further remove—it is a means of getting commodities and services. The prevalent common sense on the subject was summed up by John Stuart Mill in a famous passage:

There cannot, in short, be intrinsically a more insignificant thing in the economy of society, than money; except in the character of a contrivance for sparing time and labor. It is a machine for doing quickly and commodiously, what would be done, though less quickly and commodiously, without it; and like many other kinds of machinery, it only exerts a distinct and independent influence of its own when it gets out of order.[15]

Acting on this conviction, economists have paid a great deal of attention to the monetary mechanism—the best ways of designing it and of keeping it in order. But they treat this problem as a specialty that has little to do with general economic theory. In discussing value and distribution they take money as a tool for investigating more important matters. Thus Alfred Marshall declares that money

is the center around which economic science clusters . . . not because money or material wealth is regarded as the main aim of human effort,

[15] *Principles of Political Economy*, Ashley's ed., p. 488, London and New York, 1909.

nor even as affording the main subject-matter for the study of the economist, but because in this world of ours it is the one convenient means of measuring human motive on a large scale.[16]

The "real forces" that control behavior, on Marshall's showing, are satisfactions and sacrifices. It is these real forces, and the balancing of one set of them against the other set, that require analysis. Money is an indispensable tool for measuring the force of opposing motives; but it remains merely a tool so far as the fundamental principles of economics are concerned.

This view of the place of money in economic theory is perfectly consistent with the conception of human nature entertained by Marshall. Despite his substitution of less colorful terms for "pleasure" and "pain," he thought after Bentham's fashion. Men practice a sort of double-entry bookkeeping, satisfactions on the credit and sacrifices on the debit side of the account; they discount for futurity and for uncertainty; they are ready reckoners. To tell what they will do, one needs to know the motive force of the satisfactions and sacrifices promised by alternative lines of action. That force can best be expressed in terms of money; but the use of money does not alter the substantial character of economic behavior.[17]

Shift from Marshall's psychological notions to Veblen's, and the whole picture changes. Money becomes a most significant thing in the economy of society, because it shapes the habits of thought into which our native propensities grow. Instead of being "a machine for doing quickly and commodiously what would be done, though less quickly and commodiously, without it," the use of money "exerts a dis-

[16] *Principles of Economics*, 6th ed., p. 22, London and New York, 1910.

[17] In fairness it should be noted that Marshall's discussions of economic behavior are far more realistic than this schematic framework seems to promise.

tinct and independent influence of its own" upon our wants as consumers, upon our skill as planners, upon our methods as producers, and upon our ideals as citizens. And since the discipline that the use of money imposes upon our minds affects some classes far more than it does others, this institution produces social stresses—stresses that may disrupt the present polity.

To begin where Veblen began: In a society where money-making is the commonly accepted test of success in life, our native propensity toward emulation takes on a pecuniary twist. We wish to seem well-to-do, and to attain that agreeable rating we cultivate an air of careless affluence as much as our means permit. We like goods that look expensive, we keep up with the changing styles however uncomfortable they may be, we subject ourselves to inane and fatiguing social frivolities, we teach our children accomplishments that are elegant because they are costly. Our sense of beauty is stamped with the dollar sign. We stand in awe of the very rich, and approach as close to their reputed manner of life as we can. Though born with an instinct of workmanship that makes futility disagreeable, we get satisfaction from conspicuous waste. Though active creatures, we practice conspicuous leisure, or make our wives and menials do it for us. The higher modern technology raises our standards of living above the "minimum of subsistence," the wider the scope of our invidious consumption. Money cannot be intrinsically insignificant in the economy of a society whose inner cravings bear so deep an impress of pecuniary standards. All this and much more was set forth in Veblen's first volume, *The Theory of the Leisure Class*.

Secondly, money-making drills into us a certain type of rationality—the type that reaches its flower in modern accounting. The monetary unit provides us with a common denominator in terms of which the best drilled among us can express all values, not excepting the value of human lives. However vagrant our fancies, we are all forced by the environment of prices to be somewhat systematic in planning. We learn to reckon costs and income, to make change, to compare the advantages of different types of expenditure. It is the habit of mind begotten by the use of money that makes the pleasure-pain calculus plausible as an account of our own functioning. Thus the use of money lays the psychological basis for that philosophy of human behavior which Bentham and Mill, Marshall and Clark, represent—a philosophy which, ignorant of its origins, treats money as a thing of slight moment except in facilitating trade and research. As pointed out above, economic theory written from the private and acquisitive viewpoint becomes a system of pecuniary logic that exaggerates the importance of one institutional factor in behavior to the neglect of others.

Thirdly, money-making both promotes and obstructs the fundamental task of getting a living. Veblen pictures two sets of economic activities running side by side through the life of a modern community. One set is concerned with producing raw materials, working them up into serviceable goods, transporting and distributing the things men desire to use. The other set is the endless series of concatenated bargains by which men determine how much each individual can take to himself of what others have made. The material welfare of the community as a whole depends solely upon the quantity and quality of the goods brought to consumers by the first set of activities. Money-making conduces to material well-being just in so far as it enlarges the quantity or improves the quality of the serviceable goods obtained from a given expenditure of energy. From a common-sense viewpoint, therefore, money-making is a means to getting goods. But in practice we reverse the relation. We make goods in order to make money. Veblen never wearies of expounding that central paradox and of developing its consequences.

He grants the commonplaces about the economic advantages of this scheme of organization. Adam Smith was right: industrial efficiency requires division of labor, division of labor requires exchange, and exchange requires money. No other scheme of organization that men have tried out in practice yields so large a per capita flow of goods to consumers as the current scheme of making goods for profit. Business accounting is a marvelous device for controlling complicated undertakings. Industry requires capital and credit, and, as matters now stand, who can supply capital and credit but the capitalist and the banker? The businessman is the central figure in modern economic life, the prime mover, what you will. There is no call to quarrel with encomiums of this sort which anyone is moved to pronounce upon the present order. But it is interesting to reflect upon certain features of the situation that are less obvious to business-trained eyes.

One is that the recurrent crises and depressions which ever and again reduce the flow of goods to consumers are due to business, not to industry. There is no technological reason why every few years we should have idle factories and unemployed men walking the streets, while thousands lack the goods employers and men would like to supply. The trouble is that business enterprises are run for profit, not to meet human needs. When times are good, prices rise, profits are high, businessmen borrow freely and enlarge their output. But such prosperity works its own undoing. The substantial security behind the loans is prospective net earnings capitalized at the current rate of interest. When the rate of interest rises, as it does during prosperity, the capitalized value of a given net income declines, and the loans become less safe. More than that, net earnings in many cases prove less than had been expected in the optimistic days of the nascent boom. Prices cannot be pushed up indefinitely; the costs of doing business rise and encroach upon profits; bank reserves fall and it becomes difficult to get additional credit. When fading profits are added to high interest, creditors become nervous. In such a strained situation, the embarrassment of a few conspicuous concerns will bring down the unstable structure which had seemed so imposing. A demand for liquidation starts and spreads rapidly, for the enterprises pressed for payment put pressure upon their debtors to pay up. So prosperity ends in a crisis, followed by depression. In short, business enterprises cannot prosper without committing business errors that bring on a crisis, and from these errors the whole community suffers.

More serious in the long run than these acute fits of indigestion is a chronic malady of the present order. Businessmen seek to fix their selling prices at the maximum net-revenue point. There is always danger that an oversupply of products will reduce prices more than the increased turnover will compensate for. This danger is peculiarly great because of the "inordinate" productivity of the modern machine process. Give the engineers their heads and the markets might be swamped by a flood of goods. Businessmen are constantly on their guard against this peril. It is their office to adjust supply to demand; that is, to prevent an unprofitable rate of output; that is, to keep industrial efficiency "subnormal"; that is, to practice "capitalistic sabotage."

Indeed, by their very training, businessmen are incompetent to serve as captains of industry. Technology is becoming more and more an affair of applied science. We have

elaborate schools for engineers in which mathematics, physics, chemistry, and electrical theory are the basic subjects of
instruction. The graduates from these schools are the men
who know how to make goods. If permitted to organize
production on a continental scale, they might, with their
present knowledge, double or triple the current output of
industry. That they will not be suffered to do, so long as they
are subject to the higher authority of businessmen, who do
not understand technology and who distrust the vaulting
plans of their own engineers. And this distrust is well founded,
so long as business enterprise is organized in many units. To
set engineering science free from business shackles would
smash the independent enterprises of today, and lay out the
process of making goods on much broader lines. In the early
days of the industrial revolution, the businessman was an
industrial leader; in these later days the development of
technology has turned him into an industrial incubus.

Yet the situation of business enterprise which seems so
firmly entrenched is becoming precarious, because the habits
of thinking engendered in men by modern life are undermining the habits of thinking on which business traffic rests. If
businessmen do not speak the same language as engineers, or
enter into their thoughts, neither do engineers speak the
language or share the ideas of businessmen. The one group
talks in terms of physical science, the other talks in terms of
natural rights, particularly the right of ownership. It is increasingly difficult for the engineer to see why he should not
be allowed to develop his plans for increasing output to the
limit. He asks why the pecuniary interests of a handful of
families should stand in the way of a doubled per capita
income for the community as a whole. Demonstrations that
absentee owners have a perfect right to draw dividends from
industry without contributing personal service leave him

cold. What is more threatening than this doubting mood of the technologists is a growing disaffection among the masses of factory hands. Though not schooled in physical science, these people fall into a somewhat similar habit of thought. Their daily work with materials and machines teaches them to seek an explanation of all things in terms of cause and effect. They tend to become skeptical, matter of fact, materialistic, unmoral, unpatriotic, undevout, blind to the metaphysical niceties of natural rights. And nothing effective can be done to check the spread of these subversive habits of thought so long as the workers must be kept at their machines. So it appears that the time is coming when the present order of society, dominated by business enterprise in the interests of absentee ownership, will no longer seem right and good to the mass of mankind.

Veblen has no definite specifications for the new structure of institutions that will grow up in place of the present one, beyond an expectation that technically qualified engineers will have a larger share in managing industry. His evolutionary theory forbids him to anticipate a cataclysm, or to forecast a millennium. What will happen in the inscrutable future is what has been happening since the origin of man. As ways of working shift, they will engender new habits of thinking, which will crystallize into new institutions, which will form the cultural setting for further cumulative changes in ways of working, world without end.

V

If Veblen has descried aright the trend of cultural change, his economic theories will commend themselves to a wider circle in the next generation than in his own. For on his showing, science, like all other cultural excrescences, is a by-product of the kind of work folk do. Circumstances made a certain

Thorstein Veblen one of the early recruits in the growing army of men who will look at all social conventions with skeptical, matter-of-fact eyes. Just before his time the German historical school had perceived the relativity of orthodox economics; but they had not produced a scientific substitute for the doctrine they belittled or discarded. Karl Marx had been more constructive. In Veblen's view, Marx had made a brave beginning in cultural analysis, though handicapped by a superficial psychology derived from Bentham and by a romantic metaphysics derived from Hegel. Bentham's influence led Marx to develop a commonplace theory of class interests that overlooked the way in which certain habits of thought are drilled into businessmen by their pecuniary occupations and quite different habits of thought are drilled into wage earners by the machine process in which they are caught. Hegel's influence made the Marxian theory of social evolution essentially an intellectual sequence that tends to a goal, "the classless economic structure of the socialistic final term," whereas the Darwinian scheme of thought envisages a "blindly cumulative causation, in which there is no trend, no final term, no consummation." Hence, Marx strayed from the narrow trail of scientific analysis appropriate to a mechanistic age and attained an optimistic vision of the future that fulfilled his wish for a socialist revolution.[18] The Darwinian viewpoint, which supplies the needed working program, will spread among social scientists, not because it is

[18] See Veblen's two papers on "The Socialist Economics of Karl Marx and his Followers," originally published in *Quarterly Journal of Economics*, August, 1906, and February, 1907; reprinted in *The Place of Science in Modern Civilisation* pp. 409–456, New York, 1919. The phrases quoted are from pp. 417, 436.

After dilating upon the "disparity between Marxism and Darwinism," Veblen points out that "the socialists of today" have shifted from "the Marxism of Marx" to "the materialism of Darwin," though "of course" without admitting that "any substantial change or departure from the original position has taken place." See pp. 417, 432, 433.

less metaphysical than its predecessors or nearer the truth (whatever that may mean), but because it harmonizes better with the thoughts begotten by daily work in the twentieth century. That the majority of economists still cling to their traditional analysis is to Veblen merely the latest illustration of the cultural lag in social theory—a lag readily accounted for by the institutional approach.

Yet Veblen remains an inveterate doubter even of his own work. The Darwinian viewpoint is due to be superseded in men's minds; the instinct-habit psychology will yield to some other conception of human nature. The body of factual knowledge will continue its cumulative growth, and idle curiosity will find new ways of organizing the data. His own view of the world is date-marked "A.D. 1880–1930," as definitely as Jewish culture is date-marked "B.C."

A heretic needs a high heart, though sustained by faith that he is everlastingly right and sure of his reward hereafter. The heretic who views his own ideas as but tomorrow's fashion in thought needs still firmer courage. Such courage Veblen had. All his uneasy life he faced outer hostility and inner doubt with a quizzical smile. Uncertain what the future has in store, he did the day's work as best he might, getting a philosopher's pleasures from playing with ideas and exercising "his swift wit and his slow irony" upon his fellows. However matters went with him, and often they went ill, he made no intellectual compromises. In his retreat among the lovely coast hills of California, he died on August 3, 1929, a "placid unbeliever" to the end.

15

COMMONS ON INSTITUTIONAL ECONOMICS[1]

Institutional Economics is a militant sage's summing up of his lifetime's thinking. Despite the author's disavowal of discoveries, it is a highly original book—the product of a stubbornly independent mind, developed by intense strivings with problems of social behavior. Happily that mind has given an account of itself: *Myself*, by John R. Commons, reveals the author's personality and sketches his rich experience. Readers will get more profit and more pleasure from the 900-page treatise if they start with the 200-page autobiography.[2]

I

As a boy John Commons found difficulty in acquiring knowledge at second hand from schoolbooks. His was not a docile mind; he could not cram for examinations. Always he had to find out facts for himself and to think out the relations among his findings. As a college instructor he failed when he tried to give systematic courses. He was essentially an investigator; an investigator who observed men's theories as carefully as he observed their actions. He talked with people of all sorts and he ransacked libraries. The theories collected from books required as much working over as the theories collected from conversations; both sets had to be

[1] Reprinted by permission from *American Economic Review*, vol. XXV, pp. 635–652, December, 1935.

[2] John R. Commons, *Institutional Economics, Its Place in Political Economy*, pp. XIV, 921, New York, 1934. John R. Commons, *Myself*, pp. X, 201, New York, 1934.

thought out afresh to find what they really meant. All the materials and products of this smelting process—the formulation of his problems, the facts and theories that he observed, the interpretations that he offered, the solutions that he found—came to bear the imprint of John R. Commons.

That compound of skepticism and curiosity was the son of a Quaker father whose family had left North Carolina because they hated slavery and of a Presbyterian mother whose family came from Vermont. The two met on the Ohio-Indiana line where John Rogers was born in 1862 and named after the martyr burned in "Bloody Mary's" reign. The elder John Commons developed a discursive interest in the world at large. He read Shakespeare, Darwin, and Herbert Spencer; he drifted away from the Quaker assembly, talked politics endlessly, and acquired by swapping a country newspaper which he could not make pay. The family responsibilities fell to the strict Puritan mother, who had graduated from Oberlin College and who wished to make her eldest son a minister. With that ambition she sent John to Oberlin when he was twenty, following the next year with her two younger children and taking boarders to pay for their education. The boys had picked up printing in their father's shop and supplemented the family income by setting type both in termtimes and during vacations. The double burden of study and earning overtaxed John's strength. He suffered nervous breakdowns, took six years to graduate, and had a poor record at that. But he won the confidence of his teachers.

A thousand-dollar loan from two Oberlin trustees made possible graduate work at Johns Hopkins. There the youth met Richard T. Ely and learned that economics might include much more than the deductive analysis he has been taught in Oberlin. But his academic work did not prosper. Failure in a history examination spoiled his chances of a fellowship, a third year of study, and a Doctor's degree. Yet his teachers again showed faith in the ultimate success of this unconventional student, and got him an instructorship at Wesleyan. Another failure resulted. His effort to teach in the standard fashion satisfied no one, and Commons was dropped at the end of the year. That did not dismay him, for he had learned to teach in his own way; thereafter he used whatever he happened to be investigating as material for his classes, "regardless of logical sequence in a course of lectures."

Oberlin took him back for a year; he passed on to Indiana for three, and then to Syracuse for four years. At Syracuse he taught anthropology, criminology, charity organization, taxation, political economy, and municipal government. He took his students into the field and learned with them a surprising variety of things about contemporary life. But he also acquired the reputation of being a "radical." Chancellor Day told him that expected contributors refused gifts to Syracuse because he taught there. The trustees did not discharge him; they quietly abolished his chair. In public the Chancellor "bewailed the loss of one of their ablest and most popular professors." Commons drew two inferences: "It was not religion, it was capitalism, that governed Christian colleges." Wealth had a double meaning, "*holding* something useful for one's own use and exchange" and "*withholding* from others what they need but do not own."

Never again did he seek an academic position. To meet his craving for firsthand investigation and to give his family a meager support, research jobs turned up one after another. George H. Shibley, a bimetallist with money, financed Commons and N. I. Stone while they compiled a weekly index number of prices at wholesale covering a long stretch of years. The first figures were published in July, 1900. Prices were falling and the index made good campaign material for

Bryan. But the decline stopped in August. Shibley tele-
graphed that the figures must be wrong. Commons and Stone
could find no error. In the first week of September the index
rose and Shibley canceled the contract within twenty-four
hours. That mattered little; for E. Dana Durand asked
Commons to finish a report on immigration for the United
States Industrial Commission, and later to help in preparing
the *Final Report.* This job brought close associations with
Marxian socialists, with a flamboyant capitalist who hated
the Standard Oil Company, and with an able staff of investigators, whom Commons calls the first "brain trust." Next,
Ralph M. Easley took him into the National Civic Federation
—that well-meant attempt to solve social problems by
getting the leaders of capital and labor to sit down together.
Easley dealt with capital through Marcus A. Hanna; Commons dealt with labor through the chiefs of great unions. In
1903 the Department of Labor gave him four helpers to
investigate the restrictions and regulations of output by
capital and labor. This was the last of his casual jobs; for
Professor Ely had been "working up" a position for him
at the University of Wisconsin, and in the summer of 1904
Commons came into his own.

Seldom have a man and an opportunity been better mated.
Under the leadership of Governor LaFollette, Wisconsin was
ready to experiment with social legislation. The state expected the university to serve the people in more ways than
by giving college educations to a limited number of its sons
and daughters. Commons had learned much about the
cantankerous nature of man, the frictions and the wastes of
modern life. He thought that the pursuit of self-interest
produced efficient cooperation only when some social authority existed to judge and to enforce proper practices. What
practices are proper in different types of transactions must

be found out by studying practical experience. What forms and powers the judging and enforcing authority should have also depend upon the type of transaction. To produce satisfactory cooperation, both the practices and the social authorities should develop with changes in economic conditions. Like the Wisconsin "progressives," Commons wanted "to save capitalism by making it good" (*Myself*, p. 143). He was tireless in finding facts, he was ingenious in inventing devices, he knew how to deal with men of different occupations and prejudices. In short, he was admirably fitted to become a designer of social legislation for a "progressive" party.

The story of Professor Commons's contribution to the social legislation of his state is too long to tell. He drafted the civil service law in 1904–1905; helped to shape the extension of public-utility regulation into the municipal and interurban field; got himself investigated by the Progressives for promoting a small-loan law that authorized interest at 3½ per cent a month; suggested the Wisconsin Industrial Commission, served two years as one of the commissioners, and capped his service with the Wisconsin Unemployment Reserves law of 1932. Meanwhile he had shared in the National Civic Federation's study of municipal ownership in Great Britain and America, in the Pittsburgh Survey of 1906, in the United States Industrial Relations Commission of 1913-1915, and in the Pittsburgh-plus case of 1923. He had taken up monetary problems after the war and collaborated with Congressman Strong in preparing a banking bill that aimed at stabilizing prices. Also he had trained graduate students year after year by making them participate in his successive investigations. With the help of several coworkers he had compiled *A Documentary History of American Industrial Society* in ten volumes and written a

History of Labour in the United States in two volumes to which a third will be added this year. Besides his books published before going to Wisconsin, *The Distribution of Wealth, Social Reform and the Church,* and *Proportional Representation,* he had written six volumes dealing with various aspects of industrial problems, a learned treatise upon the *Legal Foundations of Capitalism,* and two dozen papers in technical journals.

Such in brief was Professor Commons's preparation for writing *Institutional Economics.* Few, indeed, are the men who combine intimate and varied experiences in practical affairs with so much experience in using ideas.

II

The fundamental convictions which Commons drew from experience were that men are mutually dependent creatures who must cooperate with one another; that the scarcity of goods gives rise to private property and to conflicts of individual interests; that collective action is necessary to decide these conflicts and to create a new harmony of interests, or to establish at least the modicum of order required for cooperation.

Collective control, then, is essential to economic life. It is exercised by the soverign, primarily through the courts. Such control is found in all societies, though in a well-ordered state it works so unobtrusively most of the time that economic theorists have given it scant attention.

It follows that the unit of economic investigation must be a unit that combines the three constituents of dependence, conflict, and order established by social control. This unit is a *transaction.*

Transactions . . . are not the "exchange of commodities," in the physical sense of "delivery," they are the alienation and acquisition, between individuals, of the *rights* of future ownership of physical things, as determined by the collective working rules of society [*Institutional Economics*, p. 58].

There are three types of transactions. Economists have concentrated their attention upon one type only, bargaining transactions, and have simplified unduly their presentation even of that type. In a bargain there are never just two parties exchanging goods; always in the background influencing the bargain, and sometimes coming into the foreground, are a second potential buyer, a second potential seller, and a ruling authority ready to decide disputes. In the second type, managerial transactions, there are three parties: a legal superior giving orders to a legal inferior—for example, a factory superintendent and a foreman, or a foreman and a laborer, or a sheriff and a citizen—plus the controlling authority in the background. Also in the third type, rationing transactions, there are three parties—a superior, an inferior, and a court—but here the superior is a collective body or its official spokesman prorating burdens or benefits among inferiors. Examples are a government apportioning taxes, a trade-union collecting dues from and making disbursements to its members, the directors of a corporation levying assessments upon the stockholders or declaring dividends.

These three units of activity exhaust all the activities of the science of economics. Bargaining transactions *transfer ownership* of wealth by voluntary agreement between legal equals. Managerial transactions *create wealth* by commands of legal superiors. Rationing transactions apportion the burdens and benefits of wealth creation by the *dictation* of legal superiors [p. 68].

The three types of transactions are brought together in a larger unit of economic investigation which is called a *going concern.*

THE BACKWARD ART OF SPENDING MONEY

A going concern is a joint expectation of beneficial bargaining, managerial and rationing transactions, kept together by "working rules" and by control of the changeable strategic or "limiting" factors which are expected to control the others [p. 58].

It is these going concerns, with the working rules that keep them agoing, all the way from the family, the corporation, the trade union, the trade association, up to the state itself, that we name Institutions. . . . we may define an institution as Collective Action in Control of Individual Action [p. 69].

All the activities of going concerns look to the future.

. . . The persuasions or coercions of bargaining transactions, the commands and obedience of managerial transactions, and the arguments and pleadings of rationing transactions . . . will ultimately determine production and consumption. In these negotiations and decisions, which are of the essence of institutional economics, it is always *future* production and *future* consumption that are at stake, because the negotiations determine the legal control which must precede physical control [p. 7].

This conception of economic activities carries with it psychological conceptions different from those with which most economists have worked. Man is an active creature who forms plans and strives to carry them out. His mind-body is

a *creative* agency looking towards the future and manipulating the external world and other people in view of expected consequences [p. 17].

The mind is an "organizer of impressions." It

does not wait for impressions, it is continually looking for them, breaking them up into parts, and reconstructing them into new feelings. Those new feelings are . . . active beliefs reaching forward for future action. It is this relation of the part to the whole and of the past experience to future expectations that becomes the psychology of our transactions and going concerns [p. 153].

Repetition of similar experiences makes it possible to test different modes of action by trial and error, to select those

[320]

modes that seem most satisfactory, and to test ideas about physical phenomena or human behavior. From repetition arise habits and customs that conserve the lessons of past experience and provide a basis for future expectations.

Habit is repetition by one person. Custom is repetition by the continuing group of changing persons. It has a coercive effect on individuals . . . [p. 155].

Among the most significant of customs are those investigated by economics, the working rules laid down by collective action for the conduct of the transactions among individuals belonging to going concerns.

These I take to be the basic ideas of institutional economics according to Professor Commons.

III

Had some other man grasped these ideas vividly he might have contented himself with working out a logical treatise having little reference to the history of institutions or the evolution of economic doctrines. Not so our indefatigable investigator. To him institutional economics is an evolutionary science. It

consists partly in going back through the court decisions of several hundred years, wherein collective action, not only by legislation but also by common-law decisions interpreting the legislation (culminating in the common-law method of the Supreme Court of the United States), takes over, by means of these decisions, the customs of business or labor, and enforces or restrains individual action, wherever it seems to the Court favorable or unfavorable to the public interest and private rights . . . [Also it] consists in going back through the writings of economists from John Locke to the Twentieth Century, to discover wherein they have or have not introduced collective action [p. 5].

The first of these laborious tasks was performed in *Legal Foundations of Capitalism*, published in 1924; the second is performed in *Institutional Economics* published a decade later. Since the two books should be read together, I must recall the content of the first before dealing more fully with the second.[3]

IV

Capitalism evolved slowly out of feudalism through the rise of novel practices, the exfoliation of concepts, and the formulation of new working rules by the courts, which judged what practices were beneficial under changing conditions and devised ways of legalizing them.

Under William the Conqueror, the king's property was not distinguished from his sovereignty; there were local customs on every manor, but there was no common law of the realm; the tenants of the king and the villeins on a manor owed personal services to their lords; use values dominated economic life; there was little exchanging and that little was mainly by barter. All these conditions had to undergo fundamental changes before there could come into being a system of "production for the use of others and acquisition for the use of self."

The idea of property in land was gradually separated from the idea of sovereignty by commuting the obligation of rendering military service to the king into the obligation of making money payments to him. The king substituted his own army for the retainers of his tenants and made his sovereign power indisputable; but the tenant got a clear title to his land and could buy or sell as he saw fit. By sending his circuit judges to hold court in the counties, Henry II laid the basis for the common law; for the king's court could

---

[3] For a less condensed statement, see "Commons on the Legal Foundations of Capitalism," by the present writer. *American Economic Review*, vol. XIV, pp. 240–253, June, 1924.

take cases out of the manorial courts and refuse to recognize local customs of which they disapproved. Commutation of labor dues into money payments helped to clarify and standardize the rights of the small man; it gave him control over his own time and a wider range of choice. When prices rose in the sixteenth century, new courts were created to which even villeins had access; and these courts adopted the rule that the landlord could not alter at will the customs by which lands were held. Money proved a solvent of ideas and an instrument of economic liberty in these humbler dealings as well as in the dealings of the king with his magnates.

Meanwhile capitalism was getting its start among the traders and later among the artisans of the towns which were for a time "islands of money economy in a sea of barter." The guilds secured charters from feudal superiors, largely by purchase, and were empowered to make and enforce their own working rules. But their increasing power brought the guilds into conflict with the common law. Late in the sixteenth century the king's courts ventured to condemn by-laws that established monopolies, even though the by-laws rested upon charters granted by the crown. Later the courts took over the constructive task of working out common rules of fair competition and enforcement of contracts. The promissory note was legalized; the law of copyright and of patents recognized that property rights covered not only physical things but also expected profits from business dealings. Common law that deals with physical things and punishes after the event was supplemented by equity that deals with intangible values and commands, before the event, the actions on which values depend.

These gradual achievements of English law were taken over by the American courts, though Professor Commons thinks that the lag between changes in business practice and changes in legal theory has been longer in the younger country. Not until about 1900 did our Supreme Court definitely recognize intangible property. And one important type of bargain still lacks a satisfactory set of working rules. Labor is not a commodity or a promise; the laborer is free to quit at will and the employer to lay him off at any time. The courts could not maintain the personal liberty of the worker if they assimilated the wage contract with other contracts. The legally anomalous position in which that contract stands has been made more anomalous still by the intervention of trade-unions, which have thrust themselves as third parties between employer and employee.

Apparently a "new equity" is needed—an equity that will protect the job as the older equity protected the business [*Legal Foundations of Capitalism*, p. 307].

Of this development Professor Commons could descry merely the beginnings in 1924 as the courts in deliberate fashion were taking cognizance of the practices that were developing in dealings between employers and organized labor.

V

What *Legal Foundations of Capitalism* essays to do for court decisions, *Institutional Economics* essays to do for economic concepts. Professor Commons can see nothing new in his analysis.

Everything herein can be found in the work of outstanding economists for two hundred years. It is only a somewhat different point of view [*Institutional Economics*, p. 8]. The problem now is not to create a different kind of economics—"institutional" economics—divorced from preceding schools, but how to give to collective action, in all its varieties, its due place throughout economic theory [p. 5].

[324]

Each idea here incorporated is traced back to its originator, and then the successive modifications of that idea are developed and the earlier double or treble meanings of the idea are separated, until each, as a single meaning, is combined with the others in what I conceive to be the Science of Political Economy as it is developing since the last Great War [preface].

It is this attempt to make institutional economics a history of the exfoliation of theoretical concepts that makes the book so long, so formidable to the layman, and so difficult to summarize. The advantage of this mode of treatment is that

every student of political economy repeats in his own mind the historical evolution of the schools, and a study of the history of economic theory is not an academic curiosity—it is a recapitulation of the evolution of our own thinking [p. 260].

Doubtless the candid reader will agree that he began "his working life as a Mercantilist" and arrived at more penetrating insights by degrees. But he may not now attach much importance to his early errors, and a book that recapitulates the tortuous process of his own thinking may tax his patience. He may feel that the ripe scholar who writes this book has much in common with the young instructor who failed when he tried to give a systematic course of lectures at Wesleyan in 1890. But the discursive writer of today is also the teacher who became keenly stimulating when he began to make his students participate in his own investigations. This is the opportunity offered by Professor Commons in *Institutional Economics*. The reader must do his own systematizing of the rich materials put before him; but the result will amply reward the effort.

VI

Starting with Locke's *Essay concerning Human Understanding*, Commons traces the conception of the mind as a recipient of sensations and an organizer of ideas, through

[325]

Hume's distintegrating skepticism, to the "scientific" pragmatism of Charles S. Pierce and the pragmatic ethics of John Dewey. On parallel lines, he traces the concepts of the interdependence of men, the conflict of individual interests, and the basis of social order from Locke's *Two Treatises on Civil Government*, through the writings of Hume, Quesnay, Adam Smith, Blackstone, and Bentham, to the idea of "reasonable value" worked out by the Supreme Court of the United States. He sets forth the "intellectualist fallacy" committed by the "Eighteenth Century Age of Reason," which he contrasts with the "Age of Passion and Stupidity" proclaimed by Malthus. For his own part, Commons follows Malthus rather than the ruling dynasts from Smith and Bentham to Herbert Spencer. But he prefers to speak of

Custom . . . instead of passion and stupidity, in order to avoid invidious reflections and to allow for a slow infiltration of reason provoked by uncomfortable experience [p. 246].

Efficiency and scarcity have a chapter to themselves as well as many casual passages before and after.

Scarcity is primarily distinguishable as power over others, and efficiency as power over nature [p. 387].

The conflict between engineering and business centers in the difference between these inseparables. Efficiency is the theme of engineering economics, which deals with the relations of man to nature, with the physical input and output of industrial processes, with use values. Scarcity is the theme of institutional economics, which deals with the relations of man to man, with pecuniary outgo and income, with scarcity values. Smith and Ricardo took wants for granted and explained values by scarcity; but the former traced scarcity to man's reluctance to undergo labor-pain, while the latter traced scarcity to the limitations of labor-power. The Austrians eliminated both labor-pain and labor-power as causes of scarcity by assuming that man has attained a a "pleasure economy"; they made the diminishing intensity of consumer wants the decisive variable.

Marshall coordinated the two schools by introducing the relativistic concept of changing ratios between . . . the quantities wanted by consumers (buyers) and the quantities supplied by producers (sellers)—both of which were variable independently on their own account [p. 386].

This familiar interpretation of the evolution of value theory is intertwined with an analysis of the concept of wealth. From John Locke to Alfred Marshall that term carried a double meaning: physical objects and their ownership. It was tacitly assumed that everything valuable is owned, that ownership varies exactly with the quantities of materials owned, that production can be identified with selling and consumption with buying, that exchange is both a transfer of physical objects and a transfer of legal control. Observation of actual processes shows the inaccuracy of these assumptions. Ownership, in the economically important sense of value owned, varies with prices as well as with quantities of materials; producers do not always succeed in selling; there are transfers of legal control without transfer of physical objects. Hence, institutional economics must improve upon the organization of orthodox economics. It must incorporate the theory of money and credit in its discussion of value. It must make the theory of business cycles an integral part of its account of modern processes, trying to show how difficulties in selling at remunerative prices prevent men from producing as large a national dividend as technology and natural resources make possible. So also, institutional economics must supplement the concept of corporeal property by the concepts of incorporeal property or negotiable debts, and intangible property or "the right to

[327]

fix prices by withholding from others what they need but do not own" (p. 3).

Still another variable that institutional economics must recognize is the principle of futurity, separable in thought, but inseparable in fact, from the principles of scarcity and efficiency.

The concept of Time, in economic science distinguished from physical science, has shifted from the *past* time of classical and communistic theory, into the *present* time of hedonistic theory, until it is becoming the *future* time of waiting, risking, purpose, and planning. These are the problems of Futurity, another economic "force," not found in the physical sciences, but nevertheless approximately measurable in all the diversities of reasonable value [p. 389].

The long chapter on futurity starts with debts. The large significance of that theme Professor Commons sets forth in a characteristic passage:

When the science of Political Economy began to emerge in the Eighteenth Century, it fell in line with the theory, then dominant, of an original state of liberty and rationality of human beings. . . . These theories of liberty and rationality accomplished extraordinary results in overthrowing absolute monarchies, abolishing slavery, and establishing universal education. But it was not because they were historically true—it was because they set up ideals for the future. Historically it is more accurate to say that the bulk of mankind lived in a state of unreleasable debts, and that liberty came by gradually substituting releasable debts. And historically it is more accurate to say, as Malthus said, that man is originally a being of passion and stupidity for whom liberty and reason are a matter of the slow evolution of moral character and the discipline enforced by government [p. 390].

Prior to the sixteenth century, only landlords and wealthy people could make contracts that the common-law courts would enforce. Merchants based their deals with one another on "parol" contracts. As trade expanded in volume and grew impersonal, it became necessary to give these contracts legal standing. The lawyers accomplished that desideratum very simply: they assumed that the person who received goods did so with intent to pay, and so virtually accepted a debt which he must discharge—a rule that still suffices to establish obligations between brokers on stock exchanges. The next step was to make merchants' debts, now legally enforceable, also negotiable. The foundation of the law of negotiable instruments was laid in the seventeenth century. Thus "incorporeal" property in the form of debts had become a factor of considerable consequence in economic life before Adam Smith was born. But the classical economists were so much concerned with material goods, so intent upon showing that money and all that sprang from it was a mere instrument of convenience, that they paid little attention to these legal claims of one set of people upon property in the hands of a second set. It remained for the lawyer-economist H. D. MacLeod in 1856 to recognize that "a debt is a salable commodity" and to analyze the relationship of the debt market to commodity markets.

This insight into a neglected problem proved extraordinarily stimulating, and gave rise to much of the acutest analysis of later decades.

Sidgwick's distinction of the money market and capital market (1883); Wicksell's world debt-paying community (1898); Cassel's scarcity of waiting (1903); Knapp's release of debt (1905); Hawtrey's creation of debt (1919); and Fisher's over-indebtedness and depressions (1932) . . . were all developed out of MacLeod's writings [p. 396].

Common's critical exposition of these ideas leads to a discussion of how "banker capitalism" can be made to function steadily. Left to itself, this form of economic organization tends to run now faster, now slower, in a rough rhythm.

Business activity depends upon the prospects of profits as seen by businessmen and gathers speed when these prospects are deemed bright. If the profits anticipated are to be realized, consumers must be able to buy the goods produced for them and to pay prices that include a margin above cost. But consumers' demands are limited by the money incomes they have already received, mainly from business enterprises, as wages, rent, interest, or profits. Business demands, on the other hand, are limited by the indefinite quantity of purchasing power that may be created for them outright, or transferred from savings, by the banks. And the banks, like the borrowing businessmen, keep their eyes fixed upon future profits. Thus:

> The institution of credit is the biggest factor which enables the business man to buy *more* when prices are rising, whereas the consumer buys *less* when prices are rising; and the institution of credit is the biggest factor which *compels* the business man to buy *less* when prices are falling, whereas the consumer, since he does not do business on future sales, buys *more* when prices have fallen [p. 560].

I think that these statements concerning the cyclical behavior of consumers' purchases are inaccurate; but let that pass. Professor Commons is certainly right in bringing all the factors mentioned into the business-cycle problem. He goes on to demonstrate admirably that the profit margins, on which so much depends, are very narrow.

> If any one of the cost prices rises one or two per cent, the margin for profit may be reduced 10 to 30 times as much [p. 587].

It seems, then, that the working of the whole system can be altered by making minor changes in any of the many costs of doing business. This fact points the way toward a possible social control over business cycles.

Wicksell taught that central-bank discount rates are the most promising instrument to use for this purpose. To make that instrument effective, he proposed "world-wide monopo-listic concerted action of central banks." Experience has shown that this mode of control, while effective in checking booms, is not effective in relieving severe depressions.

With the modern very narrow margins for profit, very few industries could continue on a world-wide bank rate of 10 per cent, whereas it is obvious that a bank rate as low as one per cent could not, of itself, stimulate an inflation of prices, if risk is unfavorable [p. 610].

The risk-discount, to which Irving Fisher has called atten-tion, "is the most important factor in present valuation" (p. 609). It declines in the expansion phase of business cycles and rises in the contraction phase. Bank rates can be put high enough to offset the fall of risk-discounts during booms, but not low enough to offset the rise of risk-discounts during depressions.

Hence, a more direct method of control must be resorted to, if we are to have managed revivals.

In order to create the *consumer demand*, on which business depends for sales, the government itself must create the new money and go completely over the head of the entire banking system by paying it out directly to the unemployed, either as relief or for construction of public works, as it does in times of war. Besides, this new money must also go to the farmers, the business establishments, and practically all enterprises, as well as to wage-earners, for it is all of them together that make up the total of consumer demand [pp. 589, 590].

"Reasonable value," like scarcity, efficiency, and futurity, crops up for discussion in many earlier passages and then has a chapter all its own. To Commons, reasonable value is a theory of intangible property developed by the Supreme Court of the United States since 1890. Its characteristic fea-tures are made clear by contrasts with the rival theory of intangible property developed about the same time by Thorstein Veblen.

THE BACKWARD ART OF SPENDING MONEY

Veblen took as the source of his materials the testimony of industrial and financial magnates before the United States Industrial Commission of 1901 [p. 649].

He found that these men were using a concept of property unrecognized by economists, namely, the present value of their future bargaining power. Through their legal control over the means of production, the captains of industry were able to prevent the community from producing goods except on terms profitable to themselves, and through the financial markets they could capitalize their prospects of profits, thus exploiting the community in years to come.

But during the years when Veblen was developing his scientific analysis of what the greater businessmen were doing, the Supreme Court was attacking the problem in a purposive fashion. The court recognized property rights in prospective profits, but gradually developed criteria for judging what profits a corporation might be allowed to expect—criteria that are summed up in its doctrine of reasonable value.

The court was beginning to distinguish, as Veblen did not,

between good-will and privilege, good-will being the reasonable exercise of the power to withhold, and privilege being the unreasonable exercise of that power [p. 673].

. . . the administrative machinery for research in ascertaining reasonable value . . . did not begin until the powers of the Interstate Commerce Commission were extended in 1908, followed by hundreds of state commissions on fair competition, reasonable discriminations, and reasonable values, as well as by industrial commissions after 1911, the latter to ascertain reasonable relations in the conflicts of capital and labor.

Also, the movement towards scientific management had only just begun [when Veblen was doing his pioneer work], and a professional class devoted to ascertaining and installing reasonable conditions in all the parts of managerial transactions had not yet begun to find itself.

Other applications of the principles of intangible property, especially the stabilization of prices, had not yet even been thought of, much less the administrative machinery to be devised [*sic*] [p. 676].

Since the war considerable progress has been made in these various directions, and Commons expects the future to bring higher standards of what is reasonable in bargaining, managerial, and rationing transactions, and more effective social control for enforcing reasonable practices.

He draws a lesson for economics from the two theories of intangible property. It ought to take the constructive, purposive attitude of the courts in its explanation of institutional growth, instead of the purely objective attitude of physical science that was professed by Veblen.[4]

[4] In this connection, Professor Commons becomes momentarily confused. Veblen, he says, considered that science is "matter-of-fact" science, arising from the modern inventions of machinery, wherein the scientist eliminates all of the older ideas of purpose or "animism" contained in the concepts of alchemy, or divination, and adopts merely the ideas of "consecutive change," or "process," which has no "causation" and no "final end" or "purpose."

"If this is so [Commons comments], then there is no science of human nature. Science becomes only the physical sciences" (p. 654).

He proceeds to argue that institutional economics is concerned precisely with human purposes as summed up in "worldly wisdom"—a mental attitude which Veblen regards as "at cross-purposes with the disinterested scientific spirit."

Of course, Veblen did not conceive human beings as devoid of purpose. Commons himself presently recognizes that the "instinct of workmanship" brings purpose into the foreground of behavior (p. 661). That was not the only instinct with which Veblen endowed mankind, and all instincts are purposive. His chief criticism of hedonism is that it pictures men as passive creatures, controlled by the pleasure-pain forces which impinge upon them.

What Veblen was driving at is that science assumes no purposes in "nature," or in "the course of events" outside of man. In dealing with human behavior, he tries to give an account of human purposes in terms of an evolutionary process of natural selection. For those purposes are an evolutionary product and so can be explained in the same fashion as man's opposable thumb. The scientist should refrain, so far as is possible for such a purposeful creature as man, from mixing his own purposes into his explanations of cumulative changes in the purposes of others. That rule of intellectual honesty Commons accepts in principle and practices with indifferent success, like Veblen and the rest of us.

The reason is not that the economist should be more keen to "do good" than a physical chemist, but that the problems of social behavior contain elements not present in problems of physical chemistry. The "Will-in-action, guided by purpose and expectation" (p. 648), is a cardinal factor in the behavior of all individuals, including Supreme Court justices. In so far as action is purposive, causation runs from the future back to the present; not from the past forward to the present. One cannot understand what men do, if he treats them as he would treat molecules, leaving their expectations, valuations, and purposes out of account. Concepts like reasonable value play as definite a role in shaping institutions as does the difference between the cultural incidence of machine tending and money-making, which Veblen taught us to see. Even if the economist remains an aloof spectator of social processes, with no itch to modify them, he must not leave human purposes out of his explanations.

John Commons is both a theorist and a reformer—like Adam Smith, Malthus, and Ricardo. And it is the reformer who winds up the chapter on reasonable value as follows:

The theory of reasonable value may be summarized, in its pragmatic application, as a theory of social progress by means of personality controlled, liberated, and expanded by collective action. It is not individualism, it is institutionalized personality. Its tacit or habitual assumptions are the continuance of the capitalist system based on private property and profits. It is fitted to a Malthusian concept of human nature, starting from the passion, stupidity, and ignorance whereby mankind does the opposite of what reason and rationality would prescribe, and ending in an admiration for the individual who, by initiative, persistence, taking risks, and assuming obligations to others, rises to leadership.

Unregulated profit-seeking drags the conscientious down towards the level of the least conscientious; yet a considerable minority is always above that level, no matter how high it may have been raised by collective action. These indicate the possibility of progress.

[334]

The problem, then, is the limited one of investigating the working rules of collective action which bring reluctant individuals up to, not an impracticable ideal, but a reasonable idealism, because it is already demonstrated to be practicable by the progressive minority under existing conditions. . . .

If the profit-motive, in the field of economics, can be enlisted in the program of social welfare, then a dynamic factor, more constructive than all others, is enlisted. It is an appeal to the business man to get rich by making others rich, and, if he does not respond, then to appeal to collective action [sic] [pp. 874, 875].

Commons is by no means certain, however, that the courts, industrial commissions, scientific managers, monetary reformers, and their colleagues will succeed in saving capitalism by making it good. He devotes his last chapter to the characteristics and prospects of the three forms of economic organization that dominate the world today—capitalism, fascism, and communism. What the future holds in store he makes no pretense of knowing. Nor is he sure which form of organization is to be preferred by the mass of mankind.

. . . it is doubtful whether, under modern conditions, a decision can be reached as to which is the better public policy—the Communism of Russia, the Fascism of Italy, or the Banker Capitalism of the United States. In the two European systems . . . liberty is suppressed and the intellectuals . . . are eliminated, not merely because they are physically suppressed but because individual originality and genius cannot thrive in a nation of fear.

Yet these are a small fraction of the population. The overwhelming majority are manual and clerical workers. . . . To them liberty is an illusion under institutions which demoralize them on the upturn of prices, pauperize them on the downturn, and coerce them by lack of jobs. They do not miss liberty if Communism or Fascism gives them security at low wages.

Likewise with the personal thrift which became the basis of . . . small capitalism. . . . The inflation and deflation of a twentieth-century Banker civilization scrapes off the cream of that individual proprietorship which hitherto had induced individual wage-earners and farmers to save, to economize, to take the risks which they had a chance to surmount, and to maintain the American Republic. . . .

If these thrifty individuals are eliminated from the capitalist civilization by becoming a proletariat of wage and salary earners, then it is probable that, for the overwhelming majority, a communist or fascist dictatorship may be preferable to American Banker Capitalism. It will, no doubt, promptly eliminate academic liberty and a free press, but meanwhile the economists have, for the time being, a new equipment of experimental laboratories on three grand scales, in Russia, Italy and America, for a rough and tumble testing of their classical, hedonistic, and institutional theories [p. 903].

VII

One of the chief services that Professor Commons's treatise performs is to clarify the relations of "institutional economics" to what for lack of a better term is called "orthodox economics." The institutional type is often conceived to be a rival of and would-be substitute for the types of theory that derive from Ricardo, Menger, or Walras. The leading institutionalists may be partly responsible for that misapprehension. MacLeod, whom Commons names the "originator" of institutional economics (p. 399), was an acrid controversialist, and Veblen explained the preconceptions that had prevented economics from becoming an evolutionary science as cultural lags. But whether one accepts Veblen's concept of an institution as a widely prevalent habit of thought, or Commons's concept that an institution is "collective action in control of individual action," he must acknowledge that the earlier masters of economic theory dealt with institutions at length. Certainly the mercantilism that Adam Smith condemned was an institution, or complex of institutions, on either definition, and so also was the "simple and obvious system of natural liberty" that Adam Smith praised; for his discussion of the duties of the sovereign makes it clear that there must be collective control over individual action even under a policy of *laissez faire*. The Philosophical Radicals talked explicitly about "bad institutions," showed marked ingenuity in devising paper schemes for "good institutions" and influenced powerfully the institutional development of England for three generations. Perhaps no other economist has stressed the importance of institutions in human history more incisively than did John Stuart Mill in his discussion of distribution. It certainly is not the choice of institutions as subject matter that differentiates "institutional" from other types of economics. The day must be close at hand when critics will begin to proclaim that economics has always been "institutional."

What did mark off Veblen's work from that of his predecessors was concentration upon the evolution of institutions, and the application to that problem of a fresh conception of human nature. Adam Smith, the Philosophical Radicals, and later economists had analyzed the workings of contemporary institutions, had shown how these workings promoted or obstructed public welfare as they conceived it, and had argued that the bad institutions should be abolished to make way for good ones. Institutional change to them meant a process of "reform," based upon rational insight. In this respect I do not see that MacLeod differed as an institutionalist from Mill. Karl Marx is a fitter candidate for nomination as the "originator" of the later type of institutional economics, for he focused his attention upon the process of institutional change. But Marx retained substantially the conception of human nature that the Philosophical Radicals had elaborated, and his notion of institutional evolution reeked of Hegel's metaphysics.

Veblen was the first economist to present institutional evolution in terms of natural selection, and his conception of human nature derived from Darwin and William James,

[337]

not from Bentham. To him the proper way to explain existing institutions was in terms of the cumulative changes in ways of making a living. He took that factor to be of chief importance in forming the habits of thought prevailing in successive generations, because most men and women spend more of their time in getting a living than in any other activity. When he thought about the workings of contemporary institutions, his interest centered in the changes that these great social habits are now undergoing. He was not concerned with the quasi-mechanical details of price determination, after demand schedules and supply schedules had been assumed. To him the significant problems of value were hidden from sight in these formal schedules. He asked, for example, why men desire obviously expensive goods and accomplishments however much discomfort their display may impose, and how a species of animals that owes its primacy to work can form the habit of thinking labor irksome.

Great as was the service that Veblen rendered by studying the evolution of institutions, it is clear that this theme does not constitute the whole of economics. The problems treated by orthodox theory are genuine problems, and the two sets of discussions should be put into such form that everyone can see how they supplement each other. For example, Veblen's analysis of the cultural incidence of the machine process and of business traffic takes for granted knowledge of how prices are fixed and of the bearing of prices upon the distribution of income.[5] Every scheme of institutions has an implicit logic of its own, and it is not less important to know what that logic is than to know how the institutions came

[5] Veblen was ready enough to take up these problems when one of his themes required; but on such occasions he dealt with aspects of price fixing and the distribution of income that receive slight attention in treatises upon economic theory. See for example, chapters iii–vii of *The Theory of Business Enterprise*, New York, 1904.

into being and what they are becoming. When Veblen's friend, H. J. Davenport, defined economics as the science that treats phenomena from the standpoint of price, and insisted that it must be written "from the private and acquisitive point of view," he was elaborating the logic of pecuniary institutions in much the same way that Euclid elaborated the logic of ideas about space. Though Davenport explicitly ruled cultural evolution out of economics, he was contributing toward the understanding of one set of institutions.

Professor Commons, as an institutionalist, takes this catholic point of view. Let me quote again one of his most characteristic statements:

> The problem now is not to create a different kind of economics— "institutional" economics—divorced from preceding schools, but how to give to collective action, in all its varieties, its due place throughout economic theory [p. 5].

Collective action, like Veblen's widely prevalent habits of thought, is the product of cumulative changes, and Commons studies its historical evolution with care; but he finds no difficulty in fitting the ideas of "orthodox" economists into his framework. On the contrary, the evolving ideas of economic theorists help him to elucidate the evolution of collective action. Study of institutional change taught him, as it had taught Veblen, to eschew the intellectualist fallacy; but Commons found the traits of human nature that are basic for his purposes summed up by Malthus. Veblen took a whimsical pleasure in making orthodox economics appear in the light of his workaday world as airy rationalizings, spun from conceptions that live below the threshold of consciousness and that wither in the light of common day. Commons goes to the opposite extreme. Having spent a lifetime in trying to get men to cooperate in his reforms, he is temperamentally inclined to minimize the element of novelty in his thinking and to magnify the insight of his predecessors.

VIII

No man can cover the field of institutional economics, however keen his insight and however persistent his industry. Commons's largest contribution to our knowledge concerns a specific form of collective control over individual action—that exercised by the courts. As he points out, this field Veblen did not cultivate. *Legal Foundations of Capitalism* is one of the most suggestive contributions to social history made in this generation. Repeating what is needful from the earlier volume, *Institutional Economics* sets forth the stellar role that judicial process plays in the present scheme of things in the United States. To perform that task thoroughly, Professor Commons has to clear the way by sketching men's developing conception of human nature, and the gradual discovery that social cooperation rests not upon a divinely appointed or a "natural" harmony of interests, but upon a state of order that men learn to establish among themselves. This order must control the conflicts among individuals arising from the scarcity of goods, and it must provide for the organized cooperation indispensable to efficiency. The individuals whose clashing interests must be controlled and whose mutual interdependence must be organized are creatures of passion and stupidity, but creatures who can plan. In their planning, expectations of the future are the controlling factor. These expectations gradually come to be the dominant form of property, the center of clashing interests, and the crux of interdependence. At this stage of institutional evolution, the courts are forced to develop a doctrine of reasonable value that includes the "principles" of scarcity, efficiency, and futurity in a scheme of collective control adapted to the rapidly changing needs of the day.

This brief summary of the theme, and even the fuller statements in the preceding pages, show only the skeleton of a living book. It shares the vitality of the author's career. His interest in economics has the driving force that characterized the work of Malthus and Ricardo and that declined as "political economy" turned into an academic discipline. *Institutional Economics* is the fitting crown of a real investigator's life, and it should be an incitement to other investigators to follow the various leads that Professor Commons has given.

16

THE PROSPECTS OF ECONOMICS[1]

WHETHER economics is to us a subject of thrilling
interests or a dismal pseudo science depends upon
ourselves. If we come to it with literal minds, seeing only
what has been definitely accomplished, we find the discussions dull and the conclusions dubious. But if we come thinking of man's long struggle to master his own fate, then the
effort to solve economic problems by taking thought seems
a vital episode in human history, a hopeful portent for the
future. Seen in this perspective, economic speculation represents a stage in the growth of mind at which man's effort to
understand and control nature becomes an effort to understand and control himself and his society. The beginnings of
that effort may be crude, yet they stand for a high endeavor.
And the future of economics, the question whether men will
ever succeed in establishing a serviceable science of economic
behavior, becomes one of the crucial issues on which hangs
the doubtful fate of humankind.

At present the prospect of making progress in economics is
bright. We seem to be entering upon a period of rapid
theoretical development and of constructive application.
To justify this faith is my chief task in the following pages.
But to do so I must sketch the various types of theory
developed since the Napoleonic Wars impoverished Europe,
showing what manner of thing economics has meant to suc-

[1] Reprinted by permission of F. S. Crofts and Co., New York, from *The Trend of
Economics*, ed. by R. G. Tugwell, pp. 3-34, 1924.

cessive generations, what varying outlooks it has opened before them, what hopes they have cherished for its future development, and how they have striven to apply its teachings. Against this background I can make clear where economics stands today, what it promises to become, and what uses it may serve in the years before us.

I

Orthodox economic theory as we have it today inherits its problems and its methods from classical political economy. Classical political economy in turn got its problems from English politics in the period of reconstruction that followed Waterloo, and its methods from the conception of human nature then current among philosophers and men on the street.

The Napoleonic Wars had forced England to suspend specie payments and brought on an extraordinary rise of prices. They had imposed upon the nation heavy taxes and added four billion dollars to the domestic debt. But during the long struggle England had been sustained by the rapid development of her manufactures. The industrial revolution which had begun in the eighteenth century was accelerated during the wars, and the high profits of manufacturers and merchants bore the brunt of war loans and taxes. At the same time these newly rich manufacturers and merchants gained in political cohesion and power much as the English Labor party gained in the war against Germany. But the growth of manufactures brought with it a new difficulty. The diversion of labor from fields to factories together with the rapid increase of population made England dependent upon foreign countries for a part of her food supply, despite an extension of cultivation and a marked improvement in agricultural methods. Finally, fear that the revolutionary spirit in France might spread had produced a violent reaction in English politics, not unlike the reaction that fear of the Russian revolutionary spirit produced in 1918. The Tories remained in power during the wars and for fifteen years longer; they stubbornly resisted reform and thereby stimulated the very agitation they dreaded.

On the return of peace in 1815, England faced a series of problems much like the problems she faces today. What should she do about the depreciated currency and the high cost of living, about the heavy taxes and the war debt? How could she obtain cheap foreign grain without injuring her farmers and landlords? How should she meet the demands of the new manufacturing towns for political representation and allay the unrest among the laboring classes? It was with these problems of reconstruction that Ricardo, the chief architect of classical political economy, was concerned as an economist and a member of Parliament.

Nowadays the newspapers would call Ricardo "a millionaire radical." He was a staunch champion of free speech in days when free speech was even more unpopular than it has been among us of late. He advocated the resumption of specie payments, the reorganization of the banking system, and the systematization of the taxes. Though very rich, he demanded a levy on capital to pay the war debt. Though he had entered Parliament "through his breeches pocket," he advocated parliamentary reform. Though a great landlord, he labored for the repeal of the import duties on grain. It was out of his analysis of this last problem that he developed the main lines of his economic theory.

When Napoleon was sent to Elba and trade was reopened across the Channel, the English landed interest feared they would be ruined by a flood of cheap Continental wheat. As a safeguard they proposed to raise the import duties on grain. This project roused a storm of opposition. Parliament was besieged with anticorn-law petitions from the towns and industrial districts, "the greatest number of petitions that has ever perhaps been known" said Lord Grey. Sir Robert Peel warned the Commons that "if the measure passed the manufactures of the towns would be destroyed." For it was believed that dear grain meant high wages, and that high wages meant ruinously low profits. The debate in Parliament grew into a self-conscious class struggle between the landlords and the capitalist employers. The working classes, and this touch is especially characteristic of the times, were not a party to this struggle; they had no spokesmen of their own in Parliament, they were not even supposed to have anything at stake. To talk of the laborer being interested in the bill, said Alexander Baring, was "altogether ridiculous: whether wheat was 120*s.* or 80*s.*, the labourer could only expect dry bread in the one case and dry bread in the other."[2]

This struggle over the corn laws made the distribution of income the chief issue in English economic policy. Ricardo, as a man of his day, made distribution the chief problem in economic theory. The practical problem was whether the power of the state should be used to maintain the incomes of the farmers and landlords, or whether the import duties should be reduced to safeguard the incomes of manufacturers and merchants. The theoretical problem was: What determines the proportions in which the national dividend is shared between landlords, capitalists, and laborers?

Ricardo solves this problem by propounding three separate laws of rent, profits, and wages. The poorest land in cultivation, he held, yields crops sufficient merely to pay the ordi-

[2] See the account of the corn-law debates in William Smart, *Economic Annals of the Nineteenth Century*, vol. I, pp. 450–457, London, 1910.

nary rate of profit to the farmer who works it and ordinary wages to the laborers he employs. "The natural price of labour," Ricardo goes on, "is that price which is necessary to enable the labourers, one with another, to subsist and to perpetuate their race, without either increase or diminution." Of course, the market price of labor, "the price which is really paid, . . . may, in an improving society, for an indefinite period, be constantly above" the natural rate. Further, the natural price itself is not "absolutely fixed and constant," for it "essentially depends on the habits and customs of the people." A rise in this standard of living is much to be desired, but not to be counted on. For Ricardo was a firm believer in the theory of population propounded by his friend Malthus. Practically, he held, we must face the hard fact that if wages rise perceptibly above the established standard of living, the numbers of working people will soon increase and the larger supply of laborers will again reduce wages to the old level. So in economic theorizing we may—indeed, we must—take wages as a constant, fixed by the standard of living. Such was Ricardo's version of Alexander Baring's remark that the laborer had no interest in the corn-law bill, "whether wheat was 120s. or 80s., the labourer could only expect dry bread in the one case and dry bread in the other."

With wages a fixed quantity, the law of profits presented no difficulty. The farmer cultivating no-rent land pays his workmen what is needed to enable them to maintain the established standard of living. For himself he has whatever is left after meeting his payroll. Hence, the share of the produce that goes to profits varies inversely as the share that goes to wages. In Ricardo's language "profits depend on high or low wages, wages on the price of necessaries, and the price of necessaries chiefly on the price of food." The poorer the land cultivated, the less will the agricultural laborer produce over and above what is required by his fixed standard of living, and the less produce will be left to his employer for profit.

Now, this sharing of the produce on the poorest land in cultivation "regulates" the sharing between laborers and capitalists in all other enterprises throughout the country. For under a regime of free competition farmers on one class of lands cannot long make profits either greater or less than farmers on other classes of lands. Nor can men who embark their capital in manufactures or trade expect profits greater or less than the profits of farmers of no-rent lands. For if they made higher profits, the no-rent farmers would go into manufactures or trade, and, if they made lower profits, the manufacturers and merchants would turn to farming. All over the country there is substantially one basic rate of wages and one basic rate of profits, with certain permanent differentials to compensate for the exceptional risk, difficulty, or disfavor attaching to particular occupations.

This conception of a basic rate of profits and wages in all occupations makes it possible for Ricardo to complete his theory of distribution by laying down the law of rent. Competition among farmers bidding for leases will force them to offer for every farm that is to let a rent per acre just equal to the value of the produce it yields over and above what an acre of the poorest land in cultivation would yield to a like outlay of capital and labor. For if a given farm were leased at a lower rent than this differential, the lucky tenant would receive more than the going rate of profits. Of course, competitors would not let any farmer get so good a bargain. On the other hand, no farmer would knowingly pay a rent so high that he would have left for himself less profit than he could make on no-rent land.

These three laws of wages, profits, and rents in the present, Ricardo supplements by three other laws concerning the tendencies of wages, profits, and rents to change in the future. The fundamental factors in future developments are the likelihood that population will increase and that methods of production will improve. The increase of population will require larger food supplies and force men to resort to successively poorer grades of land and more intense cultivation. We cannot expect that improvements in agricultural methods will do more than partially offset this force that is constantly making it harder to wring a living for the population from the soil. In manufactures, on the contrary, the prospect is that improved technique will more than compensate the increasing cost of raw materials. Therefore, "The natural price of all commodities, excepting raw produce and labour, has a tendency to fall."

"The natural tendency of profits" is to fall; for in the last analysis profits vary inversely as "the quantity of labour requisite to provide necessaries for the labourers, on that land or with that capital which yields no rent," and this quantity increases as the decline in the original powers of the soil to which resort must be had outruns the effects of improvements in methods of agriculture.

"In the natural advance of society, the [real] wages of labour [also] have a tendency to fall, so far as they are regulated by supply and demand; for the supply of labourers will continue to increase at the same rate, whilst the demand for them will increase at a slower rate," since the decline of profits checks the accumulation of capital.

Rent, on the contrary, tends to rise. Indeed, the landlord scores a double gain; the declining margin of cultivation means larger rents in produce, and each unit of produce means larger purchasing power over manufactured goods.

Hence, despite the checks interposed repeatedly by improvements in methods of production, the time seems coming when "the very low rate of profits will have arrested all accumulation, and almost the whole produce of the country, after paying the labourers, will be the property of the owners of land and the receivers of tithes and taxes."

Such are the chief conclusions of Ricardo's *Political Economy*. They are simple yet drastic. Wages are fixed by the standard of living, and the pressure exerted by the growth of population makes it difficult to prevent that standard from sinking slowly. Profits also will shrink as more and more labor is required to provide necessaries for the mass of the working population. The future belongs to the landlords, who will grow richer while the laborers and capitalists grow poorer. "It follows," says Ricardo, "that the interest of the landlord is always opposed to the interest of every other class in the community."

How did Ricardo reach these sweeping conclusions? How did he defend them against critics? His way of working is important for us because it exercised even more influence than the conclusions to which it led.[3]

Ricardo had been an eminently successful financier for years before he became an economic theorist. He had lived on the apex of the business pyramid, and from that lofty perch he had surveyed the surrounding realms of merchandising, manufactures, and agriculture. Concerning the details of making and selling actual commodities he had little practical knowledge, or he could never have said that "in the production of manufactured commodities every portion of capital is employed with the same results and no portion pays a rent." But he felt that he had the essential facts in

[3] [The topic is treated more fully in the essay on "Postulates and Preconceptions of Ricardian Economics."]

hand. When he came to write his book, he reread Adam Smith, Say, and Malthus; but he did not seek to collect new data concerning wages, profits, or rents, or question in any way the oversimplified analysis of human nature which he found in those writers. His conclusions rest on the broad assumptions concerning economic behavior which a thoughtful financier had found dependable, and which he saw no occasion to test critically.

For his purposes capitalists are animated by a "restless desire" to find the most profitable investments, modified by a conventional eye for the nonpecuniary disadvantages of certain trades, and a not-insuperable preference for home over foreign investments. His laborers are creatures ruled by habit and a tropismatic longing to marry. His landlords are Olympians raised above economic strife, reaping their double gains in idleness and honor. "Their rent is the effect of circumstances over which they have no control, excepting indeed as they are the law makers, and lay restrictions on the importations of corn."

Similarly, the social organization under which these three classes live is simple and enduring to Ricardo. Social organization had changed in the past, for Ricardo could look back to "that early and rude state of society which precedes both the accumulation of stock and the appropriation of land." But social organization had reached maturity and would not change materially in the future. He did, indeed, expect that "the progressive state" in which he lived would run down like a clock into "the stationary state," that is, the state in which population stops growing and capital stops accumulating. But this change implies no serious shift in social organization. In the stationary state there will be the same three classes of men dividing the fruits of industry; the same system of private property, investment for profit, and production for the market; the same dependence of the mass of mankind upon wage labor, and the same government maintaining "security." Various minor reforms are feasible, but the institutional framework of society will remain what it is. Men like Robert Owen who cherished hopes of an economic revolution were "visionaries."

Not that Ricardo had a high opinion of the existing social order—far from it. Besides the minor faults he strove manfully to mend, he saw fundamental faults that would abide. On his showing, the existing order presents an irreconcilable conflict of interests. It is true not only that "the interest of the landlord is always opposed to that of the consumer and manufacturer," but also that "there is no way of keeping profits up but by keeping wages down." And there is nothing to be done about these class conflicts; they are as much a part of the natural order as the scarcity of fertile lands. Furthermore: "Nothing contributes so much to the prosperity and happiness of a country as high profits"; yet the inevitable drift of prosperity is to stimulate the accumulation of capital, to reduce profits, and thus to destroy itself.

The reason why we must acquiesce in the present order despite its fundamental defects is found in "that principle which should ever be held sacred, the security of property." This principle is sacred for no mysterious reason: it has its ground in ordinary human nature. Even the laborers whose prospects are so drab would find any disturbance of the present order a catastrophe:

. . . for the quantity of employment in the country must depend, not only on the quantity of capital, but upon its advantageous distribution, and, above all, on the conviction of each capitalist that he will be allowed to enjoy unmolested the fruits of his capital, his skill, and his enterprise. To take from him this conviction is at once to annihilate half the productive industry of the country, and would be more fatal to the poor labourer

[351]

than to the rich capitalist himself. This is so self-evident that men very little advanced beyond the very lowest stations in the country cannot be ignorant of it.

Ricardo's type of economics, then, consisted of conclusions reached by reasoning from a few broad assumptions that oversimplified the facts. Human nature is far less simple and social organization is far less stable than he assumed. Improvements in production have been more sweeping, the rise in the standard of living has been more rapid than he expected, and the birth rate has declined. Consequently, most of the conclusions which Ricardo drew about the future have proved to be mistaken. The landed proprietors of England have not gained in wealth faster than the capitalist classes; profits probably have not declined, real wages have not been stable, it has not become harder to wring a living from the soil, England has not approached the "stationary state," but seems to be swirling in a current of change today quite as truly as when Ricardo wrote.

Yet Ricardian economics is not to be dismissed lightly as a tissue of false conclusions spun from mistaken assumptions. It may be that in good part; but it is also the first vigorous attempt to think through the tangled problems of distribution on the basis of such knowledge of human nature and social organization, and with such analytic technique, as were available when practical politics brought the capitalist class into sharp conflict with the landed interest. We learn something by dwelling on Ricardo's errors; but we can learn more by considering what use successive generations have made of his work, and how they have improved upon it.

The class that was rising to power in the two generations following Ricardo's death accepted his political economy as established truth, a safe guide to public policy.

THE PROSPECTS OF ECONOMICS

Ricardo's arguments reinforced Adam Smith's case for free trade and Malthus's case for checking the increase of population. The new poor law was enacted in 1834 and England completed the gradual abolition of her protective duties by repealing the corn laws in 1846. Sir Robert Peel followed Ricardo's specifications when he reorganized the Bank of England in 1844. Economists were seated in Royal Commissions and employed in the Civil Service. Chairs of political economy were founded in Oxford and Cambridge, and elementary textbooks were prepared for the use of schoolteachers and governesses. By popular lectures before Mechanics Institutes, newspaper articles, and propagandist pamphlets an attempt was made to spread the truths of political economy broadcast among the working classes. Miss Martineau's tales illustrating the economic verities sold by the ten thousand. Clever writers applied economic theories to questions of the day in the quarterly reviews, and liberal parsons like Sydney Smith represented economics in the church. The English classics were promptly republished in the United States, and translated into foreign tongues for the benefit of the Continent. Nor did political economy suffer from intellectual isolation. It was part of the wider growth of philosophical radicalism and so had stimulating contacts with other social disciplines. Historians like Grote, Buckle, and Thorold Rogers were among its votaries; anthropologists like Hearn wrote economic treatises, psychologists from James Mill to Alexander Bain expounded the conception of human nature that the economists took for granted, John Stuart Mill and Walter Bagehot elaborated and defended the logic implicit in Ricardo, John Austin systematized jurisprudence on lines that harmonized with economics, the revolution in biology was started by Darwin's reflections upon an economic doctrine, and Herbert Spencer began his

[353]

career with a book that set forth the political theory of the economists in uncompromising form. Never, in fact, has political economy enjoyed such popular favor and intellectual prestige, never has it exercised such practical authority as in the two generations that followed Ricardo.

One might well expect that all this popular and scientific interest, all these practical applications, would cause a rapid development of economic science. Ricardo had made a hasty survey, he had propounded sweeping conclusions; these conclusions bore directly upon current politics, they aroused keen controversies. Yet in 1848 orthodox political economy remained substantially what Ricardo had made it in 1817. What explains the scientific sterility of these thirty-one years of writing, teaching, and debating?

It is good for a social theory to be applied in practice, for the exacting test of application reveals imperfections and suggests new developments. But it is bad for a social theory to get into politics. Ricardo's conclusions had the misfortune to become a party platform. Just because his economic laws had been made to solve the political problems of his own day, they could be warped to political uses so long as the problems from which they grew held the political stage. Of course, a theory that gets into politics hardens into a dogma. It becomes a target of partisan attack and an article of partisan faith. It ceases to be a working hypothesis tentatively accepted as a guide to further investigations. Men exercise their wits as debaters in making out a case for or against it, not in critical efforts to amend or extend it.

But all this popular use and abuse of classical political economy could not have kept it from growing if its best exponents had not worked out a deadening line of defense. They pointed out that Ricardo's conclusions rested on certain postulates, that the science was hypothetical, that it was a doctrine of "tendencies." To demonstrate that the conclusions of political economy were at variance with notorious facts, therefore, did not discredit the conclusions. The tendencies it dealt with really existed though they might not be obvious; these tendencies would stand out clearly if real life answered to the economists' hypotheses; the conclusions were consistent with the postulates however the facts might stand.

Now, this line of defense was logically valid, and the men who developed it clarified the situation. But having attained clarity regarding the logical position of their science, they stopped. They were content with a type of economics that dealt with tendencies, that argued from unreal hypotheses, that rested on postulates contrary to fact. The birth rate might fall while the standard of living rose; but Malthus was none the less right. Instead of bringing poorer lands into cultivation, English farmers might restrict the cultivated area, but that did not refute Ricardo. Statistics might reveal the greatest diversity of profits, but still profits "really tended to a minimum."

Economists who took this line might be technically right in every one of their contentions; it matters little whether they were right or wrong. What does matter is that by taking this line they lost the most powerful incentive to further achievement. If economics does not attempt to explain the concrete facts of economic life, then all that Ricardian economics needed was skillful exposition, the correction of minor lapses, and certain extensions along the original lines. Economic truth had been found and would abide as long as logic lasted, no matter what paradoxical developments appeared in the world of railways, centralized banking, trusts, and trade-unions; no matter what facts the statisticians pressed, no matter what the anthropologists learned or how the psychologists shifted their ground.

THE BACKWARD ART OF SPENDING MONEY

Probably the economists would not have remained long in this stationary state if they had seen how to progress by any method other than Ricardo's. But they did not have the historical knowledge, the statistical data, the psychological insight, or the technical methods of analysis required to work effectively in a more realistic fashion. It was, indeed, possible to make a beginning in this direction, and some among Ricardo's contemporaries and successors did so. But their example was not encouraging. What results they reached seemed meager, negative, and uncertain in comparison with the large, positive, and logically proved conclusions that Ricardo had excogitated so rapidly. The orthodox economists might feel ill at ease when forced to face some awkward facts, but their self-esteem returned when they dipped into the books of their unorthodox brethren. And in 1848 came John Stuart Mill's great treatise to confirm their faith in the Ricardian tradition.

The foremost logician of his day, the moral leader to whom young liberals like James Bryce and John Morley looked for inspiration, the sympathetic yet constructively critical friend of social reform, the admirable stylist—Mill had an intellectual prestige among contemporaries such as no other economist has ever approached. His *Principles of Political Economy* had a flavor very different from Ricardo's book. It glowed with a temperate optimism concerning the future, because Mill saw that economic institutions are malleable. He believed that a cooperative management of industry would prove efficient, that capitalists might find it advantageous to lend their funds to cooperative associations for terminable annuities, and that in "some such mode, the existing accumulations of capital might honestly, and by a kind of spontaneous process, become in the end the joint property of all who participate in their productive employment: a transformation which, thus effected, . . . would be the nearest approach to social justice, and the most beneficial ordering of social affairs for the universal good, which it is possible at present to foresee." Further he thought that human instincts, particularly the instinct of sex, would be brought under control by education. Thus he escaped from the bugbear of Malthus. But with all his hopefulness and with all his social sympathy Mill yet built his political economy on the Ricardian foundation by the Ricardian methods. And the very merits of his version served to prolong the sway held by the classical type of economic theory over the minds of men.

A new type of economic theory, so its author believed, was announced to the world by Stanley Jevons in 1871. He called it "the mechanics of utility." Unlike Ricardian economics, this new type was based explicitly upon psychology. For his psychology Jevons went back to *The Principles of Morals and Legislation* printed in 1780 by one of Ricardo's elder friends, Jeremy Bentham. Thus the new economics started with a psychological system which was already ninety years old, or even more antique if we trace it back of Bentham.

Bentham represented men as dominated by two masters, pain and pleasure.[4] Therefore, said Jevons, pleasures and pains are the ultimate quantities in economics. We value goods because of the pleasures they give us in consumption; we dislike to labor and to wait in producing more goods because these efforts are painful. A science can be erected on this basis, since pleasure and pain are measurable quantities which vary continuously in magnitude according to the amount of goods we possess or of the effort we make. The last hour of the day's work is more painful than the first

[4] [Compare the preceding essay on "Bentham's Felicific Calculus."]

hour; the goods produced in the last hour give us less pleasure than the goods produced in the first hour. When we come to the moment where the pleasure to be had from further products ceases to exceed the pain of further labor we stop work. Similarly, in exchanging goods, we carry on trading up to the margin where another increment of what we obtain would give us no more pleasure than we should lose by parting with its price. Thus economic life is really systematized by calculations of utility and disutility. By following this clue the economic theorist can explain the phenomena of production, exchange, distribution, and consumption. This is the central idea that Jevons suggested and that others worked out in detail.

About the same time that Jevons brought out his *Theory of Political Economy* in England, Carl Menger expounded substantially the same ideas in Austria, and Léon Walras in France. A little later John Bates Clark followed suit in the United States. Utility analysis from these four sources impressed most economists as radically different from Ricardo's type of theory, because Ricardo had explained value mainly by cost of production, taking utility for granted. After due deliberation, lasting some twenty years, the economists became excited and began a lively controversy on the relative merits of cost analysis and utility analysis. Zealous spirits took sides, as if the issue were of the either-or variety. But more cautious men like Alfred Marshall, the most conspicuous of later English theorists, refused to subsume cost under utility or utility under cost, and held that both factors in conjunction determine values. Such men were dubbed eclectics for their caution.

I pass lightly over the controversy, because it appears in retrospect to concern a minor issue. Jevons, Menger, Walras, Clark, and their disciples did not really produce a new species of economic theory; what they had found turned out to be merely a new variety of the Ricardian species. The utility theorists and the cost theorists held the same conception of human behavior, they worked at the same problems, and employed the same methods. Under these circumstances their differences were bound to be superficial. Indeed, the two lines of analysis were so much alike that they harmonized admirably when Marshall incorporated both into a single framework.

Less noticed but more important in the long run was the issue Jevons raised by making his doctrine of utility rest explicitly upon Bentham's psychology of pleasure and pain. This foundation began to create uneasiness about the time utility theory came into favor among economists. For certain writers cultivating the borderland between economics and philosophy warned economists that the psychologists were questioning hedonism. Even Henry Sidgwick, who succeeded John Stuart Mill as leader of the English utilitarians, averred that he ate his dinner because he was hungry, not because he anticipated pleasure. The economists were perplexed. They knew no psychology and had not realized that they were implicit hedonists. Yet they did not know how to controvert the statement, and they had to believe that hedonism must be faulty if psychologists said so. What should they do? Could they find a sounder psychological basis for economics than hedonism? Could they prove that their theories remained valid though the alleged psychological foundation crumbled? Could they perhaps dispense with a psychological foundation altogether?

Of course, the easiest thing to do was to do nothing; that is, to continue expounding economic theory in the traditional fashion without raising the psychological issue.

Menger, Walras, and Clark, in developing utility analysis, had said nothing about hedonism; why not follow their example instead of the example set by Jevons? So Alfred Marshall in the later editions of his *Principles* contented himself with substituting the word "satisfaction" for the word "pleasure," as if such verbal changes cleaned his skirts of hedonism. Others, like Irving Fisher and Herbert J. Davenport, expressly repudiated hedonism and professed to dispense with psychology altogether by making economics "the science that treats phenomena from the standpoint of price." They took each individual's scale of price offers ready-made by whatever process the psychologists fancy as the starting point—a starting point which it was their business to use in explaining prices, but which it was not their business to inquire into. Professor F. A. Fetter pursued a third course. In his *Economic Principles*, 1915, he undertook to present "a quite new statement of the theory of value, one in accord with the modern volitional psychology, thus eliminating entirely the old utilitarianism and hedonism which have tainted the terms and conceptions of value ever since the days of Bentham. The basis of value is conceived to be the simple act of choice, and not a calculation of utility. Even the phrase 'marginal utility' is definitely abandoned." But one finds as he reads Professor Fetter's book that the quite new theory of value is followed by the familiar doctrines of prices, rent, wages, interest, and profits. What an economic treatise says about the psychology of value seems to make no difference in its economic theory.

All this means, of course, that our orthodox economists have a most inadequate conception of psychology—and economics also, for that matter. They write as if the economist's only concern with psychology lies in the problem of motive. If pleasure and pain are not the motives of valuation,

[360]

then what are the real motives, if any? That is the sole
psychological issue they have grasped. When they pass on
from the value problem they think themselves out of the
quagmire of psychology on firm economic ground. Obviously
this is a grand error. Economics is necessarily one of the
sciences of human behavior. Whether its votaries recognize
the fact or not, it endeavors to show how men deal with one
another in getting their livings. Now, no man can possibly
give an account of economic behavior without having some
working notions of human nature in the back of his head if
not on his tongue. No one can lay down any proposition
about business transactions without implying that men
have certain standard ways of feeling, thinking, and acting
in their market dealings with one another. It is, therefore,
naïve to talk of divorcing psychology from economics. If
Davenport's "science that treats phenomena from the
standpoint of price" helps to explain the behavior of men,
that theory is itself a piece of psychologizing, good or bad.
It is equally naïve to talk as if the economist borrowed or
could borrow all his psychological notions from the psychologists. For if economics deals with economic behavior,
then it must go beyond the contributions that the professed
psychologists make to the general science of behavior. The
economist will learn more in his own field, of course, if he
begins tilling it with sound psychological conceptions to help
him; but the soundest general conceptions of "the original
nature of man" and its modifications in the course of experience will be merely a starting point for his own researches
into human behavior.

If ideas of this sort are beginning to dawn upon economists, it is partly because the younger men are reading psychological literature, but mainly because certain among the
older men have been cultivating an unorthodox type of

economic theory—a type of theory that deals with a range of problems undreamt of in the philosophy of value and distribution. This type is perhaps best called institutional economics.

Among Ricardo's contemporaries was Richard Jones, a clergyman of the Church of England, who knew enough of economic history and of contemporary conditions outside of England to appreciate that Ricardo's whole system applied to an institutional situation recent in its development and limited in its scope. Accordingly, Jones set himself to broaden the basis of economic theory by studying the distribution of wealth in other times and other lands. The result was a book that dealt with rents under the feudal system, with metayer rents in antiquity and in modern Italy and France, with ryot rents in India, cottier rents, and finally with contract rents such as Ricardo had discussed.[5]

Jones was by no means the sole worker who studied economic institutions. For example, Sismondi, the historian of medieval Italy, investigated the development and cultural consequences of the industrial revolution in England; John Rae, who lived long in Canada and saw something of economic life among the Indians, showed how different institutions affect invention and the accumulation of capital; Robert Owen and William Thompson, Saint-Simon and Fourier, sought to devise a new set of institutions that would ensure a juster distribution of labor and income. Nor were the orthodox economists wholly hostile to this kind of work; for we have seen that John Stuart Mill emphasized the influence of institutions upon distribution and placed his hopes for the future upon institutional changes. But such excursions into institutional economics were not considered to be really

[5] *An Essay on the Distribution of Wealth*, London, 1831.

[362]

a part of economic theory—they were "applications of social philosophy" in the language of Mill's subtitle.

This mistake of differentiating economic theory from the study of economic institutions was confirmed by the rise of the German historical school in the eighteen-forties. For the German critics of English political economy gradually worked themselves up to the point where they felt it necessary to throw away the whole structure of abstract theory, devote a generation or more to the collecting of historical materials, and after that make a fresh start at generalizing. That uncompromising attitude provoked the great controversy over method. Should economics be a deductive or an inductive science?

While many of the accredited representatives of economics were wasting their time in this futile debate, a most unorthodox theorist was demonstrating how study of the evolution of institutions might be indissolubly joined with analysis of their workings. Marx's *Das Kapital*, published in 1867, seems nowadays a curious mixture of Hegelian metaphysics, Ricardian economics, historical learning, and political propaganda. Doubtless Marx's alleged science was warped by his passionate desires, his theory shaped to suit a program, quite as much as was the case with his bitterest opponents. But Marx saw the central problem of economics in the cumulative change of economic institutions; he knew how to use contemporary documents as an effective supplement of economic theory if not as its basis; and he showed how vital economic theory becomes when it is attacked from this side, especially if the current processes of change are projected into the future.

Contemporaries were too much scandalized by Marx's conclusions to profit by his methods. Indeed, they were so intent on refuting his errors that they could learn nothing in the process. It remained for younger men to whom his conclusions were an old story before they opened *Das Kapital*, to see the scientific possibilities in his way of working. By the nineties, Sidney Webb in England, Werner Sombart in Germany, and Thorstein Veblen in America were studying the evolution of economic institutions in a scientific, as opposed to a historical or a propagandist, spirit. Further, they were claiming that work of this kind is economic theory.

This sketch of the way in which economics has grown by differentiation into several types has been too brief to develop the full complexity of the present situation. There are types of theory of which I have said nothing and there are varieties within each type that I have not noticed. But even on the present showing we have several kinds of economists—neoclassicists like Marshall, the American psychological school represented by Fetter, those who cultivate pecuniary logic like Davenport, and the champions of institutional theory like Veblen.

Which of these several types of theory shows most vitality today? Must we choose some one type to cultivate and discard the others, or is there some rational way of combining the contributions of all? What prospect has economic theory of progressing in the near future? Such are the questions I shall try to answer in the last part of this paper.

II

The World War promises to give economics once again the vitality it had in Ricardo's day. That will be a marked change; for economics had settled into an academic discipline, cultivated by professors and neglected by men of action, modest in its pretensions to practical usefulness, more conspicuous for consistency and erudition than for insight, hated by few and feared by none. Even the Marxian socialists had become respectable, professing an orthodox creed and practicing an opportunist policy. Nowhere outside of Germany did economists play an active role in shaping public policy, and in Germany they were entrusted merely with certain details of imperial statecraft. There is doubtless a connection between the emergence of the later types of economic theory and the development of public affairs; but that connection is not obvious like the emergence of Ricardo's theory of distribution from the corn-law struggle. As economic theory had grown to be further removed from contemporary problems it had lost much of its early intensity, and become "sicklied o'er with the pale cast of thought." For years Ricardo and Malthus had bombarded each other with long letters about their theoretical differences, for on those subtle differences they saw dependent grave issues of national policy. In June, 1914, there were probably no two men in all the world who took their quest of economic truth with such seriousness.

When war broke out, however, the nations found that economic efficiency was a matter of life and death. The first shock forced governments and business interests to concoct immediately novel expedients to save credits from disruption. Presently all the large questions of war financing had to be faced—how much to borrow and how much to tax, how to adjust the burden of taxation, and how to manage the currency. Then it became clear that victory required drastic economic mobilization of all available resources to maintain military efficiency and civilian morale. It was not merely a problem of getting money with which to buy goods, but a problem of organizing agriculture and industry, shipping and railways, of training labor and making inventions to procure the necessary amount of food, clothing, and munitions.

Economists in every belligerent country had a share in framing the many measures for mobilizing resources. They were called in as technical advisers for the most part, but some among them became responsible officials. Both executives and advisers were plunged into a situation where they had to think constructively about economic institutions. They did a vast amount of strenuous planning, and tried to change the institutions of their several nations even more radically than they succeeded in doing.

What developments of economic theory has all this experience produced? Not much as yet on which one can put his finger beyond monographic books and articles. And there are those who expect no more than this to emerge. Economics, they say, will not change because the kind of theory we had in 1914 proved adequate to the demands made upon it. I cannot accept this view. The wartimes were too full of emergencies to permit of calm reflection, still less did they permit free writing and publishing. But the next few years should harvest heavy crops from the sowing of the war. For the influence of the war on systematic thought is not over; indeed, the war is just beginning to make its influence felt in the slow-moving social sciences.

The problems of reconstruction thrust upon us by the war offer as strong a stimulus to original analysis today as the reconstruction problems of 1815 offered to Ricardo and his circle. Europe's need of adapting her institutions to fit the altered conditions is far more pressing, but it is clear that changes must come in the United States as well—changes that call for intelligent planning. Public finance bristles with difficulties: shall we try to collect the loans to our recent allies, shall we seek to reduce the domestic debt rapidly, shall we maintain the heavy supertaxes on large incomes, can we make the federal budget a real scheme of control, are our public expenditures too large a fraction of our national income? The terms under which the railways passed back to private operation satisfy no one; how can we provide inducements for the new capital investments that are required, pay adequate wages, and yet keep freight rates moderate? The war almost stopped immigration; after the war we imposed hasty legal restrictions upon the expected inrush of Europeans; what policy shall we adopt, now that we have time for sober second thoughts? What shall we do with the huge amount of shipping that we acquired during the war? Shall we continue to export capital on a grand scale? Can we maintain our traditional tariff policy without thwarting our commercial ambitions? This list of problems bred by the war need not be completed; it is long enough to suggest how varied and how searching are the demands that will be made upon the constructive capacity of economists.

Not only has the war left us a legacy of problems through which we must flounder or think our way; it has also left us an example of bolder action in the common interest than we had been accustomed to consider. Thousands of men who participated in the work of the War Boards learned to think in terms of the nation's needs, to collect quantitative data as a guide to their planning, and to effect a strange blending of governmental and private initiative in the measures they adopted. This bold spirit has not wholly vanished. Our more competent public men and our more aggressive private citizens face their problems with an imaginative vigor that would have shocked a larger portion of the community in 1914 than it shocks today. And so our economic problems that were not begotten by the war are coming in for reconsideration. There is promise that the government and private agencies in conjunction will see and attack the problem of controlling business cycles. A more constructive attitude will animate our dealings with large-scale business enterprises. We shall become better conservators of our natural resources. We shall study economic wastes of various sorts and strive to diminish them. We shall learn more about the size and distribution of our national income, and shall evolve a more definite policy toward both the conflicts and the unity of interests that center here—a policy that will be felt in labor unions and employers' associations as well as in legislatures.

The conditions under which these problems new and old will be treated in the days to come promise to be more favorable to scientific fruitfulness than were conditions during the war. Then, it was often more necessary to settle a question promptly than to solve it correctly. Despite our national impatience, this pressure for offhand decisions has relaxed. We can take time to assemble data, to analyze them, to weigh the relative importance of different factors, and to study the bearing of each problem on the others. Decisions will not be left so largely to a small group of executives as they were during the war. In many issues appeal must be made to voters; in others, legislators and officials will seek support from competent opinions of many kinds before accepting the responsibility for a decision. Most of the economic analyses made during the war were jotted down in hasty memoranda, read by a few officials, and then tucked into filing cases. We shall return perforce to the practice of publishing the grounds of action, and economic literature will profit. Finally, the ultimate criterion by which economic policies are judged will cease to be military efficiency and become, at least in name, civilian welfare. That shift will make solutions more difficult to reach, but also far more interesting to the economist.

So far the argument has been rather obvious. We certainly face difficult economic problems, old and new. Certainly the economists will have a chance to show what they can do in a constructive way; working conditions favor their efforts: it will be strange if economic theory as well as economic practice fails to benefit. But we may go beyond these quasi certainties into a more interesting range of possibilities, and forecast some of the ways in which economic theory will change as it grows.

Of widest significance among these changes will be a firmer grasp upon the fact that economics is a science of human behavior. That conception will give the valuable contributions of past theorists their proper setting and afford a framework within which the diverse contributions of the future will find their proper places. It will show that economic history, economic theory, and applied economics have close organic relations, and it will dispel the darkness that has shrouded the relations between economics and the other sciences of behavior—psychology in particular.

As soon as an economist has assimilated this idea that he is dealing with one aspect of human behavior, he faces his share in that problem so conspicuous in current psychology, nature and nurture, the propensities with which men are born and their modifications in experience. I do not imply that the economist must read all the literature upon instincts and repressions which the psychologists publish. Doubtless acquaintance with that literature is helpful; it suggests a wide variety of hypotheses, and it makes one critical of the naïve theories about the human mind that each mind proffers in profusion. But we do not get very far with academic disquisitions upon instincts, or with general discussions of balked dispositions. They are at best a starting point for more serious work. And the economist has constructive work to do upon his aspect of behavior which the psychologist can at most help him to set about in an intelligent way.

Psychology itself makes most rapid strides when it deals with a concrete problem. The economists and psychologists share many such problems—for example, the problem known as "industrial relations." In this field the competent investigator finds an especially promising opening for work:— he can get excellent facilities for investigation; predecessors have left him working hypotheses to develop; the problem is clarified by the formal organization of the opposing interests, by the standardized behavior demanded by machine tending, the standardized reactions of the workers, and by the repetition of the same situation with instructive variations in a thousand plants. When a human situation gets organized in this fashion half the theorist's work is done for him. Adam Smith could make a great advance upon earlier economists because the economic life of England in his day was taking on a definite and fairly uniform pattern. Ricardo could formulate a theory of rent because the relations between landlord and tenant were taking shape as a business contract. So in our turn we should be able to analyze effectively the problems of industrial relations, because the underlying facts are crystallizing of themselves.

Many economists think psychology useless because it is introspective and subjective. When they grasp the idea that their business is with behavior, and that behavior is objective they will see that their psychological footing can be made secure. Indeed, one of the developments to be looked for is the rapid application of statistical technique to the study of demand for commodities, to the measurement of fatigue, to saving and other aspects of behavior that have seemed particularly baffling because particularly subjective. Psychological facts that can be measured are better data for science than most of the materials the economists have utilized in the past.

While fresh fields will thus be brought into the economist's demesne, he will find that his old fields of work gain new fertility from his new way of working. It will become evident that orthodox economic theory, particularly in the most clarified recent types, is not so much an account of how men do behave as an account of how they would behave if they followed out in practice the logic of the money economy. Now the money economy, seen from the new viewpoint, is in fact one of the most potent institutions in our whole culture. In sober truth it stamps its pattern upon wayward human nature, makes us all react in standard ways to the standard stimuli it offers, and affects our very ideals of what is good, beautiful, and true. The strongest testimony to the power and pervasiveness of this institution in molding human behavior is that a type of economic theory that implicitly assumed men to be perfectly disciplined children of the money economy could pass for several generations as a social science. The better orientation we are getting will not lead economists to neglect pecuniary logic as a sterile or an exhausted field. On the contrary, not only will it make clear the limitations of the older work, but it will also show how the old inquiries may be carried further, and how they may be fitted into a comprehensive study of economic behavior.

So also, the numerous special branches of economics, which have recently become sharply differentiated, will gain more from economic theory and contribute more to it as that theory takes on a realistic, quantitative form. For many years there has been a notable difference between the way in which economists handled economic theory, on the one hand, and the way in which they handled such problems as transportation, public finance, tariffs, money, banking, insurance, trusts, and labor, on the other hand. The monographs made little use of the theoretical treatises, and the treatises drew upon the monographs for little beyond illustrations. Textbooks often had a theoretical part and an applied part held together by nothing more intimate than the binding. When, however, economic theory is made an account of the cumulative changes in economic behavior, then all studies of special institutions become organic parts of a single whole. The viewpoint of the man who writes on railroad rates becomes that of the man who writes on the economic life of the ancient Greeks and that of the man who is concerned with the process of valuation. Thus economic theory will cease to be a thing apart from applied economics, because economic theory itself will deal with genuine issues— the kinds of issues that are now discussed in monographs.

As we work with the conception that economics is a science of behavior, we find our attention focusing upon the role played in behavior by institutional factors. That idea has been suggested casually in the preceding sections; the reason for it should be made clear.

In economics, as in other sciences, we desire knowledge mainly as an instrument of control. Control means the alluring possibility of shaping the evolution of economic life to fit the developing purposes of our race. It is this possibility, of which we catch fleeting glimpses in our sanguine moments, that grips us. Always the center of our interest lies in the changes that have taken place in economic behavior, the changes that are now taking place, the changes that may take place in the future.

From all that we know about the history of our race it seems probable that the equipment with which men are born changes little if at all through millenniums. Our reflexes, instincts, and capacity to learn are believed to be substantially the same as those of our cave-dwelling ancestors. If our lives are radically different from theirs, it is because we have developed through a long process of cumulative change more effective ways of training our native capacities. We have acquired certain ways of dealing with one another and with material things that are roughly standardized and taught to our children—ways of behaving which have their aspects of feeling, thinking, and willing. It is these widely prevalent social habits, learnt afresh with modifications by each generation, that make our behavior so different from that of our ancestors, and that will make the behavior of our descendants different from ours.

Accordingly, it is in these habits that the student of economic behavior finds his chief problems when he studies the past or the present, and his chief hope when he thinks of the future. "Institutions" is merely a convenient term for the more important among the widely prevalent, highly standardized social habits. And so it seems that the behavioristic viewpoint will make economic theory more and more a study of economic institutions.

Throughout the nineteenth century it was possible to assume with Ricardo that economic organization had attained a permanent form. Robert Owen's socialism was verily utopian, John Stuart Mill's expectation that cooperation would spread rapidly proved a genial delusion, the processes that Marx saw undermining capitalism failed to work as he prophesied. Alfred Marshall seemed justified in taking as the motto of his treatise, *Natura non facit saltum.* Changes in organization did occur; indeed, the current of change was swifter perhaps than in any preceding century. Yet with their astonishing capacity for not seeing what they were not looking for, the economists could treat these changes as negligible in their analyses. In the world thus made stable, the economist's business was merely to analyze the workings of existing institutions. A historian, it was admitted, might gratify idle curiosity by tracing the tortuous process through which economic organization had reached its final shape; but the economic theorist should stick to the serious task of understanding the present and not bemuse himself with speculations about the past or the future.

Darwinism, with its picture of the whole universe as evolving through a process of cumulative change which has no final term, disturbed this orthodox tradition, though the economists with their wonted deliberation took more than a generation to grasp the significance for the social sciences of Darwin's work. Nor did the men who sought to make economics an evolutionary science produce much impression on their fellow workers. Biological evolution as Darwin pictured it was a process of change infinitely slow, and the fact that the evolution of institutions proceeds far more rapidly was not brought home to most economists with convincing effect. By the time formal recognition was won for the evolutionary viewpoint in the social sciences, Darwinism had become outworn theology to alert biologists and Gregor Mendel had been rediscovered. In 1914 the institutional type of economic theory was still a rare form of mental aberration, to which few but the young succumbed and from which most victims made a prompt recovery.

Catastrophes, the anthropologists say, have been the potent factor in social change, the great provoker of social thinking. So it was with the war. Western civilization was not so solidly crystallized but that the belligerent nations could readjust their institutions promptly and considerably, under the intense pressure which they suffered. The institutional changes then effected, though intended to be temporary, have made a deep impression upon thoughtful minds, and shifted the perspective in which men see the future. Even in days of reaction, we cannot regain implicit faith in the stability of our prewar institutions. We cannot forget the national program of economic mobilization that was just emerging from the earlier chaos in Washington when the armistice was signed. We cannot shut our eyes to the greater changes that happened in Europe—the overthrow of dynasties in the Central Powers, the Soviet Revolution. And both those who hope and those who fear keep speculating about the further changes in prospect—the possible admission of bankruptcy in France and Italy, the growing power of the Labor party in England, the doubtful stability of the present regimes in Germany and Austria, the portentous awakening of Asia. Living amidst such uncertainties, we cannot be content with an economic theory of the "static state," except in moods when we long to escape from stern reality into a romantic world. The generation that is rising may accept as "scientific" only those theorists who make the cumulative change of institutions their chief concern.

Of course, it is mass behavior that the economist studies. Hence, the institutions that standardize the behavior of men create most of the openings for valid generalizations. That was true even in Ricardian economics, when the generalizations were made by the treacherous method of reasoning on the basis of imputed economic motives. A much more dependable set of generalizations can be attained as rapidly as objective records of mass behavior become available for analysis. The extension and improvement of statistical compilations is, therefore, a factor of the first consequence for the progress of economic theory. Gradually economics will become a quantitative science. It will be less concerned with puzzles about economic motives and more concerned about the objective validity of the account it gives of economic processes.

One of the oustanding lessons of the war to all economists who had a share in planning was the indispensable necessity of carrying their analyses beyond the stage represented in orthodox treatises. It seldom sufficed to say that a given action would have consequences of a certain kind, that would have been easy—and trifling. The important thing was to find out at least in what order of magnitude these consequences should be reckoned. Continually grave decisions turned on the questions: how many? how much? how soon? Say that the limiting factor upon our military effectiveness in France was ships—ships to carry troops and munitions. Then we should put all the available tonnage under army control. And it was wasteful to recruit and train more soldiers or to make more materials within a given time than these available ships could carry. But how large a force would each thousand tons maintain in France and how many thousand tons were available for army use? The available tonnage depended partly on how soon the new shipyards could get their vessels finished, partly on how much tonnage we could acquire from neutrals, and partly on how much tonnage was needed to provision the Allies and to bring us necessary imports. What imports, then, were necessary? That again was a quantitative problem of almost infinite detail. We might cut down the output of tires for pleasure automobiles, for example, but we needed a great deal of rubber for military and for essential civilian uses. Just how much did we need, just how much was already in stock, just how much more crude rubber should be imported each month, and where could we get it with the shortest voyages? Such questions came up—literally by thousands—and they had to be answered in figures: figures drawn from official records if there were such, figures carefully estimated if there were no records, figures intelligently guessed at if there was no real basis for an estimate.

In the economic problems of peace this quantitative element is not less fundamental than it was in the problems of the war. Here, indeed, is one of the differentiating characteristics that set off the problems that crop up in real life from those that appear in books. The theorist discoursing at large may content himself with pointing out the kinds of causes and consequences to be considered; the practitioner dealing with specific cases must calculate the magnitudes involved. In proportion as economists face real problems they will strive to cast even their general theory into the quantitative mold.

In so doing they will derive a deal of help from the statistical work done during the war, and which will be kept going or will be taken up again as the problems of peace are faced in earnest. For example, to help the price-fixing authorities the Federal Trade Commission made careful and elaborate studies of the cost of producing staples like coal and iron in different plants. Their figures give clearer insight than we ever had before into one of the oldest topics of economic disputation. So, too, the distribution of income is better known because of records of Internal Revenue. We are getting fuller data concerning the output of commodities; the Federal Reserve Board promises to measure the fluctuations of credit; studies in the physical productivity of labor are becoming feasible; some light has been shed on the volume of savings; statistical records of business cycles are being refined. And so on through a long list.

Moreover, officials, businessmen, and philanthropists are coming to see that they cannot depend safely upon "hunches" in guiding policy—they need to know the facts before they act. This growing interest in economic fact is not a conjecture, it is proved by the recent establishment of a number of organizations for social research. The Harvard Committee on Economic Research, the Wharton School's Bureau of Economic Research, the National Bureau of Economic Research, the Bureau of Industrial Research, the Labor Bureau Incorporated, the Institute of Economics, the Food Research Institute, the bureaus of business research created in several universities, and the far larger number of statistical organizations set up by business corporations and trade-unions are significant signs of the times. It seems likely, indeed, that the endowment of economic research will become as favorite an enterprise of public spirit as the endowment of medical research. With materials from all these sources to aid them, the economists will find it far easier than ever before to carry their theoretical analyses forward to the quantitative stage.

Another change that will come over economics is the recession of the theory of value and distribution from the central position it has held ever since the days of Ricardo to make room for the theory of production.

Quantitative analysis will be largely responsible for this change in emphasis. For recent studies of income not only make our present knowledge of the inequalities of income more precise, but also throw into high relief the inadequacy of the aggregate national income. It seems that even if the national income were divided equally among all inhabitants of our country—and our country has presumably the highest per capita income in the world—American families would still lack the means for a satisfactory life. If these results are valid, the fundamentally important problem is how to render production more efficient.

That problem is one that calls for many-sided cooperation. The physicists, chemists, and biologists are the men whose work lies at the basis of our struggle with nature. In the last resort, the fate of mankind hinges on the duel between science and the atom, as Professor Soddy picturesquely puts it. We must look to the engineering profession in its numerous branches to bring our industrial equipment and industrial processes abreast of our technical knowledge. The psychologist must take a larger share in selecting men for jobs, in training them, and in rearranging working conditions to evoke more energy from the workers. But, after all these specialists and others have done their best, plenty of work will remain for the economists. They must find out a great deal more than is known at present about waste. Just what benefit do Americans as a whole gain from all the effort they spend on advertising? The commercial process of getting goods from manufacturers to consumers has not been greatly improved since 1800. Is there no possibility of a commercial revolution comparable with the industrial revolution in importance? Why should a nation that needs useful goods suffer periodically an industrial depression in which men and machines stand idle by tens of thousands? To give full scope to modern engineering technique, production ought to be organized on a continental scale. Every industry ought to be carefully adjusted to every one of the industries with which it interlocks, so that the processes of making useful goods may run smoothly from the production of the raw materials to the delivery of the finished product at the door of the ultimate consumer. But there are economic obstacles in the way of meeting these technical demands. We are afraid of that very process of integration among industries which is necessary to make them mechanically efficient, and rejoice when our government dissolves the Standard Oil Company and forces the packers to give up their side lines, though by so doing it increases systematic waste. Economists must attack this whole problem of combining protection to the consumer with organization of production on a scale larger than is yet attempted.

To do that effectively, they must make a realistic analysis of present-day production. They must study the problem of distribution itself from the viewpoint of production, seeking to find out the bearings of inequality of income upon savings, personal efficiency of workers and employers, industrial depressions, and the like. This work will require courage, both because the American public at large distrusts huge organizations and because powerful private interests would be threatened by organization for efficiency. But the problem is susceptible of treatment by quantitative methods on the basis of data in which the margin of error can be approximately measured. Where scientific work is possible there is slight excuse for hesitation. Public attention is already being called to the alleged possibility of increasing output of useful goods severalfold by systematic planning of all production, and it seems likely that agitators will make much of this claim in the future. That is all the more reason why engineers and economists should work soberly in conjunction to determine what wastes of commission and omission are inherent in our present system of production, and how they may be eliminated without introducing new wastes of greater magnitude.

This last clause points to an obvious problem which the sanguine reformer is prone to slur over. Would not organization of production on a continental scale necessarily involve

bureaucratic control over production, and would not bureaucratic control lead to a new type of inefficiency worse than
the old? The answers we now give to this momentous question are based mainly on speculative opinions that get their
color from our prejudices or casual experiences rather than
from knowledge. We need careful quantitative analyses of
efficiency under various conditions before we can say with
assurance what the margin of waste is under governmental
as compared with corporation management, and before we
can say how far the causes of present governmental inefficiency are eradicable.

Yet one more phase of the change that is coming over
economics may be predicted. In becoming consciously a
science of human behavior economics will lay less stress upon
wealth and more stress upon welfare. Welfare will mean not
merely an abundant supply of serviceable goods, but also a
satisfactory working life filled with interesting activities.

At present welfare thus conceived is rather vague, but it is
capable of being made objective and definite in reference to
such matters as food, clothing, shelter, sanitation, education,
fatigue, leisure. And this realm of the definite in welfare will
be expanded steadily by quantitative methods, so that we
shall develop a criterion of welfare applicable to many lines
of effort. Intensive studies of production will show not
merely how the output of fields, mines, and factories can be
increased by better organization, but also how the human
cost of production can be diminished. The idea of cumulative
change in institutions will prepare us to try experiments
intelligently. Industrial relations will be studied not merely
to find how strikes and lockouts can be avoided and individual efficiency raised, but also to find how work itself may
be made interesting to the mass of the workers.

THE BACKWARD ART OF SPENDING MONEY

Let me give one concrete illustration of this change. To the classical theorists, production was a painful process which men performed solely to attain the pleasures of consumption. By the curse of Adam or by the laws of nature, as you please, man was condemned to eat his bread in the sweat of his brow. That was a hard fact that the economist had to accept and use in explaining other facts. It was not a fact that he need investigate or that he might hope to modify. What hope there was lay in enhancing the output of goods or in limiting the population, not in making the process of production pleasant.

The utility theorists took the same view, except that they emphasized the variations in the irksomeness of labor during the working day. After work had been fairly started it might be positively pleasant for a time, and so long the worker gained both the pleasure of exercise and the pleasure of having products to consume. This fact, however, might be set aside once it had been mentioned. For the factor that helped the economist to explain prices was the marginal sacrifice of labor—the sacrifice made in the most difficult hour of the working day. That sacrifice was taken for granted and the economist passed to other problems.

In this field so lightly tilled there is a deal of work to do. That work may start with Veblen's naïve question: Why is labor irksome? He has shown that man has an "instinct of workmanship" which finds satisfaction in the skillful performance of a job, and dissatisfaction in waste of good materials or waste of effort. He has suggested that our feelings opposed to the instinct of workmanship, pride in "conspicuous waste," and disesteem for manual labor, may have no more permanent foundation than a set of institutions that make riches the chief criterion of success in life. Is that true? If it is true, is it the whole truth? May not the conditions of work imposed by the machine process be repugnant to the kind of human nature we inherit? But if they are repugnant, is there nothing more to be done? Can we not find ways of adjusting work and workers so as to lessen the irksomeness of labor if not to make it attractive, "energizing" instead of "enervating" in Dean Schneider's phrase?

A practical movement will drive these questions home. In this country and still more vigorously in England the working classes are insisting with new vehemence on the old truth that labor is not a mere commodity to be counted among the costs of production like the coal burned in the factory furnace. For labor cannot be separated from the laborer, and the laborer is a citizen who believes he has rights to as satisfactory a life as anybody else. These rights he seems minded to enforce by peaceful methods if they suffice, perhaps by violence if that proves necessary. He wants not merely good wages and leisure hours, but also a share in the management of industry to secure satisfactory working conditions, and to gratify his craving for power.

Between such demands and current conditions there is a great gulf fixed. That gulf can be bridged only by scientific social engineering. In making and trying designs for this bridge men of constructive imagination among the employing class and among the working class will play the most active roles. But the professional students of the social sciences will also have a share in the work. Men have an extraordinary variety of aptitudes in detail; different jobs call for the most diverse qualities of mind and body. It is necessary to analyze with care both men and jobs to find the capacities of the first and the requirements of the second. If that can be done with success it should prove possible to place a large part of the workers, perhaps, in the end, all the workers, in jobs that will give ample scope to their faculties without overstrain. Then the average factory operative may get as much satisfaction from his job as the average professional man now gets, provided always that in the processes of change we shuffle off our conventional disdain of manual labor.

Such a consummation is one of the working ideals that economists will come to cherish. They will think of production not merely as a process of making goods, but also as a set of human activities in which the workers are being cramped or being developed. They will be even more concerned with what man does than with what he gets.

At the beginning I said that the prospect of making progress in economics is bright, that we seem to be entering upon a period of rapid theoretical development and of constructive application. My reasons for that faith are now in evidence. The grave problems of the war and of reconstruction will restore to economic theory the vitality it had after the Napoleonic Wars. In dealing constructively with these problems economics will develop rapidly on the quantitative side; it will lay increasing emphasis upon the production of serviceable goods; it will focus its attention upon the cumulative change of institutions; it will realize that it is one of the sciences of human behavior, and as such it will become less the science of wealth and more the science of welfare; from this new viewpoint it will gain clearer insight into its relationship to other sciences, its past accomplishments, and its future tasks.

All this is full of promise. But I must add that the task of the social sciences is supremely difficult, that progress will be checkered, that the particular changes I have prophesied in economic theory may not take place, that our generation may pass before men find a really fruitful way of attacking economic problems. How all will go we cannot forsee. Yet if we do the work of today and tomorrow according to our lights, we shall at least be helping on that long process of trial and error by which mankind is striving toward control over its own behavior. A chance to share in this work with its exacting demands, its frequent disappointments, but its thrilling possibilities, is open to all who will.

17

ECONOMICS 1904–1929[1]

WHETHER we call Adam Smith or François Quesnay the "father of political economy," the science is younger than Columbia University. Discussions of various economic problems, it is true, can be traced back to classical antiquity. But a science cannot be said to exist before a considerable body of knowledge has been systematically organized. It was four years after the chartering of King's College that Quesnay published his *Tableau économique*, exhibiting the circulation of wealth in a nation of farmers, manufacturers, merchants, and sovereign, thus supplying a framework into which a host of problems could be fitted. It was twenty-one years after our charter was granted that Adam Smith organized economics as a discussion of the relations between individual initiative in making a living and national wealth.

Since these beginnings of systematization in the eighteenth century, the nascent science has had an eventful history. Its old problems have multiplied by fission, new problems have appeared, its factual information about past and present practices of men has grown enormously, its general scheme of organization has assumed various forms.

While Adam Smith had stressed the problem of maximizing the annual production of wealth, Ricardo pushed the distribution of this social income to the fore. "Previous

[1] Address on the occasion of the one hundred and seventy-fifth anniversary of the founding of Columbia University. Reprinted by permission of Columbia University Press, New York, from *A Quarter Century of Learning*, pp. 31–61, 1931.

writers," he said, "afford very little satisfactory information respecting the natural course of rent, profit and wages. . . . To determine the laws which regulate this distribution is the principal problem of political Economy."[2] But to elucidate the distribution of income in a society where men sell their services or the use of their property for money and then buy goods produced by others, Ricardo found it necessary to begin with the problem of value. He thus fixed what still passes as the standard pattern of economic theory —the dominant themes are value and distribution.

Since the 1820's, however, this pattern has been elaborated and improved. Ricardo explained "natural" values mainly in terms of the costs of producing goods. In the seventies Jevons, Menger, Walras, and a little later, J. B. Clark, each working independently, developed an explanation of values that shifted the emphasis from cost to utility. Then in 1890 Alfred Marshall showed how it is possible to combine cost analysis with utility analysis in a systematic theory of value. He showed also how this theory can be applied to the treatment of distribution. Under his hands the problems of wages, rent, profits, and interest became special cases in a general treatise upon value, and economics became a more highly integrated science than Ricardo had conceived.

This line of development from Ricardo through the utility analysts to Marshall may be taken as the main sequence in economic theory. But other ways of organizing economics have been tried and must be mentioned. When the quarter century with which we are concerned opened, several schools of economists were flourishing. In having schools, economics was more like its mother, philosophy, than like its elder

[2] *Principles of Political Economy and Taxation*, preface to the 1st ed., London, 1817.

sisters, physics and chemistry. There was not one generally accepted scheme of work; there were several competing schemes.

The historical school distrusted the methods and results of classical economics. It proposed to start afresh by collecting a far wider range of observations and in the fullness of time to derive more trustworthy generalizations by "induction." Marxian socialism, which plumed itself upon being "scientific" in contrast to the "utopian" socialism of earlier generations, concentrated attention upon a problem that neoclassical economics slighted. It asked, how are economic institutions changing, and it professed to give the answer. Both of these schools were losing somewhat of their earlier militancy by the end of the nineteenth century. When Gustav Schmoller, the leading figure of the historical school, published his "Olympian survey" of economics in 1901, he made free (and awkward) use of the "deductive" analysis which he had formerly scorned. Meanwhile Marxian socialism was undergoing a process of revision at the hands of disciples who toned down, explained away, or frankly rejected certain of their master's most distinctive doctrines. But two other schools were coming to the front.

Pareto, an Italian engineer who had turned to social problems, was developing mathematical economics along the lines sketched by Léon Walras. Though Pareto cultivated a fine scorn for "literary economists," the difference between his work and that of men like Marshall was more technical than substantial. While those who followed the classical tradition attacked the problem of value by dealing with one or two commodities at a time and showing how their prices were affected by the prices of other goods, Walras invented and Pareto improved a method for attacking the simultaneous determination of the prices of any number of commodities in a market where every price affects and is affected by every other price.

Less like the standard pattern and more like the historical program, was the institutional approach to economics. Thorstein Veblen published his first critique of economic theory in 1898 and his first constructive study of economic institutions in 1899.[3] A student of Darwin and contemporary psychology, Veblen contended that the conception of human behavior tacitly employed by economic theorists was sadly out of date. Men are creatures of instinct and habit rather than creatures of calculation. Of these two controlling elements, instincts have remained a nearly constant factor in the life-history of the species, while habits have undergone a cumulative development. It is the cumulative change in prevalent habits of thinking—that is, in institutions—that makes the life of man today so different from his life in Neolithic times, in classical antiquity, in the Middle Ages, or even in the eighteenth century. Hence, to account for modern economic life we must study its evolution. A scientific economics is one that concentrates attention upon the cumulative change of economic institutions. The explanations of behavior that conventional theory offers in terms of choice between opposing motives are curious products of the rationalist fallacy—consistently reasoned deductions from mistaken assumptions concerning human nature. Let us turn from these futilities, urged Veblen, to study the effects that the daily discipline of life in tending machines and making money is producing upon the mass habits of thought inherited from earlier generations.

[3] "Why is Economics not an Evolutionary Science?" 1898; reprinted in *The Place of Science in Modern Civilisation*, 1919. The book referred to is *The Theory of the Leisure Class*, 1899, 10th *reprint*, 1924. [Compare the preceding essay on Thorstein Veblen.]

THE BACKWARD ART OF SPENDING MONEY

I

So much by way of background for the period to be discussed. If the background does not seem confused, I have misrepresented it. In his lecture upon economics in the one hundred and fiftieth anniversary series, Henry R. Seager commented forcibly upon the mixture of doctrines which prevailed at that time: "The dogmatic orthodoxy of the past," he said, "has been succeeded by an exuberant heterodoxy which gives so great prominence to the disagreements among economists that the agreements are easily overlooked." But he went on to speak hopeful words about the future, which is now the past we are reviewing: "This disputatious period is gradually passing in its turn and a new body of principles is emerging which entitles economics to be regarded as the most exact of the relatively inexact social sciences."[4] What has economics accomplished since Professor Seager thus summed up its status and its prospects?

One thing is certain: the problems with which economists concern themselves have expanded vastly during our period, both in the sense that old problems have unfolded new features, and in the sense that new problems have appeared. Let me begin with that certainty, and postpone the question how economics has reorganized its work.

Some problems have been thrust upon us. During the World War each of the leading belligerents undertook to mobilize its economic forces with a drastic thoroughness quite unprecedented in history. Many economists had an active share in formulating and administering the policies

[4] Henry R. Seager, *Economics; A Lecture Delivered at Columbia University*, Jan. 2, 1908, p. 14, 1909.

that were adopted; but they had little time for reflecting upon the implications of the stern work they were helping to put through with a rush. After the armistice came the problems of economic reconstruction, with which nations did not deal in so vigorous a spirit. And as a pendant to the war came the stupendous experiment that Russia is trying— the effort to establish a new economic order.

All these catastrophic changes occurred so suddenly, they constituted such an overwhelming mass of strange experiences, that economists have only begun to make piecemeal use of the data they offer for analysis. Fortunately, the Carnegie Endowment for International Peace seized the opportunity to compile an elaborate record of what happened behind the fighting fronts. Its *Economic and Social History of the World War* is one of the large contributions made in our period to man's knowledge of mankind. But this factual record consists mainly of raw materials: to work them up and incorporate the results into our social sciences will take time. The way in which the volume of physical production was maintained when so many of the most vigorous workers had been drawn into the fighting forces; the social consequences produced by marked changes in the distribution of property and income; the criteria by which national policies of mobilizing economic resources may be guided in war or peace—these are but three of the many significant problems suggested by the war. Perhaps the lecture on economics delivered when Columbia celebrates her two hundredth anniversary will deal at length with what has then been learned from the study of the war and the period of reconstruction. Certainly the Russian experiment must have yielded instructive results by that time. As yet there is not much to report beyond the dazed perception that social organization is more flexible for good and ill than we had realized, more amendable to purposeful control, and more exposed to man-wrought disaster.

Science deals with humdrum processes more successfully than it deals with dramatic episodes. This general rule applies to the present case. So let us turn from the heady theme of war to developments that get their significance from slow but steady cumulation of results. To stress the transition, take next that workaday matter, the rise of business schools.

For years business has been claiming an ever-growing proportion of college graduates in this country, and business has been making ever more exacting demands upon its leading personnel. The universities, our own among the leaders, have responded to the need and begun training students for business careers as they have long been training men for the church, for the law, for medicine, and for engineering.

The organization of these new courses was a difficult pioneering job. It was possible in some cases to draw into faculties experienced businessmen with scholarly tastes. But for the most part the universities had to develop teachers. Economists knew more about business than did any other group of accredited investigators. To them fell the lion's share of the new opportunity and the ass's share of the new labor. As fast as possible, young economists made themselves specialists in banking, insurance, accounting, merchandising, salesmanship, transportation, corporation finance, commercial geography, business statistics, advertising, and the like. All these men owed a certain loyalty to economic theory; but they did not always find clear guidance for their new tasks in the standard treatises, and many went their own way without much regard to what they had been taught. By this time they have amassed and organized for their immediate needs a vast fund of factual information concerning business problems and business practices. This knowledge is taking its place in the general stock of data at the disposal of economists. Much of it is exceedingly difficult to use for scientific purposes along traditional lines. But its existence affords an opportunity and a challenge that the students of economic behavior cannot blink.

In our country there are traces of an inclination to draw a dividing line between "business economics" and economics proper. Foreign colleagues tell us that this distinction is more sharply insisted upon in other lands that are beginning to develop schools of commerce. One of the hopeful expectations we entertain of the near future is that the two groups of workers will realize the common character of their interests more clearly than they have so far done. As the men in business economics pass beyond the pioneering stage of their work, they will develop standards as scholarly as those cherished by the strictest adepts in economic theory. On the other hand, if economic theorists seek to understand what is going on about them, they can find no more helpful allies than their colleagues teaching in business schools and working in business enterprises. Perhaps many of the most important contributions to economics will come in future from men who carry into business careers the habit of disinterested analysis of social processes for which economic science stands.

A further embarrassment of riches has come to economics from the multiplication of statistical data and the improvement of statistical technique. All of us know somewhat about the debt that the physical and the biological sciences owe to telescopes, microscopes, spectroscopes, and a host of highly specialized devices for peering into matters invisible to the human eye. Until the present time the social sciences have received but little technical help in observation. Their devotees have had to work mainly on what an individual could see for himself. But the turn of economics and its sisters has come. Governments and business enterprises, mainly for their own ends, are making and publishing an ever-increasing array of records touching an ever-increasing variety of human activities. These records afford mass observations upon the production and exchange of commodities, transportation, prices, wages, interest, profits, and similar phenomena which economists have long been watching as best they could. The new materials are far from perfect data for scientific analysis; they are laborious to manipulate; but they extend enormously the factual information at the disposal of an investigator. They make it possible in many cases to substitute measurements for the vague distinctions of former days between factors of major and factors of minor importance.

So economists with an aptitude for quantitative work have thrown themselves into statistical research. Their laboratories are beginning to merit the borrowed name; they are real workshops where masses of objective data are subjected to ingenious analysis. This type of work has made such headway that, in the United States at least, candidates for the research degree are commonly required to show proficiency in statistical technique. Outside of the universities several research institutes, well equipped mechanically and well staffed, have been set up since the war, primarily for fact-finding work on a quantitative basis in the social sciences.

While a series of substantially new problems has been pressed to the fore by the rapid development of business education and by the progress of statistics, many problems intensively studied in the past have expanded enormously in scope. In discussing the development of economics, for brevity's sake I stressed what have been regarded by successive leaders as the central issues of economic theory. But these central issues have never constituted the whole field of work. Since Quesnay and Adam Smith organized the science, their followers have continued the old practice of devoting special attention to particular problems of outstanding interest. In the last twenty-five years specialization has grown so rapidly that it sometimes seems to threaten the unity of economics.

Public finance is a problem in point. Adam Smith devoted Book V of the *Wealth of Nations* to "The Revenue of the Sovereign or Commonwealth." Ricardo discussed the shifting and incidence of taxation at considerable length. Elaborate monographs upon public finance have been part of our literature for two or three generations. But never have the problems of public finance received so much attention from economists as within the period we are reviewing. The enormous expansion of national debts, the heavy taxes imposed during the period of reconstruction, the huge reparations and indemnities, the growth of municipal expenditures, the cost and value of social betterment programs —these and a host of related developments have busied our specialists in such matters.

The field of labor problems has developed in somewhat the same way. Always deeply concerned with the wage-earning classes, economists used to preach sermons on the advantages of limiting families and on the futility of trade-unions. A later generation became interested in the structure and policies of labor organizations. In recent years economists have taken a wider view of labor problems and a more constructive attitude toward them. They think of labor not merely as disagreeable effort undergone to get wages, but as activities that yield abiding satisfaction and personal development, if the worker is adapted to his job. How to get men of varied temperaments and capacities into positions that suit their personalities; how to arrange working conditions so as to minimize fatigue and irritation; how to enhance output per man-hour by eliciting interest in the work; how to fix compensation in ways that appeal to the employees' sense of fairness; how to make all parties feel that they are sharing in a common interest—in short, how to give the mass of the operatives a share in the joys as well as the burdens of work, is the bold program which the specialists in labor problems are daring to conceive.

Needless to say, this program represents more aspiration than accomplishment. To attain their aims, economists are realizing that much more than economic analysis of the problems is required. They are cooperating with business executives, engineers, accountants, psychologists, physiologists, social workers. Some are serving as "impartial chairmen" in plans for collective bargaining; others are employed in the personnel departments of business corporations; a few are retained by trade-unions as advisers. In these varied activities economists are learning a great deal about behavior that finds no place in their traditional discussions of economic motives.

Third, the problem of money and prices, which has exercised the wit of man for many centuries, has entered upon a new phase. Of course, the war brought in its train a series of revolutions in price levels, and these startling changes were recorded with unprecedented fullness. Hence, the specialists in money have had better material offered them than ever before for tracing the relations between changes in the volume of the currency and changes in prices. It was as if the ordinary processes had been placed under a powerful microscope for the benefit of investigators. Into the analysis of monetary experiences in Germany, France, England, the United States, and the neutral nations—experiences of a singularly varied character—Europeans and Americans have thrown themselves with energy. The old debate concerning the validity of the quantity theory has given place to search for the different ways in which money and credit influence prices and the physical volume of trade, and the different ways in which prices and the volume of trade influence money and credit. The compilation of index numbers of prices at wholesale has been supplemented by similar efforts to measure the trends of prices at retail, the physical quantity of goods produced and exchanged, velocities of circulation—indeed, all the factors in the "equation of exchange." And each one of these factors is being broken down for more intensive study of its parts. A growing group of investigators cherish the daring belief that the world's monetary systems can be reorganized in such a fashion as to "stabilize the price level"—thereby removing many of the business uncertainties that have hitherto been considered inevitable.

Quite a different aspect of the price problem appears in the efforts of business enterprises to control prices for their own profit. Establishing monopolies is an old scheme to that end, which keeps developing ever new variants. It is a scheme which has great economic advantages under certain conditions; for there are services that can be rendered to communities more efficiently by a single large concern than by competing companies. How to gain these advantages and yet protect consumers against extortionate charges is a question that grows in scientific and practical interest as society becomes more complex. Study of it leads on to the more

[397]

complicated cases in which there are a few very large enterprises with some of the attributes of a monopoly, but supposedly competing with each other. Perhaps most characteristic of the day are the efforts of numerous industries to end "price competition," while continuing to compete in quality of service. Not merely economists who take the consumers' viewpoint, but also businessmen who for one reason or another are forced to buy in a controlled market and sell in a competitive market, are deeply interested in these developments.

To take one more example: It is within the last twenty-five years that the old problem of commercial crises has been reorganized as the study of business cycles, and under this guise has won celebrity. Scientific progress in this field owes much to the increasing volume of statistical data and the refinement of statistical technique. Similarly, the public attention given to the subject owes much to the growing bond between economic research and business practice—or rather, that attention is one of the salient examples of the bond. I have lost count of the number of agencies engaged in the hazardous task of business forecasting. And once more we find bold spirits who believe that their studies of business fluctuations have great potential value for society. Insight won by research may make it possible to devise measures that will mitigate the recessions and depressions from which modern nations suffer.

II

If time sufficed, I might comment upon a much longer list of substantially new problems on which economists have begun working since 1904, and of old problems that have expanded enormously under their hands. But I can give a more lifelike impression of the change coming over economics if I leave my catalogue of special problems incomplete and turn to certain characteristics of the work in progress that mark it off in a measure from earlier efforts.

In the nineteenth century, economic theory passed through a highly abstract stage. At a time when facilities for observation were narrow, the most effective way of treating many problems was that of setting up in the inquirer's mind an imaginary state of society and considering what would happen under the conditions supposed. These conditions were made simple enough to facilitate analysis; yet the intention was to include among the suppositions the fundamental features of the real world. To make definite analysis possible, these features were usually given an unreal sharpness and rigidity. For example, the wage earner's standard of living was treated as incompressible, capital funds were assumed to be perfectly fluid, competition was unlimited. Ricardo set this fashion. The most brilliant example of it is Professor John Bates Clark's treatise on *The Distribution of Wealth*, published just before our period opened. I like to call the method in question "imaginary experimentation." Of course, it is a favorite and a useful device of other sciences, notably of physics.

The weak point in this method when applied to economics is that one cannot be sure how far conclusions irrefragably established under the imaginary conditions apply to the world we wish to understand. The major economists have sought to explain what actually happens, and have regarded their imaginary constructions as valuable in so far as they shed light upon reality. In this respect the workers of today are no more earnest than their predecessors. But many of our contemporaries have gained faith in the possibility of a more direct attack. Instead of imagining a realm "that never was, on sea or land," they prefer whenever possible to look directly at Main Street and see what they can make of the behavior of the crowd. Current work is decidedly more realistic in form than was the work of the preceding generation. The shift is one in degree only: it seems to be less marked in Europe than in America, perhaps because our facilities for observing what is going on and for utilizing mass observations are better than those in other countries. And even here there are individuals, not all of them elders, who continue to rely largely upon the method of imaginary experimentation. Also, there are problems that it is still exceedingly difficult to treat realistically. But I think there is no doubt that the trend of current work sets strongly in the direction of dealing directly with the concrete and the actual rather than with the abstract and the imaginary.

Closely related to this shift toward realistic treatment is the growing emphasis upon measurement.[5] Of course, that is made possible by the increase of statistical data, the refinement of statistical technique, and the provision of statistical laboratories already mentioned. In a celebrated address delivered early in our period, Alfred Marshall applied the terms "qualitative analysis" and "quantitative analysis" to economics. He suggested that qualitative analysis, such as he had himself practiced for the most part, had "done the greater part of its work," and that the future task was the more difficult one of developing quantitative analysis. But "this higher and more difficult task," he said, "must wait upon the slow growth of thorough realistic statistics."[6] In the United States, at any rate, the growth of "realistic statis-

---

[5] [Compare the preceding essay on "Quantitative Analysis in Economic Theory."]

[6] "The Social Possibilities of Economic Chivalry," *Economic Journal,* vol. XVII, pp. 7, 8, March, 1907.

tics" has been less slow than seemed likely when Marshall spoke. The new data are not "thorough" in the sense of covering anything like the whole field of economic behavior, and they do not yet make it possible to reorganize economics as a genuinely quantitative science. But many more problems can now be treated by statistical methods than could be attacked in this fashion in 1904. There is a marked disposition to utilize quantitative analysis just as far as the necessary data are available; also, I think, a growing disposition to prefer problems that can be treated in quantitative terms. Moreover, it is often possible to restate one of the traditional problems of the science, not open to statistical attack as commonly formulated, in such a fashion that existing data can be used. Thus, subtly but cumulatively, the character of economics is undergoing a transformation. Out of the statistical laboratories is coming a new conception of what economics should be, as well as a new program of work. Many of our ablest students are attacking "the higher and more difficult task" of quantitative analysis with a faith in its possibilities that may work wonders.

The active participation of economists in practical affairs promotes, and is promoted by, the realistic treatment of problems that is coming into vogue, and the increasing emphasis upon statistical observations. One who tries to be of service in business, government, or social movements finds himself perforce thinking realistically, or at least shaping his abstract thinking with a definite view to pragmatic testing. Also, he is impelled to measure the factors involved in his problems as accurately as conditions permit. On the other hand, interest in what is actually happening and ability to measure social phenomena make economists more useful in practical affairs and so bring them more openings in business and more calls to public service.

THE BACKWARD ART OF SPENDING MONEY

With these changes comes another. The economist who participates in planning policies finds that he must consider factors that are not commonly regarded as strictly economic. That used to be cited as a reason why economists should stand aloof from practice—they are not competent to advise outside of their own specialty, and their own specialty is never the only thing to be considered. The conclusion now drawn quite as frequently is that an economist should associate himself with men who can supply his deficiencies—engineers, accountants, business executives, lawyers, psychologists, and an indefinite list of other specialists. In speaking of labor problems, I have already mentioned one example of such cooperation.

While the need for a combined attack upon social problems may be clearest in practical affairs, it is dawning upon us that the several social sciences must cooperate all along the line. The more realistically minded we become, the stronger grows this conviction. We have no inclination to check specialization; but we wish to know more of one another's viewpoints, methods, and results, so that we can utilize more intelligently one another's help. The economic man who buys and sells has a family, he belongs to a political party and votes, he has strictly personal idiosyncrasies and yet shares in the ideas of his generation, he is a historical product. All these characteristics affect his behavior whether we look at him from the economic, the sociological, the political, the psychological, or the historical angle. Quite literally, we cannot understand any phase of social behavior apart from all the other phases. It is easy to make this admission—ours is not the first generation to do so; but to accept its consequences in practice and to develop a genuine program of cooperation among the social sciences is hard. On that constructive task our generation has made a beginning—but no more than a beginning.

But while economists in common with other students of social problems are realizing that to get the best results specialization and cooperation must walk hand in hand, those who are most serious in this endeavor best realize how hard it is really to fuse the knowledge won by different groups. To make mutual understanding easier for our successors, we are introducing courses on social science at large into the high schools and colleges. The boys now being brought up on books that treat human geography, political institutions, social organization, and economic activities as parts of a single subject should be free from some of the limitations which still hamper their teachers.

III

The developments of the last twenty-five years in economics that seem to me most characteristic of the time are the developments I have been describing: expansion of the problems upon which investigators are working, and changes in the spirit and technique of treating problems. What has been happening meanwhile to economic "theory"? That strikes me as a rather outmoded question; but let me discuss it first in old-fashioned terms.

Since 1904 there has appeared no systematic treatise upon economic theory that exercises an influence comparable to Marshall's *Principles of Economics*, to J. B. Clark's *Theory of Distribution*, or to Schmoller's *Volkswirtschaftslehre*. There have been significant treatises such as Pareto's *Manuel d'économie politique*, and Cassel's *Theory of Social Economy*, improving upon the mathematical theory of pricing started by Walras; von Wieser's *Theorie der gesellschaftlichen Wirtschaft*, a comprehensive presentation of marginal analysis; Schumpeter's *Theorie der wirtschaftlichen Entwicklung*, attributing economic change to the restless activities of a small class of imaginative innovators who leaven the inert mass of routineers; Pigou's *Economics of Welfare*, building upon the foundations laid by Marshall; Sombart's *Der moderne Kapitalismus*, painting upon a broad canvas the development and the workings of capitalistic institutions; Fetter's *Economics*, seeking to reestablish economic theory upon a sounder psychological basis; Davenport's *Economics of Enterprise*, confining economics to the theory of prices and seeking to get rid of psychology.

I might double this list of examples, and illustrate an even wider range of experimenting with different ways of systematizing economics. Experimenting is the significant point, I think. In dealing with specific problems we are realizing the limitations of our older framework; the systematically inclined among us are trying out various methods of conceiving the subject as a whole; the rest of us are watching their efforts with varying degrees of attention, crossed by sympathy or skepticism, while absorbed primarily with problems of detail. There is no consensus of opinion that any of the types of theory suggested is wholly satisfactory or that any is futile. The German historical school seems to have collapsed largely for adventitious reasons, and Thorstein Veblen died in August, 1929, leaving no real successor. But surely there is no diminution of historical interest among economists—quite the contrary. So, too, the institutional approach to economic problems is adopted by many who suppose they are following the lead of common sense rather than the lead of Veblen.

A significant sign of the experimental temper of the time is the subsidence of controversy about the larger issues of economic theory. Turn over the old volumes of our technical journals and you will find them featuring papers dealing with methodology and fundamental concepts. Not so today. The acrimonious quarrel between Schmoller and Menger over the

merits of deduction and induction, and the courteous exchanges between Clark and Böhm-Bawerk over the nature
of capital, have few recent parallels. This slackening of doctrinal controversy is not a symptom of declining fervor; on
the contrary, it seems to me that economists are more heartily
interested in their work at present than they have been at
any time since the generation of Malthus and Ricardo. The
science has greater vitality and cherishes larger expectations
than in the quarter century that closed in 1904. I think that
we debate broad issues less, because increasing concern with
factual observation is breeding in us a more scientific and a
less dialectical temper. Also, we are rather bewildered by the
multifarious extensions of our tasks and scarcely know how
to conceive our science as a whole.

The generation to which I belong was brought up on some
system of economics—most of us on classical political economy as modernized by Marshall. We learned to draw a line
between economic theory and applied economics. Supposedly,
our central body of theory held together our wide-ranging
studies in public finance, money and banking, agricultural
problems, tariff problems, labor problems, and the like. But
now that the problems upon which we specialize have grown
so numerous, now that each of them has been subdivided for
more detailed inquiry, and now that we are so immersed in
factual researches, we often feel, as said above, that the
science is disintegrating. Frequently a specialist will say
boldly that he gets little help from economic theory. Our
monographs confirm that impression. Writers on the money
market seldom take their cues from Böhm-Bawerk's, Fisher's,
and Fetter's disquisitions on the theory of interest. Writers
on labor problems do not often start their discussions of wage
rates with the general theory of value and distribution. And
when definite contact is made between factual investigations

and economic theory, it is rather to test theory than to verify it. That change in wording from "verification" to "testing" is significant.

The declining authority over many of the factual investigators exercised by what is still spoken of as economic "theory," the lessened prestige of "general principles," is explained by doubts that are spreading concerning the scientific significance of what I have called the main sequence in the development of the subject. From Ricardo to Marshall our masters have explained how rational beings conduct themselves in seeking to minimize the sacrifices of labor and waiting, and to maximize the satisfactions of consumption—or, rather, to maximize the net balance of satisfactions over sacrifices. Now, the tacit assumption that men value goods according to the pleasures or the gratifications these goods will yield; that they work and save up to the points at which further effort or parsimony will impose pains just equal to the anticipated pleasures, has been vigorously challenged by a line of critics who knew how hedonism has fared at the hands of psychologists. More influential in discrediting the old assumptions has been the increasingly realistic work with concrete problems. The man who studies strikes and lockouts, the shifting fortunes of business combinations, modern methods of overcoming "consumer resistance," or business booms and depressions, does not confirm the impressions of human rationality conveyed by our theoretical treatises. Economists who find themselves working with political scientists are infected by skepticism of the average voter's intelligence. Those who consort with psychologists hear more about habits, conditional reflexes, action patterns, configurations, complexes—a score of fluctuating terms—than they hear about the felicific calculus, declining

utility, or curves of indifference. Those who deal with international problems find themselves ascribing potency to
suspicions, rivalries, fears, hatreds, and stupidities that do
not yield to reason.

Granted the artificiality of old notions about "the springs
of action," what shall we do to mend matters? That has been
a puzzling question for economists.

One answer is to substitute a more modern brand of psychology for hedonism. Thus Schmoller gave a list of human
instincts, just passing out of fashion in his prime, and proposed to work with them in explaining economic actions.
More recently Fetter has offered "a quite new statement of
the theory of value, one in accord with the modern volitional
psychology."[7] Still later writers flirt with psychoanalysis
upon occasion. The trouble with this solution is, of course,
that psychology gives no finished answer to the question
about human motives that the economist can borrow.

A second escape which has been tried is to throw psychology out of economics. In practice this means abandoning
the theory of valuation, which has passed as the very cornerstone of the whole structure. That resort is recommended by
Pareto, Davenport, and Cassel, for example. These innovators hold that it is none of our concern, as economists, why
people attach importance to commodities or why they will
not work or save beyond vague limits. All that economic
theory needs as a foundation for its work are schedules of
demand prices and supply prices—that is, supposedly objective statements of how many units of different commodities
people will buy and sell at various prices within a given time
and market. That sounds innocent enough until someone
asks what justifies an economist in supposing that people
have such schedules in their minds. If that question incites

[7] *Economic Principles*, preface, p. ix, 1915.

inquiry into the actual behavior of consumers, the psychological unreality of the whole assumption of definite demand schedules becomes uncomfortably clear. Nor is the theory of value the only part of our traditional doctrines that rests upon psychological premises. The whole structure is in the same precarious position. For one cannot reason about how men will behave without making tacit assumptions concerning human nature—and assumptions about human nature are psychological assumptions.

A third way of dealing with our quandary about psychology remains open. It is the one that I think economists find themselves taking in their current work—usually without thinking much about the significance of their procedure. The business of the economist is to gain understanding about a certain type of human activities. He does not need a set of preconceived or borrowed notions about the character of human motives for this undertaking, provided he takes human behavior as the problem to be studied. Instead of starting with a set of motives and showing how human beings thus constituted may be expected to act, he can inquire how actual men conduct themselves. Knowledge of current psychological viewpoints and methods improves his equipment for this task and safeguards him against making naïve errors; but he should not expect the psychologist to solve the riddles of economic behavior. The economist must himself contribute toward the understanding of human nature. Economic theory, thus conceived, becomes part and parcel of the social psychology we are gradually developing through the cooperation of all the social sciences. And not of the social sciences alone; for all the sciences dealing with living matter and with man's environment have their contributions to offer.

This analysis of the changing attitude of economists toward their share in the problem of human nature suggests the way in which we seem most likely to work out a new framework for our science. That framework is quietly developing out of our studies of specific problems. In any growing science there is a continual give and take between system making and fact finding. Systematic ideas keep suggesting new relations, and new facts to be looked for; in turn, new facts as they are established confirm or modify systematic ideas. There are periods in which there is elaborated a system that embraces and accounts for all the known phenomena in so consistent and comprehensive a fashion that factual research seems for the time being a hunt for further decimal places. There are other periods in which new factual discoveries discredit the systematic notions in vogue and call for radical reconstruction. Various schemes of organizing the materials, old and new, are tried; finally there emerges some system that serves the intellectual needs of the workers until they come upon more things in heaven and earth than are dreamed of in their philosophy—and so realize that they need a new system.

In economics we are now passing through one of these periods when factual investigations are straining the framework that is supposed to contain them. As already said, the work in business economics, in statistical laboratories, in realistic studies of many kinds is being pushed forward with little reference to the lines marked out by economic theories that are themselves systematizations of an earlier and a less comprehensive body of factual knowledge. Our current monographs contain within themselves not only the data, but also the tentative outlines, of the new generalizations that will reorganize the science for further work. No one yet knows precisely in what form this outline will crystallize; but I venture a surmise, which may seem very quaint in twenty-five years more.

Years ago John Dewey pointed out the path on which all the social sciences seem to be entering. In his Chicago days he was preoccupied by the problem of how we think. That was part of the broader problem of how men behave. In describing the role of thought in practical life, Dewey revealed the role played by other modes of acting. Also, he made it clear that his inquiry is one in which not only the philosopher and psychologist, but also the educator and all the social scientists, are engaged, whether they realize the fact or not. Doubtless this philosophic formulation of the proper study of mankind remained unknown to the vast majority of economists, political scientists, sociologists, and anthropologists. But what a prescient philosopher could glimpse a generation ago has grown clearer in the course of experience. Many a worker in the social sciences has discovered for himself that his technical problems of pricing, constitutional law, imitation, kinship systems, or what not, are really bits of the great problem of human behavior. Dewey interprets to ourselves what we are doing in the social sciences, much as Adam Smith showed his law-flouting generation that they had been building up unwittingly a new economic polity. Our adumbrations of what we are about explain that rapidly expanding cooperation among the several social sciences of which I have spoken.

What is true of the social sciences as wholes is true likewise of the numerous sets of specialties within each social science—economics among the rest. The fears that economics is disintegrating are well founded from the viewpoint of one who takes conventional economic theory to be the common bond. But if we think of economics as concerned with human behavior, all the specialists, however schismatic, are enclosed within the fold. Studies of marketing, of personnel administration, of business cycles, of public-utility regulation, of any special problem in the long and shifting list, deal with some aspect of the mundane task of getting a living. Everyone who throws light upon these activities is contributing to economics—indeed, he is contributing to economic theory.

Thus the old distinction between economic theory as a peculiar avocation and the study of special problems is wearing thin, like the walls that shut off one social science from another. This does not mean that there is less specialization in current work than there used to be. Quite the contrary, the expansion of factual knowledge and the refinement of technical methods make whatever problem a man feels drawn to a more exacting mistress. But in dealing with his special problem, however intensively, the man who grasps the modern view sees how the bit he is doing fits into the program as a whole. Thus specialization gains in significance, while cooperation among the specialists, like cooperation among the several social sciences, becomes easier.

The acceptance of this conception of economics as one of several sciences of human behavior does not lead to the rejection of any of the several types of theory now current. Rather, this conception unites, interprets, and gives fresh meaning to these types. Obviously, institutional economics, such as Veblen stood for, has a conspicuous place in the study of human behavior. Widely current habits of thinking play a leading role in social activities; we must learn all we can about the cumulative changes that have brought these habits to their current form and about the trend of the further changes they are now undergoing. In the work of economic historians like Vladimir Simkhovitch the fusion of history and economics is so thorough that one cannot separate the two. As economics becomes increasingly realistic, historical studies of the most varied sorts are absorbed into its working program. But the rationalizing type of work practiced by economists of the main sequence does not drop out. Among the most significant institutions of the current age are the highly elaborated habits of thinking about making and spending money. All of us acquire perforce something of these habits and in so doing we standardize and rationalize our behavior in some measure. Even as consumers we count the costs of different goods offered for sale and make dim comparisons of benefits expected. In business we carry this rational scheme of control to a point that we often feel paradoxical—our absorption in the technical game may defeat the ends for which we suppose ourselves to be striving. The exploration of this rational aspect of social life is in no danger of suppression; rather, it gains fascination when we see the part of life that the orthodox economist sketches in black and white side by side with life as the modern novelist paints it with his lurid palette. There is a place in the behaviorist setting even for that most abstract type of economic speculation—the mathematical theory of general equilibrium. For our pecuniary institutions really make every price dependent upon every other price, directly or through devious and tenuous connections. It is important to explore these bonds which unite all prices in a system. If Henry L. Moore and his coworkers succeed in getting their equations into a form that permits them to use statistical data, this type of work will appeal to the most realistically minded inquirer. For it, too, sheds light on social behavior.

Thus the constructive work of various schools of economic theorists promises to combine harmoniously in the framework that is becoming visible. Nor is the combination an eclectic affair. On the contrary, each contribution gets whatever place it can hold on its merits, as an aid to understanding social ways of thinking and acting. That is a severe test, and doubtless many of our traditional speculations will undergo considerable revision in passing it. Imaginary experiments will still be made, but more distinctly as steps toward understanding actual processes. The fiction of the static state will not lose all its usefulness, though men interested in human behavior will be eager to find less roundabout and less cumbrous methods of attacking their problems whenever possible. So, too, the notion of equilibrium between opposing forces, and the method of variations appropriate to it, are not likely to disappear wholly from economic analysis; but they will be used with a keener sense of their limitations. Human behavior is such a complicated affair that those who seek to understand it can ill dispense with any line of attack.

The parts of past work that have poor prospects of survival are the negative parts—the attempts to prove that there is no value or no place in economics for methods and results differing widely from one's own. The men who prefer some single line of work will have a clearer view of the value of what their colleagues with different interests are doing as they come to understand better the bearing of their own contributions. For example, the critics who have said that, whatever else it may be, Veblen's analysis of institutions is not economic theory are right when economic theory deals with the way in which a general equilibrium is attained between marginal sacrifices and marginal satisfactions. People who think of economic theory as dealing with human behavior in getting a living will take no such exclusive stand. Nor does the effort to read the theory of value out of economics fit into the new perspective. Certainly the question how men have come to attach such varying scales of importance to different commodities and different activities in successive

generations is one of the problems that must intrigue the
student of economic behavior. Contemporary aspects of that
problem keep thrusting themselves forward. How does an
advertiser influence willingness to buy? How do new products find their way into the standard of living? What reactions do the new demands which develop produce upon the
old demands? These and the similar questions I might put
are questions that realistic students of the present day must
face, and such questions concern social processes of valuation.
It is vain to tell one of our colleagues who teaches marketing
in a School of Commerce that these problems lie outside
the pale of economics; that in touching them he is trenching
upon psychology, which he is not licensed to practice. You
will not shake his confidence that he may learn something
about the behavior of consumers that is not in the books
on psychology and that belongs in books on economics. But
when we recognize that all of us are working at problems of
human behavior, who will raise such issues? The decline of
controversies on doctrinal issues is quite in line with the
gradual emergence of the behavioristic conception and is
likely to persist as that conception gains ground.

All this talk about the future framework of economics is
speculation. In the nature of things it must be colored by my
personal equation. I see what I take to be tangible evidences
of the movement, and in many quarters. Yet there are economists who would challenge my forecasts. There are others
who would say that the conception of economics as a science
of behavior is too vague to give us guidance, whereas my
expectation is that it will prove a vigorous organizer of working programs. In view of these differences of opinion, you will
do well to take this part of my lecture with caution. One
thing, however, admits of little doubt. Economics is develop-

ing its old problems, attacking its new problems, improving its technique, and widening its alliances with vigor. If we do not reorganize the framework of our science as we move forward, it will be because the scheme excogitated by our predecessors proves more adaptable to changing needs than many of us now venture to believe.

18

BUSINESS CYCLES

BUSINESS CYCLES are a type of fluctuation characteristic of economic activities organized in the form of "business economy" or "high capitalism," to use the German term. They have a wavelike pattern—each cycle includes a phase of revival, expansion, recession and contraction. These successive changes in activity spread more or less promptly over a large part, seldom over all, of the economic processes of a country. The cycles are recurrent, but not periodic. Their average duration varies in communities at different stages of economic development from about three to about six or seven years.

This list of features makes a thumb print which is useful in identifying business cycles amidst the welter of changes to which economic activities are subject. But a vivid impression of the part they play in modern life and the problems they present to economics can best be had from a historical approach.

The Development and the Discovery of Business Cycles

Trade crises must be as old as trade itself and must have affected the fortunes of increasing numbers as trading grew in social importance. The early crises of record were commonly attributed to what would now be classed as random causes, such as governmental aggressions, riots, wars or "acts of God." As economic activities became more highly organized, random factors continued to make business troubles; but new sources of difficulties appeared within business itself. For example the outstanding feature of the Mississippi bubble and the South Sea scheme, which ran their parallel courses to disaster in 1720, was a mania for speculation. In the later crises of the eighteenth century commercial miscalculations were held responsible in increasing degree. By the close of the Napoleonic wars it was realized that "commercial crises" are recurrent, and economists began to devise explanations which applied not merely to a particular case but to crises at large.

Gradually the problem of accounting for "periodic crises" expanded in scope. In 1833 John Wade suggested casually that "the commercial cycle is ordinarily completed in five or seven years, within which terms it will be found by reference to our commercial history during the last seventy years, alternate periods of prosperity and depression have been experienced." This idea occurred to others and spread rapidly. Economists who still wrote under the caption "crises" came to deal with the full round of cyclical changes. Thus the term "business cycles," or "trade cycles" as the English say, is a twentieth century rechristening of a nineteenth century discovery.

Sources of Information

Commercial crises were dramatic departures from the ordinary course of affairs which could scarcely be overlooked by the least skilful of observers. Hardly less striking were periods of boom and depression. The earlier investigators of these phenomena harbored no doubts about their genuineness. Descriptive materials such as merchants, bankers and newspapers provided sufficed to show the facts which required explanation. What statistical data were available concerning bankruptcies, imports, exports, discount rates and the like seemed merely to make this common knowledge more definite.

[417]

THE BACKWARD ART OF SPENDING MONEY

As statistical data grew more abundant it became possible
to attempt more penetrating inquiries. Yet efforts in this direction led to difficulties and doubts, for time series show
several distinct types of fluctuations in combination. To pick
out the cyclical fluctuations for intensive study was a difficult
task. Indeed the question as to what constitutes a business
cycle, a question which seemed simple when few but descriptive materials were used and those in a broad way, now
became complicated. The statistical investigator had to develop a sharper concept of the cyclical component in the
changes of a given series; he had also to discover what sort
of whole the cyclical fluctuations of different series make up.
These are problems on which investigators are actively working, spurred on by critics who hold that "the so-called business cycle" is a myth.

While reliance is now placed largely on analysis of the
increasingly abundant statistical data the older type of descriptive material has not dropped out of use. On the contrary such materials have been collected more systematically
than before and condensed into "business annals," showing
the changes from year to year in the state of trade. Collections of this sort extend our knowledge of cyclical fluctuations over countries and periods for which the statistical record
is scanty. And where the statistical record is fullest business
annals are a useful adjunct to the analysis of time series.

Analysis of Time Series

Most economic time series show four distinct types of
changes: secular trends, cycles, seasonal variations and random perturbations. Less definitely established are certain other
fluctuations called by their discoverers "long waves" and "secondary trends."

The secular movements are ascribed to factors which influence an economic variable in some uniform or regularly changing fashion over periods of time which for present purposes may be defined as long in proportion to business cycles. Examples are the gradual decline in American canal traffic which accompanied the development of transportation by rail, and the growth of the latter-a growth very rapid at first, then moderating its pace.

Swerving about a line of secular movements there may be several sets of wavelike fluctuations differing from each other in duration and presumably arising from complexes of causes which contain different elements. Thus Kondratieff, on analyzing a considerable number of the longest European and American time series, concludes that the capitalistic world experienced two and a half "long waves" between 1785–95 and 1914–20. The duration of these waves he gives as 40 to 60 years. Kuznets, using a larger number of series, finds waves which he calls "secondary movements" averaging not quite 25 years from trough to trough. Both of these results have still to pass through the process of critical testing by other investigators.

Seasonal variations arise partly from climatic and partly from conventional or institutional factors. Examples are the increase in coal consumption during the winter, holiday shopping in December and large dividend disbursements at the beginning of each quarter. In some series the seasonal variations are so prominent as to obscure all other fluctuations. When no regular seasonal change can be detected in a series the activity represented is presumably influenced by so many independent seasonal factors that they cancel one another's effects.

Random perturbations are as universal in their incidence as seasonal factors. Every economic process is affected at all times by a host of influences which cannot be classified under any other recognized head. When these many influences are not markedly unequal in magnitude and not closely connected by causal bonds they may be expected to offset each other so as to leave few detectable traces in a statistical record. At any moment, however, one or more factors having similar effects may rise to dominance in the constellation of random influences and produce marked perturbations in the net resultants of all the forces operating. Violent aberrations from the expected course of affairs are often plausibly attributed to a particular random cause such as a strike, a new law or a war. But the "expected course of affairs" is a vague concept. Analysis of a given time series over a period when no violent aberrations appear cannot determine what role the constellation of random factors is playing. And when some sudden break can be attributed to a definite cause it is impossible to say just how much of the observed effect that particular cause accounts for.

Interwoven with the preceding types of fluctuations are wavelike movements which recur more or less regularly, with a time span longer than a season and shorter than that of the problematical secondary trends. In numerous series such fluctuations stand out boldly. In other series they can be traced by one on the lookout for such phenomena. In still other series they seem to be lacking. All recurrent fluctuations in individual time series with an average duration of more than a year may be called "specific cycles" to differentiate them from the general movements called "business cycles."

Even when cyclical fluctuations are readily discernible they are always shrouded by a veil of other changes—a mixed fabric woven in varying proportions of secular, seasonal and random changes, perhaps also long waves and secondary secular movements.

One of the obvious tasks of research is to draw aside this veil of other changes in order to see the cyclical fluctuations more clearly. The technique developed for this purpose consists in measuring and then eliminating such types of fluctuations as can be seized by statistical methods.

Current efforts toward isolating business cycles seldom go beyond computing and eliminating the secular and seasonal movements by methods which are described in the articles on these topics. Combined, trends and seasonals produce a curve which is usually characterized by regular wavy movements of a year's span superimposed upon smooth sweeps covering considerable periods. If long waves or secondary secular movements are found in a series and measured, an investigator may combine them with the secular-seasonal curve. But this is a stage of refinement not yet methodically attempted, although many empirical trend determinations presumably include secondary secular movements without the investigator's knowledge. Whatever the fluctuations independently measured, their values, in combination or by successive operations, are divided point by point into the corresponding values of the original data. The quotients, multiplied by 100 or treated as deviations from zero, are taken to show the cyclical-random fluctuations of the series.

Of course this stage represents but a partial segregation of cyclical fluctuations. How to press the segregation further by eliminating the random variations is one of the current problems. Perhaps the most promising suggestion is the following: (1) After eliminating the secular trend of a series, its seasonal variations and any other type of fluctuation susceptible of direct measurement, break up the residual cyclical-random fluctuations into segments on the basis of the cyclical turning points, which can usually be located with some confidence on a chart. (2) Find the average value of the first segment, take this value as 100 and turn the series into relatives. This procedure applied to each segment in turn yields comparable figures showing cyclical-random fluctuations in as many cycles as the series covers. (3) From the relatives for successive revival dates, or for a few months centered on these dates, derive whatever average best represents the central tendency of the array. Make similar averages for the reference dates for successive recessions. In these averages the distorting influence of random perturbations will be attenuated generally in proportion to the number of cycles represented. (4) Elaborate the observations as far as desired by breaking the intervals between revival and recession and between recession and the next revival into fractions, computing averages of the relatives for each fraction and drawing representative averages from the array for each fraction, just as averages were drawn for revivals and recessions.

The number of cycles which a series must cover to yield fairly representative cyclical patterns depends on the character of the series and the character of the period covered. Frequently half a dozen cases or even fewer suffice to establish the general character of the special cycles found in a series; but of course an investigator likes to have more evidence at his disposal.

Specific Cycles and Business Cycles

Not all the specific cycles found in time series are systematically related in time to business cycles. For many economic activities have a rough rhythm peculiar to themselves, arising from technical circumstances not closely connected with the condition of general business. For example Warren and Pearson find a fifteen-year cycle in the purchasing power of farm prices for beef cattle in the United States. Pigou holds that in England "ten years seem to be, not merely the average, but also the markedly predominant" working life of machinery. Hence any period of active machine buying gives rise to subsequent cycles of a ten-year span in machine buying, although these cycles may run down gradually with the lapse of time.

To determine in what economic activities the specific cycles conform to business cycles is an additional task. One may proceed empirically, sorting the series into groups based on the timing of their cyclical turning points and then studying the interrelations among the cycles of the several groups. A more systematic and in the end a quicker method is to begin by drawing up a set of "reference dates" marking off successive revivals and recessions in "general business." Such reference dates may be taken from some time series believed to reflect changes in business tides. An index number of prices at wholesale might serve, or an employment index, or bank clearings in Anglo-Saxon countries. But uncertainty regarding the role played by random factors in any single series and the difficulty of finding fit series which have been maintained in trustworthy form for long periods of time favor the choice of a broader base. Business annals when carefully compiled seem to offer the safest guide, and they can be carried as far back in time as is required. The indications they give regarding the timing of revivals and recessions can be made more definite and checked by supplementary use of such time series as are available.

There is an element of unreality in giving precise dates for revivals and recessions in general business; for these changes really take place during transition periods rather than at turning "points." But some set of bench marks is needed from which to measure the various turning points of individual series. The lack of uniformity in the materials on which decisions must be based makes it impossible to fix reference dates over long periods and in different countries in strictly consistent fashion; but if the dates are used merely as points from which to measure the leads and lags of different series,

STANDARD REFERENCE DATES FOR BUSINESS CYCLES,
UNITED STATES, 1855–1927

Expansion		Contraction		Duration in Months		
				Ex-pan-sion	Con Trac-tion	Full Cycle
Revival	Peak	Recession	Trough			
Jan. 1855 to June	1857	July 1857 to Dec.	1858	30	18	48
Jan. 1859 to Oct.	1860	Nov. 1860 to June	1861	22	8	30
July 1861 to April	1865	May 1865 to Dec.	1867	46	32	78
Jan. 1868 to June	1869	July 1869 to Dec.	1870	18	18	36
Jan. 1871 to Oct.	1873	Nov. 1873 to March	1879	34	65	99
April 1879 to March	1882	April 1882 to May	1885	36	38	74
June 1885 to March	1887	April 1887 to April	1888	22	13	35
May 1888 to July	1890	Aug. 1980 to May	1891	27	10	37
June 1891 to Jan.	1893	Feb. 1893 to June	1894	20	17	37
July 1894 to Dec.	1895	Jan. 1896 to June	1897	18	18	36
July 1897 to June	1899	July 1899 to Dec.	1900	24	18	42
Jan. 1901 to Sept.	1902	Oct. 1902 to Aug.	1904	21	23	44
Sept. 1904 to May	1907	June 1907 to June	1908	33	13	46
July 1908 to Jan.	1910	Feb. 1910, to Jan.	1912	19	24	43
Feb. 1912 to Jan.	1913	Feb. 1913 to Dec.	1914	12	23	35
Jan. 1915 to Aug.	1918	Sept. 1918 to April	1919	44	8	52
May 1919 to Jan.	1920	Feb. 1920 to Sept.	1921	9	20	29
Oct. 1921 to May	1923	June 1923 to July	1924	20	14	34
Aug. 1924 to Oct.	1926	Nov. 1926 to Dec.	1927	27	14	41
Average Duration						
19 cycles 1855 to 1927				25.4	20.7	46.1
13 cycles 1885 to 1927				22.8	16.5	39.3

this defect is not vital. The order in which the various series turn up or down is the important matter and it does not depend upon the dates chosen.

Equipped with a schedule of reference dates showing the time when each cycle in general business began, culminated and ended, an investigator can determine in what series the specific cycles conform in number and timing to business cycles. Further, he can make a second set of measurements showing the cyclical behavior of different series within the standard periods marked off by revivals and recessions; that is, he can take the turning points in general business, instead of the low-high-low points in each series, as the chronological basis for deriving cyclical patterns in the way described above. For many purposes this second set of measurements, made on a common time schedule, is even more significant than the first set. Finally, an investigator can express degrees of conformity between specific cycles and business cycles in numerical terms, and classify all the series he uses according to "indexes of conformity" which run in practise from +100, indicating perfect positive conformity, through zero, indicating no conformity, to −100, indicating perfect inverse conformity. Of course, in a theoretical inquiry, series which conform irregularly or not at all to business cycles require quite as careful attention as series which conform perfectly.

Half a dozen illustrations of special cycles and their relations to business cycles are provided by the annexed chart. In each graph a comparison is made between the average behavior of the variable within the periods marked off by its own cyclical turning points and within the periods marked off by the cyclical turning points of general business (standard reference dates). Seasonal variations have been eliminated from all these series except the wholesale price index, which has no regular seasonals. Secular trends also are eliminated from the "index of general business activity" compiled by the American Telephone and Telegraph Company; in the other series they are eliminated in part and in part retained. The process of turning a time series into relatives on the bases of successive cycle segments leaves undisturbed what-

THE BACKWARD ART OF SPENDING MONEY

INDEX OF GENERAL BUSINESS ACTIVITY
AMERICAN TELEPHONE AND TELEGRAPH CO.
UNITED STATES - BY MONTHS : 1879 - 1927

•••• 14 SPECIFIC CYCLES
——14 REFERENCE CYCLES

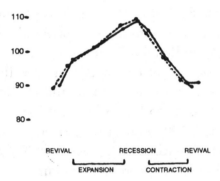

INDEX NUMBER OF WHOLESALE PRICES
U.S. BUREAU OF LABOR STATISTICS
UNITED STATES - BY MONTHS : 1892 -1927
•••• 11 SPECIFIC CYCLES
——11 REFERENCE CYCLES

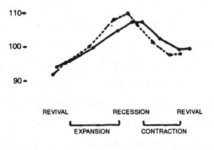

BUSINESS CYCLES

LAWFUL MONEY - NEW YORK CITY
UNITED STATES - BY CALL DATES - 1879 - 1914

•••• 9 SPECIFIC CYCLES
━━━ 10 REFERENCE CYCLES

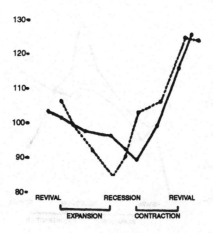

BANK CLEARINGS OUTSIDE OF NEW YORK CITY
UNITED STATES - BY MONTHS : 1878 - 1927

•••• 14 SPECIFIC CYCLES
━━━ 14 REFERENCE CYCLES

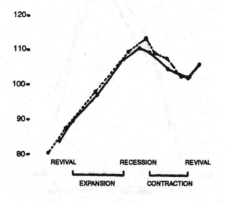

[427]

THE BACKWARD ART OF SPENDING MONEY

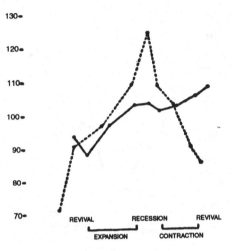

FLOUR SHIPMENTS - MINNEAPOLIS
UNITED STATES - BY MONTHS : 1878 - 1927

---- 13 SPECIFIC CYCLES
—— 14 REFERENCE CYCLES

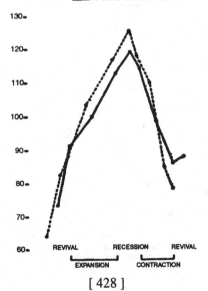

PIG IRON PRODUCTION
UNITED STATES - BY MONTHS : 1885 - 1927

--- 13 SPECIFIC CYCLES
—— 13 REFERENCE CYCLES

ever trend is present within the time span of an average cycle, but excludes the trend from one cycle to the next.

All six series show well marked specific cycles. In three cases the specific cycles agree perfectly in number and closely in timing with business cycles. Bank clearings outside of New York City skipped the recession at the close of the late war, and the lawful-money holdings of New York City national banks skipped the revival Of 1897. Yet the chart shows a close correspondence between the average cyclical movements of these series and those of general business. Quite different is the case of the one agricultural series. Flour shipments from Minneapolis have clearly marked specific cycles, a little longer on the average than business cycles. However, the relation in time between these specific cycles and business cycles is so irregular that when this series is chopped into segments on the basis of the standard reference dates the specific cycles almost cancel each other. Crop series commonly yield this result when similarly analyzed.

One example is given of an "inverted" pattern. The lawful-money holdings of New York banks before the war declined in periods of expansion and rose in periods of contraction. Other examples of inversion are unemployment, bankruptcies and many records of commodity stocks, though by no means all.

In amplitude of cyclical rise and decline there is a marked difference between the wide fluctuations of pig iron output and the narrow movements of wholesale prices. More extreme contrasts would be provided by taking series of discount rates, stocks of commodities or net earnings on the one hand and retail prices on the other.

Finally, the present sample illustrates the variety of time relations between specific cycles and reference cycles. The specific cycles of bank clearings outside New York City, partly because of their marked intra-cycle trend, lead the reference cycles by 3.3 months at revival and lag behind the latter 2.2 months at recession. The specific cycles of pig iron production lead the reference cycles by 3.5 months at revival and are virtually synchronous with them at recession. Wholesale prices, on the other hand, lead a bit at revivals and at recessions. In lawful-money holdings of New York banks the inverted specific cycles lag some four months at revivals, decline for a short while and then have an uncommonly long advance. As for flour shipments from Minneapolis, the irregular time relations between the specific cycles and the reference cycles make it impossible to establish significant leads or lags. On the chart the two curves are arbitrarily started at the same vertical line.

Business Cycles as Wholes

All the statistical analysis so far spoken of applies to individual time series taken one by one. To the theorist the finished results are merely raw materials useful in his effort to understand business cycles as wholes.

This effort has been likened to that of ascertaining changes in the general level of wholesale prices from quotations for individual commodities. The analogy is suggestive but there is a vital difference between the two problems. Price quotations for different commodities can be made into index numbers by some process of summation. But a mere summation of the cyclical fluctuations of time series representing different types of economic activities has no meaning. To understand business cycles it is necessary to understand the relations among the cyclical fluctuations characteristic of different processes. Working hypotheses concerning these relations should determine what cyclical measurements shall be combined to get significant indexes and how the individual series or indexes representing different types of activities shall be used.

BUSINESS CYCLES

At this point the quantitative study of business cycles connects with earlier work. We have noted that efforts to explain the frequent recurrence of "commercial crises" began before any but the most meager statistics were available. Hence numerous "theories of crises and depressions" were developed by men in no position to test their validity by appeal to measurements. When the accumulation of data and the development of statistical technique had made a more searching type of work possible those who took advantage of the new materials and methods could avail themselves also of the old hypotheses, as well as of any fresh ideas they got while working with time series.

Leading Explanations of Business Cycles

These explanations may be summarized in three classes according to the nature of the causes stressed most heavily.

1. Physical explanations run back to the idea of Jevons announced in 1875 that the activity of solar radiation controls mundane weather, weather dominates crop yields and crop yields dominate business conditions. The leading contemporary explanation of this type is Henry L. Moore's theory of eight-year "generating cycles." Moore holds that generating cycles are "the natural, material current which drags upon its surface the lagging, rhythmically changing values and prices with which the economist is more immediately concerned." As for their origin he suggests that weather cycles are caused by the planet Venus, which at intervals of eight years comes directly into the path of solar radiation to the earth.

2. John Mills gave a "psychological" explanation of "credit cycles" in 1867. Among present writers perhaps Pigou lays most stress upon the emotional factor in business, although he recognizes that "industrial fluctuations" are probably due to a combination of several factors. When trade is active business men tend to become over-optimistic concerning their prospects. Hence they invest freely in industrial equipment. While this equipment is being constructed the active demand

[431]

for products makes prices remunerative. But when a large part of the new equipment begins to turn out products prices fall and the error of optimism is revealed. The new condition breeds an opposite error of over-pessimism which checks investment until the reduction of carried over stocks and the gradual growth of demand develop a profitable market once more and so generate a new wave of over-optimism. 3. Institutional explanations trace business cycles to the workings of various economic processes: banking, saving and investing, producing and consuming, disbursing and using incomes, profit seeking and economic innovations.

R. G. Hawtrey's analysis of the cyclical impulses arising from banking runs as follows: When banks have large reserves they reduce discount rates and so encourage borrowing and business expansion. Once started an expansion mounts cumulatively until the growing requirements for cash created by active trade and large wage disbursements impair bank reserves. Then the banks raise their discount rates, thereby contracting loans and hence the volume of trade. Thereupon cash requirements become smaller and funds accumulate in the banks once more. Competition for the reduced volume of business leads the banks to reduce their discount rates and a new cycle begins.

John A. Hobson's "savings theory" makes business cycles an indirect result of inequalities in the distribution of income. In a period of prosperity large incomes swell so rapidly that the recipients cannot increase their personal consumption proportionately. An automatic increase in savings results. The investment of these huge sums brings about an increase in the equipment for making goods which exceeds the growth in the capacity to buy. A check comes when many of the new plants are finished and seek to market their products. Prices fall and large incomes are so reduced that over-saving ceases. Consumption then gradually overtakes production, restores profitable prices and starts a new cycle.

BUSINESS CYCLES

The modern theory of general over-production is best represented by Aftalion. Good trade leads to rapid increase of industrial equipment, then to an increase in the output of consumers' goods and finally to a decline in their marginal utilities. Meanwhile money is in active demand—its marginal utility tends to rise. These two changes combine to reduce the demand prices for consumers' goods, thus lessening the profits of business enterprises and checking the growth of industrial equipment. Depression sets in and lasts until the slow growth of consumers' demand has restored a profitable market for the existing plants—whereupon the cycle repeats itself.

Spiethoff denies that consumers' goods or goods in general are over-produced. He attributes recessions to over-production chiefly of industrial equipment and of the materials from which industrial equipment is made. The construction, steel, cement and similar industries depend for their market upon capitalized income. When steel and cement are made into steel and cement plants they increase the production of steel and cement themselves, forcing down prices and profits in the equipment trades. As matters now go it is practically impossible to maintain for long a tolerable balance between the growth of capitalized income on the one hand and the growth of the industries in which such income is chiefly invested. A relative excess of capitalized income leads to expansion; a relative excess of the goods in which capital is invested leads to contraction.

The income theory is associated with the names of Foster, Catchings and P. W. Martin. If the goods sent to market are to be sold at profitable prices the incomes disbursed to buyers must equal the full selling value of the goods turned out, and buyers must use their incomes promptly in taking goods off the market. But in practise business enterprises do not pay out the full selling value of their products. When times are active they retain a considerable part of their receipts to add to working capital, to provide dividends in lean years and the like. Hence a period of brisk business gradually accumulates an excess of goods offered for sale over the purchasing power of the market. This malproportion might be prevented if producers' and consumers' credit could be expanded in just proportion to the deficiency in disbursed income, business and personal; but that is a feat of economic rationality which no banking system can yet perform.

Veblen and Lescure have organized their explanations around the theme of profits. An increase in the physical volume of sales does not produce a corresponding increase in wages or overhead costs. Hence profits rise and business men seek to enlarge their working funds. Their chief resort is to banks, which are as eager to exploit the favorable prospect as any other group of enterprises. Supported by the increasing volume of credit, the business public bids up prices, enters into heavy future commitments and enlarges its plant capacity. These developments support each other so that business expansion becomes a cumulative process which runs on until one or more of the internal stresses which it accumulates reach the breaking point. Sometimes the first factor to be overtaxed is the banks. Prosperity causes a larger volume of cash to remain suspended in hand-to-hand circulation, and so tends to reduce bank reserves. At the same time demand liabilities grow apace because the expansion of loans increases deposits. If the banks find themselves compelled to restrict the granting of further loans, or even to charge very high discount rates, this check will bring on a recession. Or prospective profits may be undermined by the encroachments of increasing costs of doing business. Though lagging behind wholesale prices, wage rates rise. It is difficult to prevent the efficiency of labor from declining after the élite of the industrial army has already been enlisted, and difficult to prevent an even more menacing decline in the efficiency of management when the rush of business interferes with careful planning. The one way to protect profit margins against increasing unit costs is to raise selling prices. For a considerable time this remedy works; but it has to be applied again and again. And there is an elastic limit beyond which it cannot be carried; for rising prices increase the volume of credit required by business and so add to the strain on the banks. Moreover there are important groups of enterprises which cannot raise their selling prices effectively, such as public utilities, contractors not working on a cost-plus basis, manufacturers who follow a fixed-price policy. And in every period of rapid expansion there are some industries in which the increase of plant capacity so outstrips the growth of demand that selling prices are forced down. Thus expansion itself sets going processes which reduce prospective profits in an increasing number of enterprises. But prospective profits, capitalized at the going rate of interest, are the basic security on which rests the towering structure of credits. The mere rise in the rate of interest, which accompanies the later stages of expansion, forces a downward revision of capitalized values. When to this is added an actual decline in the profits which are capitalized creditors begin to take alarm and call for reduction of outstanding debts. Thus the weakness of a minority of business enterprises sets in operation a new process—liquidation of indebtedness—which leads to recession. In turn, recession leads to contraction. Credit ratings are revised downward; financial obligations are gradually cleared off or readjusted; unit costs are reduced faster than selling prices; and the bulk of enterprises gradually get into a position where their prospects of profits begin to grow brighter— thus laying the basis for a new revival and period of expansion.

Finally, business cycles are held to be a result of the changes in organization which are such a characteristic feature of a business economy. Schumpeter's "innovation theory" may serve as an example. Most business men are "routineers"—systematic people competent to run affairs on customary lines. A few are "innovators"—restless, inventive, daring men whose imaginative minds are ever planning new schemes. Such men produced the "commercial revolution" by reorganizing European methods of production. By exploiting mechanical inventions they made the industrial revolution what it was and still is. Today they are devising ever greater corporate combinations, upsetting selling methods, launching novel products, developing new sources of supply and cultivating new wants. When a wave of innovation mounts, business has a season of hectic activity. Prices of raw materials and of finished products, the kinds of goods demanded by buyers, the competitive position of different enterprises, methods and costs of obtaining capital, financial alliances—indeed most of the elements on which business plans rest, go through a series of changes. These unsettled conditions create difficulties for the mass of routineers. Failures increase, confidence dwindles and there comes a crisis, followed by a period of dull times. Dullness checks innovation because it prevents the disturbers of the business peace from getting the capital necessary for carrying out their hazardous schemes. Dullness also allows the routine business men to work out a passable readjustment of their plans on the new basis. But no sooner is quasi-stability re-attained and confidence restored than the innovators are again able to put some of their schemes into effect. Followed by a host of imitators they set going a new crop of changes, which multiply rapidly and bring on another crisis.

BUSINESS CYCLES

The various explanations sketchily presented here, and the numerous other explanations which might be cited, are not to be thought of as contradicting each other. Even from the viewpoints of the authors the differences consist mainly in emphasis. Each writer selects from the cyclical changes going on in modern society the process which seems to him of greatest importance and analyzes that in detail. But he may also make elaborate use of theories presented with an emphasis other than his own. Thus Pigou, who stresses emotional aberrations of business judgment, can take account also of construction, monetary and crop factors; Schumpeter can utilize Pigou's analysis as a side line; and the profits theorists can comprehend any change which appears to affect prospective profits in a rhythmical manner.

This inclusive use of what were originally offered as independent explanations is especially congenial to statistical workers. The task of a theory of business cycles, seen from their angle, consists in finding out what cyclical fluctuations are characteristic of different processes, searching for explanations of the idiosyncracies revealed and tracing the connections among different processes. In seeking to trace these various connections they need and can consistently make use of working hypotheses concerning the numerous processes which are parts of the whole. So far as their effort succeeds it weaves the elements into a common pattern. The end result aimed at is not eclectic patchwork but a systematic account of all the relevant phenomena.

The Phases of a Business Cycle

A systematic account of cyclical fluctuations, taken seriously, becomes an analytic description of the processes by which a given phase of business activity presently turns into another phase. The obvious framework for such a description is provided by the successive phases of the cycle. Historical changes in the character of the phenomena, as well as advances in knowledge, have led to significant modifications in the scheme and names of these phases favored at different periods.

From crises, the first focus of attention, the interest of investigators extended to the subsequent depressions. Prosperity was recognized as a problem when it became clear that the causes of crises are to be sought among the developments of the preceding booms. Somewhat later began definite attempts to find out how business recuperates from depression. Thus the four-phase business cycle of prosperity, crisis, depression, revival, came to be accepted. The suggestion that the transition from prosperity to depression be subdivided into two phases, "financial strain" and "industrial crisis," making a five-phase cycle, encounters two objections. In numerous cycles the phenomenon of financial strain has been conspicuous by its absence; in other cycles periods of acute financial strain have occurred within the phase of depression instead of during the transition from prosperity to depression.

Moderation in the violence of cyclical changes has led to revision of the old nomenclature. During the 1860's British bankers discovered methods of "panic financiering" enabling them greatly to moderate the credit strains which had been a prominent feature of past crises. Arrangements which assured all solvent borrowers of bank accommodation adequate to their needs, though at a high rate of interest, put an end to panic fears. Adaptations and extensions of the peculiar British measures in other countries, in combination with other lessons learned from past experience, have given many of the later transitions from prosperity to depression so mild a character that the word "crisis" seems scarcely fitting. Nowadays the term "recession" is widely used. Only a recession of a severity now uncommon, like that of 1920, is called a crisis.

Corresponding doubts are beginning to be harbored about the terms "prosperity" and "depression." There have been cycles in various countries in which the phase of increasing activity has not reached the pitch which "prosperity" suggests and in which the phase of declining activity seems not to justify the use of so strong a word as "depression." As substitutes the terms "expansion" and "contraction" are used here.

Even the latter pair may prove to have no more than a passing historical fitness. Statistical studies of cyclical behavior reveal not a few cases in which important processes have shown no actual shrinkage during the contraction phase of mild cycles. A stoppage of expansion is observed, or merely a retardation in the rate of growth. If the many sided efforts now under way to control business cycles succeed gradually, this attenuation of cyclical fluctuations will become common. Then the terms "expansion" and "contraction" will be replaced by some other pair such as "acceleration" and "retardation."

Differences among Business Cycles and the Task of Explanation

Business cycles, then, are not a fixed species but an evolving one. To the familiar notion that individual cycles differ from each other because each is influenced by a unique constellation of random influences must be added the notion that business cycles are subject to secular changes. Coming into existence gradually with a certain form of economic organization, they have changed as this organization has changed. The geographical and the industrial scope of the oscillations has grown wider; their amplitudes have grown narrower. Needless to say this is a checkered development; but the trend is clear if one compares cycles separated by a century. Further, while the modem business world has a common pattern, every country has its own peculiarities of economic organization and development which affect its cyclical fluctuations.

The secular, national and random differences among business cycles have exercised not a little influence upon theoretical inquiries. The peculiarities of the case with which a writer is most familiar are likely to color his impressions of the general character of the phenomena, much as his personal idiosyncracies color his notions about human nature. The best safeguard against such misconceptions is study of objective records covering numerous cycles which occurred in different times and countries. Such study suggests that a complete theory of business cycles would explain not merely the tendency of all business economies to develop rhythmical alternations of expansion and contraction, but also the secular changes in the manifestations of this tendency, the differences among the cycles of different countries and the roles played by random factors. Though so ambitious a scheme may be visionary it is desirable to consider just what part of the full task any given theory essays to perform.

The following analytic description of a business cycle aims merely to sketch the leading features generally found in the recent cycles of such countries as the United States, England and Germany. It does not dwell upon the characteristic differences among the cycles of these countries, upon the secular changes which can be traced in each or upon the effects of random influences. Even the striking perturbations of the late war are passed over.

BUSINESS CYCLES

The Phase of Expansion

Since revivals are conceived to grow into periods of expansion, expansions into recessions, recessions into contractions and contractions into new revivals, a description of cyclical fluctuations may start with any phase. But whatever phase is chosen as the starting point, the business conditions out of which that phase arises must be taken for granted. How these conditions develop can be shown only by working forward through the cycle until the starting point is reached again. The present exposition breaks into the round of events at the point where a revival has gotten well under way. How the revival started is the last question to be answered.

Among the fruits of revival are an increase in the physical volume of production and trade, fuller employment, an upturn in commodity prices, brighter prospects of profits, an advance in the prices of stocks, the prevalence of optimism, a desire to expand business enterprises, larger borrowings, heavier investments in industrial equipment and rising interest rates.

For a time each of these developments supports and stimulates the further progress of all the others. Thus the increase in physical production and trade enlarges the demand for labor and swells the stream of income even before wage rates rise. Large wage disbursements broaden the market for consumers' goods and so support the increase in production not merely of goods which families consume but also of the materials and equipment from which and by which they are made. These swelling demands push up the prices of the goods which are being bought freely and of the materials from which they are made. The greater volume of trade betters business prospects and makes men optimistic; the rise of prices reenforces these factors. Optimistic expectations of profits promote the further expansion of production and trade,

[441]

the employment of more labor and the advance of prices. All these factors combine to encourage investment, which stimulates construction work, which adds fresh impetus to the demand for goods, the rise of prices, the employment of labor, the disbursement of incomes, the growth of retail trade and the optimistic spirit, thus returning through a spiral of reactions to heighten investment itself.

Once started, then, the expansion of business becomes a cumulative process. In the absence of unfavorable random factors, when well under way even in the face of such factors, the movement seems to generate momentum. Nor is there anything mysterious about this appearance. For in modem nations, where most people get their livings by selling services or goods for money incomes and then spending money for goods, everyone helps to make the market for everyone else. The more one man gets the more he buys of consumers' or of producers' goods, and so the more other people are able to buy of what he has to sell. Hence an increase of activity at any point in the whole organization tends to spread and, through a series of reactions, to intensify the activities with which it started.

The Phase of Recession

Because of this interdependence among economic processes, however, expansion in any one process cannot exceed certain limits set by the synchronous expansion in other processes. These limits are neither uniform nor rigid; for economic organization is a rugged affair which does not require precise adjustments among its growing parts. Yet, since there is no adequate provision for keeping a balance, in every period of acceleration the cumulative expansion of different processes is so uneven as to produce a series of minor checks. The difficulties which are overcome reappear or are succeeded by more threatening stresses, and soon or late the cumulation of favorable influences turns into a cumulation of business troubles.

Profits are the focus of economic activities in a business economy. A pervasive but mild check upon the growth of profits comes into operation when expansion reaches the stage at which most enterprises have as much business as they can readily handle with their existing equipment of standard efficiency and with the trained personnel at their disposal. Before this stage was reached every additional order secured at current prices had promised a more than proportionate addition to profits because it distributed over-head costs over more units without raising operating costs per unit. But thereafter unit costs rise. A further expansion of business now requires the use of substandard equipment, the breaking in of new employees, who are likely on the average to be less efficient than the old, and additional overhead commitments. Raw material prices, wage rates and interest charges mount rapidly when business enterprises of many kinds are competing eagerly for supplies, labor and loans. Also it becomes difficult to maintain a high standard of operating efficiency when overtime is common, when discharge is a trifling penalty and when everything must be done in a rush both in the office and in the workshop.

The sovereign remedy for increasing unit costs is to raise selling prices. That remedy can be applied without checking the volume of trade while people expect the rise of prices to continue; but there are enterprises which cannot resort to it readily. Public utilities whose charges are regulated by governmental commissions, contractors who have taken long jobs for fixed sums and makers of goods which are sold at widely advertised prices cannot pass on the mounting costs to their customers promptly and in full. Thus a not insignificant minority of business enterprises may find their prospective profits shrinking as expansion runs on.

Another way to take business advantage of rising demands and to counteract rising costs is to increase plant capacity and to make the new plants more efficient than the old. That plan contributes to the activity of business for a time, but presently encounters difficulties. A wave of expansion usually brings an increase of contracts for new equipment before the old equipment is all in use; for business men try to anticipate their opportunities. The demand for new business buildings, factories, machinery, rolling stock and the like depends less on the physical volume of production than on changes in this volume. Any check in the rate at which the physical volume of business is growing will bring a positive decline in the contracts for new equipment. Then the equipment trades suffer, and all the more if, as is likely, the plants which themselves make steel, cement, machines, etc. have extended their facilities.

Such a check can scarcely be avoided as business is now conducted; for it is not possible to forecast accurately the growth in consumers' demand for all types of commodities and to adjust to this growth the expansion of industrial equipment, all of which depends in the last resort upon personal consumption for its market. Of course the equipment trades themselves give a powerful impetus to retail demand for commodities while they are disbursing wages for the making of goods which are not sold through retail shops. But when the new equipment is ready for use and begins adding to the supply of consumers' commodities offered for sale, not all the investments will prove profitable. Cases of "over-production" or "under-consumption" occur in every cycle. If they prove numerous they give rise to an impression that industry is "overbuilt" and check new orders for equipment. In any case it is not likely that the growth of physical demand for goods will long maintain the rapid pace characteristic of the early stages of expansion. All the other difficulties accumulating tend to moderate the rate of growth and so to produce acute difficulties in the equipment trades which will augment whatever troubles give rise to the check.

Meanwhile the intricate task of financing the swelling volume of trade at rising prices is becoming a problem. The best available data indicate that Americans spend some 50 to 60 percent of their money incomes at retail shops. Also it appears that individuals and business enterprises together "save" sums which average some 15 percent of the national income—that is, they spend this proportion of their net receipts for income bearing goods. There remains a considerable slice of income for rents, personal service, taxes and miscellanies. To maintain business activity the flow of incomes to individuals and from individuals to retail shops must expand with the dollar value of the consumers' goods flowing into shops for sale. At the same time the flow of "savings" from individuals and business enterprises must be kept growing at a steady pace, or the enterprises which make industrial equipment will suffer a slump.

It is argued that the whole congeries of business enterprises cannot long disburse as income sums which exceed the value of the goods they produce, and that if they disburse any smaller sum, part of the goods they sent to market must remain unsold or be sold at a loss. Prosperous enterprises do not disburse the full value of what they contribute to national production; they require larger working capitals and they deem it wise policy to accumulate reserves, which may not all be invested promptly in ways which sustain the demand for goods. Hence there is danger that the flow of individual and corporate incomes will lag behind the volume of goods seeking sale.

[445]

THE BACKWARD ART OF SPENDING MONEY

This deficiency of current income may be made up by bank loans, which put additional purchasing power at the disposal of the public. But that raises a new question of adjustment. If the banks extend their loans too freely the chief effect may be to accelerate the rise of prices and so presently to recreate the difficulty of finding enough purchasing power to buy all the goods sent to market. If the banks do not lend enough, or if they do not distribute their advances among different classes of buyers in the proportions required by business needs, some section of trade will suffer. Economists who stress this line of analysis commonly hold that consumers' incomes require supplementing by bank credit on a larger scale than is practised.

There remains the question as to how far the banks can go in furnishing the community with the additional credit required by expanding trade and rising prices. An increase of loans leads to a more or less equivalent increase of deposits and notes. While reserves are usually high in proportion to demand liabilities at revival, the ratio declines in the course of expansion, not only because deposits and notes grow with loans but also because the public keeps a greater volume of coin and paper money in its pockets and tills when wages are high and retail trade is active. Banks raise their discount rates; but that does not check promptly the demand for loans. They may get additional gold. But no matter how the banking system is organized there are limits below which it is not safe to let reserve ratios fall. When these elastic limits are approached the banks must discourage new applications for credit by very high discount rates and also set very exacting credit standards for new loans or even for renewals. If many enterprises cannot get loans at rates which leave a margin of profit business expansion will cease and there may be an epidemic of bankruptcies.

BUSINESS CYCLES

Although the preceding list of adjustments which must be maintained among different processes is not complete it suggests that, in the process of expanding, the business system may develop any one of numerous disorders. Neither business history nor business statistics supports the view that the decisive break always comes about in the same way. The sequence in which different time series reach their highest points and turn down varies from recession to recession. Usually several stresses seem to be accumulating during a period of expansion and the only question is which will overtax the factors of safety first. Random influences, such as harvest fluctuations, business conditions in foreign countries, the pet miscalculations of the day and the like, seem to exercise a considerable influence upon that event. And there seem to be secular changes in the character of expansions and recessions. Certain of the wilder excesses which characterized early booms seldom attain prominence today. But the fundamental difficulty remains of keeping all the important processes of a business economy duly adjusted to each other in a period when all are expanding. The more one studies the variety of cyclical patterns characteristic of different processes and the intricate ways in which different processes affect each other the more remarkable it appears that phases of expansion sometimes last several years. Two years is the average term in the United States, though four years was approached during the Civil War and again in the years 1915–18. In European countries the average duration exceeds three years, and periods of expansion outlasting four years are not uncommon.

Once a recession starts it commonly proceeds faster than does a revival, especially when the expansion has been accompanied by a marked growth of interlocking credits. A few conspicuous bankruptcies may alarm creditors and set them pressing for the prompt settlement of their claims. Unless the banks are able to reassure every solvent enterprise that it can get whatever accommodation it is entitled to, the recession will degenerate into a crisis or a panic. Granted this assurance, however, there may be little evidence of financial strain. Indeed, if the preceding phase of expansion has not reached the proportions of a boom and if the banking system is well organized and wisely managed, the recession may be as mild in character as are most revivals.

The Phase of Contraction is in many respects the reverse of the phase of expansion. Optimism gives way to pessimism, prices fall, production shrinks. In this general decline of activity there are significant differences of degree.

Consumers' demand, particularly for nonessentials, falls off appreciably in consequence of shrinking employment, the gradual spending of individual hoards and balances and the reduction of many non-wage incomes. Merchants require smaller stocks and cut their orders more than sales fall off. A similar policy is followed by other enterprises. Thus the reduction in volume of trade is amplified stage by stage as it travels back through wholesale dealers to manufacturers and producers of raw materials. Particularly severe is the decline of orders for new industrial equipment. Few enterprises care to sink money in extensions and betterments while most existing plants are either operating at but a fraction of their capacity or standing idle. Of course these changes react upon one another. Every reduction in production means less employment, less wage disbursements and thus less ability to buy at retail, still less production and less employment.

Similar differences mark the decline in prices. Wholesale prices fall faster than retail, the prices of producers' goods faster than the prices of consumers' goods, and the prices of raw materials faster than the prices of finished commodities.

The prices of crops may not follow this course because of harvest conditions; raw metal prices show the market conditions best. Wage rates (not wage disbursements) and interest on long time loans decline less than wholesale prices, while discount rates and common stock prices decline more. The one important class of prices which commonly rise in contraction are the prices of high grade bonds.

. These developments reduce the profits of almost all enterprises and bring deficits to many. The number of bankruptcies usually grows larger in contraction than it was during recession, although the average liabilities decline. Losses must be written off and reorganizations submitted to. With the reduction of inventories, current accounts and payrolls, less working capital is required and bank loans shrink.

As in the phase of expansion, so in that of contraction, there is an early period when every change seems to work in the same direction. One shrinkage forces others and is made more drastic by roundabout reactions from its own effects. But in the later phase as in the earlier the concatenated changes presently begin to raise obstacles to their own continuation.

The Phase of Revival

As unemployment increases and retail trade declines men have less money left in their pockets and shops need less in their tills. Idle cash accumulates in the banks and flows from the country districts toward the great financial centers. Combined with the net decline in bank loans, this flow raises reserve ratios. Discount rates fall very low, call rates lower still—sometimes so low that there is a margin of profit in buying gilt edged securities with borrowed funds. Such a condition in the leading money markets presently reinvigorates the demand for stocks and bonds. The stock market often revives in this way while general business is still at low ebb. An increased demand and rising prices of stocks are hailed as an encouraging sign.

Meanwhile the difficulty of making profits has put pressure upon business managements to improve their practise. The wastes, big and little, which often creep in during the rush of prosperity are discovered and eliminated. The reduced volume of business can be handled with the best of existing equipment and the most efficient personnel. There is plenty of time to supervise current operations closely, and also to devise plans for heightening efficiency. Overhead costs are in many cases cut by financial readjustments and operating costs by the fall in the prices of materials as well as by more skilful management. In some cases these changes are sufficient to restore a not unsatisfactory rate of earnings even while selling prices remain low.

An abundance of loan capital to be had at moderate rates has somewhat the same effect upon construction work that it has upon the demand for securities. Building materials can be had cheaply, building labor is eager for jobs, contracting firms will figure closely, prompt deliveries and prompt construction can be counted on. Even though the current demand for new housing or equipment is slight, investors are found who think it well to anticipate revival and build while work can be done at low costs and long time financing arranged on easy terms.

Even the business in consumers' goods must presently look up. When times are dull retail merchants let their stocks run as low as they can without losing too many sales through broken assortments. This possibility of reducing stock was one of the factors which had enabled them to cut their purchases for a time more than their sales fell off. But once their stocks are reduced to the minimum of safety they must order at least as much as they sell. This means some increase of business for wholesale and manufacturing concerns. Indeed, if the rate at which their sales are shrinking becomes smaller, retailers must order more than they sell. Thus the mercantile demand for consumers' goods may begin to increase at the same time that retail sales are still contracting.

Also there are physical reasons compelling an expansion of consumer demand for certain types of goods. Shoes, clothing, house furnishings of many kinds can be kept in use a longer or shorter time according to the state of peoples' pocketbooks. When hard times come many families economize by using these semi-durable goods as long as possible. Hence the demand for such articles falls off more in the early stages of contraction than the demand for staple groceries. But the time comes when an increasing number of the old articles are literally worn out. Then the indispensables at least must be replaced, if money or credit can be had in any wise. And that means another fillip to trade.

A similar observation applies to industrial equipment. Under pressure of hard times repairs, upkeep and renewals may be neglected for a while, not to speak of extensions and betterments. But that can be but a temporary policy. Whatever equipment is used must be kept in running order. The more it is neglected for a time the more work must presently be given to repair shops and equipment houses. Even the hardest pressed and most conservative enterprises are forced into this policy, if they stay in business. The more enterprising in trades which have been growing rapidly sometimes grasp the breathing spell of a slack year to build anew, planning to "junk" their old plants when the more efficient equipment is ready. Thus while the equipment trades may have an exceedingly lean season they are sure of some increase in business after a while.

Nor can prices keep on falling rapidly for an indefinite time. In the face of threatened bankruptcy an embarrassed house may sacrifice accumulated stocks for what can be had. But men will not buy materials and make up new supplies unless they can get back at least their operating costs. These costs in turn are aggregates of prices, including the prices of labor, and it is difficult to beat them all down. Nor can the still more resistant overhead costs be left out of selling prices for long without disastrous consequences. As prices get lower and lower the rate of decline flattens out. Buyers see less gain in holding off for still better bargains, and begin to fear they may wait overlong and get caught on a rising market. The first sign that the low point has been reached in any line is likely to bring out a flood of orders and to encourage other sellers to resist further concessions.

Business sentiment also becomes less pessimistic. As the liquidation wears on the worst becomes known and proves less serious than many had expected. Bankruptcies grow fewer again; everyone realizes that others are being cautious; the majority of enterprises have proved their solvency; outstanding debts have been reduced. Confidence slowly revives, and men begin to remind each other that every past period of depression has been followed by a revival. How soon business will turn the next corner becomes the question of the day.

None of these encouraging developments has great momentum. Though each favorable change reenforces the other elements of strength, unfavorable random or secular factors may check one slight improvement after another. Thus the phase of contraction is sometimes prolonged in a most discouraging fashion, as has been the case in England, for example, since 1921. In the United States the depression of 1873–79 dragged on for nearly five and a half years, whereas the longest period of expansion in times of peace since the

1850's has not exceeded three years. But cyclical developments of a favorable cast keep cropping up. The time comes when they are not offset by "disturbing causes," or when they are reenforced by favorable developments from outside the realm of business. Then a revival makes itself felt and a new cycle begins. On the average in this country from 1855 to 1927 the phases of contraction lasted some twenty or twenty-one months as compared with twenty-five months for phases of expansion.

WESLEY C. MITCHELL

Afterword
The Optimistic American Empiricist

I RECENTLY had the opportunity, together with other econo mists, to participate in the fiftieth anniversary commemo- ration of the death of my teacher, mentor, and friend, Wesley Clair Mitchell, held at the 3–5 January 1998 meeting of the Allied Social Science Associations sponsored by the History of Economics Society.

The fact that the meetings were held in Chicago, where Mitchell had earned his undergraduate and doctoral degrees from the University of Chicago, and my remembering that he was born and grew up in Rockford, Illinois—less than one hundred miles away—struck a rich and resonant chord. While preparing my remarks, I thought again about Mitchell's ap- proach to economics, particularly the influences of his for- mative years on the development of his value system, his disciplinary preferences, and how they shaped his views of empirical research. Most succinctly, it was to the advance- ment of empirical research in business cycles that he devoted his long and productive life.

Several points stood out in my reflections as I sought new understanding of the ways in which Mitchell directed his ener- gies and efforts during his lengthy career in economic research. I was struck first by the fact that Mitchell early came to appreci- ate that despite periodic depressions—some of which were se- vere—the U.S. economy was headed towards ever higher levels of output and income. True, there was nothing good about depressions, but their importance should not be exaggerated.

AFTERWORD

While Mitchell called attention on several occasions to the influence of two of his Chicago teachers on his intellectual development—Thorstein Veblen and John Dewey—on further consideration it struck me that neither Veblen nor Dewey became a role model for Mitchell. In fact Mitchell had no role model, a recognition that had earlier escaped me.

This brought to mind a related observation that also had eluded me before the Chicago commemoration. Mitchell had little positive to report about his extended years at the University of Chicago, the University of California at Berkeley, or Columbia University—which was his long-term academic home. And there is no evidence to suggest that Mitchell was impressed with the graduate year that he spent in Germany at Halle, the year he later visited at Harvard, nor the year in the early 1930s when he served as the second Eastman Professor at Oxford.

I can report from conversations with Mitchell that he held most academic administrators in low esteem, and he warned me to be wary when negotiating with them. Mitchell resigned from Columbia in 1918 to join the newly established faculty at the New School of Social Research, but returned within two years, after negotiating a new salary arrangement. But I must quickly add that Mitchell returned to Columbia not for reasons of an enhanced salary but rather because he had come to recognize that he would be unable to attract doctoral candidates to write dissertations at the New School.

As part of preparing my remarks for Chicago, I reread Mitchell's concluding chapter to *Recent Economic Changes*[1] which was forwarded to the publisher less than six months before the stock market crash of October 1929. And I also

[1] *Recent Social Changes in the United States,* Report of the Committee on Recent Economic Changes of the President's Conference on Employment, Herbert Hoover, Chairman, New York, McGraw-Hill, 1929.

read his summary statement to President Hoover in 1932, when presenting the results of the inquiry which he had chaired on *Recent Social Trends*.[2] Two points impressed me. First, Mitchell was by no means clear that the New Era, which had had a good run for seven years, might not falter in the near-mid term; in his view, such a reversal did not warrant a downbeat assessment of the future of the U.S. economy. The United States had suffered periodic depressions in the past and would undoubtedly be able to overcome such challenges in the future.

The letter to President Hoover was more surprising. Mitchell pointed out that the U.S. economy was doing very poorly in 1932, and he offered no reassurance that the economy would soon turn itself around. But once again he kept his composure and suggested that the future would be upbeat.

I suddenly saw Mitchell in a new light. I realized that he had little or no use for the ideologists and theoreticians at home or abroad who offered sweeping views of the economy based on excogitations, not supported by facts and figures. I realized that Mitchell was greatly impressed by empirical research carried out by laboratory scientists in other disciplines, and he hoped to replicate their methods by turning economics into an empirical enterprise.

As suggested above, Mitchell would be patient, so long as his goal held promise of eventually being successful. It early became clear to Mitchell that speculative theorizing was not the way to strengthen the basis of economic knowledge or to advance its potential. The best way to make progress was to dedicate oneself to adding solid facts and figures so that one could gain a better understanding of how the economic system could and should work. Admittedly there was nothing easy or quick about adding one piece of solid information to another so that one could gain a broader and deeper understanding of how a modern economy, dependent largely on the interactions among markets, operated.

But what options did the serious investigator face other than to make progress in slow, steady steps? So long as new knowledge led to more incisive understanding about how a dynamic economy operated, there was surely nothing wrong and much that was right of enlarging and strengthening the foundations with more and better facts and figures. There was nothing spectacular about a process that advanced knowledge and understanding one step at a time, but in the absence of any clear-cut superior alternative slow progress was surely better than pseudo-progress based on spinning ever more elaborate theories. Mitchell was willing to bet on the future of empiricism, even if that future would be slow in arriving. Empiricism seasoned with optimism would lead to a more upbeat future.

ELI GINZBERG

Index

A

Agriculture, Department of, 64
Albee, Ernest, 178n.
American Economic Association, 28, 29, 37, 43, 54
American Statistical Association, 42-43, 53-57
Ampère, André, 263
Anderson, B. M., Jr., 175n.
Austin, John, 353
Ayres, C. E., 195n.

B

Bagehot, Walter, 116, 149-150, 152n., 153, 203n., 204, 353
Bain, Alexander, 353
Baring, Alexander, 345, 346
Beccaria, Marchese di, 178
Bentham, Jeremy, 27, 79, 86, 98, 116, 152n., 154, 155, 160, 177-202, 210-213, 216, 219-220, 223, 252, 300, 303, 306, 311, 326, 338, 357, 359
Bernoulli, Daniel, 189
Bessemer, Sir Henry, 264
Bismarck, 262
Blackstone, William, 326
Böhm-Bawerk, E. von, 156n., 157n., 226n., 228, 232, 405
Bonar, James, 154
Bosanquet, Charles, 216n.
Bowering, Sir James, 194n.
Brookings Institution, 80
Bryan, William Jennings, 316
Bryce, James, 356
Buckle, Henry Thomas, 353

Burke, Edmund, 179
Bureau of Industrial Research, 378
Bureau of Municipal Research, 66
Bureau of Research and Tabulation of Statistics, 47
Bureau of Social Hygiene, 66

C

Cairnes, J. E., 33, 73-74
Cambridge University, 353
Carleton College, 282
Carlyle, Thomas, 109
Carnegie Endowment for International Peace, 391
Carnegie Institution of Washington, Department of Historical Research, 66
Cassel, G., 329, 403, 407
Census office, 55, 64
Central Bureau of Planning and Statistics, 47, 56
Central Statistical Board, 47n.
Central Statistical Commission, 43
Charlemagne, 273
Chicago, University of, 72-82, 284, 410
Local Community Research Committee, 81
Clark, J. M., 175n.
Clark, John Bates, 154, 282, 292, 306, 358, 360, 387, 399, 403, 405
Clerk-Maxwell, James, 34, 35, 263
Cleveland, Frederick, 74
Colbert, J. B., 84n.
Columbia University, 386
Columbia University Commission, 94n.
Commons, John R., 115, 157-159, 313-341

[459]

Condorcet, M. J. A. N. C., 196
Cooley, C. H., 175n.
Cornell University, 283–284
Council of National Defense, 45
Cournot, A., 168–169, 171–172
Cumberland, Richard, 178
Cummings, John, 43

D

Darwin, Charles, 74, 116–117, 287, 290,
  292, 296, 297–300, 302, 311–312,
  314, 337, 353, 374, 389
Davenport, Herbert J., 74, 155n.,
  158n., 159, 160n., 233, 296, 339,
  360, 361, 364, 404, 407
Davy, Sir Humphry, 60
Day, Chancellor, 315
Dewey, John, 49, 73, 78–80, 326, 410
Dumont, A., 195
Durand, E. Dana, 316

E

Easley, Ralph M., 316
Edgeworth, F. Y., 153–155, 161, 186,
  198–199, 232, 233, 297
Edgeworth, Maria, 212n., 218n., 223
Edison, Thomas A., 60, 265
Ely, Richard T., 314, 316
Euler, L., 263

F

Fabians, 98
Faraday, Michael, 60, 263
Federal Reserve Board, 64, 377
Federal Trade Commission, 377
Fetter, Frank, 156–160, 233, 360, 364,
  404, 405
Field, James A., 213n.
Fisher, Irving, 155, 156n., 157n., 159,
  166, 233, 329, 331, 360, 405
Food Administration, 45, 297n.
Food Research Institute, 22, 66, 378

Förster, Wilhelm, 242
Fourier, F. M. C., 362
Frank, Lawrence K., 32n.
Fuel Administration, 45

G

Galileo, 60, 263
Galton, F., 297
Gauss, K. F., 263
Gay, Edwin F., 47
Giessen, University of, 72
Glasgow, University of, 138
Godwin, William, 179, 196
Goldenweiser, A. A., 80, 81
Gossen, H. H., 155, 156n.
Gray, Asa, 292
Grey, Lord, 345
Grote, G., 353

H

Halévy, Elie, 179, 180, 182n., 183, 184,
  186n., 187, 188n., 195n., 196n.
Hamilton, Alexander, 122, 130
Hanna, Marcus A., 316
Harper, William Rainey, 284
Hartley, D., 178, 194
Harvard University, 104, 105, 133
  Bureau of International Research, 67
  Committee of Economic Research,
    22, 378
Hawtrey, R. G., 329
Hearn, W. E., 353
Hegel, G. W. F., 311, 337, 363
Helvetius, C. A., 178, 196
Henry II, of England, 322–323
Hertz, H., 263
Hill, William, 73
Hobson, John A., 174
Hoff, Jacobus H. van't, 263
Hollander, Jacob, 37n.
Hoover, Herbert, 60–61
Hoxie, Robert, 74
Humboldt, Alexander, 223

INDEX

Hume, David, 178, 197, 279, 280, 281, 283, 326

I

Indiana University, 315
Industrial Relations Commission, 317, 332
Institute of Economics, 22, 66, 378
Institute of Government, 66
Institute of Law, 80
Institute of Research in Land Economics and Public Utilities, 66
Interstate Commerce Commission, 332

J

James, William, 294, 298, 300, 337
Jevons, W. Stanley, 24, 25, 34, 88, 119–120, 152–155, 232, 300, 357–360, 387
Johns Hopkins University, 315–316, 282–283
Johnson, Alvin, 80, 157n., 158n.
Jones, Richard, 204, 362

K

Kant, Immanuel, 283
Kekule, F. A., 263
Keynes, J. M., 37n., 117, 151n.
King, Mackenzie, 74
Knapp, G. F., 329

L

Labor, Department of, 316
  Statistical Committee of, 47
Labor Bureau Incorporated, 378
LaFollette, Robert, 316
Lagrange, Count Joseph Louis, 263
Lauderdale, Earl of, 112–113
Laughlin, J. Laurence, 73, 74, 284
Lavoisier, A. L., 263
Liebig, J. von, 72, 263
Linnaeus, C., 200

List, Friedrich, 246
Locke, John, 321, 325–327
Loeb, Jacques, 297n.

M

McCulloch, J. R., 208n., 211n., 213, 215n., 221n.
Mackenzie, J. S., 154
Mackintosh, Sir James, 179
Maclaurin, Colin, 263
McLean, S. J., 74
Macleod, H. D., 329, 336, 337
Malthus, T. R., 70, 87, 116, 171n., 179, 203–204, 211n., 212n., 219n., 221n., 224n., 290, 326, 334, 339, 341, 346, 350, 353, 355, 357, 365, 405
Marshall, Alfred, 20, 21, 23–25, 29, 33, 34, 36–37, 150, 155, 164–168, 172n., 186, 232–233, 276, 303–304, 306, 327, 358, 360, 364, 373, 387, 388, 400–401, 403–406
Martineau, Harriet, 353
Marx, Karl, 97, 204, 209n., 258, 273, 276, 277, 311, 316, 337, 363–365, 373, 388
Mayer, Robert, 263
Meade, Edwin, 74
Mendel, Gregor, 297, 374
Menger, Carl, 154, 228, 229, 236–237, 247, 248, 336, 358, 360, 387, 404–405
Merriam, Charles E., 81
Merz, J. T., 34n.
Mill, James, 185, 194, 213, 353
Mill, John Stuart, 29, 73–74, 107, 139, 150–151, 166, 168, 225–226, 228, 247, 303, 306, 337, 353, 356, 357, 359, 362, 363, 373
Miller, Adolph, 73
Millis, Harry, 74
Mills, Frederick C., 35n.
Moore, Henry L., 23, 24, 33, 169n., 257, 412
Morgan, J. Pierpont, 273
Morley, John, 356

[461]

N

Napoleon, 123, 342–344, 384
National Bureau of Economic Research, 22, 66, 142n., 378
National Civic Federation, 316, 317
National Planning Board, 101–102, 133–136
National Resources Board, 89n.
Newcomen, Thomas, 137
Newton, Sir Isaac, 33, 34, 60, 180, 200, 263
North Carolina, University of, Institute for Research in the Social Sciences, 67, 80
Nourse, Edwin G., 94n.

O

Oberlin College, 314, 315
Ogburn, William F., 80, 81
Ogg, Frederick, A., 65
Ohio Institute, 66
Owen, Robert, 194, 196, 208, 213, 351, 362, 373
Oxford University, 353

P

Paine, Thomas, 179
Paley, William, 179n.
Pareto, Vilfredo, 161, 233, 388–389, 403, 407
Pearson, Karl, 297
Peel, Sir Robert, 353
Pennsylvania University, W h a r t o n School, Bureau of Economic Research, 378
Personnel Research Federation, 66
Philippovitch, E., 226n.
Philosophical Radicals, 337
Pierce, Charles S., 326
Pigou, A. C., 174, 404
Pittsburgh Survey, 317

Place, Francis, 213
Poinsot, Louis, 263
Pollack Foundation, 22, 66
Priestly, Joseph, 178, 196, 263
Princeton University, Industrial Relations Section, 67

Q

Quesnay, François, 326, 386

R

Radcliffe College, Bureau of International Research, 67
Rae, John, 361
Railway Administration, 45
Ricardo, David, 29, 70, 114, 139, 151n., 152n., 171n., 203–224, 231, 247, 252, 292, 326, 334, 336, 341, 344–359, 362–366, 373, 386–387, 395, 399, 405, 406
Rogers, John, 314
Rogers, Thorold, 353
Roosevelt, Franklin D., 99, 124, 130
Russell Sage Foundation, 66

S

Saint-Simon, Comte de, 362
Say, J B., 350
Schmoller, Gustave von, 37–38, 225, 258, 388, 403–405
Schneider, Dean, 383
Schumpeter, Joseph, 37–38, 40, 162, 225, 403–404
Scripps Foundation, 66
Seager, Henry R., 390
Seligman, Edwin R. A., 80
Senior, Nassau, 15, 204
Shakespeare, William, 314
Shaw, Bernard, 247n.
Shibley, George H., 315
Shipping Board, 45
Sidgwick, Henry, 329, 359

INDEX

Simkhovitch, Vladimir, 411
Sismondi, J. C. L. S. de, 362
Smart, William, 227n., 345n.
Smith, Adam, 29, 59, 83–95, 106–121,
   138, 139, 151n., 152n., 195–196,
   207, 209n., 303, 307, 326, 329, 334,
   336–337, 350, 353, 370, 386, 395,
   410
Smith, Sydney, 353
Social Science Research Council, 22,
   70, 80, 81
Solvay, E., 264
Sombart, Werner, 171, 258–278, 364,
   404
Southern California, University of,
   Social Research Society, 67
Spencer, Herbert, 28, 283, 314, 326,
   353–354
Standard Oil Company, 316, 380
Stinnes, H., 273
Stone, N. I., 315, 316
Strong, Nathan L., 317
Stuart, Henry Walgrave, 74, 154
Supreme Court, 321, 331, 332, 334
Syracuse University, 315

T

Tanners' Council, 55
Taussig, F. W., 207n.
Taylor, H. C., 204n.
Thompson, William, 362
Trower, Hutches, 208n., 212n., 213n.,
   215n., 217n., 220n., 221n., 222n.

U

United States Industrial Commission,
   316
Ure, Andrew, 263

V

Veblen, Andrew, 282
Veblen, Oswald, 282

Veblen, Thorstein, 15, 29, 73, 78–80,
   113, 151–152n., 155, 156n., 157n.,
   173n., 176n., 203n., 257, 277,
   279–312, 331–334, 336–340, 364,
   382–383, 389, 404, 411, 413
Viner, Jacob, 37n.
Voltaire, F.-M. A. de, 180

W

Wagner, Adolf H. G., 225
Walras, Léon, 154, 162, 336, 358, 360,
   387, 388, 403
War Industries Board, 45
   Division of Planning and Statistics, 47
War Trade Board, 45
Watt, James, 95, 138
Webb, Beatrice (Lady Passfield), 59–60
Webb, Sidney (Lord Passfield), 59–60,
   364
Weber, E. H., 263
Weber, Max, 269
Wesleyan University, 315
Whittaker, A. C., 151n.
Wicksell, Knut, 329–331
Wicksteed, P. H., 161–162, 233
Wieser, Friedrich von, 151n., 159n.,
   225–257, 403
William the Conqueror, 322
Willis, H. Parker, 74
Wilson, E. B., 37n., 40
Wilson, Woodrow, 47
Wisconsin Industrial Commission, 317
Wisconsin University, 316
Wöhler, F., 263

Y

Yale University, 283
   Institute of Human Relations, 67, 80
Young, Allyn A., 43–44, 152n., 158,
   166n., 223n.

Z

Zawadzski, W., 161

Printed in the United States
by Baker & Taylor Publisher Services

Printed in the United States
by Baker & Taylor Publisher Services